SILMAN'S COMPLETE ENDGAME COURSE

Other Siles Press books by Jeremy Silman

How to Reassess Your Chess, 3rd Edition (1993)
The Complete Book of Chess Strategy (1998)
The Amateur's Mind, 2nd Edition (1999)
The Reassess Your Chess Workbook (2001)
Pal Benko (2003)

SILMAN'S COMPLETE ENDGAME COURSE

FROM BEGINNER TO MASTER

INTERNATIONAL MASTER
JEREMY SILMAN

SILES PRESS   LOS ANGELES

First Edition

20 19 18 17 16

Library of Congress Cataloging-in-Publication Data
Silman, Jeremy.
[Complete endgame course]
Silman's complete endgame course : from beginner to master /
by Jeremy Silman.
p. cm.
Includes bibliographical references and index.
ISBN 978-1-890085-10-0 (alk. paper)
1. Chess--End games. I. Title. II. Title: Complete endgame course.

GV1450.7.S56 2007
794.1'24--dc22

Cover design and photography by Wade Lageose for Lageose Design

SILES PRESS

a division of Silman-James Press, Inc.
www.silmanjamespress.com
info@silmanjamespress.com

*To my friends Shihan Anthony "Big Tony" Katsoulas
and Baron Clement von Franckenstein*

Contents

Preface

There was a time when endgame books were fairly scarce—only those by Fine, Keres, Averbach, and a couple other authors could be found on the bookshelves. Now, with a torrent of new chess books pouring into stores every year, that has changed—endgame books are a dime a dozen.

Most chess writers think that chess players want as many positions as possible in an endgame book. And that *sounds* like a good idea! Give the chess hopeful the most bang for the buck! Stuff everything into one book! This would be reasonable for an endgame encyclopedia, and such books are good research tools. But must every chess author daze his readers with this kind of "overkill"? Of course not! In fact, more than one player has been demoralized by the sheer mass of information that many endgame books offer—it all seems so dull and so hard to grasp.

Almost all players who dream of endgame improvement experience the same frustrating scenario: They buy the latest critically acclaimed and usually over-stuffed endgame title, open it up (hands quivering with the exciting prospect of gleaning arcane knowledge), and read the author's assurances that they now possess the book of ultimate endgame enlightenment. However, after they spend a few days looking over several examples, they inevitably shelve it alongside all their other unread chess tomes.

Pondering this common story led me to ask an important question: *How can the whole endgame genre be done differently?* That question led to *Silman's Complete Endgame Course*, which stresses individual guidance and instruction and, yes, hope for players of every rating group. This book is designed to make players who are disgusted with endgame study feel that there *is* light at the end of the tunnel, and it assures you that you *can* become an accomplished endgame player with just a little effort.

By offering instruction that's tailor-made to fit a player's individual rating group, and is in accord with that player's future goals, I make endgame study easy to grasp and extremely practical for players and coaches. Of course, each coach will have opinions as to what endgames are appropriate for each rating group, so personal adjustments can always be made. Nevertheless, coaches will find my book to be an invaluable teaching tool that they can use with confidence.

Silman's Complete Endgame Course is the endgame book that everyone always wanted but couldn't find. Now it's in front of you, and I hope it proves to be everything you always dreamed such a book could and should be.

Jeremy Silman
Los Angeles, CA

Introduction

All chess players want endgame skills, but doing the work to actually achieve this much-needed knowledge is anything but easy. My goal in writing this book was to take a subject that most see as boring and make it palatable, educational, and yes, even fun. Thus the following six essential points make up the philosophy behind *Silman's Complete Endgame Course*:

- *Rating is important.* Players of different strengths need to know different (and level-appropriate) kinds of endgames.

- *Guidance is the key.* Chess students need to be told which endgames are important for their particular level. Studying endgames that are too advanced for their rating-level will only depress them and waste their time, since they'll rarely (if ever) have need of such knowledge in the kinds of games/positions that players of their ratings usually reach.

- *Give players hope.* By telling players that they only need to know a finite amount of easily digestible material (based on their strengths/ratings), you give them hope and confidence. Now they'll be willing to invest time in learning the recommended positions and ideas because everything is mapped out and accessible.

- *Every player should receive well-rounded training.* The correct study of chess calls for balance. For example, a beginner needs to spend very little time on the endgame. (Basic mates are all he or she needs.) Instead, the beginner's main efforts should be devoted to gaining as much tactical acumen as possible. On the other hand, a tournament player in the 1500 range needs quite a bit of critical but easy-to-learn endgame knowledge if he or she wants to move up the rating ladder. However, such a player shouldn't indiscriminately study random endgame positions. The balanced study of tactics, strategy, opening theory, and appropriate endgames is more important here than ever.

- *Create a love for the endgame.* Most players seem unable to appreciate anything but a mating attack or a tactic/combination. This is really a shame since they are missing a lot of the game's beauty. An appreciation of its final phase will not only allow them to become stronger in that area, but also add to their enjoyment of chess as a whole.

- ● **Introduce a "Unified Field of Endgame Study."** Every player needs to master a certain amount of endgame material that's pertinent to his or her strength. This means that a class "B" player (1600-1799), in order to absorb the material presented in the class "B" section, must have learned everything presented for the lower rating groups! All endgames, even the most difficult theoretical quagmires, are based on basic foundation positions—if you don't learn these, your endgame growth will suffer.

How to read this book

In the introduction to his excellent *Dvoretsky's Endgame Manual*, Dvoretsky writes, "Amazingly enough, I have not yet found a single endgame manual which I could recommend wholeheartedly to my pupils. Most existing books are either elementary and useful for novices only, or are useless methodologically, or do not cover endgame theory fully."

I'm left wondering about the average strength of Dvoretsky's students. Also, how does he define "novice"? In my experience, a book that "fully" covers the endgame is exactly what players under 2400 *don't* need! Thus, I strongly recommend that you put aside all other endgame books and trust your endgame study to *Silman's Complete Endgame Course*. There *is* an important place for the various fine endgame books found in my recommended book list. However, they will only prove useful once you finish my course and have gained a solid master's grasp of endgame theory. Remember, I'm trying to make your precious study time count. Jumping from book to book is a fast track to nowhere.

Silman's Complete Endgame Course is *not* organized by endgame type, which is how it's been done in the past. Unfortunately, organizing the study of endgames by type ultimately fails the student by offering too much information too fast. Instead, I've divided my book by rating—*by what you personally need to know* so that your endgame IQ is equal to your overall playing strength.

For example, if you have just learned to play, all you need to study is the section designed for beginners (Part One). After mastering the material there, put the book away and spend your time studying tactics and a few strategic concepts. Once your overall strength tightens up and you feel you're ready to break into class "E", re-open this book and master the material that's been designed for players rated from 1000 to 1199 (Part Two), then repeat this process as you move up the rating ladder.

If you already possess a high rating, let's say class "B" (Part Five), you *must* make sure you completely understand everything in the earlier sections before tackling the "B" material. If you fail to do this, you'll find yourself lost, confused, and frustrated. Patiently go through each part of the book up to or, at most, one part above your present rating. Make sure you thoroughly *understand* the lessons in each part of the book. Memorization is a very poor substitute for true understanding.

Once you attain Expert strength (2000-2199), or once you're a strong "A" player and wish to step up to the next level, the book's material changes somewhat and a concept I call "flowcharts" is explored. Nothing in this section will make sense if you haven't carefully studied and absorbed everything I presented earlier.

Next, we come to the Master lessons (Part Eight), which embrace concepts more than positions or memorization. Oddly, I think class "A" players and Experts can get a lot out of this section, so feel free to leap ahead and read it if you've already reached these levels.

Part Nine is Endgames for Pure Pleasure. Here anyone of any rating can enjoy the comic look of entombed or dominated minor pieces, tactics in the endgame, and a study of The Five Greatest Endgame Players of All Time. You might not necessarily understand all of this section's nuances if you're of less than Expert strength, but that shouldn't prevent you from deriving a good deal of pleasure from the examples.

When studying this book, please remember that I've deliberately left out many endgames. Why? Because I don't feel they are important to players under the 2400 level. For example, I heretically decided not to include Bishop and Knight vs. Lone King because it's far from easy to master, and it occurs very rarely in over-the-board play. In fact, I only got it once in my entire career, while IM John Watson and IM John Donaldson never got it at all! Is such a rarity really worth the two or three hours it would take to learn it? I say no. Ultimately, this is what *Silman's Complete Endgame Course* is all about: Learning what's useful, and devoting the rest of your precious study time to other areas of the game.

Acknowledgements

This book owes its existence to the endgame-laments of countless frustrated players that I've encountered over the course of my chess career.

I would like to express my gratitude to Jack Peters, Yasser Seirawan, Anthony Saidy, and John Watson. They all deserve far more than mere thanks for the help they have supplied in the writing of this book.

Finally, I also need to thank my old Haight-Ashbury buddies Sky Monkey and Penguin Delight, who told me that repeated exposure to the Door's "This is the End" would eventually result in the creation of a chess tome on the same subject. Amazingly, they were proved right.

Part One

Endgames for Beginners (Unrated–999)

Contents

We all have to start somewhere, and though endgames should take a back seat to tactics and the basics of strategy when you're a beginner, it *is* annoying (if you equate pain, agony, and self-loathing to annoying) to find yourself with an extra Queen in the endgame and not know how to deliver checkmate.

Since you'll be called on to perform these endgame mates over and over again, spending the hour or two it will take to master these extremely easy-to-learn positions is a *must*! Think about it: an hour of work for a lifetime of endgame confidence. Quite a deal, isn't it?

When players first learn the game, they are often taught to always play to the last breath since "nobody ever won a game by resigning." Though the defender's fate is more or less a foregone conclusion when he's a Rook or more down, it doesn't hurt him to continue and watch the final mating net unfold—thus learning how to do it when he is on the winning side. Eventually, the beginner will resign such situations when he begins to play against experienced tournament players, but at first it's not a bad idea to always play them out and see if the opponent knows his stuff. Don't doubt that your opponents *will* play them out, so this chapter is a must if you've just learned to play the game.

Beginners only need to be aware of two endgame situations: **Overkill Mates** (one side has an enormous amount of material versus the lone enemy King) and **Stalemates** (one side has no legal moves, but is *not* in check).

Overkill Mates

You've played a pretty good game (no shame in feeling proud after a great effort). Though you were not able to get an early mating attack, you picked up some extra material and, as the game continued, added to your booty until you found yourself way, way ahead. Trading and more devouring of enemy units ensues until an overkill endgame is reached. What do you do now?

To win an overkill endgame, you only need to learn two techniques: the **Staircase** and the **Box**.

The Staircase

When you are up by a Queen and a Rook, or even by two Queens (or more!), one must wonder if your opponent (who could give up and show a bit of respect) is bullheaded or simply enjoys suffering and/or pain. Whatever his reasons for continuing might be, you are the one who must now demonstrate how easy it is to score the victory.

Though there are many ways to force a quick mate in such situations, the simple device recommended here (the Staircase) makes all endgames where you are up by two major—also known as **heavy**—pieces (Q + Q or Q + R or R + R) a no-brainer to win. The three key components of the Staircase are:

> 1 ▷ Push the enemy King to one of the four sides of the board.

Diagram 1

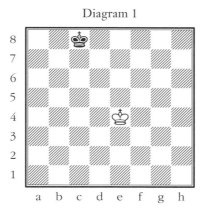

Black's King is on the side of the board

3

In diagram 1, we see black's King situated on the side of the board, while white's King stands proudly in the middle.

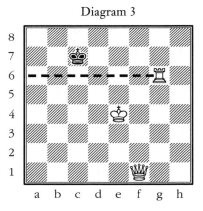

Diagram 2

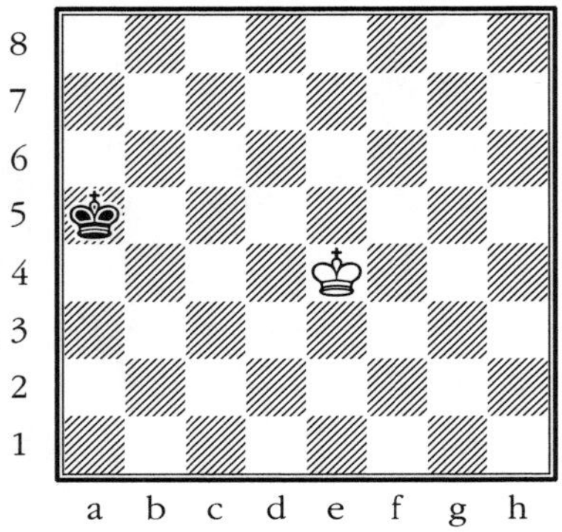

Black's King is still on the side of the board

In diagram 2, black's King still resides on the side of the board. There are four sides to the board, and trapping a King on any of them is good.

2 ▶ Use one of your heavy/major pieces (Rook or Queen) to cut the enemy King off from a rank or file.

Diagram 3

The Rook traps the enemy King

In diagram 3, the Rook traps the enemy King on the last two ranks. The line from the Rook to the queenside (g6-a6) represents an imaginary force field that black's King can't pass through.

3 ▶ Use the other major piece to check the King off the next file or rank.

In diagram 4, White has just played Qf7+. Black's King can't move towards the middle due to the Rook's "force field," thus it must step to the board's side.

Diagram 4

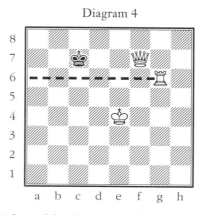

Kicking black's King off the 7th rank

After **1...Kc8** (or 1...Kb8 or 1...Kd8), the Queen now stops the King from moving forward. This frees the Rook from "King-containing duty," allowing it to administer the final blow with **2.Rg8** mate. Note how the movements of the Rook and Queen resemble steps up or down a Staircase.

Repeating this information in paragraph form: As in almost all mating end-games, you need to push the enemy King to one of the four sides of the board. The point of the Staircase is to use one major piece (Rook or Queen) to keep the enemy King from stepping onto a rank or file. Then the other major piece will give check along the next rank or file, forcing the target King to step closer to its doom on the side of the board.

Play over the positions in this section quickly (it's not rocket science, so there's no need to ponder it), and the Staircase will rapidly become engrained in your mind.

King and Two Queens vs. Lone King

Diagram 5

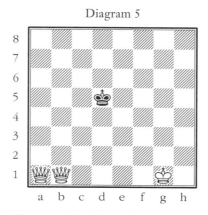

Misery is black's only companion

White uses his two Queens to push the black King to one of the board's edges (once there, it can't step backwards out of harm's way), where it will be mated.

1.Qb5+ Ke6

Or 1...Ke4 2.Qaa4+ (The quicker 2.Qae5+ Kf3 3.Qbe2 mate doesn't follow the advocated Staircase method, so we'll "pretend" it doesn't exist and stick to our theme—trust me, nobody cares if you mate in three or five, as long as you succeed every time!) 2...Ke3 3.Qbb3+ Kd2 4.Qaa2+ Ke1 5.Qbb1 mate.

Diagram 6

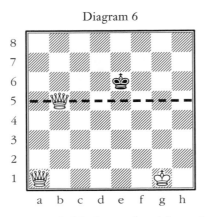

Force field along the 5th rank

After 1...Ke6 the whole 5th rank is "mined" by white's b5-Queen.

2.Qaa6+

Note how black's King can't move up to the 5th rank since the Queen on b5 controls all the squares there. Even faster is 2.Qae5+ Kf7 3.Qbe8 mate, but this has nothing to do with our recommended (easier to learn) technique.

2...Ke7 3.Qbb7+

Diagram 7

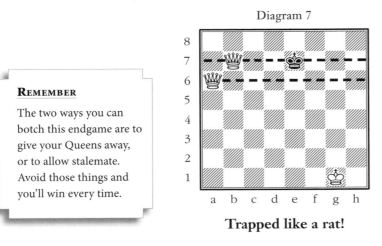

> **REMEMBER**
>
> The two ways you can botch this endgame are to give your Queens away, or to allow stalemate. Avoid those things and you'll win every time.

Trapped like a rat!

Black's King is forced back to the last rank

3...Kf8 4.Qaa8 mate.

King, Queen, and Rook vs. Lone King

This calls for the same rank-by-rank or file-by-file Staircase technique as in the two-Queen example.

Diagram 8

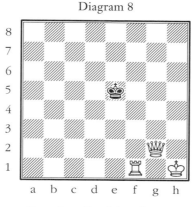

> **REMEMBER**
>
> Watch out for your Rook—unlike the two Queens, the Black King can approach the Rook and threaten to take it.

Let the checking begin!

1.Qg5+

White elects to push the King to the edge of the board rank-by-rank. He could have done the same thing file-by-file with 1.Qe2+ Kd5 2.Rd1+ Kc5 3.Qc2+ Kb4 4.Rb1+ Ka5 (or 4…Ka3 5.Qb3 mate) 5.Qa2 mate.

1…Kd4

Or 1...Ke6 2.Rf6+ Ke7 3.Qg7+ Ke8 4.Rf8 mate.

2.Rf4+

Notice how White is making sure his Rook is guarded by its Queen!

2…Ke3 3.Qg3+

Diagram 9

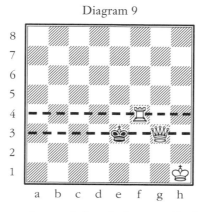

The crowned goat is herded towards the 1st rank.

Both the 3rd and 4th ranks can no longer be stepped on by the black King, and White is slowly but surely herding it towards the edge of the board.

4...Ke2 4.Rf2+

Not 4.Qh2+ since that would free up the 3rd rank and allow 4...Ke3 (though that tiny mistake could easily be rectified by 5.Qg3+ Ke2 6.Rf2+, transposing back into the game.

4...Ke1 5.Qg1 mate.

King and Two Rooks vs. Lone King

Once again, the stronger side should push the opponent's King towards the edge of the board since, once it's there, it can no longer step backwards out of harm's way. Of course, this example is harder than the previous two since the King can approach white's Rooks and threaten them.

USEFUL ADVICE

Keep your Rooks as far from the enemy King as possible. That way the King can't attack them.

Diagram 10

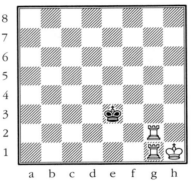

Push black's King to the side

1.Re1+

The plan is as follows: take files/ranks away from the enemy King while pushing it towards the side of the board, and keep your Rooks as far away from the beleaguered monarch as possible. Your goal (trapping the King on the side), mixed with patience and safety, will always get the job done.

1...Kd3

Now black's King can't cross over the e-file since it is controlled by a white Rook. Also possible was 1...Kf3 when 2.Rf2+?? Kxf2 is the stuff of nightmares. However, mate will occur fairly quickly if White remembers to keep his Rooks far away from black's King: 1...Kf3 2.Rg8! Kf2 (Threatening the other one.) 3.Re7 (And not 3.Ree8 since then our "Staircase footwork" wouldn't be possible.) 3...Kf3 4.Rgf8+ Kg4 5.Rg7+ Kh5 6.Rh8 mate.

2.Rg8

Gaining distance from the black King so the Rook can give check without being attacked.

2...Kd2

Threatening this Rook is an act of defiance, but White won't let it be taken.

3.Re7

This Rook creates checking distance while retaining its grip on the e-file fence. Now White is finally ready to push the black King to the queenside, where it will meet its doom.

3...Kd3 4.Rd8+

> **REMEMBER**
>
> Rooks usually prefer to check at a distance!

Diagram 11

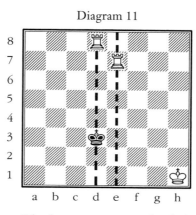

Black must step to the left

The two Rooks control the e- and d-files, thus forcing the black King to the left.

4...Kc4

The King was forced to step to the left since the d-file has been annexed by one Rook, while the e-file is untouchable due to the presence of the Rook on e7.

5.Rc7+

Now the Rooks control the c- and d-files, and black's King must get even closer to the dreaded edge of the board.

5...Kb5 6.Rb8+

Black's King has finally been forced to the side of the board.

6...Ka6

Stopping 7.Ra7+ due to 7...Kxa7.

7.Rc1

Diagram 12

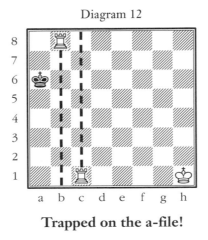

Trapped on the a-file!

The Rook on the b-file leaves black's King trapped on the a-file, waiting to be mated. Now the other Rook steps a safe distance away from the enemy King in preparation for the final, soul-destroying check.

7...Ka7

The impudent King threatens the other Rook too.

8.Rb2

Both Rooks are out of the black King's reach and mate can finally be administered.

8...Ka6 9.Ra1 mate.

That's it for the Staircase! Play around with it a bit more and, when it becomes mindlessly easy, move on to our next technique.

The Box

This is a very important endgame idea, and chances to use it will occur remarkably often throughout your chess career. Keep in mind that the Box isn't always the fastest way to mate, merely the easiest to learn.

In the case of both King and Queen vs. King, and King and Rook vs. King, the goal is to imprison the enemy monarch in an ever-shrinking Box.

The point about using both King and Queen to force mate is an important one. Chess is a team game where your pieces depend on your whole army to get a job done. Since a lone Rook or even Queen can't mate the enemy King, you will have to get your King involved if you wish to score the full point.

In most endgames—basic and complicated—King participation is a huge part of a successful winning campaign or defensive stand.

Two mandates for a successful Box:

➤ Use your King!

Diagram 13

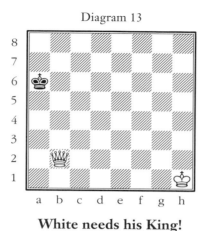

White needs his King!

In diagram 13, White can't mate without the aid of his King. Thus he needs to march it over to the queenside immediately!

➤ Trap the enemy King in an ever-shrinking Box and then slowly but surely tighten it.

Diagram 14

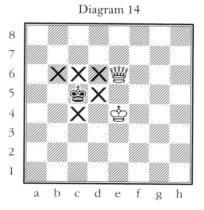

Black's King is running out of room

In diagram 14, White has just moved his Queen from g6 to e6, taking a whole group of squares away from black's King (as shown by the X's). After **1...Kb5 2.Kd4 Kb4 3.Qb6+** one can see how quickly the Box shrinks. Mate follows **3...Ka3 4.Kc3 Ka4** (or 4...Ka2 5.Qb2 mate) **5.Qb4** mate.

In diagram 15, black's King is trapped on the a- and b-files. However, by playing **1.Rc3**, the King's available territory shrinks into a small Box on a2, a1, b2, and b1. Notice that white's King firmly defends its Rook on c3.

Diagram 15

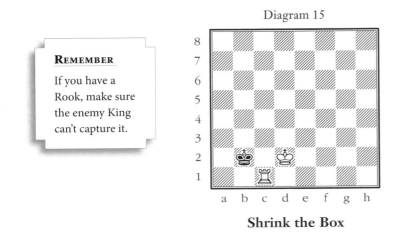

Shrink the Box

King and Queen vs. Lone King

Diagram 16

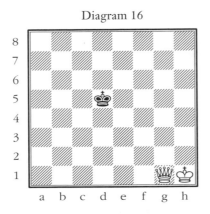

White needs to use both Queen and King

1.Qe3

This move immediately traps the black King in the diagramed Box.

Diagram 17

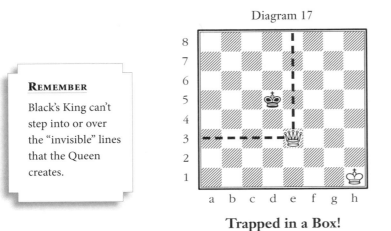

Trapped in a Box!

Of course, 1.Qe3 isn't the only way to win. One other way (though there are many—some are faster, but this doesn't concern us since we want to stick with our Box theme) is: 1.Qg4 (creating a Box from g4-a4 and g4-g8) 1...Ke5 2.Kg2 Kd5 3.Qf4 (tightening the Box, which now runs from f4-f8 and f4-a4) 3...Ke6 4.Qg5 (black's world continuously shrinks) 4...Kd6 5.Qf5 Kc6 6.Qe5 Kb6 7.Qd5 Kc7 8.Qe6 Kb7 9.Qd6 Kc8 (Or 9...Ka7 10.Qb4 Ka8 and now White rushes his King up so it can help deliver mate: 11.Kf3 Ka7 12.Ke4 Ka6 13.Kd5 Ka7 14.Kc6 Ka8 15.Qb7 mate) 10.Qe7 Kb8 and now that black's King is trapped on the back rank, White need only swing his King over to end the game: 11.Kf3 Kc8 12.Ke4 Kb8 13.Kd5 Kc8 14.Kc6 Kb8 15.Qb7 mate.

1...Kc4 2.Kg2

White's King rushes up so it can help its Queen push the enemy monarch to the edge of the board.

2...Kd5 3.Kf3 Kc4 4.Ke4

Depriving the black King of the use of the d5-square.

4...Kb4 5.Kd5

Diagram 18

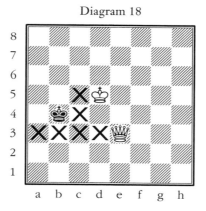

White's King and Queen are a team

The poor black King is running out of options since white's two pieces are taking more and more squares away from it.

5...Kb5

The end comes even faster after 5...Ka4 6.Kc5 Ka5 7.Qa3 mate.

6.Qb3+ Ka6

Already trapped on the side, the end is very near.

7.Kc6

White's King must come close so it can support the Queen's final move.

7...Ka5

Or 7...Ka7 8.Qb7 mate.

8.Qb5 mate.

Study this endgame carefully until you can easily checkmate your friends and your computer from the starting position of diagram 16.

King and Rook vs. Lone King

This ending is by far the hardest we'll study in this beginner to 1000 section. As in Queen and King vs. Lone King, White can only mate if his King participates in the process. And, as with the other positions we've explored, we'll solve this one by using the "shrinking Box technique."

First, let's start from the end and show the most basic winning situation.

Diagram 19

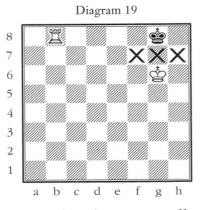

A mate based on a team effort

A team effort has led to the mating of the black King. White's King has deprived its counterpart of f7, g7, and h7, while the Rook calls check and dominates the whole back rank.

Clearly, White needs to do two things to win the King and Rook vs. lone King endgame:

➤ He needs to employ both his King and Rook. The lone Rook can't mate the enemy King.

➤ He needs to drive Black to the edge (any edge!) of the board.

Our next position shows how we reached that final mate.

Diagram 20

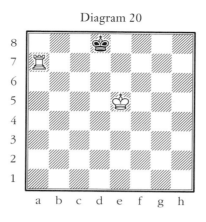

White's King to the rescue

Black is trapped on the back rank. However, a mate isn't possible without help from the white King.

1.Kd6

The move to d6 (1.Ke6 is just as good) threatens mate, but black's King doesn't intend to stay around and let it happen!

1...Ke8

Or 1...Kc8 2.Rh7 (giving Black a move he doesn't want and putting distance between the Rook and the black King) 2...Kb8 3.Kc6 (calmly walking the black King down) 3...Ka8 4.Kb6 Kb8 (an example of forced suicide) 5.Rh8 mate.

2.Rb7

The only way White can win is to force the black King to step in front of white's. The direct approach doesn't work: 2.Ke6 Kd8 3.Kd6 Ke8, etc. The seemingly innocuous 2.Rb7 gives away a move and sets up a situation where Black will be forced to do the very thing he dreads: to step in front of the white King and allow an instant mate.

2...Kf8

Putting off the inevitable, which would have instantly occurred after 2...Kd8 3.Rb8 mate.

3.Ke6

Now we can see white's strategy: Not wanting to play 3...Ke8 due to 4.Rb8 mate, Black is forced to flee to the right. However, he will soon run out of board and this will force him to dance the other way—right into white's web!

USEFUL ADVICE

White will usually mate his opponent by forcing the enemy King to self-destructively step in front of white's (thus giving us the kind of position shown in diagram 19).

REMEMBER

In general, put as much distance as possible between your Rook and the enemy King!

Diagram 21

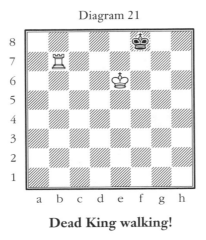

Dead King walking!

3...Kg8 4.Kf6

Calmly walking the enemy King down. White prepares for black's forced self-immolation.

4...Kh8 5.Kg6

Now Black has nowhere to go, so with head held high he steps into Death's embrace.

5...Kg8 6.Rb8 mate.

We are finally ready to see how to get black's King to the side of the board. It can't be mated in the middle, so chasing it to any edge is absolutely essential!

Diagram 22

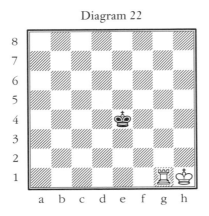

Black's King can't be mated in the middle

1.Rg3

This move creates our first Box from g3-g8 and g3-a3, as shown in diagram 23.

Diagram 23

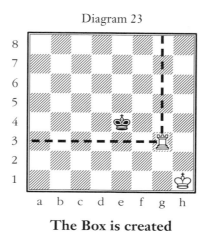

The Box is created

1...Kf4 2.Kg2

It is imperative that you use your King in this endgame! Both of white's pieces MUST work together if he wishes to succeed in pushing the black King to one of the edges of the board.

2...Ke4 3.Rf3

Tightening the Box, which now runs from f3–f8 and f3–a3.

3...Kd4 4.Kf2

4.Re3?? tightens the Box again, but also allows the "unfortunate" 4...Kxe3.

4...Ke4 5.Ke2

White's King, which will take squares away from the enemy monarch and will defend the Rook, always wants to be right in the midst of the action!

5...Kd4

No better is 5...Ke5 6.Kd3 Kd5 7.Rf5+ Ke6 8.Ke4 Kd6 9.Re5 when White returns to the same kind of Box tightening that we see in our main line.

6.Re3

Diagram 24

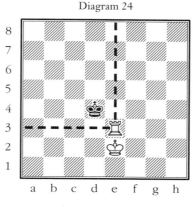

Slow and steady

You should be getting a feel for the method by now: shrink the Box with the Rook, move the King, shrink the Box with the Rook, move the King. Repeat until mate occurs.

> **REMEMBER**
>
> White is *not* in any hurry. Just follow the prescribed process and the game will literally win itself.
>
> **USEFUL ADVICE**
>
> In general you want to keep your Rook as far away from the enemy King as possible. One of the few exceptions is when you're creating Boxes in an effort to push the enemy King back to one of the board's corners or sides.

6...Kc4 7.Rd3

Forming a new (and rapidly shrinking!) Box from d3-d8 and d3-a3.

7...Kb4 8.Ke3 Kc4 9.Ke4

As before, there are many ways to win (don't screech that your computer announces a faster mate—the word "faster" has absolutely no meaning in the present context!), but putting the white King in the enemy's face is always a good idea in this particular endgame.

9...Kc5 10.Rd4 Kb5 11.Kd5

Diagram 25

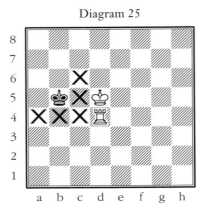

White's King takes away c5 and c6 from Black

The white Rook and King join forces to dominate black's only existing unit.

11...Kb6 12.Rb4+ Kc7

Black doesn't want to play 12...Ka5, 12...Ka6, or 12...Ka7 since that would instantly trap his King on the edge—something he's trying desperately to avoid.

One sample: 12...Ka6 13.Kc6 Ka7 (13...Ka5 14.Rc4 Ka6 15.Ra4 mate) 14.Rb1 (black's King will soon be forced to commit suicide) 14...Ka8 15.Kc7 Ka7 16.Ra1 mate.

13.Rb2

A quiet move that forces Black to move to the back rank or step in front of white's King. Naturally, 13.Rb5, 13.Rb3, or 13.Rb1 would all have the same effect.

13...Kd7 14.Rb7+

Black is finally forced to the edge.

14...Kd8 15.Kd6

Diagram 26

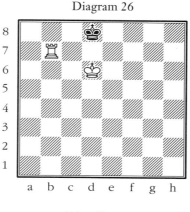

It's all over

15...Ke8

Or 15...Kc8 16.Rb6! when Black must commit suicide by 16...Kd8 17.Rb8 mate. After 15...Ke8 we get the scenario from diagram 21—black's King tries to avoid stepping in front of white's King, but it soon runs out of board and must embrace Armageddon against its will.

16.Ra7 Kf8 17.Ke6 Kg8 18.Kf6 Kh8 19.Kg6 Kg8 20.Ra8 mate.

That's it! You now know the winning ideas for all overkill endgames.

Stalemate Alert!

When I played in my first tournament (at age twelve), it suddenly occurred to me that I didn't know the difference between checkmate and stalemate. Later in life I got a long distance phone call from a couple in New York who had somehow found my number. It seems they had a disagreement over what a checkmate and stalemate were, and had placed a bet. The man was positive that he was going to win the wager, and he was stunned when I explained that he was completely wrong.

Just in case you are suffering from the same confusion I (and that couple) did, let's clarify both (using Black as the weaker side):

<u>STALEMATE</u>: Black's King is *not* in check, but there is no legal move on the board that would not result in the King's capture. Since you're not allowed to purposely place your King on an attacked square, a state of "stalemate" is said to exist and the game is declared a draw.

<u>CHECKMATE</u>: When White is threatening to capture the black King and Black can't do anything to prevent its loss, the game is declared over due to checkmate, with White winning the game as a result.

Diagram 27

Suicide is not allowed!

If White has the move in diagram 27, he wins by 1.Qb1 mate or 1.Qb2 mate or 1.Qa3 mate or 1.Qa4 mate. In each case the black King is threatened with capture and has no way of preventing it!

If *Black has the move* in diagram 27, there are only three possible places for the black King to go: ...Ka2, ...Kb2, or ...Kb1. However, ...Ka2 would allow Qxa2, ...Kb2 would allow both Qxb2 and Kxb2, and ...Kb1 would allow both Qxb1 and Kxb1. A King is not allowed to step onto an attacked square, which means Black doesn't have a legal move. Thus, the game ends in stalemate and is declared drawn.

Diagram 28

Black to move
Many pieces, still a stalemate

> **REMEMBER:**
> The difference between checkmate and stalemate: in the case of a checkmate, the enemy King is in check and can't escape capture. In the case of a stalemate, the enemy King is *not* attacked, he has no legal move, and thus the game is drawn because a player can't be forced to do something illegal.

A stalemate can occur when Black has a lone King or several pieces. In diagram 28, a close look tells us that none of black's pieces can legally move—any move of the e1-Bishop hangs the King to Rxa1, any move of the Knight hangs the King to Bxa1, the pawn is blocked by its white counterpart and can't move, and black's King can't move to a2 (due to Qxa2) or b1 (due to Kxb1). However, at the moment black's King isn't under attack, which means that the game will be declared drawn by stalemate since you are never allowed to make an illegal move.

Diagram 29

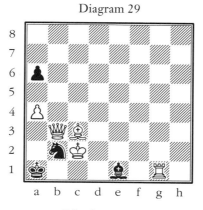

Black to move
Not a stalemate

In diagram 29 Black does *not* draw by stalemate because he has a legal move: **1...a5** (which he must play), which should be met by **2.Qxb2** mate, or **2.Bxb2** mate, or **2.Qa3** mate, or **2.Rxe1** mate.

Diagram 30

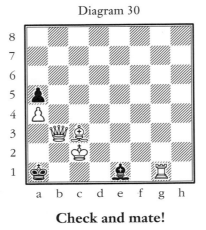

Check and mate!

This is similar to diagram 28, but this time black's King is under direct attack by the c3-Bishop. Since 1...Ka2, 1...Kb2, and 1...Kb1 all illegally place the King on an attacked square, and since 1...Bxc3 isn't legal since it allows Rxa1, the game ends with checkmate and a white victory.

> **USEFUL ADVICE:**
> Mastering the overkill checkmates means you have also become acutely aware of stalemate disasters.

It's very important to know what a stalemate is—when you are winning the game you want to avoid falling for one and tossing your win into the garbage. However, when you are the weaker side, being aware of possible stalemate swindles will occasionally save you a precious half point.

Our next example illustrates a nice blend of basic mate strategy with a stalemate spider-sense.

Diagram 31

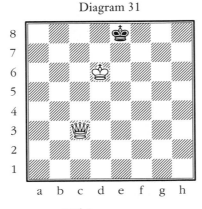

White to move

1.Qg7! This is the move that best fits in with our endgame philosophy: trap the King on the back rank and mate will surely follow. After **1...Kd8** (forced) **2.Qd7** it's mate.

Another move that fits in with this concept is 1.Qc7, trapping the black King, when **1...Kf8 2.Ke6 Kg8 3.Kf6 Kh8 4.Qg7** is mate.

Notice how nice and simple these moves are, but what about **1.Qf6?** This seems effective, but there's one problem: the game suddenly is drawn due to stalemate! That's right, Black has no legal moves because he's not allowed to move his King into check.

Summing Up

- In the endgame, the enemy King can rarely be mated in the middle of the board. You almost always want to chase it to one of the four sides, or to a corner.

- The Staircase maneuver is the easiest way to make use of a lopsided material count such as two Queens vs. lone King, Queen and Rook vs. lone King, or two Rooks vs. lone King.

- The Box is a technique that enables you to limit the enemy King's space. As you shrink the Box, you force his King to eventually retreat to the side of the board, where you will finally be able to mate it.

- If you are left with King and Queen vs. lone King, or King and Rook vs. lone King, you can't mate with the major piece alone. You will need to use both your major piece and King to finish the enemy off.

- Watch out for stalemates! There is nothing worse than setting your opponent up for the killing blow, then botching the whole thing to a draw by overlooking that you've stalemated his King! In situations where stalemates might be possible (i.e., the King has limited squares to move to), always take a moment before moving and ask, "When I play this move, will his King have a legal square to go to?"

Tests and Solutions

TEST 1

Diagram 32

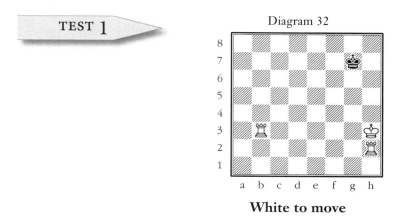

White to move

White has a forced mate in four.

TEST 2

Diagram 33

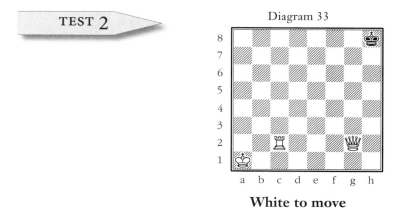

White to move

Is it wise to play 1.Rc7, trapping the enemy King on its back rank?

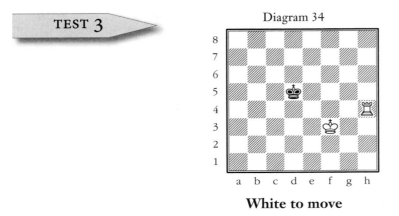

Diagram 34

White to move

Trap the enemy King in the smallest possible Box.

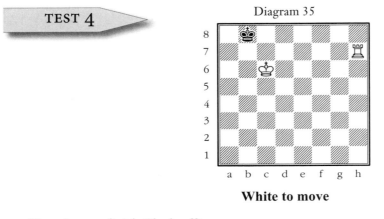

Diagram 35

White to move

How do you finish Black off?

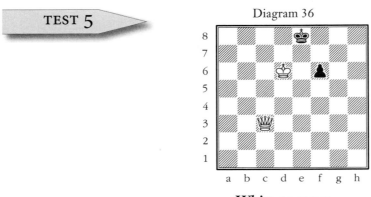

Diagram 36

White to move

Can White safely take the pawn on f6 with his Queen? Should he do so?

TEST 6

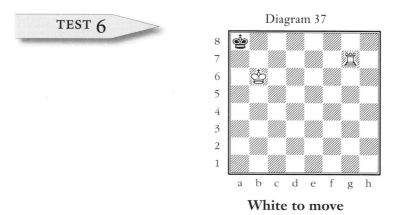

Diagram 37

White to move

It's mate in one, can you find it?

*   *   *   *   *

SOLUTION 1

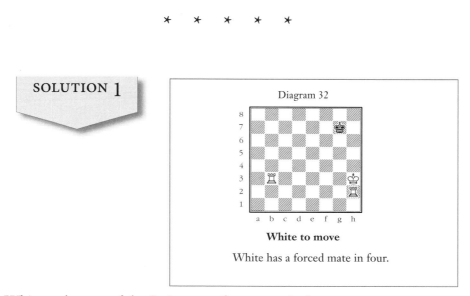

Diagram 32

White to move

White has a forced mate in four.

White makes use of the Staircase to force mate in four:

1.Rb6!

This traps black's King on its 2nd rank. An alternative solution is 1.Rf3! Kg6 2.Rg2+ Kh5 3.Rf4 Kh6 4.Rh4 mate.

1...Kf7 2.Ra2!

This sets up a Staircase and also makes both Rooks safe from attack by placing them as far from the enemy King as possible.

2...Ke7 3.Ra7+

A perfect Staircase: one Rook stops the enemy King from stepping up to its 3rd rank while the other Rook forces the King back to the vulnerable 1st rank.

3...Kd8 4.Rb8 mate.

SOLUTION 2

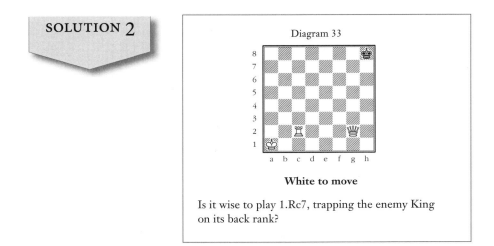

Diagram 33

White to move

Is it wise to play 1.Rc7, trapping the enemy King on its back rank?

No! Though 1.Rc7 seems very strong, you are taking the h7 square away from the defending King, while the Queen is depriving the black monarch of g7 and g8. This means it doesn't have any legal moves and a draw by stalemate results. Instead, the simple **1.Rc1** (1.Rc3, 1.Rc4, or 1.Rc5 also mate on the h-file, while 1.Qb7 followed by 2.Rc8 mate also does the job) **1...Kh7 2.Rh1** mate is quick and painless.

SOLUTION 3

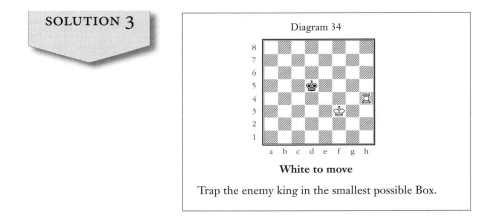

Diagram 34

White to move

Trap the enemy king in the smallest possible Box.

1.Re4! immediately traps the black King in a Box whose borders are from a4 to e4 to e8. Once you learn to recognize and create such Boxes, mating with a King and Rook vs. King will prove easy.

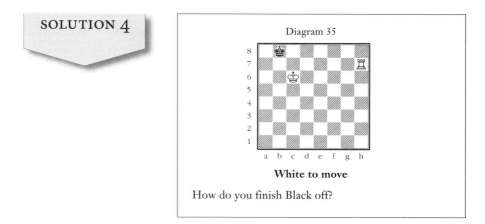

Diagram 35

White to move

How do you finish Black off?

To mate, you need black's King standing in front of yours. However, if you play 1.Kb6 he skips away by 1...Kc8, while the tempting 1.Rb7+ Ka8 2.Kb6?? is a draw by stalemate.

1.Rg7

White just wants to give Black the move so he will step in front of white's King. There are many ways to do this (1.Rg7, 1.Rf7, 1.Re7), though one nice alternative is 1.Rh8+ Ka7 2.Rg8 (Any Rook move along the back rank from h8 to c8 would serve the same purpose, which is to force black's King to commit suicide by stepping in front of white's King.) 2...Ka6 3.Ra8 mate.

Note that 1.Rd7 isn't as good since 1...Kc8 stops Rd8+

1...Ka8

Of course, 1...Kc8 is met by 2.Rg8 mate.

2.Kb6 Kb8 (No choice!) **3.Rg8** mate

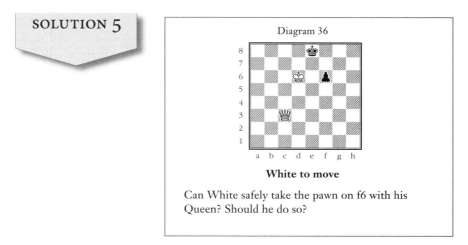

Diagram 36

White to move

Can White safely take the pawn on f6 with his Queen? Should he do so?

Taking the pawn is a horrible blunder since a stalemate occurs after 1.Qxf6??. Sticking to our "trap the enemy King on the side of the board" rule via 1.Qc7 is simplest *and* safest!

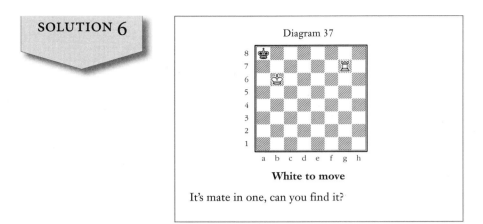

SOLUTION 6

Diagram 37

White to move

It's mate in one, can you find it?

If you know the difference between checkmate and stalemate, the right move is obvious: **1.Rg8** mate. However, if you don't know that difference, then 1.Rb7?? might prove attractive. Sadly, this creates a stalemate and a draw. If you didn't get this right, please go back and study the material under Stalemate Alert!

Final Thoughts

So you've learned to play chess, you've played a bunch of games online or with friends face to face, you've picked up an opening idea or two by glancing in a chess book, and you've also begun to recognize a few tactical tricks—often by painful experience! Now, having carefully gone over this chapter, you're able to finish-off an opponent if you reach an Overkill endgame situation.

It's time to put aside this book and continue to gain valuable over-the-board experience by crossing swords with players equal to or a bit better than yourself. If money is available, you can accelerate your progress by taking lessons. Of course, going over tactical quizzes is always a great idea—books featuring mates in one, two, and three, plus "White to play and win" tactical puzzles are plentiful and very useful.

Or, Study Part Two—which will put you one step ahead of your expected endgame IQ—and *then* put aside this book and follow the earlier advice.

In either case, once you feel you've improved and reached a higher rating/skill level, it will be time to crack open this book anew and move on to the next series of endgame lessons.

Part Two

Endgames for Class "E" (1000–1199)

Contents

My first rating was 1068. Aside from the overkill mates (see Part One), I knew nothing at all about endgames. This didn't seem to affect me too much because I lost the vast majority of my games rather quickly and rarely had need of any endgame skills at all. However, now—as an International Master—I'm very aware of the plight of the beginning tournament player, and can't allow the level of total endgame ignorance I possessed when I was a class "E" neophyte to carry over to my students. Instead, I always demand that they learn a few endgame basics that, though easy to absorb, will create a simple but highly useful foundation for later moves up the rating ladder.

Here in Part Two, you'll learn what material advantages do and don't win, and you'll take your first step into the world of serious endgame knowledge— you'll develop an appreciation for the powers of the King, the mysteries of the **Opposition**, and the drawing proclivities of the rook-pawns.

Sound daunting? It's all far easier to understand than you might imagine, and a couple hours effort will make you the master of this extremely important material.

What Can (or Cannot) Mate vs. Lone King

When you reach a position where your opponent has lost everything but his King (which, of course, can't be captured), it's a *must* to know what material you'll need to force a checkmate. On the other hand, you can save many poor positions by leaving your opponent with an insufficient amount of mating material when you are the one with the lone King. Clearly, a knowledge of what can (or cannot) mate vs. a lone King is extremely important!

1 > **Queen** = CAN!

2 > **Two Rooks** = CAN!

3 > **Rook** = CAN!

4 > **Two Bishops** = CAN!

5 > **Bishop and Knight** = CAN!

6 > **Pawn** = CANNOT! (Unless it can successfully promote.)

7 > **Bishop** = CANNOT!

8 > **Knight** = CANNOT!

9 > **Two Knights** = CANNOT!

We've already seen (in Part One) that a King and Rook (or more) vs. a lone King mates easily. Thus, the first three items on our list need no comment. (If you are not 100% sure that you can mate in those situations, go back and master those endgames!) Two Bishops (4) is too complex for this section but will be examined later in the book (though, considering your specific target rating, you might find that you will never have a need to learn it). Bishop and Knight (5) might never occur in your whole chess lifetime and is far too difficult to waste your precious study time on (in other words, this book won't examine Bishop and Knight vs. King at all). The basics of a lone pawn (6) will be presented here in Part Two, and a deeper knowledge of King and pawn vs. King will be presented in Parts Three and Four. Bishop (7) and Knight (8) are sad facts, but you simply can't mate your opponent with King and minor piece vs. King even if he's trying to help you! This leaves us with the final item on the list, two Knights vs. a lone King.

The odd case of two Knights vs. King is the most frustrating and unfair situation on our list. Two pieces up and White can't win against proper defense! How is that possible? Let's take a look.

Diagram 38

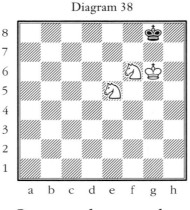

One move draws, one loses

The first thing that must be understood is that White only has a chance to deliver mate in this endgame if black's King blunders into a mate in one. Two Knights and King versus lone King can never force a mate (it takes help from the defender). In general, almost all self-mates in this endgame occur in the corner, so if black's King has been herded in that direction he needs to show a bit of care.

In the diagramed position, White has correctly chased black's King to the side of the board and has even driven him near that dangerous corner square. Black is in check by the f6-Knight and only has two legal moves. If he moves to the poisoned square on h8 he'll be mated by Nf7, however if he avoids it with 1…Kf8 then White will never be able to force mate. In other words, Black can only get mated if he blunders.

USEFUL ADVICE

Since the vast majority of blunder-mates in this endgame occur in the corners, make sure you dance away from them (and/or away from the enemy King) whenever possible and you'll be completely safe.

Minor Piece vs. Queen

Inexperienced players occasionally think that a lone minor piece (i.e., a Bishop or Knight) might be able to put up some resistance versus a lone Queen. Let me assure you that nothing could be further from the truth! We will explore both possibilities (Bishop vs. Queen and Knight vs. Queen) and demonstrate beyond any shadow of a doubt that the poor minor piece is completely outgunned.

Bishop vs. Queen

This is a no contest! One poor Bishop can't hope to face off against a mighty Queen!

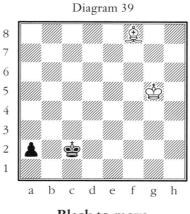

Diagram 39

Black to move

1...a1=Q

It's important that Black promote his pawn immediately else White will prevent it by Bg7.

Black should treat a Queen vs. Bishop situation in the same way as a King and Queen vs. lone King. The only difference: you must be a bit careful about stepping onto the colored squares controlled by the Bishop.

2.Bd6 Kd3

The game can't be won without help from the King!

> **USEFUL ADVICE**
>
> In a Queen vs. dark-squared Bishop endgame, stay on light-squares as often as possible and the Bishop becomes a non-entity.

3.Kf5 Qf1+

Black will patiently kick the enemy King around a bit and, after some prodding, make it give ground to black's monarch.

4.Ke5 Qe2+

Black's Queen continues to torment white's King.

5.Kf5 Qh5+

Finally pushing the enemy King back, since 6.Kf4 Qh2+ wins the Bishop.

6.Kf6 Ke4

Black's King will always step closer to white's whenever it's possible to do so.

7.Bf8

Trying not to move the Bishop too far from its King since that could easily lead to its loss. For example: 7.Bg3 Qf3+ snares the adventurous Bishop.

Other tries are certainly no better: 7.Bc7 Qh6+ 8.Ke7 Kd5 9.Bd8 Qg7+ 10.Ke8 Ke6 and mate follows next move; 7.Be7 Qh6+ 8.Kf7 Kf5 and black's progress is obvious.

7...Qe5+

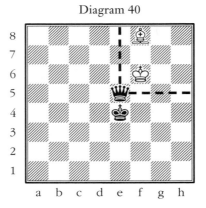

Diagram 40

Making use of the Box technique

8.Kg6 Qe8+

Threatening the King and Bishop at the same time.

9.Kg7 Kf5

Tightening the Box until mate occurs.

10.Ba3 Qg6+ 11.Kh8

11.Kf8 Ke6 followed by 12...Qf7 mate.

11...Ke6

Intending 12...Kf7 followed by 13...Qg8 mate.

12.Be7 Kf7!

Not falling for 12...Kxe7?? when the game is drawn by stalemate!

13.Bf8

"Please take my Bishop!" Of course, Black is on to the stalemate and will avoid touching white's Bishop.

13...Qg8 mate. Black won by treating the endgame as a King and Queen vs. lone King ending—the Bishop was more ghost than threat, and in some cases its presence helped Black avoid stalemate!

Knight vs. Queen

As with Queen vs. Bishop, Queen vs. Knight is a fairly simple win, but here the Knight's strange leaping powers create some nasty forking possibilities!

Diagram 41

White to move

1.Kh2

Bringing the King over to help its Queen, but not falling for the horrific 1.Kg2?? Nf4+ when white's Queen and King are forked.

1...Ke6 2.Qd4

> **REMEMBER**
>
> A Knight can be tricky! If you're not paying attention, it can fork and win a Queen, so be careful!

The Queen moves up and takes command of a few more squares. White's King and Queen will continually do this so that, slowly but surely, the enemy King will be pushed to the side of the board.

2...Ne7

A trick! Do you see what Black is hoping for?

3.Qe4+

Again, White's on guard and doesn't fall for 3.Kg3?? Nf5+ when the pesky
Knight has saved the day.

3...Kf6 4.Kg3

White's King has to get as close to black's King as possible.

4...Ng6 5.Kg4

Threatening Qf5+ followed by Kg5.

5...Ne5+ 6.Kh5

White's King and Queen are surrounding black's King and Knight. Soon he'll
be forced to step back to the fatal sidelines.

6...Ke6

On 6...Nd7, White would continue the squeeze by 7.Qc6+ Ke7 8.Kg5 (and
not 8.Kg6?? Ne5+ and there goes white's Queen!).

7.Kg5 Kd6 8.Kf5 Nd7 9.Qd4+ Ke7

Also hopeless is 9...Kc6 10.Ke6 Nc5+ 11.Ke7 Kb5 12.Kd6, etc.

10.Qd5

Diagram 42

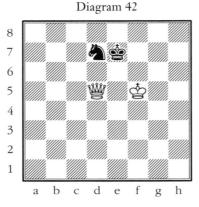

Patience is a useful quality

Patiently taking more squares away from black's pieces. Though 10.Qb4+ Kf7 11.Qb7 Ke7 12.Qc7 Ke8 13.Ke6 Nf8+ 14.Kd6 is even faster, our basic Box plan will make your life easier by offering a constant (and highly effective) idea to follow.

10...Nf8

And not 10...Nf6? 11.Qe6+ when the Knight is lost.

11.Qc5+ Kf7

Obviously, moves like 11...Kd7?? and 11...Kd8 allow 12.Qxf8.

12.Qc7+ Ke8

Black's King has finally been pushed back to the side of the board.

13.Kf6

Threatening 14.Qe7 mate.

13...Nd7+ 14.Ke6 Nf8+ 15.Kd6

There are no more checks and Qe7 mate is still a threat. The noose is tightening around black's neck!

15...Ng6

Covering the e7-square and giving the black King a place to run to on f8.

16.Qg7

A complete killer that hits the Knight and also takes away the f8-square from black's King. The Knight is hanging but any Knight move allows 17.Qe7 mate. That only leaves one other choice.

16...Kd8 17.Qd7 mate.

As we saw, to safely win this endgame you should:

➤ Always be on the lookout for Knight forks!

➤ Use your King and Queen as a team.

➤ Chase the enemy King to the side of the board.

➤ Be patient! As your Queen and King cut off more and more of the board, he'll eventually be forced to give ground and run for the sidelines, which is just where you want him!

Understanding the King

Players that are starting out tend to think of the King as an annoyance—something that demands constant protection, but gives very little back in the life and death battles that ultimately determine a game's result. This view is as wrong as wrong can be, and the following material shows just how critically important the King is to success in chess.

Use Your King!

In chess, the opening and middlegame is a dangerous time for each side's King—both of them suffering from a "wanted dead-or-alive" mentality. The enormous threat of enemy pieces crashing through the center and mating one's King has led books and teachers to give the student a bit of excellent advice: castle as quickly as possible (this gets it out of the center and activates the Rooks) and shield the needy monarch behind its pawns.

Sadly, wisdom in one situation isn't always wisdom in another, and what passes for correct opening and middlegame strategy can often be wrong in the endgame. The truth is, *the King is a very strong piece* (at least as strong as a Bishop or Knight)! Unfortunately, the terror created by the game's early phases causes most players to lose sight of this piece's true worth.

The endgame poses very different problems and needs than the other phases. With minimal material remaining on the board, both players need to make use of everything they have left. Furthermore, in the endgame, pawns and Kings take on enormous significance. Since the threat to the Kings is no longer real (the enemy's limited army no longer poses any danger to his Majesty), both players should rush their King to the center of the board as quickly as possible!

LET ME REPEAT: Once the board clears of pieces, a player must make use of everything he has. The time has come for the King—which is finally safe from a possible assault by a large enemy force—to emerge and lead the remains of his army to the final victory. The message here is very simple: when an endgame occurs, rush your King to the center of the board!

Because of the King's importance, the tournament "E" player (i.e., those with a rating under 1200) needs to take the first steps in understanding the basic movements of the King and the white and black King's relation to each other. It is *very* important to look over the following examples again and again until the ideas are fully absorbed.

To start, let's take a quick look at a critically important endgame that occurs all the time:

Diagram 43

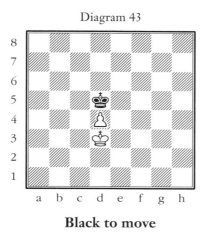

Black to move

Though White cannot mate with a King and lone pawn, he CAN promote his pawn to a Queen—a Rook will do, but why not go for the biggest gun possible? As a result of this fact, every King and pawn vs. King situation is all about one thing: can the pawn promote? The position in diagram 43 is a common one and shows a simple but intense battle: White wants a new Queen (which will lead to an easy win), and Black wants to stop this from happening (which will lead to a draw).

1...Kd6 2.Ke4 Ke6 3.d5+ Kd6 4.Kd4 Kd7 5.Ke5 Ke7 6.d6+ Kd7 7.Kd5 Kd8 8.Kc6 Kc8 9.d7+ Kd8 10.Kd6 stalemate.

Black managed to achieve his goal (draw). But do you know how he did it? Could White have improved his play? To understand what was going on and what the moves for both sides meant, you need a basic knowledge of Opposition. So, let's leap into that subject, thoroughly master it, and then return to the position in diagram 43.

Opposition

The quest for domination between two opposing Kings is called the Opposition, whereby one King tries to become stronger than the other.

Diagram 44

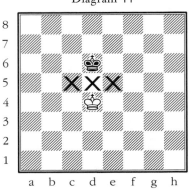

Basic Opposition
Whoever moves loses the Opposition

This diagram illustrates the most basic and direct form of Opposition (Of course, the absence of other material means that neither side can win. I'm just illustrating Opposition here and nothing else!). Both Kings would like to advance and gain ground, and both Kings have moved into a position that prevents the other from doing so. In such a situation it is a *disadvantage* to have the move since you must give up control of one of the blockade squares (shown by the three Xs in the diagram) and thus allow the opponent a way into your position. Thus Black to move would give White the *power of the Opposition* or, more simply put, the Opposition.

1...Kc6

Poor Black would like to say "pass" but this luxury is denied him. Note that 1...Ke6 would allow White to make inroads by 2.Kc5 while 1...Kd7 allows White to advance and keep the Opposition by 2.Kd5.

2.Ke5 White has successfully penetrated into the enemy position.

As you can see, owning the Opposition often allows your King to make advances into enemy territory. While this means nothing in a barren King vs. King situation, basic Opposition and the need to effect penetration into the hostile camp has enormous importance in a pawn endgame.

Let's go back to our earlier King and pawn vs. King position and study it more deeply.

Diagram 45

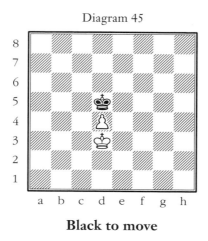

Black to move

In this initial position, White has an extra pawn *and* also possesses the Opposition (i.e., King's facing off with Black to move). Sounds good for White, doesn't it? Yet, the game is a dead draw *if* Black stops the white King from penetrating to the front of its pawn. This can only be done by using the knowledge you've gained of basic Opposition.

1...Kd6!

Though not strictly necessary at this early stage, it shows good form and an understanding of what eventually must be

> **RULE**
>
> When your King has to step away from the pawn, always go straight back!

done to save the game. The easiest way to fathom the importance of 1...Kd6 is by looking at what happens after 1...Ke6, namely 2.Ke4, when White has the Opposition. Compare this with the actual game continuation.

2.Ke4 Ke6

It seems that the positions after 1...Ke6 2.Ke4 and 1...Kd6 2.Ke4 Ke6 are the same. However, this isn't quite true. In the position after 1...Ke6 2.Ke4 it's Black to move and this means that White has the Opposition. In the game continuation—1...Kd6 2.Ke4 Ke6—it's White to move, meaning that Black has taken the Opposition and stopped white's King from stepping past its pawn. Please ponder this small but subtle difference until the concept of Opposition and the importance of who has the move completely sinks in.

An important mistake—that we will fully explore in Part Three—is 2...Kc6??. This let's white's King move forward (and step in front of its pawn) by 3.Ke5 when White wins (again, you can jump ahead to Part Three if you want an immediate explanation of this). Moves like 2...Kc7?? 3.Ke5, 2...Kd7?? 3.Kd5, and 2...Ke7?? 3.Ke5 also allow white's King to step in front of its pawn and *should be avoided*!

> **RULE**
>
> Don't let white's King step in front of its pawn unless you have no choice.

3.d5+

Retreating by 3.Kd3 or 3.Ke3 achieves nothing due to 3...Kd5.

3...Kd6

Once again stepping in front of the pawn and denying white's King access to the e5-square.

> **RULE**
>
> When you can step in front of your opponent's pawn, do so!

4.Kd4 Kd7!

Faithfully adhering to our rule of stepping straight back from the pawn. As shown previously, stepping to the side via 4...Ke7 allows White to take the Opposition by 5.Ke5.

5.Ke5

Nothing is to be gained by 5.Ke4 due to 5...Kd6.

5...Ke7

And Black once again has the Opposition.

6.d6+ Kd7 7.Kd5

Diagram 46

A do or die position

Black has three legal moves to choose from. One draws, two explode in black's face.

7...Kd8!

This is where things get serious! Now stepping to the side loses: 7... Kc8?? 8.Kc6 (taking the Opposition) 8...Kd8 9.d7 and we reach an enormously important situation:

Diagram 47

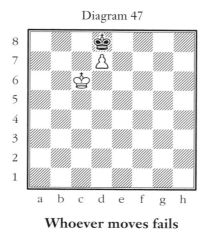

Whoever moves fails

If it's Black to move (as it is here), White wins because Black is forced to step to the side via 9...Ke7 and allow White to take ownership of the critical queening square on d8 with 10.Kc7. In the game, we reach this same position, except that White will have the move.

8.Kc6 Kc8 9.d7+ Kd8

This is the same position as was reached in the note to black's 7th move (diagram 47). However, now it's White to move instead of Black, and this means the game is drawn.

10.Kd6 stalemate and thus drawn. Of course, any other King move by White would have allowed 10...Kxd7.

Rook-Pawns

In most endgames, the presence of rook-pawns (a-pawns or h-pawns) gives the defending side drawing chances that normally would not exist. The reason for this resides in the diminished activity of any King that steps in front of such a pawn (since that King can now only move towards the center of the board—going the other way would make the poor monarch fall off the edge of the world). This diminished activity allows many stalemate possibilities that simply don't occur with other pawns.

Diagram 48

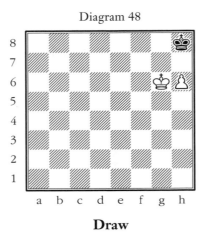

Draw

In this position White to move would win if he possessed any other pawn but a rook-pawn. However, the fact that it's an h-pawn ensures an easy draw:

1.h7

Normally Black would be forced to step to the other side of the pawn, allowing the white King to step forward and take control of the all-important queening square (as illustrated in diagram 49). However, because the blasted thing is an h-pawn, the game ends in immediate stalemate!

> **RULE**
>
> King and rook-pawn vs. lone King: If the defender's King gets in front of the pawn, the game will *always* be a draw!

Let's look at the same position pushed one file to the left.

Diagram 49

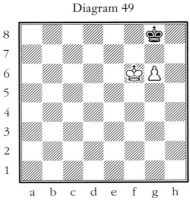

White to move wins

As in the previous position, it's White to move (Black to move would draw since he can retain the Opposition: 1...Kf8 2.g7+ Kg8 3.Kg6 stalemate). However, though this led to an immediate draw when White had an h-pawn, the fact that the pawn is now on the g-file gives White instant victory:

1.g7 Kh7

Here we see the difference! With the h-pawn, black's King could not step to the right. Here he can, and that proves to be his undoing.

2.Kf7

Grabbing control over the queening square.

2...Kh6 3.g8=Q Kh5 4.Qg3!

The most accurate move. White forces black's King to step back towards the white ruler.

4...Kh6 5.Qg6 mate.

In general, if you are defending a King and pawn endgame, the presence of rook-pawns enormously increases your chances for a successful (drawn) result.

Summing Up

➤ Two Knights vs. Lone King is a draw. Since the vast majority of blunder mates in this endgame occur in the corners, make sure you dance away from them (and/or away from the enemy King) whenever possible and you'll be completely safe.

➤ Queen vs. Bishop (no pawns for either side) or Queen vs. Knight (no pawns for either side) is easily winning for the Queen.

➤ The King is a strong piece and *must* be used in the endgame.

➤ The Opposition is an extremely important tool that allows one King to become stronger than another.

➤ Rook-pawns add to the defender's drawing chances in most endgames.

Tests and Solutions

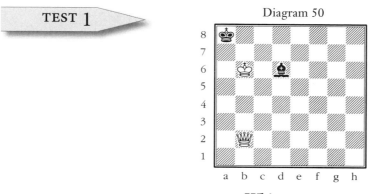

Diagram 50

White to move

Does White have anything to worry about?

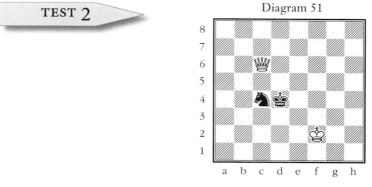

Diagram 51

White to move

Is 1.Kf3 a good move?

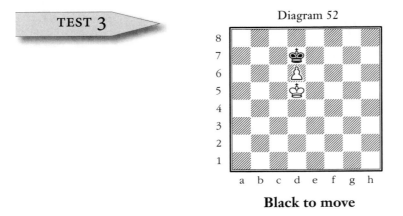

TEST **3**

Diagram 52

Black to move

Where should Black move his King?

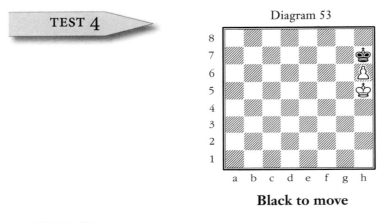

TEST **4**

Diagram 53

Black to move

Which King move is correct?

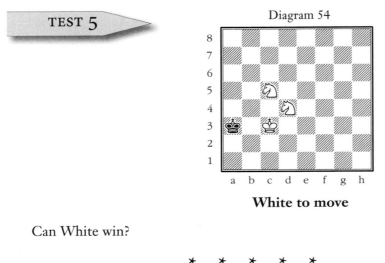

TEST **5**

Diagram 54

White to move

Can White win?

*   *   *   *   *

SOLUTION 1

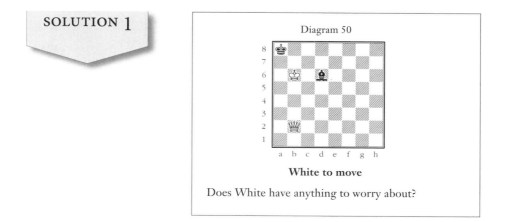

Diagram 50

White to move

Does White have anything to worry about?

A Queen easily overpowers a poor Bishop. In this position White has many ways to end the game, however, most face certain stalemate potholes:

➤ 1.Qh8+ (a good move) 1...Bb8 2.Qc8?? and the game ends via stalemate (and a draw) since Black can't legally move his King or his Bishop. Instead, 2.Qh1 mate ends matters in a happier way.

➤ 1.Qg7 (another good move) 1...Bc7+ 2.Qxc7?? stalemate (and draw). Always make sure your opponent has a legal move and this won't happen to you. Instead, 2.Kxc7 (giving black's King the a7-square) 2...Ka7 3.Qa1 mate is the way to go.

➤ 1.Ka6 (threatening Qb7 mate) 1...Bb4 2.Qxb4?? stalemate (and drawn). Why didn't White ask, "If I eat that Bishop, what can my opponent do?" If White had posed this simple question, he would have instantly seen that 2.Qxb4 was a move to avoid! One (of many) sufficient alternative was 2.Qh8+ Bf8 3.Qxf8 mate.

➤ 1.Qg2+ (by playing on light squares, White avoids any tricks by the enemy Bishop) 1...Kb8 2.Qb7 mate.

As in all endgames, stalemates play an important part in the defender's hopes and must always remain in the stronger side's mind as something to avoid at all costs.

SOLUTION 2

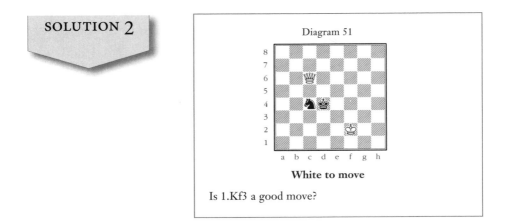

Diagram 51

White to move

Is 1.Kf3 a good move?

No, 1.Kf3?? allows Black to draw by 1...Ne5+, forking the King and Queen. Though Black will end up a whole Knight to the good, a lone Knight can't mate and so the game must be abandoned as a draw.

In a Queen vs. Knight endgame, there are only two ways the stronger side can blow it: stalemate or missing a Knight fork. If you have the side with the Queen, simply use some care and make sure neither of these possibilities occur.

SOLUTION 3

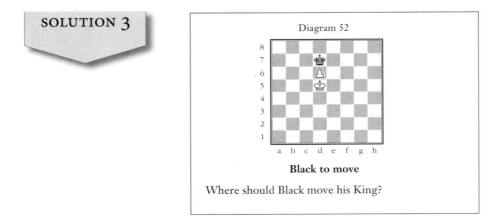

Diagram 52

Black to move

Where should Black move his King?

1...Kd8

If you didn't instantly play this move, go back and read over the material that covers this endgame! Remember: the defender must keep his King in front of the enemy pawn and, when it does have to move, it should go straight back so it can take the Opposition when the other King moves forward.

2.Ke6 Ke8

Taking the Opposition and stopping the white King from moving forward.

3.d7+

Or 3.Ke5 Kd7 4.Kd5 Kd8, etc.

3...Kd8 4.Kd6 stalemate.

SOLUTION 4

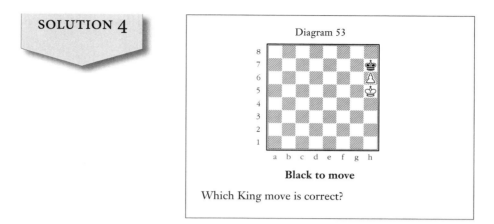

Diagram 53

Black to move

Which King move is correct?

Normally, the defender always wants to go straight back with his King in such situations. However, if he is facing a rook-pawn then it doesn't matter; either move suffices for a draw.

1...Kg8

Of course, 1...Kh8 would show good form, but here you simply can't go wrong.

2.Kg6 Kh8

Everyone in the room would know that the fix was in if Black played 2...Kf8?? (Where is that King going?) because 3.h7 forces resignation.

3.h7, ½-½. If this were any other pawn (other than another rook-pawn), White would win because the black King would have to step to the other side of the pawn. However, since there isn't another side to the pawn the game is drawn by stalemate.

SOLUTION 5

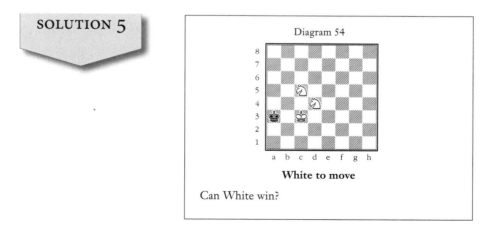

Diagram 54

White to move

Can White win?

No, two Knights can't win against correct defense:

1.Nb5+ Ka2 2.Kc2

Two pieces up and White has black's King cornered. Incredibly, it's still a draw!

2...Ka1 3.Nb3+

What else? 3.Nc3 is an immediate stalemate.

3...Ka2 4.Nd2 Ka1 and White can't put his opponent away.

Final Thoughts

Mastering these easy to learn endgames has given you your first taste of serious endgame theory. Knowing what can and can't mate is *must know* information, while a basic knowledge of the Opposition is crucial if you wish to thrive in the arena of players rated over 1000! These set up the foundation for the far more complex endgames you'll be learning as your overall chess strength continues to rise.

Part Three

Endgames for Class "D" (1200–1399)

Contents

Beyond Basic Opposition
King and Pawn Endgames
 King and Pawn vs. Lone King (Stronger Side's King
  is in Front of its Pawn)
 Another Rook-Pawn, Another Draw
 Non Rook-Pawn (One Square in Front, is it Enough?)
 Non Rook-Pawn (Two Squares in Front Always
  Does the Trick!)
 Fox in the Chicken Coup
 The Deep Freeze (When One Pawn Kills Two)
Minor Piece vs. Lone Pawn
 Bishop vs. Lone Pawn
 Knight vs. Lone Pawn
Rook vs. Lone Pawn
Summing up
Tests and Solutions
Final Thoughts

I remember going to my first tournament at age twelve. It was all quite magical, and as I watched other player's games in the under 1600 section I recall being amazed at their skills—skills which were far beyond anything I could fully understand at that time. Indeed, my view of 1200-1399 players as being demigods is not that out of line. Someone in this range is beginning to grasp many aspects of chess that would have seemed too difficult a short time before. If he plays in tournaments, he holds his own against many experienced players. If he competes against non-tournament playing friends, he most likely dominates them.

If you are reading this section, you either are a class "D" player, or you have learned all the material in the first two parts and wish to use this additional knowledge to help you break into the "1200-club." By this time you know a few openings, you have a reasonable grasp of tactics, and you've learned a positional concept or two. However, if you study with others in this rating range, you will quickly discover that endgames are not a priority, and endgame knowledge is often non-existent. That's one reason why players get stuck at a certain strength, and this is a shame since learning the material in the first three parts is within everyone's grasp—both talent-wise and time-wise.

So, before reading this section, make sure that you are thoroughly familiar with all the material presented in the first two parts of this book. Now it's time to gently add on to the knowledge we've already gained. You won't find anything too intense or profound here; all we're going to do is expand on the previously assimilated concepts and, when the smoke clears, leave you with a very solid endgame base. You'll need this for Part Four, which will take us far beyond anything presented thus far.

Here you'll add to your knowledge of Opposition, gain a deeper understanding of King-and-pawn vs. King positions, take a quick look at the drawing possibilities of rook-pawns, and be introduced to the simple but oh-so-important concept of Fox in the Chicken Coup.

Beyond Basic Opposition

In Part Two we learned all about basic Opposition—the battle of Kings that are only one square apart. This begs an obvious question: does Opposition exist if the Kings are more than one square away from each other? The answer is a resounding YES! In fact, Opposition exists from a distance, on diagonals, and even if the Kings don't seem to connect at all!

Sound terrifying? Too complicated? Trust me when I assure you that it's not. Carefully look over the material that follows (several times if necessary) and it will eventually begin to make sense. Then, after even more viewings, it will suddenly seem to be simplicity itself!

Diagram 55

White to move

Distant Opposition

Distant Opposition is similar to basic Opposition (i.e., King's facing each other with only one square separating them), only in extended form.

> **RULE**
>
> Whoever moves with an odd number of squares between the Kings *does not* have the Opposition (it's the same in basic Opposition situations: one/odd square separates the Kings and the person to move doesn't have the Opposition). Conversely, the person to move with an even number of squares between the Kings *does* have the Opposition.

In diagram 55, there is an even number of squares between the Kings and it's White to move. This means White has the Opposition, since by playing **1.Kd2** he changes it to an odd number with his opponent to move. If they continue to walk towards each other (via 1...Kd7 2.Kd3 Kd6 3.Kd4) we would get diagram 44 again.

The same idea holds true for diagonal connections.

Diagram 56

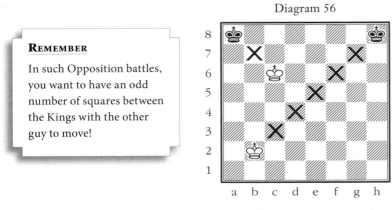

> **REMEMBER**
>
> In such Opposition battles, you want to have an odd number of squares between the Kings with the other guy to move!

Immediate and Distant-Diagonal Opposition

Diagram 56 shows both the immediate and the distant forms of Diagonal Opposition. Whoever moves *does not* have the Opposition.

It can be seen that it is not difficult to determine who has the Opposition when the Kings "connect" on a rank, file, or diagonal. But what if they fail to connect altogether? Does one have to get out a pocket calculator and solve prolonged mathematical formulas? Not at all!

Diagram 57

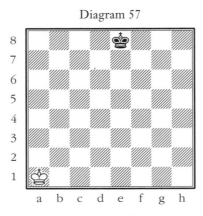

> **RULE**
>
> In this type of situation, the rule is to make a square or a rectangle in which each corner is the same color *with the other guy to move.*

Opposition without a direct connection

Take a long look at diagram 57.

White to move plays **1.Ka2!**, when we get a clear picture of what we're after in diagram 58.

Diagram 58

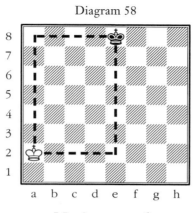

Magic rectangle
Each corner is the same color

This diagram shows the connecting points a2-a8-e8-e2. Note how each corner of this "rectangle" has the same colored square (in this case, a white square). After 1.Ka2, White has the Opposition. Here's proof:

1...Kf8 2.Kb2

Now b2, b8, f8, and f2 are the connecting points.

2...Ke8

Other moves allow quicker proof. For example 2...Kf7 3.Kb3 with Diagonal Opposition, or 2...Kg8 3.Ka2 with more of the same.

3.Kc2

Diagram 59

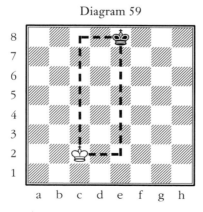

White still maintains the Opposition: the new
connecting points are c2, c8, e8, e2

3...Kf8

Similar is 3...Ke7 4.Kc3, while 3...Kd7 4.Kd3 is a basic form of Distant Opposition.

4.Kd2

Now d2, d8, f8, and f2 are the connecting points.

4...Kg8 5.Ke2

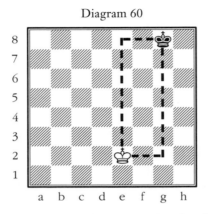

Diagram 60

New connection points are: e2, e8, g8, and g2

5...Kh8 6.Kf2

Can you make out the connection points? They are: f2, f8, h8, and h2.

6...Kh7

White's point is proven after both 6...Kg8 7.Kg2 and 6...Kg7 7.Kg3.

7.Kf3

The noose tightens. Connection points: f3, f7, h7, h3.

7...Kh8

There is nothing else since 7...Kh6 8.Kf4 makes a square (f4, f6, h6, h4) *and* gives direct Diagonal Opposition to boot!

8.Kf4 and now Black can't avoid our final proof since 8...Kh7 9.Kf5 gives Diagonal Opposition while 8...Kg7 9.Kg5 and 8...Kg8 9.Kg4 both give basic Direct Opposition.

King and Pawn Endgames

King and Pawn vs. Lone King (Stronger Side's King is in Front of its Pawn)

We've seen that the defender can usually draw if he gets his King in front of the enemy pawn. However, the stronger side's winning chances go way up if he manages to place his own King in front of his pawn. When this happens, three questions will decide the issue:

> **1** Is the pawn a rook-pawn?

> **2** Is the stronger side's King one square or two squares in front of its pawn?

> **3** Who possesses the Opposition?

Another Rook-Pawn, Another Draw

Unless the defending King is on vacation elsewhere on the board, the presence of a rook-pawn will make the game a draw.

Diagram 61

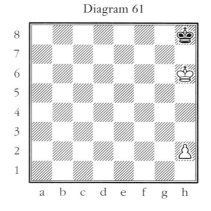

USEFUL ADVICE

If you're trying to win and you can enter a pawn up endgame where you have a rook-pawn, be careful! The words "rook-pawn" and "draw" seem to be bound at the hip!

Such a beautifully placed white King would ensure victory if the pawn was anything other than a rook-pawn. Unfortunately for White, black's King can't be chased out of the corner.

1.h4 Kg8

Black's moves are not hard to find!

2.Kg6 Kh8 3.h5

Even more pathetic is 3.Kf7 Kh7 (Again, the only legal move!) 4.Kf6 Kh6 followed by 5…Kh5 and 6…Kxh4.

3…Kg8 4.h6 Kh8

Of course, 4…Kf8?? 5.h7, 1-0, would leave us wondering about the state of black's mental health.

5.h7 stalemate.

Non Rook-Pawn
(One Square in Front, is it Enough?)

When the stronger side gets his King (on the 3rd, 4th, or 5th rank) directly in front of his pawn, the only question that matters is, "Who owns the Opposition?" If the defender has it, then the game is a draw. If the stronger side has the Opposition, then the game is won.

Diagram 62

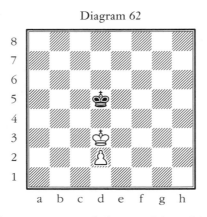

Whoever moves fails to achieve his goal

In diagram 62, whoever has the move *fails* to achieve his goal since that would give the opponent the Opposition. Let's first see what happens if White has the move (which means that Black has the Opposition).

> **REMEMBER**
>
> When the stronger side gets his King (on the 3rd, 4th, or 5th rank) directly in front of his pawn, the only question that matters is, "Who owns the Opposition?"

1.Ke3

Obviously 1.Ke2 Ke4 is our basic draw, studied in Part Two.

1...Ke5!

Retaining the Opposition and *not allowing white's King to come forward.* Losing is 1...Kc5 (it retains the Opposition but lets white's King dance forward) 2.Ke4 when White wins. We'll see how this is done in a moment.

2.Kd3

The basic draw is reached after 2.Kf3 Kd4, so White squiggles a bit before accepting the inevitable.

2...Kd5! 3.Kc3 Kc5 and White can't make any progress at all.

If Black moves first (from diagram 62), though, things are very, very different:

1...Ke5

Note that on 1...Ke6 2.Ke4, 1...Kc6 2.Kc4, and 1...Kd6 2.Kd4, White manages to move forward and retain the Opposition.

The other move, 1...Kc5, runs into 2.Ke4 with the same kind of play as will be seen against 1...Ke5.

2.Kc4

Retaining the Opposition by 2.Ke3 takes us back to our original position after 2...Kd5.

Diagram 63

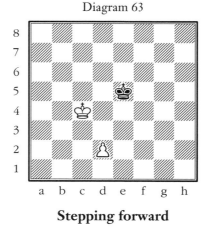

Stepping forward

Stepping forward is the most important thing, with Opposition taking a back seat to this. Why? Because White can only win if he gains control of the queening square, while also making sure that his pawn is safe. This takes us to the winning formula for such positions.

RULE

Move as far forward with your King as possible, while always making sure that your pawn is safe!

2...Kd6

Other moves:

2...Ke4 is aggressive, and hopes for 3.Kc5?? (Moving forward but forgetting the part about making sure the pawn is safe!) 3...Kd3 followed by ...Kxd2 with an immediate draw.

Thus, after 2...Ke4 White should play 3.d4! (Also good is 3.d3+ Ke5 4.Kc5!, and not 4.d4+?? Kd6 with a basic draw.) when black's King can't get back in front of the pawn: 3...Kf5 4.Kd5! (moving forward and depriving the black King of a host of important squares) 4...Kf6 5.Kd6 Kf7 6.Kd7 Kf6 7.d5 Ke5 8.d6 Kf6 9.Kc7 when White makes a Queen and wins the game.

2...Ke6 (This takes the Diagonal Opposition but fails to prevent the advance of white's King.) 3.Kc5 (and *not* 3.d4?? Kd6 with yet another basic draw) 3...Kd7 (another try, as hopeless as all the rest, is 3...Ke5 4.d4+! [avoiding 4.Kc6?? Kd4 when the white pawn falls] 4...Ke6 5.Kc6! [again, 5.d5+?? allows the basic draw by 5...Kd7] 5...Ke7 6.d5 Kd8 7.Kd6! Kc8 8.Ke7 and it's all over) 4.Kd5! (Not falling for 4.d4?? Kc7 when 5.d5 Kd7 is a basic draw, while 5.Kd5 Kd7 is also drawn since Black has the Opposition.) 4...Kc7 5.Ke6 Kc6 (5...Kd8 6.Kd6 Ke8 7.d4 Kd8 8.d5 Ke8 9.Kc7) 6.d4 (Making sure the pawn is safe. Moving forward by 6.Ke7?? Kd5 would be a true tragedy.) 6...Kc7 7.d5 (7.Ke7 Kc6 would force White to repeat after 8.Ke6) 7...Kd8 (else White would play Ke7) 8.Kd6! Kc8 (8...Ke8 9.Kc7) 9.Ke7 followed by pushing the pawn to the 8th.

3.Kd4

Diagram 64

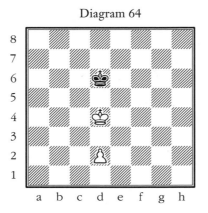

A very important moment. White was not able to advance his King safely anymore (i.e., 3.Kb5?? Kd5! and White can't stop his opponent from marching forward and eating the pawn), so it's time to regain the Opposition and once again force his opponent backward.

3...Ke6 4.Kc5

Continuing to trudge down the board, always getting closer and closer to that all-important d8-square.

4...Kd7

Black's defenses also fail after 4...Ke5 (still hoping for 5.Kc6?? Kd4, picking up white's pawn) 5.d4+ Ke6 6.Kc6 (Again, *not* 6.d5+?? Kd7 with a basic draw) 6...Ke7 7.d5 Kd8 8.Kd6! Kc8 9.Ke7 followed by pushing the pawn to the conquered d8-square.

5.Kd5

His pawn is safe, so White regains the Opposition. Naturally, 5.d4?? Kc7! would be a draw since white's King is only one square in front of the pawn with Black holding the Opposition.

5...Kc7 6.Ke6

More penetration, and a step closer to d8.

6...Kd8

One hopeless move among many. For example, 6...Kc6 7.d4 Kc7 8.d5 Kd8 9.Kd6 Ke8 10.Kc7 and wins.

7.Kd6

Also good enough is 7.d4 Kc7 8.d5 Kd8 9.Kd6.

7...Ke8 8.d4 Kd8 9.d5

This takes the Opposition and prepares one final bit of King penetration.

9...Ke8 10.Kc7 Ke7 11.d6+, 1-0.

Non Rook-Pawn
(Two Squares in Front Always Does the Trick!)

Diagram 65

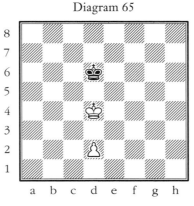

RULE

When the stronger side's King manages to get two squares in front of its pawn (unless it's a rook-pawn, of course), the game is always a win (and an easy one at that).

White wins, no matter who moves

Here it doesn't matter who has the move, White wins. Obviously if Black were to move, White would have the Opposition. But even if White has the move, he can take the Opposition by playing:

1.d3!

Suddenly it's Black to move, White has the Opposition, and we only have to follow the rules in our previous example to make the win a simple matter (1...Ke6 2.Kc5, etc.).

Fox in the Chicken Coup

Imagine a basic King and pawn vs. King endgame. Then add some (one vs. one, two vs. two, etc.) frozen pawns (meaning that they are locked together and can't move) on the other side of the board. Though a pawn up, how does the stronger side go about winning this kind of very common position? The answer: Fox in the Chicken Coup (yes, a pun)!

Diagram 66

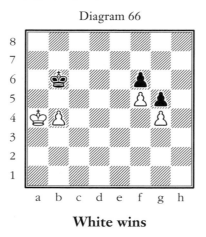

White wins

White wins in a walk by pushing the black King back and then abandoning it for the unguarded "chickens" on the kingside.

1.b5 Kb7

No better is 1...Kc5 2.Ka5 and the pawn queens.

2.Ka5 Ka7 3.b6+ Kb7 4.Kb5 Kb8 5.Kc6

> **REMEMBER**
>
> Fox in the Chicken Coup refers to a situation where the stronger side's King (the "fox") rushes to the other side of the board to feast on helpless enemy pawns ("chickens") while the defending King is busy dealing with a pawn on the other wing.

This position is a basic draw if the kingside pawns didn't exist. Unfortunately for Black, the fact that they are there leaves him dead in the water.

5...Kc8 6.Kd6!

White abandons his b-pawn, secure in the knowledge that while Black is busy dealing with it, White will capture all of black's bits on the kingside. Note that 6.b7+ Kb8 7.Kb6?? (7.Kd6 was still good enough) is a draw by stalemate.

6...Kb7 7.Ke6 Kxb6 8.Kxf6

Ah, chicken is indeed on the menu!

8...Kc7 9.Kxg5 and the rest is mindlessly easy: **9...Kd8 10.Kg6 Ke8 11.Kg7** (controlling the promotion square) followed by f5-f6-f7-f8=Q.

The Deep Freeze (When One Pawn Kills Two)

In King and pawn endgames, it's very important to avoid having your pawn majority devalued by allowing a smaller force to freeze a larger one in its tracks.

Diagram 67

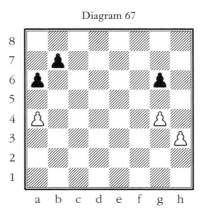

All sorts of interesting things are going on in this impossible diagram (no Kings!). For example, Black to move could create a passed pawn by 1...b5, while White to move could prepare the creation of a passer by 1.h4 followed by 2.h5.

However, the possibility to devalue the opponent's respective majority is also present. White to move could play 1.a5 when that one queenside pawn freezes black's two. On the other hand, Black to play could try 1...g5, when his one kingside pawn freezes both of white's.

Diagram 68

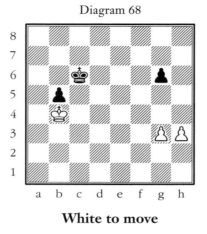

White to move

Though Black has a passed pawn, white's ability to create one of his own on the kingside ensures that the game will be drawn. However, disaster struck:

1.g4??

Correct was 1.h4 Kd5 (and not 1...Kb6?? 2.g4 Kc6 3.h5 gxh5 4.gxh5 and white's pawn will soon turn into a Queen) 2.g4 Ke4 3.Kxb5 Kf4 4.h5 gxh5 5.gxh5 Kg5 6.h6 Kxh6, ½-½.

1...g5

Diagram 69

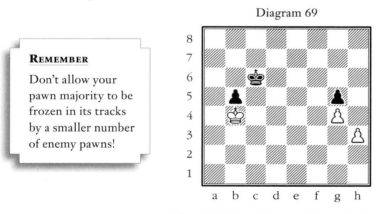

The Chicken Coup will seal the deal

Suddenly white's kingside majority is frozen and useless. Now Black is, in effect, a pawn up and he wins the game by using the Chicken Coup technique.

2.Kb3

Sacrificing the h-pawn in an effort to promote the g-pawn doesn't work: 2.h4 gxh4 3.g5 Kd6! 4.g6 Ke7 and Black stops white's g-pawn while White has no way of stopping black's h-pawn.

2...Kd5

While White has to deal with the b-pawn, black's King rushes over and demolishes white's two kingside bits.

3.Kb4 Ke4 4.Kxb5

Diagram 70

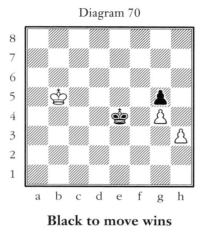

Black to move wins

4...Kf4!

Black must be careful since the natural looking 4...Kf3?? allows White to force a draw by the surprising 5.h4!! gxh4 6.g5.

5.Kc4

Now 5.h4 gxh4 is hopeless.

5...Kg3 6.Kd3 Kxh3 7.Ke3 Kxg4 8.Kf2 Kh3!

Making use of the rule that states, "When your King is in front of your pawn, go as far forward as possible until the pawn is in danger."

Mistaken is 8...Kf4 9.Kg2 g4?? (9...Kg4 would still win) 10.Kf2 with a basic draw.

9.Kg1

Or 9.Kf3 g4+ (avoiding the humiliation of 9...Kh2?? 10.Kg4 followed by Kxg5) 10.Kf2 when both 10...Kh2! and 10...g3+ 11.Kg1 g2 win.

9...g4 10.Kh1

White thinks he has the Opposition. Is this true?

10...g3

No, Black has it!

11.Kg1 g2, 0-1. There was no reason to play on and watch 12.Kf2 Kh2 transpire.

As you can see, a player must always be on the alert for such "freezing" moves!

Minor Piece vs. Lone Pawn

In positions where a minor piece (Bishop or Knight) faces a lone pawn, any winning chances that might exist lie with the pawn. This might seem strange, but it makes perfect sense: a lone Bishop or Knight can't mate, but a pawn has the potential to become a Rook or Queen. In such situations, players sometimes refer to pawns of this nature as "baby Queens" since they have one purpose in life: to reach the end of the board and become an adult!

The question, then, is very basic: can the Bishop or Knight stop the pawn from reaching its final destination? If it can, then a draw results. If it can't, the game must be immediately resigned since a lone minor piece can't withstand the raw power of a Queen (as we saw in Part Two)!

Bishop vs. Lone Pawn

This tends to be a ridiculously easy draw, since the Bishop can stop the pawn's march from a distance (which it can usually do even without help from its King).

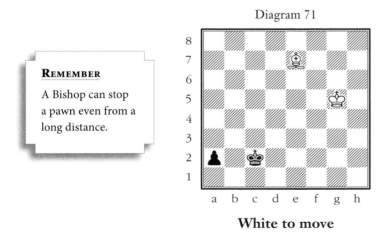

Diagram 71

REMEMBER

A Bishop can stop a pawn even from a long distance.

White to move

If it was Black to move he would win the game by 1...a1=Q, when the resulting Queen vs. Bishop endgame is completely hopeless for White. However, White to move draws easily (even though his King is far from the action) by **1.Bf6 Kb1**

70

2.Kf4 (white's King doesn't have to take part in this battle. The game would also be drawn if the Bishop endlessly shuttled back and forth along the a1-h8 diagonal.) **2...a1=Q 3.Bxa1**, ½-½.

Though a pawn can beat a piece if it can promote, there is one way that the piece can win.

Diagram 72

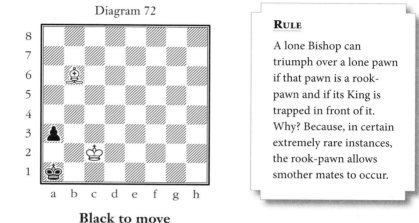

Black to move

> **RULE**
>
> A lone Bishop can triumph over a lone pawn if that pawn is a rook-pawn and if its King is trapped in front of it. Why? Because, in certain extremely rare instances, the rook-pawn allows smother mates to occur.

Black's pawn doesn't have any hope of promoting since his King is blocking its path to a1. A draw can be obtained by 1...Ka2 (one of only two legal moves!) when 2.Bd4 is a stalemate. However, if Black was in an "end it all mood" and couldn't find a noose, then an alternate form of suicide can be created by **1...a2?? 2.Bd4** mate.

Knight vs. Lone Pawn

The Knight doesn't have the long distance powers of a Bishop, but it can usually stop an enemy pawn even without help from its King *if* it's close to the pawn and can maintain control over the square in front of the pawn.

Diagram 73

Draw

The position in diagram 73 is drawn no matter whose turn it is. First, let's see what happens if White has the move.

1.Nb4+

Covering the c2-square. The Knight is more than happy to sacrifice itself for black's remaining pawn.

1...Kc4

Nothing is gained by 1...Kd2 2.Kg7 c2 3.Nxc2.

2.Nc2 Kb3 3.Nd4+

This Knight dance around the enemy pawn is the usual way such Knight vs. pawn endgames are saved—it allows the Knight to keep a permanent eye on the square in front of the pawn, thus stopping it from safely advancing. Such endgames are almost always drawn (the one exception is a rook-pawn) if the Knight can actually land on (or maintain a connection with) the square in front of the pawn (as it did on moves one, via 1.Nb4+, and two, 2.Nc2). Instead, 3.Na1+?? loses to 3...Kb2, winning the Knight and the game.

3...Kb2 4.Kg7 c2 5.Nxc2, draw.

Going back to diagram 73, we now give Black the move. However, the game is still a draw since White can target two squares in front of the pawn: c2 and c1.

> **RULE**
>
> If the Knight can safely land on (or keep connected to) the square (or squares, if the pawn isn't on the 7th rank) in front of the pawn, the game will be drawn (a rook-pawn being the one case where exceptions might occur).

1...Kc4!

A good try that doesn't allow the Knight access to the c2-square. An immediate draw follows the tempting 1...c2?? 2.Nb4+ followed by 3.Nxc2. Knight forks like this are common fare in Knight endgames, so be on the lookout for them!

2.Na5+

White also saves the game with 2.Ne5+, which leads to the same kind of play that is seen after 2.Na5+

2...Kb4

Things are easy for White after 2...Kb5 3.Nb3 Kb4 4.Nc1.

3.Nc6+ Kc5

Since 3...Kc4 4.Na5+ repeats the position, the only other aggressive move is 3...Kb5 but that falls on its face to 4.Nd4+ followed by 5.Nc2.

4.Na5 c2 5.Nb3+ Kc4 6.Nc1

Now White comfortably controls the square in the front of the pawn.

6...Kc3 7.Kg7

White has no reason to leave c1 unless he's attacked. However, even 7.Ne2+ works: 7...Kd2 (7...Kd3 8.Nc1+ Kd2 9.Nb3+) 8.Nd4! (threatening Nxc2) 8...c1=Q 9.Nb3+ picking up the newly born Queen before it even has a chance to blink!

7...Kb2

Black also has no chance to win after 7...Kd2 8.Nb3+ Kd1 (8...Kc3 9.Nc1 repeats the position) 9.Kf6 and the Knight on b3 is a rock that forever eyes c1.

8.Nd3+

Continuing with the Knight-jig. However, a calmer way to end things is 8.Ne2 when it's time to agree to the draw.

8...Kc3

8...Kb1 9.Kf6 also gives Black no hope at all.

9.Nc1 and Black is not able to make any progress and must (now or soon) agree to the draw.

> **REMEMBER**
>
> If the Knight can take control of any square in front of the pawn, the game is drawn.

As mentioned earlier, Rook pawns pose a problem for a Knight that doesn't enjoy the support of its King. Why is this? Because the Knight can't leap from one side of the pawn to the other because there is only *one* side to a rook-pawn!

Diagram 74

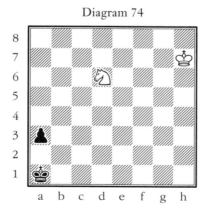

White to move draws, Black to move wins

We'll first give White the move from diagram 74.

1.Nb5 a2 2.Nc3 when Nxa2 with a draw can't be stopped.

Going back to the initial position in diagram 74, we'll now see what happens if Black has the move.

1...a2!

Simply intending 2...Kb1 followed by ...a1=Q and wins. Oddly, other moves don't work for Black:

> 1...Kb2?? 2.Nc4+ followed by 3.Nxa3.

> 1...Ka2?? 2.Nb5 followed by 3.Nxa3.

> 1...Kb1?? 2.Nb5 (2.Nc4?? a2 wins for Black) 2...a2 3.Nc3+ followed by 4.Nxa2.

2.Nc4

Hopeless is 2.Nb5 Kb2 when the Knight can't approach the pawn.

2...Kb1

Black's only legal move, but a winner nonetheless!

3.Na3+

Or 3.Nd2+ Kc2 and the "baby Queen" turns into an adult!

3...Kc1, 0-1.

Of course, White would have drawn this position if his King had been close:

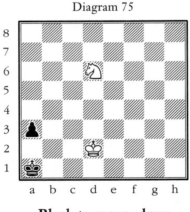

Diagram 75

Black to move, draw

1...Kb1

Or 1...a2 2.Kc1, draw. White could also draw by 2.Nc4 Kb1 3.Na3+ Kb2 4.Nc2 covering the queening square.

On 1...Kb2 White draws immediately with 2.Nc4+ followed by 3.Nxa3.

2.Nb5 a2 3.Nc3+ followed by **4.Nxa2, =.**

Here's another tweak in the general situation we've been looking at:

Diagram 76

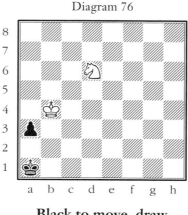

Black to move, draw

The pawn's hanging, and both 1...Ka2 and 1...Kb2 fail to 2.Nc4. Thus black's move is forced.

1...a2

Now 2...Kb1 or 2...Kb2 (depending on what White plays) followed by 3...a1=Q is threatened, so White has to put his Knight into overdrive if he wants to prevent this.

2.Nc4!

2.Nb5?? Kb2 (not 2...Kb1?? 3.Nc3+) forces the creation of a new Queen.

2...Kb1 3.Nd2+ Kb2 4.Nb3, ½-½.

The Knight can comfortably maintain its defense of the promotion square (a1) thanks to the secure protection of its King. Teamwork really is a wonderful thing!

As with the lone Bishop vs. lone pawn, the piece can occasionally win (in very rare instances!) only if the pawn is a rook-pawn and its King is trapped in front of it. Here's one such example of this occurring.

Diagram 77

White to move

1.Nb4!

Taking the a2-square away from black's King and forcing the pawn to advance. This leaves the black monarch stalemated, which means that any check will be mate.

1...a2 2.Nc2 mate.

> **REMEMBER**
> A lone Knight can only triumph over a lone pawn if that pawn is a rook-pawn and if its King is trapped in front of it. Why? Because, in certain rare instances, the rook-pawn allows smother mates to occur.

Rook vs. Lone Pawn

Unlike Bishop and King, which can't mate, Rook and King is a potent partnership. In this case the Rook will win if the pawn can be stopped or won. In this endgame, the side with the pawn can only hope to draw if the stronger side's King is too far from the action.

Diagram 78

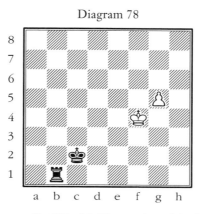

Leko - Kramnik, World Championship Match 2004

White to move

> **RULE**
>
> If the enemy pawn is well into its journey towards promotion, and if its King is helping, and if the Rook's King is off on vacation, then a draw will result.

In the present position, the pawn is too far and black's King is a non-participant. Thus, White won't have any problem saving the half point.

1.g6

The pawn is close to promoting, and black's King is too far to help stop the pawn's rush to g8.

1...Kd3 2.Kf5

It's very important that the King escort the pawn to the promised land. The immediate 2.g7?? would lose to 2...Rg1.

2...Rb5+

Also drawn is 2...Rf1+ 3.Ke6 Rg1 4.Kf7 Ke4 5.g7.

77

3.Kf6 Rb6+ 4.Kf7 Rxg6

Ending the game. Instead, 4...Rb7+ 5.Kf8 Ke4 6.g7 would still lead to the loss of black's Rook.

5.Kxg6, ½-½

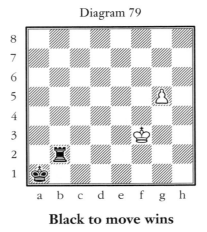

Diagram 79

Black to move wins

In diagram 79 we get to see an important winning maneuver:

1...Rb4!

This traps white's King along the 3rd rank and, as a result, also defuses the pawn. This idea doesn't work if white's King gets to the 4th rank or beyond (as it was in the Leko-Kramnik game).

2.g6

Or Black will calmly walk his King over to the kingside.

2...Rb6!

The point! Suddenly the poor pawn is on its own—its King is too far away to help it.

3.g7 Rg6, 0-1.

> **RULE**
>
> A pawn on the 5th rank and a King trapped on the 3rd rank by the enemy Rook is always a win for the side with the Rook.

In our next position (diagram 80), White wins (even though Black has the move!) because his King is close enough to the pawn to help the Rook stop it. A team effort between and Rook and King often allows White to fight successfully for control over the queening square.

Diagram 80

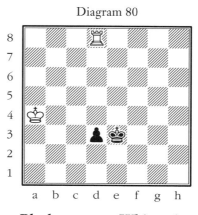

Black to move, White wins

1...d2

No better is 1...Kd2 2.Kb3 when black's pawn is going nowhere.

2.Kb3 Ke2 3.Kc2 and the pawn is lost, and with it the game.

Summing Up

Beyond Basic Opposition

➤ If the Kings are connected on a file, rank, or diagonal, then you can easily ascertain whether or not you possess the Distant Opposition—it's as simple as counting from one to six.

➤ The formula for Distant Opposition: You want an odd number of squares between the Kings with the *other* guy to move! (Conversely, if there is an even number of squares between the Kings, then you want to *have* the move.).

➤ To create Indirect Opposition, you want to create a square or rectangle connecting the Kings with every corner being the same color.

King and Pawn Endgames

➤ Rook-pawns often pose exceptions to all the normal endgame rules.

➤ In a King and pawn (any pawn *but* a rook-pawn!) vs. King endgame, the stronger side wins if his King (on the 3rd, 4th, or 5th rank) is one square in front of its pawn and he has the Opposition.

➤ In a King and pawn (any pawn *but* a rook-pawn!) vs. King endgame, if the stronger side's King is two squares in front of the pawn (which, of course, should be safe from capture!), he always wins.

Fox in the Chicken Coup

➤ Fox in the Chicken Coup is *the* way to win multi-pawn King endgames where one side possesses an outside passed pawn.

➤ The Fox in the Chicken Coup technique is: At the right moment, let the opponent win the passed pawn. While he's doing that, your King should be rushing towards the unprotected mass of enemy pawns, where it can eat them at will.

Minor Piece vs. a Lone Pawn

➤ A minor piece (Bishop or Knight) vs. a lone pawn is usually drawn, since the piece will sacrifice itself for the pawn and create a King vs. King draw.

Tests and Solutions

TEST 1

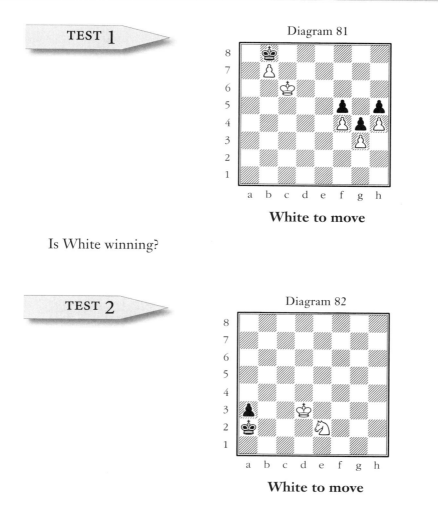

Diagram 81

White to move

Is White winning?

TEST 2

Diagram 82

White to move

Is White in any danger?

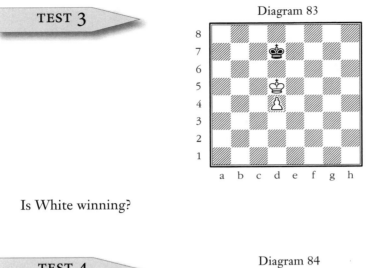

TEST 3

Diagram 83

Is White winning?

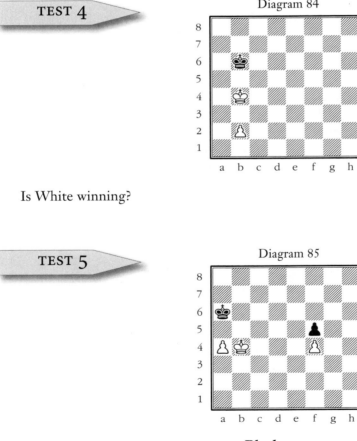

TEST 4

Diagram 84

Is White winning?

TEST 5

Diagram 85

Black to move

Can White win?

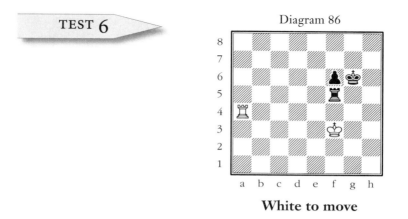

TEST 6

Diagram 86

White to move

Is the King and pawn endgame after 1.Rf4 drawn?

TEST 7

Diagram 87

White to move

Is White lost?

*   *   *   *   *

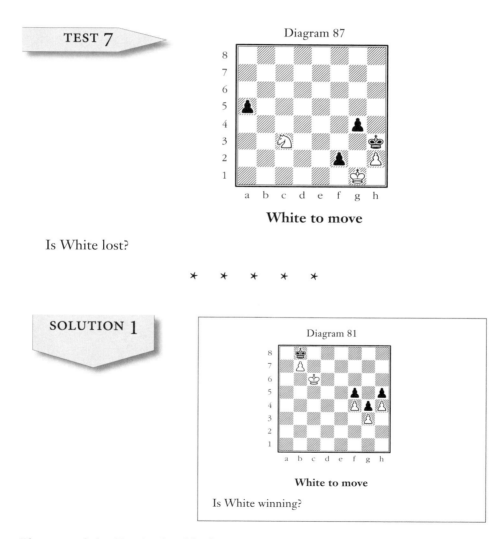

SOLUTION 1

Diagram 81

White to move

Is White winning?

If you used the Fox in the Chicken Coup concept by 1.Kd6 or 1.Kd5 or even
1.Kd7, you did well since 1...Kxb7 2.Ke6 Kc6 3.Kxf5 is completely decisive: 3...

Kd5 4.Kg5 Ke4 (of course, 4...Ke6 5.Kg6 [5.Kxh5 Kf5 6.Kh6 also wins] 5...Ke7 6.Kxh5 followed by 7.Kxg4 is hopeless) 5.f5 Kf3 6.f6 Kxg3 7.f7 Kh2 8.f8=Q is game over.

However, if you decided to hang onto your passed pawn by 1.Kb6?? you clearly have to rethink things since you've just stalemated your opponent and drawn an easily won game.

REMEMBER

As in all endgames, stalemates play an important part in the defender's hopes and must always remain in the stronger side's mind as something to avoid at all costs.

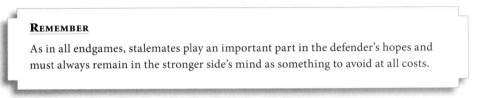

SOLUTION 2

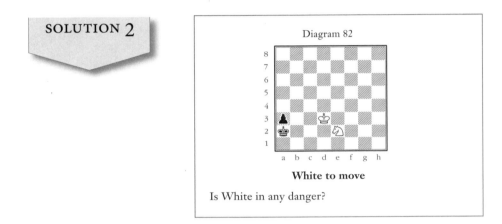

Diagram 82

White to move

Is White in any danger?

No, White's not in any danger at all. Even if Black had the move, the game would be drawn: 1...Kb2 2.Nc3 a2 3.Nxa2, draw. However, it's White to move and this turns out to be one of those rare instances where the lone Knight beats the pawn.

1.Kc2!

This traps the enemy King in the corner, where it will block its own pawn.

1...Ka1

The only legal move.

2.Nc1!

Takes away the a2-square from the black King and leaves him no choice but to push the pawn. However, this leaves the poor King completely immobile (meaning any check is mate!).

2...a2 3.Nb3 mate.

SOLUTION 3

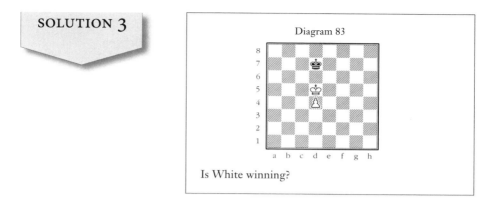

Diagram 83

Is White winning?

If you answered "yes" or "no," you're wrong on both counts. The correct answer is, "It depends on who has the move!" If it's White to move, then the game is drawn since Black holds the Opposition:

1.Ke5 Ke7 2.d5 Kd7 3.d6 Kd8 4.Ke6 Ke8 5.d7+ Kd8 6.Kd6 stalemate.

If it's Black to move, White wins since now White is in possession of the Opposition.

1...Ke7 2.Kc6 Kd8

2...Ke6 3.d5+ Ke7 4.Kc7! and the pawn pushes through and promotes.

3.Kd6 Kc8 4.Ke7 Kc7 5.d5 followed by d5-d6-d7-d8=Q.

SOLUTION 4

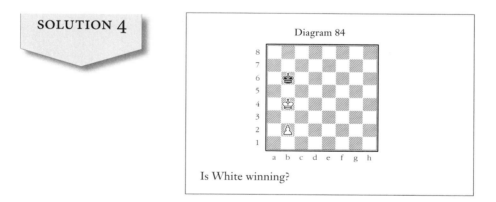

Diagram 84

Is White winning?

If you answered, "It depends on who has the move." you're wrong. White wins no matter who moves first. If Black moves first the win should be obvious:

1...Kc6 2.Ka5 Kc5 3.b4+ Kc6 4.Ka6, etc.

If this isn't clear, go back and carefully reread the material on this kind of endgame, but at this point in your studies the win if White moves first should also be a no-brainer:

1.b3!

Taking the Opposition.

1...Kc6 2.Ka5, etc.

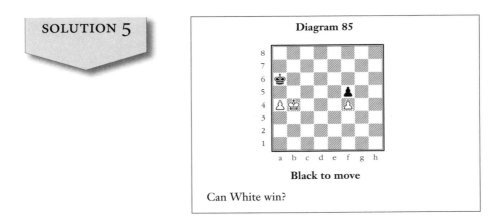

SOLUTION 5

Diagram 85

Black to move

Can White win?

I'm pleased if you thought that White might have problems because his passer is a rook-pawn, even though this isn't correct here (just the fact that you are now aware of the problems a rook-pawn can pose is a great sign!). The fact is, White wins no matter who moves, and the rook-pawn has no significance since White intends to sacrifice it anyway!

What we have here is another Fox in the Chicken Coup situation—White will give up the a4-pawn in order to win the f5-pawn, while also gaining a winning King position:

1...Kb6

If White had the first move then 1.Kc5 or Kc4 would both do the trick.

2.Kc4

White could also toss in 2.a5+ Ka6 3.Ka4 Ka7 4.Kb5 but it would lead to the same basic situation as reached after 2.Kc4.

2...Ka5 3.Kd5 Kxa4 4.Ke5

Black's King is far from the action, seemingly on vacation.

4...Kb5 5.Kxf5 Kc6 6.Ke6

6.Kg6 is also sufficient for an easy victory.

6...Kc7 7.Ke7

7.f5 also wins, but why let black's King get closer to the key f8-square?

7...Kc6 8.f5 followed by f5-f6-f7-f8=Q.

SOLUTION 6

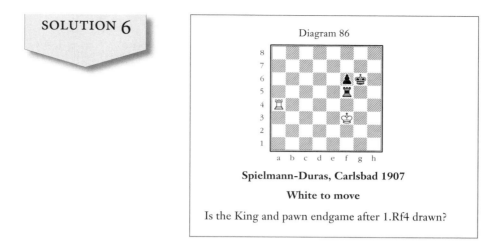

Diagram 86

Spielmann-Duras, Carlsbad 1907

White to move

Is the King and pawn endgame after 1.Rf4 drawn?

Even grandmasters blunder in the simplest of endgames. This position is hopelessly drawn and literally any King move would save the game. However, White decided to exchange Rooks and enter a "completely drawn" King and pawn vs. King endgame.

1.Rf4??

Expecting 2...Rxf4+ 3.Kxf4 with an immediate draw, he must have fallen out of his chair when Black played ...

1...Kg5!, 0-1. After 3.Rxf5 Kxf5 black's King has gotten in front of his pawn and has the Opposition. So the answer was yes, the King and pawn endgame was indeed drawn after 1...Rxf4+, but White is completely lost in the King and pawn endgame that arises after 1...Kg5!

SOLUTION 7

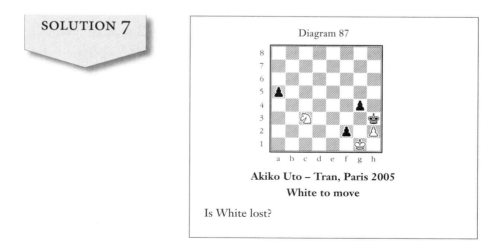

Diagram 87

Akiko Uto – Tran, Paris 2005

White to move

Is White lost?

In this position White, suffering from the illusion that her King was needed on the kingside, resigned since black's pawns appeared to be unstoppable. However, the game is dead drawn:

1.Kxf2 Kxh2

Things seem bad for White since 2.Ne4 or 2.Ne2 is met by 2...a4 when both pawns can't be stopped.

2.Ke2!

This is what White missed—this changing of the guard (white's King runs to the queenside to deal with the a-pawn while the Knight will take on the g-pawn by itself) easily saves the half point.

2...g3 3.Kd2 g2 4.Ne2, ½-½. The Knight has no problem dealing with the g-pawn, while white's King will march over and snap off the a-pawn.

Final Thoughts

I've clearly ratcheted up the difficulty level in this section—diagonal and non-connecting forms of Opposition, King and pawn endgames, Fox in the Chicken Coup, the Deep Freeze. All this is a far cry from the overkill mates in Part One!

Nevertheless, the fact is that all these endgames and their accompanying rules are extremely easy to absorb if you give the information a bit of time to sink in. Just because things appear hard due to a wide-eyed first impression doesn't mean that they are.

Yes, it will take more time than previously asked to thoroughly master this material. But you *do* have to master it—you shouldn't continue in this book until every nuance of Opposition, Fox in the Chicken Coup, and Deep Freeze is completely assimilated.

Part Four

Endgames for Class "C" (1400–1599)

Contents

The need to know endgames becomes a much higher priority once you reach the 1400-1599 range. In the United States, this rating group represents the average tournament player, and this means that you've probably become serious about moving up the ranks. To successfully do that, you'll need to expand your endgame arsenal and master a series of easy to learn but critically important positions and concepts. Now it's time to take it to another level, to digest ideas that might appear difficult and even profound, but will turn out to be easy to grasp and remember—once you put a little effort into it, of course!

This chapter is far larger than any other chapter in this book. Why? Because a quantum leap in endgame understanding is necessary if one wishes to be a solid class "C" player who has aspirations for advancement. Thus, here you'll hone the skills already acquired in this book, and come face to face for the first time with many of the most important "must know" positions and concepts in chess.

King and Pawn Endgames

Thus far we've mastered the Opposition and basic King and pawn vs. lone King theory—If you haven't mastered this material, stop (or this book will self-destruct!), go back to Part Three, and catch up! Now we'll hone the King and pawn skills you already possess, and give you some new, extremely useful, tools.

King and Pawn vs. Lone King (A Quick Tussle for Opposition)

King and pawn vs. lone King endgames are, for the most part, pretty simple affairs. In fact, a glance is usually enough to let you know who will own the Opposition and whether or not the defending side will be able to set up the basic drawing position. However, there are a few cases where some subtlety is demanded from one or both players.

Diagram 88

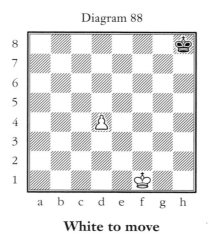

White to move

This position is actually quite confusing. If one follows our rules of Opposition with 1.Kf2—creating a rectangle whose connection points are on f2, f8, h8, and h2 and taking the Opposition—then the game will be drawn after 1...Kg7 2.Ke3 Kf6 when both 3.Kf4 and 3.Ke4 are met by 3...Ke6 with a basic draw. If this doesn't make any sense, run, don't walk, to Part Three and read the section on Indirect Opposition again.

White failed to win this position because he wasn't able to get his King in front of his pawn.

So, tossing immediate thoughts of Opposition out the window, the only way to get white's King in front of its pawn is:

> **USEFUL ADVICE**
>
> If taking the Opposition fails to accomplish the goal of getting the King in front of its pawn, then it's useless to take the Opposition in the first place.

1.Ke2!

This advances the King *and* moves it away from the enemy monarch

1...Kg7

Black can take Indirect Opposition by 1...Kg8 but this leads to the exact same position as our main line after 2.Kd3 Kf7 3.Kc4 Ke6 4.Kc5.

2.Kd3

Since black's King is on the kingside, White heads for the queenside so it can avoid a direct confrontation. As seen earlier, 2.Ke3?? Kf6 3.Ke4 Ke6 is an easy draw.

2...Kf6 3.Kc4 Ke6 4.Kc5 Kd7 5.Kd5 with a basic win for White, as seen in Part Three.

Diagram 89

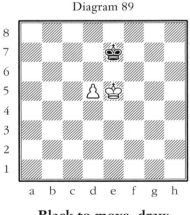

Black to move, draw

In Part Two we saw that, even though White has the Opposition, this position is dead drawn: **1...Kd7 2.d6 Kd8** (the ability to move straight back when the pawn hits the 6th rank is a critical one, as we'll see in diagram 91) **3.Ke6 Ke8 4.d7+ Kd8 5.Kd6** stalemate.

We've also learned that, when the stronger side's King gets one square in front of its pawn (we're taking it for granted that it's a non rook-pawn), the result of the game depends on who has the Opposition.

Diagram 90

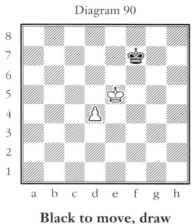

Black to move, draw

White to move wins easily by Kd6, but Black to move draws by taking the Opposition: **1...Ke7 2.d5 Kd7 3.d6 Kd8 4.Ke6 Ke8**, ½-½.

This rule—if the stronger side's King gets one square in front of its pawn the result of the game depends on who has the Opposition, illustrated in Part Three, Diagram 62—only flounders if the pawn is a rook-pawn, or if the pawn is on the 5th rank and its King is on the 6th.

Diagram 91

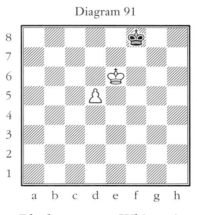

Black to move, White wins

Black to move seems to be okay since he can take the Opposition by **1...Ke8**. However, he's actually dead lost since **2.d6 Kd8 3.d7** highlights the fact that he can't move straight back (as in diagram 89). This means that Black should resign after **3...Kc7 4.Ke7**.

Our oft-repeated rule (i.e., if the stronger side's King gets one square in front of its pawn the result of the game depends on who has the Opposition), shockingly, turns out to have two exceptions! This can prove confusing to many players, so look at the differences between the last three examples (Again and again, if need be!) until you fully understand what has occurred. Once you've done this, we're ready for our next position.

> **RULE**
>
> If the stronger side's King gets one square in front of its pawn, the result of the game depends on who has the Opposition *unless* one of two exceptions are present:
> - The game is drawn if the pawn is a rook-pawn;
> - If a non rook-pawn is on the 5th rank and its King is on the 6th, taking the Opposition won't save the defender.

Diagram 92

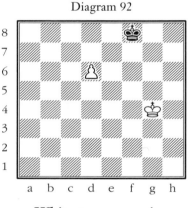

White to move, wins

A quick look might make us believe that the position is drawn since Black will get the Opposition, but a closer examination proves that Black won't survive:

1.Kf5

White can't allow ...Ke8-d7 with a draw.

1...Kf7

Taking the Opposition and stopping white's King from advancing. So far, so good. But white's next move would quickly bring Black back to reality.

Of course, 1...Ke8 2.Ke6 Kd8 3.d7 is completely hopeless.

2.Ke5

And suddenly White pries the Opposition away from Black since 2...Kg7 (taking Diagonal Opposition) 3.Ke6 is game over.

2...Kf8

A good try that allows Black to hold his breath and pray for a miracle. 2...Ke8 3.Ke6 leads to our main line.

3.Kf6!

No miracles today! Of course, 3.Ke6?? lets Black take the Opposition back with 3...Ke8.

3...Ke8 4.Ke6 Kd8 5.d7 Kc7 6.Ke7, 1-0.

Diagram 93

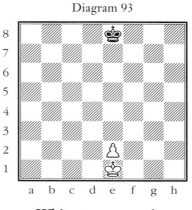

White to move, wins

This position is easy since White to move wins by simply marching his King in front of his pawn:

1.Kd2 Kd8

1...Ke7 2.Ke3 Ke6 3.Ke4 leads to a basic win, as seen in Part Three (i.e., the stronger side always wins if his King gets two squares in front of his pawn, unless it's a rook-pawn).

2.Kd3 Kd7 3.Ke4 Ke6 4.e3! and White, with his King in front of his pawn *and* with the Opposition, will have no problem scoring the full point (if there *is* a problem, go back to Part Three and reread the material).

Diagram 94

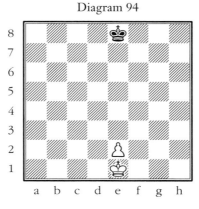

Black to move, draw

Black to move is quite another matter, and after some mutual finesses the game turns out to be drawn:

1...Ke7 2.Kd1!

What's this? Has White gone mad? Actually, White is setting a nice trap since he sees that the direct 2.Kd2 Ke6 3.Kd3 Kd5 4.Ke3 Ke5 is an easy draw.

2...Ke6 3.Kd2

Diagram 95

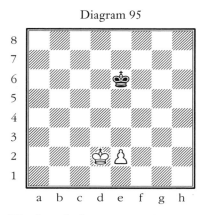

Black only has one saving move

Believe it or not, Black only has one way to draw!

3...Kd6!

Taking the Distant Opposition. Losing alternatives are:

➤ 3...Kf6?? (taking the Indirect Opposition) 4.Kd3 (and not 4.Ke3?? Ke5 with a draw) 4...Ke5 5.Ke3 and White wins (Banish yourself to Part Three if white's win isn't obvious to you after 5.Ke3.).

➤ 3...Ke5?? 4.Ke3, 1-0.

➤ 3...Kd5?? 4.Kd3 Ke5 5.Ke3, 1-0.

➤ 3...Kf5?? 4.Kd3 Ke5 5.Ke3, 1-0.

4.Kd3

4.Ke3 Ke5 amounts to the same thing.

4...Kd5, ½-½.

Sneaking into a Winning King and Pawn vs. King Position

By now you should know when a basic King and pawn vs. lone King position is lost or drawn. This knowledge allows you to correctly gauge more complex situations where the prospect of pawn exchanges forces you to decide whether the resulting position is favorable to your cause.

Diagram 96

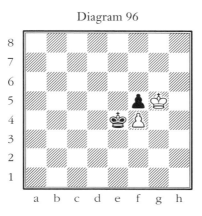

Trébuchet: Whoever moves loses

This kind of position, which can occur with any set of pawns other than rook-pawns (with both Kings in front of their respective pawns), is known as a *Trébuchet*. There is not much to learn, since a glance will make things pretty clear: whoever moves is in zugzwang—he is forced to move away from the defense of his pawn, which will result in an obviously lost King and pawn vs. lone King situation. Thus, if White has the move:

1.Kh4 Kxf4

With black's King in front of his pawn, the win in easy.

2.Kh3 Kf3

Making sure that his King will have full control over the queening square on f1.

3.Kh2 f4 4.Kg1 Ke2 followed by ...f4-f3-f2-f1=Q.

Though this "base" position is easy to grasp, being conversant with it allows you an easy plan when faced with what seems to be a tough battle.

> **RULE**
>
> A Trébuchet situation is a dead loss to the player with the move.

Diagram 97

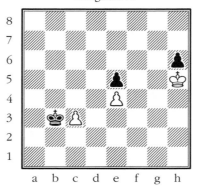

White to move, what's going on?

This is the kind of position that sends many players into a panic. Who is better? What in the world is going on? Is there anything to grasp onto that will enable us to make a quick and easy assessment? The idea of something definable which can help us understand the right path in seemingly tough positions is an important one, and we'll be searching for such "crutches" all through this book. In the present case, that crutch is our basic Trébuchet—after the c-pawn and h-pawn are taken, the result will depend on who can force the other into zugzwang via Trébuchet. Since black's King will be closer to the two center pawns (meaning that he can make first contact), White will end up a loser in the coming battle.

1.Kxh6 Kxc3 2.Kg5 Kd3!

The key move! The obvious 2...Kd4?? would be a game losing blunder since after 3.Kf5 Black would be on the sour side of the Trébuchet.

3.Kf5

Forced.

3...Kd4! and White must part with his pawn. He could resign here, but we'll continue: **4.Kg4 Kxe4 5.Kg3 Ke3** (Not letting white's King get in front of the pawn.) **6.Kg4 e4** (Avoiding the embarrassing 6...Kd2?? 7.Kf5, =) **7.Kg3 Kd2** followed by ...e4-e3-e2-e1=Q.

This example shows us that a firm grasp of the following rule can prove very useful indeed.

> **RULE**
>
> In a near (upcoming) Trébuchet position, the side whose King can make first diagonal contact with the enemy pawn can force a winning Trébuchet.

Though Trébuchets happen fairly often, far more common is the following type of situation:

Diagram 98

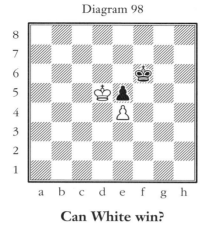

Can White win?

It doesn't matter who has the move since the e5-pawn falls in any case (White to move would play 1.Kd6). The real question is, can White win after he captures black's final pawn? Using your understanding of King and pawn vs. lone King, you should be able to ascertain that the game is drawn since Black can get a position where white's King is in front of his pawn (which is good for White), but Black can gain the Opposition (which is good for Black) and hold the game.

Let's give Black the first move:

1...Kf7!

The only way to draw! 1...Ke7?? loses to 2.Kxe5 (taking the Opposition!) 2...Kf7 (or 2...Kd7 3.Kf6) 3.Kd6 Ke8 (3...Kf6 4.e5+ Kf7 5.Kd7) 4.Ke6 (Continuing to use the Opposition to push black's King away from the queening square. White can also win by 4.e5 Kd8 5.e6 Ke8 6.e7 Kf7 7.Kd7, etc.) 4...Kd8 5.Kf7 Kd7 6.e5 and the pawn promotes.

2.Kxe5 Ke7!

Taking the Opposition and, as seen in Part Three, drawing easily.

3.Kd5 Kd7 4.e5 Ke7 5.e6 Ke8!

Black could still lose by 5...Kd8?? 6.Kd6 (Opposition) 6...Ke8 7.e7 Kf7 8.Kd7, etc.

6.Kd6 Kd8 7.e7+ Ke8 8.Ke6, ½-½.

> **USEFUL ADVICE**
>
> You can often solve seemingly difficult situations by steering the game towards the many basic situations you have mastered.

> **REMEMBER**
>
> The ability to see whether or not you or your opponent can gain the Opposition in key moments is extremely important. Successful endgame play is impossible without this skill.

Diagram 99

Black to move

As in the previous position, White to move would still pick up the pawn by 1.Kd7, but we'll give Black the move here simply because it's more instructive to do so. Unfortunately for the second player, Black now loses, even though it appears he can get the Opposition.

1...Kf8

The best try, since it allows Black to take the Opposition after White devours the e6-pawn. There's no hope at all after 1...Ke8 2.Kxe6 Kf8 3.Kd7 when the pawn quickly turns into a Queen.

2.Kxe6 Ke8 3.Kd6 Kd8

Doesn't Black have the Opposition?

4.e6

No, he doesn't! Suddenly Black is the one who must move.

4...Ke8 5.e7 and he's not able to use the "move the King straight back" rule since he's run out of board! After **5...Kf7 6.Kd7** the game would end quickly. What happened? It looked like Black should have drawn, but somehow he failed to do so!

Diagram 100

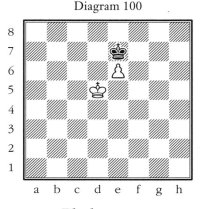

Black to move

Diagram 100 should help to clarify black's previous failure. In diagram 99, Black's King was not able to step backwards after the pawn reached e6 and, as a result, he lost. Here though, Black draws easily since he *can* step backwards and take the Opposition at will: **1...Ke8 2.Kd6 Kd8 3.Kd5 Ke7 4.Ke5 Ke8 5.Kf6 Kf8 6.e7+ Ke8 7.Ke6** stalemate.

There is a bit of an optical illusion in diagram 99, so carefully compare the last two positions until the "why" and "how" becomes clear.

King and Two Doubled Pawns vs. Lone King

King and two (doubled) pawns vs. lone King always win unless the pawns can't be properly defended, or unless they are rook-pawns. The defender's only hope lies in winning one of the two pawns, or in tricking the opponent into some lucky stalemate. Thus, when you have this two-pawn advantage, be very careful to avoid stalemate by making sure the enemy King always has a legal move.

Diagram 101

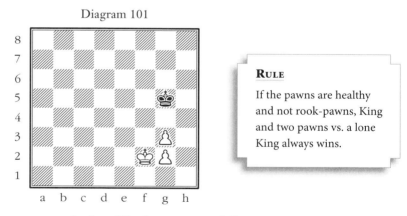

> **RULE**
>
> If the pawns are healthy and not rook-pawns, King and two pawns vs. a lone King always wins.

White moves and wins, Black moves and draws

Black to move draws immediately by 1...Kg4 when the g3-pawn is lost. The resulting King and pawn vs. lone King position is hopelessly drawn (which, if you're reading this section, you should be well aware of). White to move is a different story.

1.Kf3 Kf5 2.g4+ Kg5 3.Kg3

White does best to play this endgame as if it were a King and pawn vs. lone King situation. His extra pawn will come into effect later when a key tempo move is needed.

3...Kg6 4.Kf4 Kf6 5.g5+ Kg6 6.Kg4 Kg7 7.Kf5 Kf7 8.g6+ Kg7 9.Kg5 Kg8 10.Kf6 Kf8

Black, by following the drawing formula for a King and pawn vs. lone King position, has done the best he could. If White didn't have that extra g-pawn, then the game would now be drawn after 11.g7+ Kg8 12.Kg6. However, White *does* have that extra pawn, and this makes all the difference.

11.g7+ Kg8 12.g3

This move, in effect, says, "Excuse me, but could you kindly move your King away from the front of my pawn?"

12...Kh7 13.Kf7 and wins.

Okay, that seemed simple enough, but why didn't White push both his g-pawns down the board at the same time? The answer is that doing so would increase black's chances for a stalemate (as illustrated in the next example).

Diagram 102

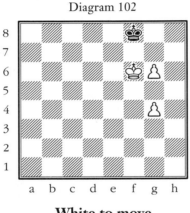

White to move

In our previous example, White only touched his extra g-pawn at the end. However, he could have pushed both, which might have led to this position. White still wins, but he has to be careful!

1.g7+ Kg8 2.g5 Kh7 3.g8=Q+!

Forced but adequate. Instead, 3.Kf7?? draws by immediate stalemate! Note how the advanced g5-pawn restricts the movement of the enemy King and thus turns into a traitor. After 3.g8=Q+, White forces a winning King and pawn vs. lone King position.

3...Kxg8 4.Kg6 Kh8 5.Kf7 Kh7 6.g6+ and wins.

> **USEFUL ADVICE**
>
> When you possess King and two doubled pawns vs. lone King, don't push both pawns up the board together since that increases the weaker side's chances for a lucky stalemate.

Rook-Pawn
(Stalemating the Stronger Side)

In general, in a King and pawn vs. lone King position, the weaker side loses if he can't get his King in front of the enemy pawn—if you can't block and stop the pawn from queening, then you're a goner! However, rook-pawns often allow all sorts of exceptions due to the fact that there isn't a file to the side of the pawn (which creates many odd stalemate possibilities).

Diagram 103

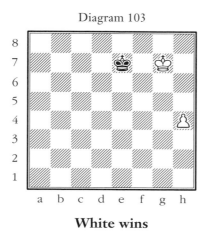

White wins

If black's King stood on h8 and white's on h6, then the game would be an easy draw since the pawn won't ever be able to get past the blocking defensive King without giving stalemate. In the diagrammed position, though, the black King isn't blocking anything (in fact, white's King has a firm grasp on the critical h8-queening square) and has no way of stopping h4-h5-h6-h7-h8=Q. Thus, he might as well resign.

Diagram 104

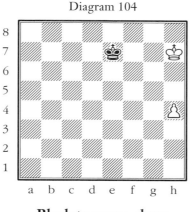

Black to move, draw

If White had the move, he would simply play 1.Kg7 and force resignation. However, Black to move draws with either 1...Kf8 or 1...Kf7. Let's take a look:

1...Kf7

Keeping white's King cornered and thus forcing it to block its own pawn!

2.h5

Of course, 2.Kh8 Kg6 followed by ...Kh5 and ...Kxh4 ends things immediately.

2...Kf8

Actually, 2...Kf6 would also draw since 3.Kg8 Kg5 picks up the pawn, while 3.h6 Kf7 takes us back into safe territory. Careful though! In general the defender wants to keep his King on f8 and f7, which allows him to leap to g8 if allowed.

3.Kh8

By now you should know that the position after 3.Kg6 Kg8 is hopelessly drawn.

3...Kf7 4.h6 Kf8

Even faster is 4...Kg6 5.h7 Kf7 stalemate!

5.Kh7

White's King is caught in a net and can't clear a path for his pawn! You might have noticed that 5.h7 Kf7 led to immediate stalemate and a draw.

5...Kf7

Not letting the snared white King out of its cage!

6.Kh8 Kf8 7.h7 Kf7 stalemate. This is a rare example of the side with no pieces left stalemating the stronger side's King.

Taking the position in diagram 104 and adding a second or even third h-pawn has absolutely no effect on the result:

Diagram 105

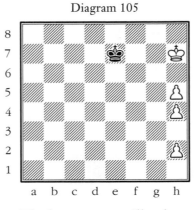

Black to move, still a draw

This strange position is a dead draw, despite the fact that White is no less than three pawns ahead!

1...Kf7 2.h6 Kf8 3.Kh8

Just as useless is 3.Kg6 Kg8 when Black just moves his King back and forth between h8 and g8 until White finally stalemates him.

3...Kf7 4.h5 Kf8 5.h4 Kf7

Notice black's subtle defensive maneuvers.

6.Kh7 Kf8 7.Kh8

Again, 7.Kg6 Kg8 is nothing for White.

7...Kf7 8.h7 Kf8 9.h6 Kf7 10.h5 Kf8, stalemate! The final position deserves a diagram:

Diagram 106

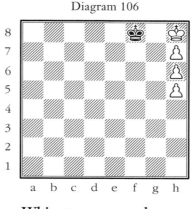

White to move, stalemate

The position in diagram 106 should, once and for all, burn the lessons we've explored concerning rook-pawns deeply into your brain.

Diagram 107

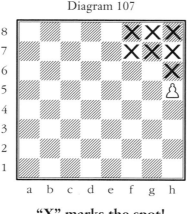

"X" marks the spot!

This diagram should make it easy to know whether or not a King and rook-pawn vs. lone King position is drawn. If the defender's King stands on any of the "X" squares the game will be a draw (the position of white's King won't change the result).

Entering the Square of the Pawn

When an enemy pawn is trying to outrace your King down the board, it's always nice to be able to see with a glance if you (or your opponent) can draw. Sadly, most players feel that they must do the old "he goes there and I go there" routine for an endless series of moves to see if their King can make it back in time to stop an unescorted enemy pawn. Fortunately, there *is* an easier way!

Diagram 108

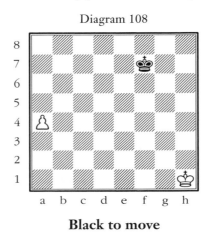

Black to move

This position (diagram 108), in which white's King is far from the action, poses a simple question: Can black's King stop (or even win) the enemy pawn? The game hangs in the balance—if the black King can stop the pawn, then the game is drawn, while the game is lost if the King can't. The answer lies in a technique called the ***Square of the Pawn***.

Diagram 109 shows the same position as the previous one, but now the normally invisible Square of the Pawn is drawn and clear for all to see. How does one create such a square? Here's the trick (in the direction of the stalking King):

▶ Draw a diagonal extension from the pawn to the end of the board.

▶ Draw a rank extension from the side of the pawn to the file where the diagonal extension ended. In this case that would be the e-file since the diagonal extension ended at e8.

▶ Connect all the lines and you'll get the square in the diagram.

Diagram 109

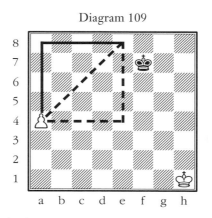

RULE

If black's King can step into this square, it will stop the pawn. If it can't, the pawn will run for a touchdown.

Black to move steps into the Square

Now we can see at a glance that black's King can indeed step into this square and thus stop the pawn. However, if it was White to move, 1.a5 is a winner because a new square would be created.

Diagram 110

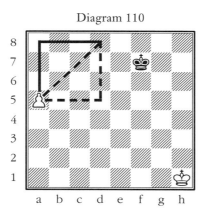

Black can't step into the Square

Even if it's his move, Black can't step into this new square and thus can't stop the pawn.

If all this seems confusing, think about it, try to move the King towards the pawn on your own board, and imagine the square shrinking each time the pawn moves. After a bit of time the whole Square of the Pawn idea will be an easy and natural part of your chess arsenal.

Outside Passed Pawns

In Part Three, we learned that many pawn endgames could be won by the Fox in the Chicken Coup technique. I didn't mention it then, but this is really just one example of the usefulness of an ***Outside Passed Pawn***.

What is an Outside Passed Pawn? It's a passed pawn that stands to the side of the main sphere of battle. Such a pawn is usually a very valuable commodity since it can be far from the enemy King and thus pose a serious promotion threat, and/or it can force the defending King over to deal with it, leaving the embattled area (where most of the pawns reside) bereft of a defender.

Diagram 111

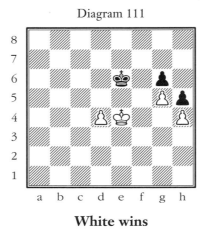

White wins

White easily wins this position (it doesn't matter who has the move) thanks to his outside passed d-pawn, which allows him to make use of the Chicken Coup idea.

1.d5+ Kd6 2.Kd4

Black's King is now forced to relinquish control over the key e5-square. Why is e5 so important? Because this is a steppingstone square that takes White closer to the tasty morsels on g6 and h5.

2...Kd7 3.Ke5 Ke7 4.d6+ Kf7

Black's last stand. He didn't fancy 4...Kd7 5.Kf6! (The key idea: White gives up his pawn—which was used as a diversion—so he can feast on the unprotected black army.) 5...Kxd6 6.Kxg6 followed by 7.Kxh5.

5.Kd5

Also good enough is 5.d7 Ke7 6.d8=Q+ Kxd8 7.Kf6 and all of black's pawns fall.

5...Kf8

On 5...Ke8 White would turn his d-pawn into a Queen by 6.Ke6 (taking the Opposition) 6...Kd8 7.d7 Kc7 8.Ke7.

6.Ke6 Ke8 7.Kf6, 1-0.

That was easy! But White started out with an extra pawn, so the result is hardly surprising. Can White use the Outside Passed Pawn in the same manner if material is even? Yes, he often can!

Diagram 112

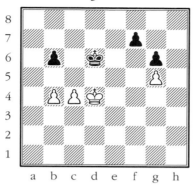

White to move

This is a win for White for two reasons:

 He has the Outside Passed Pawn.

 Black's kingside majority is devalued since white's one kingside pawn freezes both black units.

1.c5+ bxc5+ 2.bxc5+ Ke6

Trying desperately to turn his own majority into a passed pawn. The routine 2...Kc6 offers no hope at all: 3.Ke5 (of course, 3.Kc4 Kc7 4.Kd5 with Ke5 and Kf6 to follow is also game over) 3...Kxc5 4.Kf6 Kd6 5.Kxf7, 1-0.

3.Kc4!

Clearly bad is 3.c6?? Kd6 4.c7 Kxc7 5.Ke5 Kd7 6.Kf6 Ke8.

However, isn't 3.Ke4 just as good? The answer is no, since Black could then create a passed pawn: 3...f5+ 4.gxf6 e.p. Kxf6 (and not 4...g5?? 5.c6 and one of white's pawns will soon turn into a Queen). After 4...Kxf6, black's King can step into the Square of white's c-pawn after 5.c6 Ke6. So, White should try: 5.Kd5 Ke7! (not falling for 5...g5?? 6.Kd6! when black's King can't approach the white pawn. This Opposition also has another, very evil, point: 6...g4 7.c6 g3 8.c7 g2 9.c8=Q g1=Q

Diagram 113

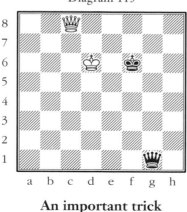

An important trick

This position illustrates an important trick: 10.Qf8+ when black's King is forced to step onto the fatal g-file. After 10...Kg5 11.Qg8+ the black Queen falls and with it the game.)

Let's go back to the position after 5...Ke7!

Diagram 114

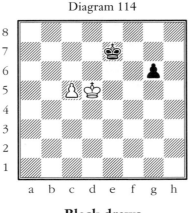

Black draws

6.Kc6 (This allows White to wrest control over the queening square on c8. Completely ineffective is 6.c6 when both 6...g5 or 6...Kd8 force a draw) 6...g5 (black's King can't help anymore, as shown by 6...Kd8?? 7.Kb7 g5 8.c6 g4 9.c7+, 1-0. Fortunately, black's own passed pawn manages to save the day.) 7.Kb7 g4 8.c6 g3 9.c7 g2 10.c8=Q g1=Q, ½-½.

It's clear that 3.Ke4 failed to get the job done and that white's King needs to be on the queenside where it can help its pawn rush for a touchdown. Hence the strength of 3.Kc4.

Diagram 115

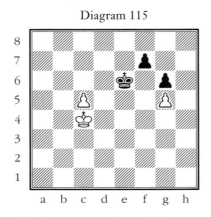

Black to move, but White wins

3...f5 4.gxf6 e.p. Kxf6

Defeat comes even faster after 4...g5 5.c6 when black's King can't deal with both onrushing pawns.

5.Kb5!

White's pawn is farther advanced than black's, so he can afford taking time to use his King in the fight for the key c8-square. The immediate 5.c6?? lets black's King set up shop on c8 after 5...Ke7 6.Kb5 Kd8 7.Kb6 Kc8.

5...g5 6.c6 Ke7

It's now clear that the pure race via 6...g4 fails: 7.c7 g3 8.c8=Q g2 9.Qg4 and it's all over.

7.Kb6 g4

Or 7...Kd8 8.Kb7 when White has won the battle for c8.

8.c7 Kd7 9.Kb7, 1-0.

> **REMEMBER**
>
> An Outside Passed Pawn is a valuable endgame commodity. It can pose a serious promotion threat, and/or it can force the defending King over to deal with it, leaving the embattled area (where most of the pawns reside) bereft of a defender.

Minor Piece Endgames

Very few people study minor piece endgames, and this is certainly not the place to enter into the many complex situations that can occur when Bishops and Knights rule the board. However, the "C" class is an excellent place to dip your toes into shallow minor piece endgame waters. Don't worry, it will be painless and very useful, since the few positions we will explore all turn up regularly and allow you to save many situations that, at first glance, seem completely hopeless.

Bishop and Wrong Colored Rook-Pawn vs. Lone King

One of the most surprising and common "miracle-saves" features a position where White enjoys a Bishop and pawn vs. a lone King! This sounds like it should be resignable, yet it can be salvaged *if*:

▶ The pawn is a rook-pawn.

▶ The pawn's queening square is a different color than its Bishop.

▶ The defender's King can reach the queening square (or any of the squares touching the queening square).

This still sounds crazy, doesn't it? Let's take a look at a few Bishop and pawn vs. King positions and, before you know it, you'll soon completely understand the dynamics behind the miracle save mentioned above.

Take a hard look at diagram 116. One would think that an extra Bishop and pawn should be child's play, and here they would be right! White wins because the rules just listed are not all present—his pawn isn't a rook-pawn.

Diagram 116

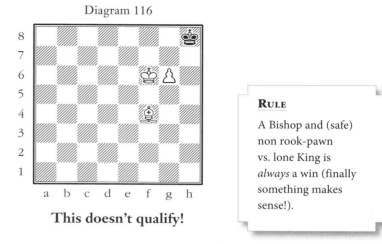

This doesn't qualify!

> **RULE**
>
> A Bishop and (safe) non rook-pawn vs. lone King is *always* a win (finally something makes sense!).

1.g7+ Kg8 2.Be5

Avoiding nasty tricks like 2.Kg6 stalemate or 2.Be3 Kh7 3.Kf7 stalemate (again!). Since the only way White can screw this up is to allow a stalemate or give away his pawn or Bishop, make sure you are safe from these pitfalls each time you move!

2...Kh7 3.Kf7 Kh6 4.g8=Q Kh5 5.Qg3 (quickest) **5...Kh6 6.Qg6** mate.

Okay, let's take a look at a position with a rook-pawn, since that is what makes this trick happen (though I have yet to prove it!).

Diagram 117

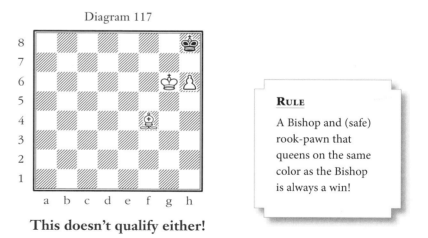

This doesn't qualify either!

> **RULE**
>
> A Bishop and (safe) rook-pawn that queens on the same color as the Bishop is always a win!

This position also loses for Black (it doesn't matter who has the move), even though White is left with a rook-pawn. Do you see why black's defensive stance won't succeed? If you noticed that the pawn's queening square is the same color as the Bishop then you have a sharp eye. As a result, white's win is ridiculously easy via **1.Be5+** (alertly avoiding 1.h7 stalemate!) **1...Kg8 2.h7+ Kf8 3.h8=Q+.** As you can see, the fact that the Bishop can kick the defending King off of h8 is extremely important!

In our next position (the one I've been promising!), White doesn't have this luxury.

Diagram 118

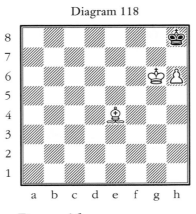

Draw with anyone to move

Ah, this is more like it! All our Bishop and rook-pawn of the wrong color rules are finally present! Now Black draws easily since White just can't get that blasted King away from h8! Still don't believe it? Let's try:

1.Bf5

Okay, this is hardly a brain-shattering move, but 1.h7 is an immediate draw by stalemate, while 1.Bd5 is yet another way to stalemate black's King.

1...Kg8 2.h7+

Other tries also get nowhere. For example, 2.Be6+ Kh8 3.Kg5 Kh7 4.Be4+ Kh8 and White isn't making any progress.

2...Kh8 3.Kg5 Kg7 and Black just moves back and forth between g7 and h8 until stalemate is delivered, White gives up his pawn, or the universe as we know it ceases to exist.

> **RULE**
>
> Bishop and rook-pawn (that queens on the opposite color as the Bishop) vs. lone enemy King is a draw.

Clearly, once you achieve this endgame, it's a no-brainer to draw. That means that the only hard part is creating it (if you were in trouble) or avoiding it (if you were winning). The rest plays itself. Here is an illustration of both these possibilities in one example:

Diagram 119

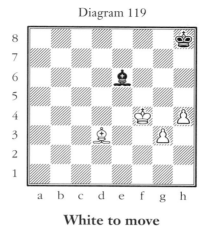

White to move

1.Ke5

Rushing the King to a dominating position is almost always a good idea in just about any kind of endgame. But do you have any idea how many people would decide to get their pawns rolling by 1.g4, only realizing their epic mistake when you spank them with the "bring them back to reality" move 1...Bxg4!. After 2.Kxg4 Kg7 Black can dance around the table, celebrating the fact that the game is a dead draw!

1...Bc8 2.Kf6

The King annexes even more ground before getting his pawns moving.

2...Bd7 3.Bf5 Be8

Of course, trading Bishops leads to a resignable King and two pawns vs. lone King endgame.

4.g4

Now this pawn can safely move up the board.

4...Kg8

A funny try is 4...Bh5, hoping for 5.gxh5?? when we have a draw even though Black is down a Bishop and two pawns! Fortunately for White, the simple 5.g5 keeps the win well in hand.

5.g5 Kh8 6.Bg4

Again White avoids the tempting but game-ruining 6.g6?? due to 6...Bxg6 with an immediate draw. Moving the Bishop to g4 prepares to safely advance the h-pawn.

6...Kg8 7.h5 Kh8 8.h6 Kg8 9.Be6+ Kh8

Or 9...Kf8 10.h7 followed by 11.h8=Q+.

10.Bf7 Bb5 11.g6, 1-0. The killing 12.g7+ will follow.

As you can see, it's imperative that you know of this trick so you can avoid it, and that you keep it in mind when things are going badly so you can salvage a half point when everyone else has counted you out!

Lone King vs. Knight and Rook-Pawn on the 6th or 7th

We've just seen an important instance where a Bishop and pawn can't beat a lone King. Surely the flexible Knight is immune from such anomalies? One would think that a Knight and (safe) pawn would always beat a lone King, but there is one important exception!

> **RULE**
>
> A Knight and a (safe) pawn vs. a lone King is always a win for the material advantage, except when the extra pawn is a rook-pawn and that rook-pawn is on the 7th rank.

We've seen that rook-pawns often create exceptions to otherwise ironclad rules, and this is yet another case of the "rook-pawn curse."

Our next example shows why the Knight and pawn win under normal circumstances (i.e., the pawn's not on the 7th rank).

Diagram 120

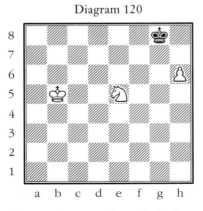

Black is doomed, even though he has the move

Even though white's King is in another time zone, Black has no chance at all in this position because the pawn can easily be protected by its Knight.

1...Kh7 2.Ng4!

And not 2.Nf7?? Kg6 3.Kc5 Kxf7 4.h7 Kg7, =.

> **USEFUL ADVICE**
>
> When you have to guard your pawn with your Knight in this kind of endgame, it's usually correct to defend the pawn from behind and not from the front or the side (as we saw in the note to White's 2nd move). Why? Because an undefended Knight on the side or front allows the defending King to capture it and still be in a position where the pawn can be stopped. Capturing a Knight that's behind its pawn allows the pawn to turn into a Queen.

2...Kg6 3.Kc5 Kh7

Of course, 3...Kg5 4.h7 leads to a new Queen for White.

4.Kd5 Kg6 5.Ke6 Kh7 6.Kf7 Kh8 7.Kg6

Be careful, 7.Nf6?? is a draw by stalemate!

7...Kg8 8.Ne5

Avoiding the tragic 8.h7+?? Kh8 when White has to give up his pawn (which is an immediate draw since a mate with King and Knight vs. lone King isn't possible) or allow stalemate.

> **USEFUL ADVICE**
>
> White wins these positions by taking control of the queening square with his Knight.

8...Kh8

Also elementary is 8...Kf8 9.h7 Ke7 10.h8=Q, etc.

9.Nf7+

Chasing black's King off of the critical promotion square.

9...Kg8 10.h7+ Kf8 11.h8=Q+, 1-0.

It seems that the Knight's ability to control any colored square (unlike the Bishop's) assures the Knight and pawn victory over a lone King in all sane situations. However (as stated earlier) there is one trick situation that must be avoided (or played for, if you're the side in trouble).

Diagram 121

Black to move, draw

Here we have the miracle save that was promised in this section's introduction. Black's King controls the queening square and the rook-pawn is on the 7th rank. Incredibly, White has no way of making the annoying black King leave the h8 or g7 squares!

1...Kh8 2.Ke6

Or 2.Kf6 stalemate.

2...Kg7 3.Kf5 Kh8

Again, Black welcomes 4.Kf6 or 4.Kg6, since both lead to an immediate draw by stalemate.

4.Kg4 Kg7 5.Kh5 Kh8 and again White can't approach the pawn via 6.Kg6 or 6.Kh6 since that would lead to immediate stalemate. The game is drawn since the pawn can't move, the Knight is stuck babysitting the pawn, and white's King can't touch its pawn without stalemating its evil counterpart.

Many players don't see this coming, so add it to your arsenal of emergency endgame weapons!

Bishops of Opposite Colors

Tournament players love to bandy about the term "Bishops of opposite colors," though they often don't really know much about this interplay of minor pieces. In the middlegame, Bishops of opposite colors is thought to be an advantage for the attacker since one Bishop can't defend what the other attacks. However, in the endgame Bishops of opposite colors can give the defender serious drawing chances in positions that one would think are losing. For example, a one-pawn advantage is often inadequate to score the full point.

Diagram 122

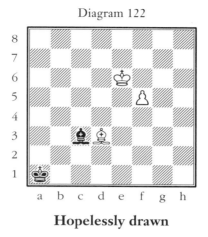

Hopelessly drawn

Even though black's King is off on vacation, White has no chance whatsoever of winning this position since Black will just snap off the pawn if it ever moves to f6.

Diagram 123

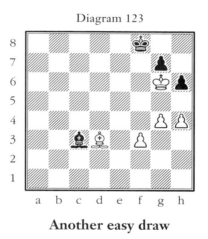

Another easy draw

White enjoys a dominating King position and an extra pawn. Nevertheless, Black draws in mindless fashion by moving his Bishop back and forth along the a1-h8 diagonal, trading pawns whenever the opportunity presents itself, and finally giving up his Bishop for the final enemy pawn. Here's a sample of how play might proceed:

1.f4 Ba1 2.f5 Bb2 3.g5 hxg5 4.hxg5

Also useless is 4.h5 g4 5.f6 Bxf6 6.h6 gxh6 7.Kxf6 and though the Bishop has been lopped off, White has run out of pawns and can't win.

4...Ba1 5.Kh7

A tricky try. The immediate 5.f6 gxf6 6.gxf6 Bxf6 is an obvious draw.

5...Bb2 6.f6 gxf6

Black could also play 6...Bxf6! 7.gxf6 gxf6, =.

7.g6

Actually threatening to win by 8.g7+.

7...f5! 8.Bxf5 Ba1 with ...Ba1-b2-a1-b2, etc. to follow until White agrees to the draw out of sheer boredom.

Diagram 124

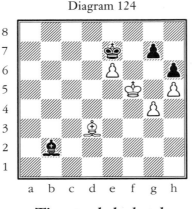

Time to shake hands

This position shows one of the main problems the stronger side faces when Bishops of opposite colors exists: the passed pawn on e6 is firmly blocked by black's King and white's light-squared Bishop is unable to influence anything on that color. Thus, it can't make the King step away from its blockade, nor can it attack black's kingside pawns!

Black draws by keeping his King planted on e7, and by keeping his Bishop on the a1-h8 diagonal. In this way, the passed pawn on e6 will never get anywhere, the h6-pawn is defended by the other pawn, and the g7-pawn is firmly (and permanently) guarded by its Bishop. Again, mindless "back and forth" action by ...Ba1-Bb2-Ba1-Bb2 is all it takes to split the point.

We'll continue our look at Bishops of opposite colors in Part Five.

USEFUL ADVICE

When you are in trouble, an excellent "last stand" strategy
is to trade into a Bishops of opposite colors' position.

Rook Endgames

Most players feel helpless when they enter a Rook endgame. This is quite unfortunate since Rook endgames occur often—in fact, they are more common than any other kind of endgame.

One thing that keeps players from studying such endgames is their apparent complexity. Who can understand and/or memorize such things? Which endgames are important, and which ones are complete wastes of time?

Here we'll begin our Rook endgame education with two must know positions: The *Lucena Position* and the *Philidor Position*. Are they hard to understand? Do they take hours of effort to master? No, the basics of the Lucena and the Philidor can be completely assimilated in thirty minutes to an hour. In return, you'll find they occur remarkably often, and they will both serve as lifelong guideposts on how to handle all other, far more complex, Rook endgames.

The Lucena Position (The Sacred Key to All Rook Endings)

It's time to learn (yes, you will completely master this particular ending in the next few minutes!) the Holy Grail of Rook endings; the sacred key that allows you to know what to avoid when defending a pawn down Rook endgame, while also giving you the knowledge to know what to head for if you have the superior side.

USEFUL ADVICE

This is one of those bits of chess knowledge that *every* serious player *must* possess. It's that important.

The Lucena Position, first published in 1634 by Salvio (for some reason it wasn't in an earlier book by Lucena), is a simplified position where one side has a Rook and a non rook-pawn on the 7th rank (the King in front of its pawn), while the other side just has a Rook. The position in diagram 125 shows us the particulars.

Diagram 125

White to move

White wins no matter who has the move, though for clarity's sake we'll give White the move here. The key feature of the Lucena is the extra pawn on the 7th rank, one square away from turning into a Queen. Also, both Kings are joined in battle, with the white King in front of his pawn and the enemy King as close to the area of battle as possible. Clearly, White needs to do two things if he wants to win:

- Move his King off of d8 so he can push his pawn.

- Promote the pawn to a Queen.

Simple goals indeed, but is it really that easy? Of course not! The problem is that white's King is blocking his own pawn and, at the moment, the black King and Rook are preventing it from getting out of the way. Since the black Rook can't be budged, White must make the black King give ground.

The first way to try and accomplish this goal is: 1.Re7+? (Many players try this, but it simply doesn't get the job done.) 1...Kf8 (And not 1...Kf6?? 2.Ke8 followed by 3.d8=Q with an instant win.) 2.Re8+ Kf7 3.Re7+ Kf8. White is getting nowhere fast.

Since this fails, White should play:

1.Rf2+!

USEFUL ADVICE

Trapping the enemy King away from the action is almost always a good thing to do.

Diagram 126

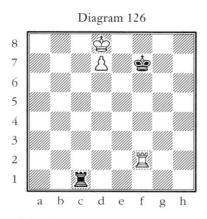

Making black's King leave the scene of battle

This is far more to the point! Since 1...Ke6?? allows 2.Ke8 followed by 3.d8=Q, Black has to step to the side and give the white King room to wander.

1...Kg7

Now comes a key moment. Of the following moves, which one do you think is correct?

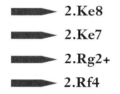 **2.Ke8**

2.Ke7

2.Rg2+

2.Rf4

Let's take a look at each choice (and *do* study the flaws of every move since it will help you acquire a clear understanding of what to avoid):

Wrong:
   2.Ke8?
   Threatening to promote the pawn.
   2...Re1+ 3.Kd8 Rc1 and White hasn't made any progress at all.

Wrong:
   2.Ke7?
   Again threatening to promote the pawn. This is the move almost everyone tries!
   2...Re1+ 3.Kd6
   It seems the White King is at last free to roam. This is true, but its inability to support its pawn in the face of the upcoming relentless barrage of enemy checks makes the whole idea invalid.
   3...Rd1+ 4.Ke6
   And not 4.Ke5?? Rxd7, draw.
   4...Re1+ 5.Kf5

Diagram 127

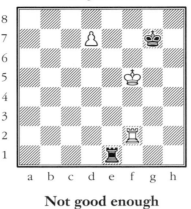

Not good enough

White's King is safe. Is he going to win?

5...Rd1

No, he's not! This Rook move brings White back to reality. The pawn can't safely advance, and it's threatened with capture. White has no choice but to defend with his King.

6.Ke6 Re1+ and White is again making no progress.

Wrong:

2.Rg2+?

This silly move helps Black by allowing him to move back to f7, once again rendering the white King immobile.

Thus, the *right* move for White is:

2.Rf4!

Diagram 128

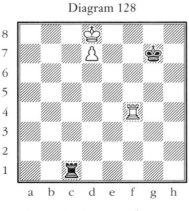

A mysterious rook move

This certainly looks odd, doesn't it? However, the idea of using the Rook to shelter its King from upcoming checks makes sense. The legendary Nimzovich described this maneuver as "building a bridge."

> **RULE**
>
> The "Building a Bridge" maneuver is the winning idea in a Lucena Position.

Let's see how it works:

2...Rc2

Black can't improve his position so he marks time.

3.Ke7

Only now should the white King leave the cover of the pawn. Since promotion is threatened, Black must go into checking mode.

3...Re2+ 4.Kd6 Rd2+ 5.Ke6

Don't toss the win out the window with 5.Ke5?? Rxd7, draw.

5...Re2+ 6.Kd5 Rd2+ 7.Rd4!

Diagram 129

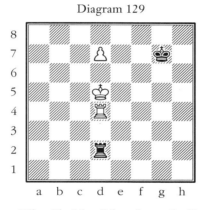

The "bridge" has been built

The bridge has been built and the pawn's promotion to a Queen can no longer be prevented. Black resigns.

We can now sum up the winning ideas:

➤ Force the black King away from the action via Rf2+.

➤ Prepare to use your Rook as a check-blocking ("bridge-building") agent with Rf4.

➤ Move your King away from the front of the pawn.

➤ Block the opponent's desperate checks with the Rook, which effectively ends the game.

Congratulations! You have now mastered the Lucena Position.

The Philidor Position
(A Critical Defensive Stand!)

Now that you've mastered the Lucena Position (You *did* master that position, didn't you?), we will take a look at something that's almost as important: the Philidor Position.

Okay, who can remember such strange names? Fair enough. Let's follow the old adage that says a picture is worth a thousand words.

Diagram 130

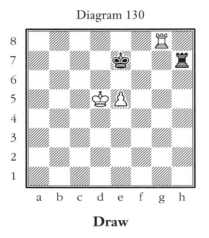

Draw

White's a pawn up, enjoys the superior King position, and apparently has the more active Rook. Though I just listed three serious plusses for White, this is a dead draw. However, people lose this kind of position every day, so you *must* know what you're doing. Fortunately, the drawing idea is very simple, and by the time you finish reading the material about the Philidor in Part Four, you'll be able to draw any grandmaster in the world with ease.

We'll return to the position in diagram 130 soon, but first let's take a look at some things that can go wrong for the defender.

Passive Rook

Though a Phildor Position should be drawn, things can turn ugly if the defender's Rook becomes passively placed, giving the stronger side free reign to do whatever he wishes to do.

Diagram 131

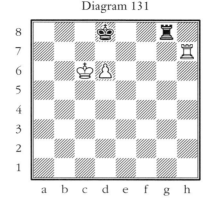

Black's passive rook leads to his doom

In diagram 131, White wins because black's Rook is stuck on his 1st rank (moving the Rook off the 1st rank allows Rh8+). Since black's Rook is a bystander and can't bother the white King, the first player can calmly play **1.Ra7!** when 2.Ra8+ can't be stopped. Black would then have to resign.

Let's glance at another, equally hopeless, passive Rook position (diagram 132).

Diagram 132

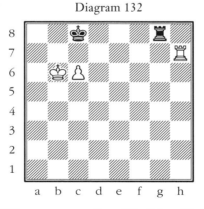

Different pawn, but Black's still dead

White scores the point by using that same "swing the Rook to the other side" technique: **1.Ra7 Kb8** (Not a happy choice, but 2.Ra8 mate had to be stopped. If 1…Kd8 2.Ra8+ picks up black's Rook.) **2.c7+ Kc8 3.Ra8+ Kd7 4.Rxg8** and Black might be well advised to resign and find something better to do with his time.

Sometimes, though, you can play horribly and still exit with your skin intact. In diagram 133, Black has allowed his Rook to become passive, but it doesn't matter because White can't win if he's left with a knight-pawn or rook-pawn.

Diagram 133

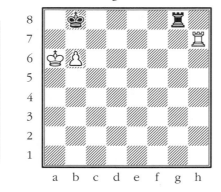

Black draws despite himself!

If only White could swing his Rook over to the file left of the a-file! Sadly, such a file doesn't exist. Because of this, White can't force a catastrophic back rank check (as occurred in diagram 131 after 1.Ra7) and, as a result, can't win the game: **1.Rb7+ Ka8 2.Ra7+ Kb8** and no progress can be made since 3.b7?? Rg6+ wins for Black!

REMEMBER

These kinds of passive Rook positions are winning for the stronger side if the pawn (which is on the 6th rank) is a bishop-pawn, queen-pawn, or king-pawn (thanks to the possibility of swinging the Rook over to the other side). However, a knight-pawn or rook-pawn is hopelessly drawn, since this "swing the Rook over" maneuver is no longer possible.

Pure Philidor

Having taken a look at the key passive Rook positions, it's finally time to return to the position in diagram 130 (recreated for your viewing pleasure in diagram 134) and study a basic Philidor Position in all its glory.

Diagram 134

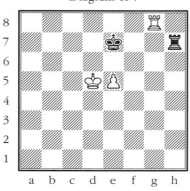

Black to move draws easily

Remember how I promised that you would be able to draw any grandmaster with ease from this position? I wasn't joking! The big idea here is to take away the whole 6th rank from the white King:

1...Rh6!

Believe it or not, this simple move ices the draw.

Black was aware that passive play failed due to our old "swinging Rook crouching check" trick: 1...Rf7 ("Why let White check our King?" is a common line of reasoning. But stopping such a check turns out to be unrealistic after …) 2.Ra8! when Ra7+ can't be prevented.

But why didn't Black play for the active Rook by 1...Rh1 (threatening to check on d1)? Because after 2.Rg7+ Ke8 White has the strong 3.Kd6!.

Diagram 135

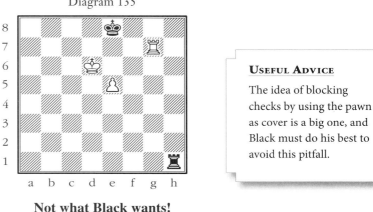

Not what Black wants!

USEFUL ADVICE

The idea of blocking checks by using the pawn as cover is a big one, and Black must do his best to avoid this pitfall.

Suddenly Black can't maintain a cascade of checks since 3...Rh6+ runs into 4.e6 (using the pawn to block the check and threatening Rg8 mate) when 4...Rh8 leads to the lost passive Rook positions already discussed in diagrams 131 and 132. Also note that 3...Rd1+ fails to 4.Ke6 when the checks are over and Rg8+ is once again "on."

By the way, the position in diagram 135 turns out to be drawn after all, but it's far from easy and is anything but "basic." Look for a discussion of this in Part Seven, where Black faces his fears and survives against impossible odds. For our purpose (i.e., proving that the Philidor Position is an easy draw), we'll say that you would be smart to avoid the position in diagram 135.

Fortunately, playing 1...Rh6! (from diagram 134) makes life good (and easy!) again.

2.Rg7+ Ke8 3.Ra7 Rg6

Diagram 136

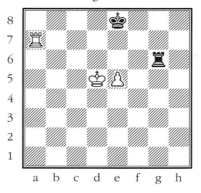

"You shall not pass!" shouts the black Rook to the white King

The "deep" defensive idea (also known as the *3rd Rank Defense*) is now clear. If left alone, Black will bravely play …Rh6 and …Rg6 until the cows come home (or wrist-cramp sets in). Of course, if Black lusts for adventure then he can toss in …Rb6 (a "longer" and more flowery move), but it all amounts to the same thing: white's King desperately wants to step forward but can't due to the blocking power of the black Rook!

4.e6

Not what White wanted to play, but he has no other choices since 4.Ra8+ Ke7 makes Black happy. Now White threatens the strong Kd6 when black's King will feel some serious heat.

4…Rg1!

Only now does this active move work. Since white's King can't hide behind his pawn any longer, the upcoming avalanche of checks makes the draw obvious.

Diagram 137

No cover for the white King

In diagram 135 White was able to use his pawn as cover. Here (in diagram 137) he cannot. You would be wise to compare the two positions!

5.Ra4

No better is 5.Kd6 Rd1+ 6.Ke5 Re1+ and White should be a good sport and shake hands.

5...Ke7

Also fine is 5...Rd1+ 6.Rd4 Rxd4+ 7.Kxd4 Ke7 8.Kd5 Ke8 9.Kd6 Kd8 10.e7+ Ke8 11.Ke6, draw.

6.Ra7+ Ke8 when White can't make any progress at all.

I strongly recommend that you ponder the ideas in this very common endgame. These themes will help you save games when down a pawn and win games when you possess that extra bit against an unschooled opponent.

> **RULE**
>
> The defender's drawing plan in the Philidor Position is to use his Rook to block the stronger side's King from stepping onto the rank in front of the pawn. Go back and forth with the Rook until the pawn is pushed (destroying the enemy King's pawn cover). Then leap to the back rank (putting maximum distance between the defending Rook and enemy King) and begin checking like a berserk demon!

Trap The Enemy King Away From the Action

As we saw in our study of the Lucena Position, trapping the enemy King away from the action was an important idea in the winning process, *and* is also a key idea for the defender. The logic is easy to grasp: If a heated battle is raging on Hill One, and a portion of the enemy army is confined to Hill Two, then you simply have your opponent outnumbered!

Diagram 138

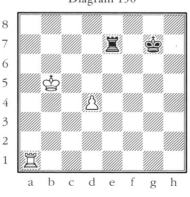

White to move

Thanks to the extra pawn and the fact that black's King is so far away, White is clearly winning the game. Black is still holding on to some small shred of hope, though. If he can get his King in front of the pawn he might (Ah, the joy of hope!) be able to create a Philidor Position. However, why should White allow Black to hold onto his dreams when he can immediately show black's helplessness by the simple **1.Rf1!** Suddenly black's King has no hope of taking part in the battle since 1...Rf7 2.Rxf7+ is a very easy win.

Our next example shows this "trapping the King away from the action" idea used defensively.

Useful Advice

Trapping the enemy King away from the action for either defensive or offensive reasons is often a very effective strategy.

Diagram 139

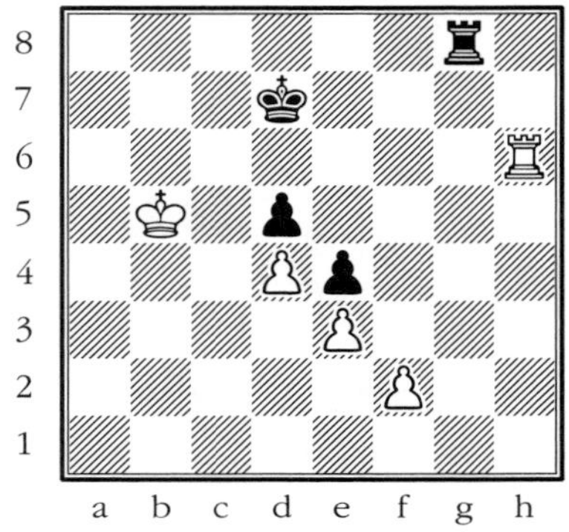

Black to move and draw

White to move would win by 1.Kc5 when the d5-pawn would fall: 1.Kc5 Rg5 2.Rd6+ Ke7 3.Rxd5. However, Black to move saves the game by ...

1...Rc8!

Suddenly white's King can't join in the battle against d5.

2.Kb6

It's clear that 2.Rh7+ Kd6 only helps Black, while 2.Rh5 Kd6 has the same effect.

2...Rc2

Letting White know that his f2-pawn isn't a tower of strength either!

3.Rf6 Rc1

Black has no intention of giving up his control over the c-file! Without a King, White can't hope to win. Drawn.

Queen vs. King and Pawn

This is a no-contest, especially if the stronger side's King—who we'll suppose is White—is close to the pawn. However, even if the white King is on the other end of the universe, a Queen can beat a King and pawn (occasional exceptions occur if the pawn is on the 7th rank) in two ways:

➤ The Queen lands on the queening square. Since the pawn then has no chance of promoting, the vacationing King can calmly walk back to the endangered area and eventually eat the pawn.

➤ The Queen forces the black King to step in front of its pawn. Since the pawn can't move for a moment, the white King can take a safe step closer to the pawn's position. This will be repeated until white's King joins with its Queen to pick off the pawn.

Queen vs. Pawn on 6th Rank

Diagram 140

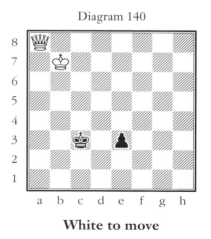

White to move

White ends things quickly by permanently stopping black's pawn in its tracks. **1.Qa5+ Kd3 2.Qe1 e2 3.Kc6** and Black can't prevent White from marching his King to the pawn: **3...Ke3 4.Kc5 Kd3 5.Kd5 Ke3 6.Kc4 Kf3 7.Kd3** and the pawn is lost.

Diagram 141

White to move

Rook-pawns often prove the exception to various general rules. In this case White doesn't want the pawn to get to the 7th rank (we'll discuss that in a moment), but he also can't get his Queen to h1, which would allow White to win as he did in the previous example.

However, he can win easily in the following manner:

1.Qg5+ Kh1

1...Kh2 blocks the pawn and let's White safely move his King closer to the action by 2.Kc7. It also allows White to instantly win the pawn by 2.Qg4, as seen at the end of our main line and in diagram 142.

Diagram 142

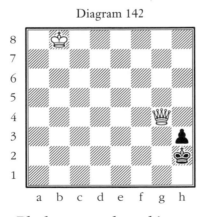

Black to move loses his pawn

The position in diagram 142 is white's main winning idea when a rook-pawn is on the 6th rank.

After 1...Kh1 (from diagram 141, which continued 1.Qg5+ Kh1), all of white's subsequent moves are geared towards creating the position in the diagram.

2.Qd5+! Kg1

2...Kh2 3.Qf3 wins the pawn.

3.Qd4+

Never giving Black a chance to push his pawn to h2.

3...Kh1

We already know that 3...Kh2 falls victim to 4.Qg4, while 3...Kf1 also loses to 4.Qf4+ Kg2 (4...Ke2 5.Qh2 is completely hopeless) 5.Qg4+ Kh2 6.Kc7, winning the pawn.

4.Qe4+

Forcing black's King to h2 or g1, both poor squares.

4...Kg1

4...Kh2 5.Qg4.

5.Qg4+ Kh2 6.Kc7 and Black is forced to jettison his pawn by **6...Kh1 7.Qxh3+** when the game is over.

> **RULE**
>
> Lone Queen vs. King and pawn on the 6th rank is almost always a win for the Queen.

Queen vs. Pawn on the 7th Rank

Though I personally leapfrogged over the "C" class (jumping directly to class "B"), I must admit that I remember the first time I ever came into contact with this endgame. I was fourteen-years-old (with a 1600 rating) and a friend called and gave me the following position over the phone.

Diagram 143

White to Move

"White's a Queen up!" I said.

"Yes, but I bet you can't win it."

I laughed at him, agreed on a fifty-cent wager, and proceeded to lose my money when I just couldn't do it! Humiliated, I finally asked for the solution.

1.Qb4+ Kd1

Otherwise White plays Qe1, forever stopping the pawn in its tracks.

2.Qd4+ Kc2 3.Qe3!

As a child, I wasn't able to find this endgame "key." The idea is to force black's King in front of his pawn, and then step a square closer to the action with the white King.

3...Kd1 4.Qd3+

Forcing Black to block his own pawn.

4...Ke1 5.Kb7

The first step of many towards black's pawn.

5...Kf2

Now White just has to repeat the same process again and again until his King helps win the pawn.

6.Qd2 Kf1

Again, 6...Kf3 7.Qe1 would be very easy for White.

7.Qf4+ Kg2 8.Qe3! Kf1 9.Qf3+ Ke1 10.Kc6 Kd2

Note that 10...Kd1 allows 11.Kd5 since the e-pawn is pinned.

11.Qf2 Kd1 12.Qd4+ Kc2 13.Qe3! Kd1 14.Qd3+ Ke1 15.Kd5 Kf2 16.Qd2 Kf1 17.Qf4+ Kg2 18.Qe3! Kf1 19.Qf3+ Ke1 20.Kd4

Now things end quickly since white's King is in striking range.

20...Kd2 21.Qd3+ Ke1 22.Ke3 Kf1 23.Qxe2+ Kg1 24.Kf3

And not 24.Qf2+ Kh1 25.Kf3?? stalemate. When the game seems ridiculously easy to win, don't get overconfident and overlook a stalemate!

24...Kh1 25.Qg2 mate.

Once I saw how it was done (we went over it several times) he made me set up another position.

Diagram 144

White to move

"I bet you can't win this."

Angry at the insult, I said, "What are you talking about? You just showed me how to do it! *Of course* I can win it!"

He was adamant. "I'll bet you double or nothing you can't."

So we went at it again:

1.Qb5+ Ke1 2.Qe5+ Kd2 3.Qf4+ Ke2 4.Qe4+ Kd2 5.Qf3!

I was quite proud of myself since I had clearly mastered this winning idea. There was no question in my mind that I was going to win this bet!

5...Ke1 6.Qe3+ Kf1 7.Kb7

At this point I decided that enough was enough. "Okay, I think I've showed you that I know how to win it. Let's end this farce!"

He just laughed and played...

7...Kg2 8.Qe2 Kg1 9.Qg4+ Kh2 10.Qf3 Kg1 11.Qg3+ Kh1!—Doh! I froze in my tracks! Suddenly I realized that the game was indeed a draw since 12.Qxf2 is a stalemate, while checks like 12.Qh3+ Kg1 simply repeat the position and never allow the white King to complete its long journey to the afflicted area.

> **RULE**
>
> A b/g-pawn, e-pawn and d-pawn on the 7th almost always lose to a Queen.

> **RULE**
>
> A c/f-pawn on the 7th rank can draw against a Queen if the stronger side's King is far away from the action.

What about a rook-pawn (a/h-pawn) on the 7th? We've seen how rook-pawns often prove the exception in many endgame positions, and this rook-pawn paranoia holds true here too.

Diagram 145

White to move, draw

Black's drawing idea in this endgame can be instantly grasped after 1.Qg3+ Kh1!, when the hoped for march of the White King (via 2.Kc7, for example) leads to an immediate stalemate and draw. Unfortunately for White, Queen checks also get nowhere: 2.Qe1+ Kg2 3.Qe4+ Kg1 (and not 3…Kg3?? 4.Qh1, winning) and the threat to promote the pawn means that white's King will never be able to help out. Thus the game's a draw.

> **RULE**
>
> A rook-pawn (a/h-pawn) on the 7th rank draws against a Queen if the stronger side's King is far from the action.

Summing Up

King and Pawn Endgames

➤ In general, in a king and pawn vs. lone King position, the weaker side loses if he can't get his King in front of the enemy pawn—if you can't block and stop the pawn from queening, then you're a goner! However, rook-pawns often allow all sorts of exceptions due to the fact that there isn't a file to the side of the pawn (which creates many odd stalemate possibilities).

➤ You can gauge the result of an upcoming Trébuchet position in this way: the side whose King can make first contact with the enemy pawn can force a winning Trébuchet.

➤ King and two (doubled) pawns vs. lone King always win unless the pawns can't be properly defended, or unless they are rook-pawns.

➤ You can calculate the square of a pawn by: drawing a diagonal extension from the pawn to the end of the board; drawing a line from the side of the pawn to the edge of the board; connecting all the lines. If the defender's King can step into this square, it will stop the pawn. If it can't, the pawn will run for a touchdown.

➤ An Outside Passed Pawn is a passed pawn that stands to the side of the main sphere of battle. Such a pawn is usually a very valuable commodity since it can be far from the enemy King and thus pose a serious promotion threat, and/or it can force the defending King over to deal with it, leaving the embattled area (where most of the pawns reside) bereft of a defender.

Minor Piece Endgames

➤ A Bishop and (safe) pawn vs. a lone King sounds like it should be resignable, yet it can be salvaged *if*: the pawn is a rook-pawn; the pawn's queening square is a different color than its Bishop; the defender's King can reach the queening square (or any of the squares touching the queening square).

➤ A Knight and a (safe) pawn vs. a lone King is always a win for the material advantage, *except* when the extra pawn is a rook-pawn and that rook-pawn is on the 7th rank. We've seen that rook-pawns often create exceptions to otherwise ironclad rules, and this is yet another case of the "rook-pawn curse."

▸ In the middlegame, Bishops of opposite colors is thought to be an advantage for the attacker since one Bishop can't defend what the other attacks. However, in the endgame Bishops of opposite colors can give the defender serious drawing chances in positions that one would think are losing.

Rook Endgames

▸ The Lucena Position is the Holy Grail of Rook endings; the sacred key that allows you to know what to avoid when defending a pawn down Rook endgame, while also giving you the knowledge to know what to head for if you have the superior side. The Lucena Position is a simplified position where one side has a Rook and a pawn (any pawn but a rook-pawn) on the 7th rank (the King in front of its pawn), while the other side just has a Rook.

▸ The Philidor Position is a Rook and pawn vs. Rook position where the defender's King is in front of the enemy pawn. In general, such a position is drawn.

▸ In a Rook and pawn endgame, it's important to not allow your Rook to become passively placed!

▸ In a Rook and pawn endgame, always trap the enemy King as far away from the action as possible by using your Rook to cut it off from a file or rank. The logic is easy to grasp: If a heated battle is raging on Hill One, and a portion of the enemy army is confined to Hill Two, then you simply have your opponent outnumbered!

Queen vs. King and Lone Pawn

▸ Queen vs. lone pawn is a no-contest, especially if the stronger side's King is close to the pawn. However, even if the stronger side's King is on the other end of the universe, a Queen can beat a King and pawn (occasional exceptions occur if the pawn is on the 7th rank) in two ways:

- The Queen lands on the queening square. Since the pawn then has no chance of promoting, the vacationing King can calmly walk back to the endangered area and eventually eat the pawn.

- The Queen forces the defending King to step in front of its pawn. Since the pawn can't move for a moment, the stronger side's King can take a safe step closer to the pawn's position. This will be repeated until the King joins with its Queen to pick off the pawn.

➤ Queen vs. pawn observations (with the stronger side's King far from the action): A Queen vs. any pawn on the 6th almost always wins for the Queen; A Queen vs. a knight-pawn, king-pawn, queen-pawn on the 7th almost always wins for the Queen; A Queen vs. a bishop-pawn or rook-pawn on the 7th is a draw.

Tests and Solutions

Diagram 146

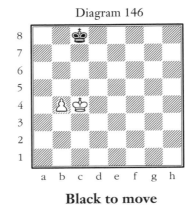

Black to move

Is White winning, or can Black save the game?

Diagram 147

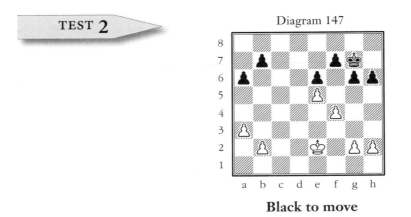

Black to move

Black played 1...g5 in this position. Is this a good move, or should he have preferred 1...Kf8?

TEST **3**

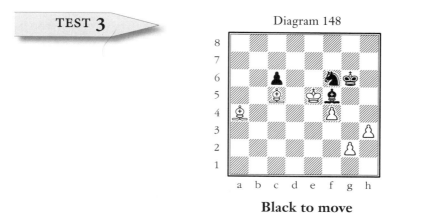

Diagram 148

Black to move

White has a dominating King, two active Bishops vs. a Bishop and Knight, and two extra pawns. Is it time to resign?

TEST **4**

Diagram 149

White to move

What is white's best move?

TEST **5**

Diagram 150

White to move

Can White win this position?

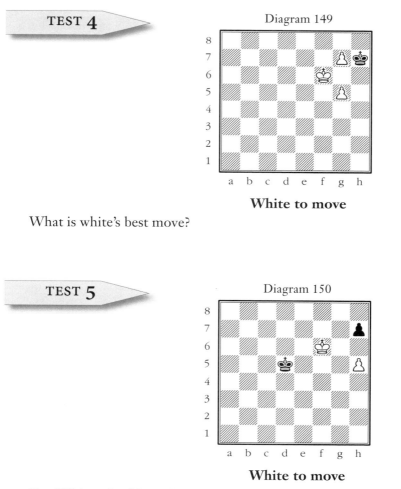

TEST 6

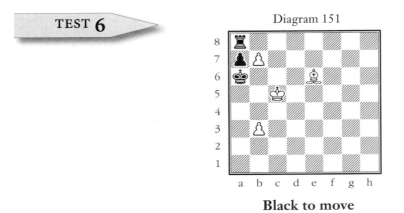

Diagram 151

Black to move

Black has a problem-like draw here that you're *not* expected to find (though have fun trying!). However, can you see the chess oddity that will allow Black to save himself? We're looking for an idea, not moves.

TEST 7

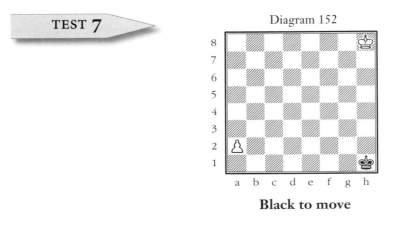

Diagram 152

Black to move

It's a race between black's King and the a-pawn. Can Black draw?

TEST 8

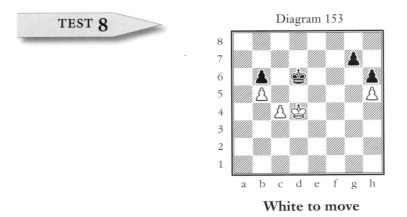

Diagram 153

White to move

White has the better King position, so he should be the one with all the chances. Can White win?

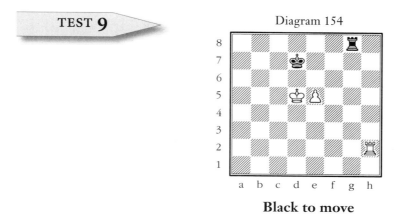

TEST 9

Diagram 154

Black to move

White threatens the unpleasant Rh7+. How can Black defend himself?

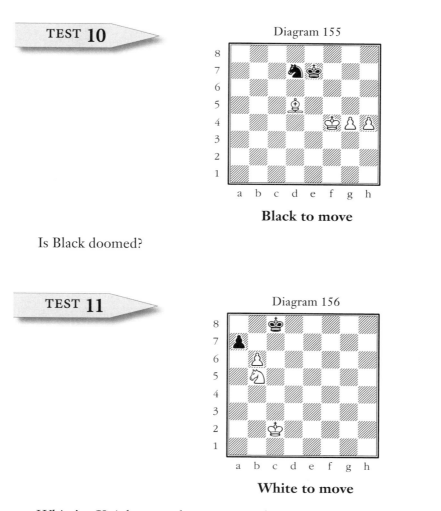

TEST 10

Diagram 155

Black to move

Is Black doomed?

TEST 11

Diagram 156

White to move

White's a Knight up and can capture the a7-pawn two different ways. Can he win?

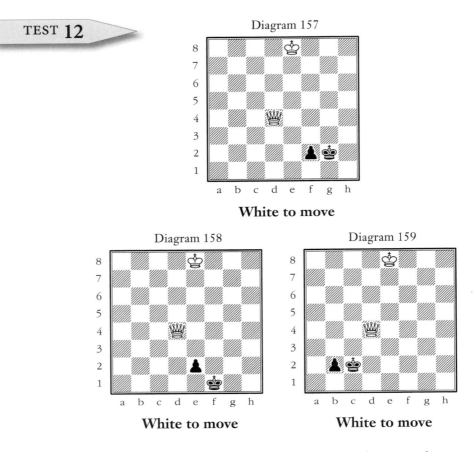

TEST 12

Diagram 157

White to move

Diagram 158

White to move

Diagram 159

White to move

Of these three diagrams (157, 158, and 159), which one (if any) is salvageable for Black (White has the move in each case)?

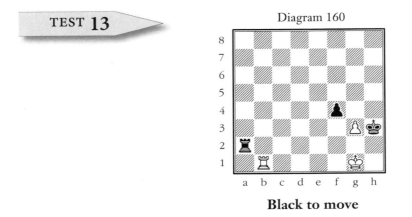

TEST 13

Diagram 160

Black to move

Black has four ways to play this position: 1...Kxg3, 1...fxg3, 1...Rg2+, and 1...f3. Do any of these choices win?

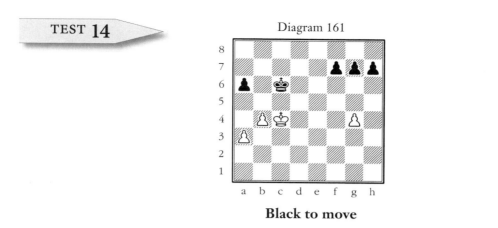

TEST 14

Diagram 161

Black to move

Black is a pawn up and enjoys a three to one pawn majority on the kingside. Wanting to create a passed pawn, he played 1...g6. Is this a good move?

*   *   *   *   *

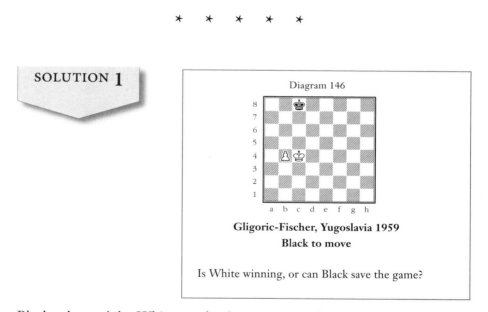

SOLUTION 1

Diagram 146

Gligoric-Fischer, Yugoslavia 1959
Black to move

Is White winning, or can Black save the game?

Black, who can't let White get the Opposition, and can't let white's King get two squares in front of its pawn, only has one move that draws:

1...Kb8!

This move sits back and waits for White to advance and give Black the Opposition. Other moves lose because White either gets the Opposition or is allowed to bring his King too far forward:

➤ 1...Kc7?? 2.Kc5 Kb7 3.Kb5 Kc7 4.Ka6, 1-0.

➤ 1...Kb7?? 2.Kb5, 1-0.

➤ 1...Kd7?? 2.Kb5, 1-0.

➤ 1...Kd8?? 2.Kb5 Kc7 3.Ka6, 1-0.

The game was agreed drawn after **1...Kb8** due to the following possibilities:

➤ 2.Kd5 Kb7 3.Kc5 Kc7 4.Kb5 Kb7 with a simple draw.

➤ 2.Kb5 Kb7, ½-½.

➤ 2.Kc5 Kc7, ½-½.

➤ 2.Kd4 Kb7 with a draw (and not 2...Kc7?? 3.Kc5 when White gets the Opposition and wins).

SOLUTION 2

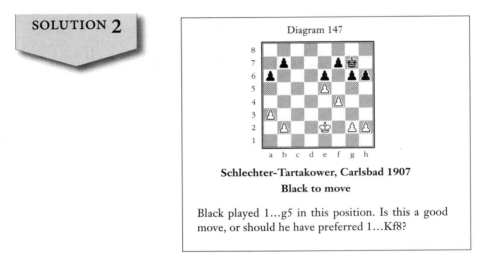

Diagram 147

Schlechter-Tartakower, Carlsbad 1907
Black to move

Black played 1...g5 in this position. Is this a good move, or should he have preferred 1...Kf8?

1...g5??

This loses since it allows White an Outside Passed Pawn (1...Kf8 2.Kd3 Ke7 3.Kc4 Kd7 would have drawn.)

2.fxg5 hxg5 3.Kf3 Kg6 4.Kg4 f5+ 5.exf6 e.p. Kxf6

Though Black has a passed pawn, he's dead lost due to the fact that White can create a far more valuable Outside Passed Pawn by g3 and h4.

6.g3! a5 7.a4 e5 8.h4! gxh4 9.gxh4

This Outside Passed Pawn allows White to make use of our Fox in the Chicken Coup concept.

9...Kg6 10.b3 b6

10...e4 11.Kf4 is easy for White.

11.h5+ Kf6

11...Kh6 12.Kf5.

12.h6 Kg6 13.h7 Kxh7 14.Kf5, 1-0. White marches over and wins black's remaining pawns.

SOLUTION 3

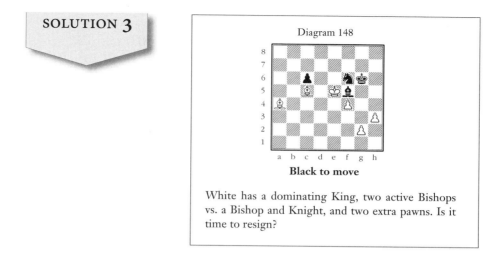

Diagram 148

Black to move

White has a dominating King, two active Bishops vs. a Bishop and Knight, and two extra pawns. Is it time to resign?

It's clear that pedestrian play like 1...Nd5 2.g4 doesn't offer Black any hope. So black's survival depends on whether or not he has some tricky saving resource. If you saw **1...Nd7+ 2.Kd6 Nxc5 3.Kxc5 Bxh3** then kudos for being very aware of the wrong rook-pawn drawing device! Now 4.gxh3 Kf5 saves the day since, after ...Kxf4, White will be left with a Bishop and wrong colored rook-pawn (5.Kd6 Kxf4 6.Bxc6 Kg5 7.Ke7 Kh6 8.Kf8 Kh7 and Black safely makes it to h8).

This example shows how a player must always be on the lookout for the Bishop and rook-pawn of the wrong color save. However, it turns out that White wins after 3...Bxh3 by 4.Bc2+!, which forces immediate resignation (4...Bf5 5.Bxf5+ Kxf5 6.g3).

SOLUTION 4

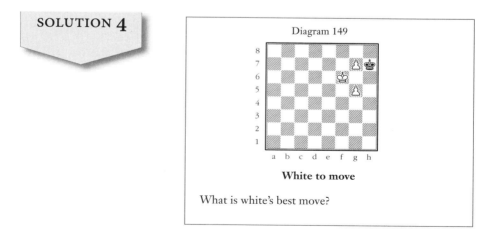

Diagram 149

White to move

What is white's best move?

White has made the mistake of pushing his doubled pawns down the board together. This actually hampers the winning process and now White only has one way to secure victory:

1.g8=Q+!

This allows White to grab the Opposition and reach a basic winning King and pawn vs. King position. Other moves throw the win away: 1.Kf7?? is an immediate stalemate, while 1.g6+?? Kg8 forces White to give up the g7-pawn and accept a basic draw.

1...Kxg8 2.Kg6!

And not 2.g6?? Kf8 3.g7+ Kg8 4.Kg6 stalemate.

2...Kh8 3.Kf7 Kh7 4.g6+ and the pawn queens.

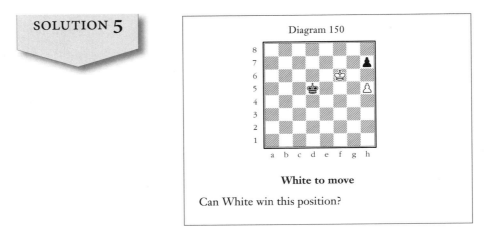

SOLUTION 5

Diagram 150

White to move

Can White win this position?

No, Black draws. Though White wins the final black pawn, his King will end up trapped in the corner, or he'll allow the enemy King to take up residence on g8 or h8.

1.Kg7

On 1.h6 Black simply waits with 1...Kd6 when 2.Kg7 Ke7 3.Kxh7 Kf7 traps white's King and forces a draw after 4.Kh8 Kf8 and now 5.h7 is an instant stalemate, while 5.Kh7 Kf7 gets White nowhere.

1...Ke6 2.Kxh7

As in our note to move one, 2.h6 Ke7 3.Kxh7 Kf7 is also drawn.

2...Kf7 3.Kh8 Kf8 4.Kh7 Kf7 5.h6 Kf8 6.Kg6

White gets nowhere with 6.Kh8 Kf7.

6...Kg8 and black's King can't be chased away from the front of white's pawn.

SOLUTION 6

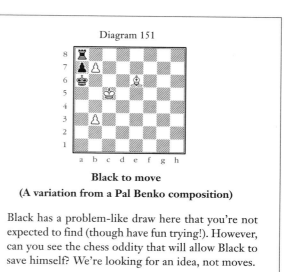

Diagram 151

Black to move
(A variation from a Pal Benko composition)

Black has a problem-like draw here that you're not expected to find (though have fun trying!). However, can you see the chess oddity that will allow Black to save himself? We're looking for an idea, not moves.

1...Kxb7!

The only good move. Other moves lose:

➤ 1...Re8 2.Bc8 and White makes a new Queen.

➤ 1...Rb8 2.Kc6 Rxb7 (2...Ka5 3.Kc7 Rxb7+ 4.Kxb7 a6 5.Bc4 and Black loses his a-pawn) 3.Bc4+! (3.Bc8?? Ka5 4.Kxb7 Kb4 5.Be6 a5 followed by ...a4, =) 3...Rb5 (3...Ka5 4.Kxb7 and White wins the a-pawn and retains a b-pawn, which gives Black no hope) 4.Bxb5+ (and not 4.b4?? stalemate!) 4...Ka5 5.Kc5 a6 6.b4 mate.

The whole point of this chess problem (starting with the brilliant 1...Kxb7) is in the possibility of creating a rook-pawn draw. Did you notice that such a thing might be possible (even if you didn't quite see how)? If so, your intuitive grasp of patterns is very impressive!

2.Bd5+ Kb8 3.Be4!

Forcing black's pawn to advance to a vulnerable square. The "obvious" 3.Bxa8 Kxa8 is an easy draw.

3...a5 4.Bxa8 a4!!, =. White is left with a basic rook-pawn draw after 5.bxa4 Kxa8.

Again, I didn't expect you to solve this problem, but trying to do so should ram home the idea that "salvation by rook-pawn" can occur from "out of the blue."

SOLUTION 7

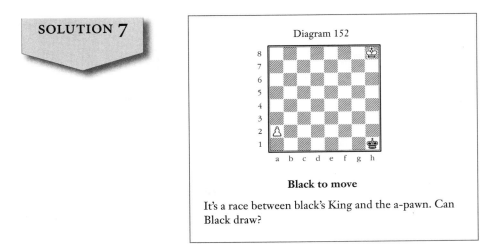

Diagram 152

Black to move

It's a race between black's King and the a-pawn. Can Black draw?

No, Black loses. Though it seems that 1...Kg2 steps into the square of white's pawn, this turns out to be an illusion since the pawn can leap two squares at once:

2.a4 Kf3 3.a5 Ke4 4.a6 Kd5 5.a7, 1-0.

SOLUTION 8

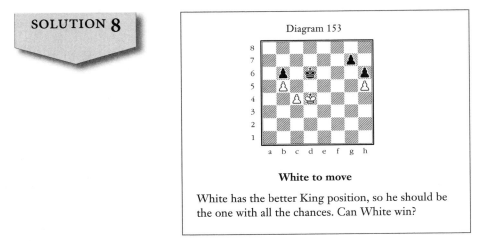

Diagram 153

White to move

White has the better King position, so he should be the one with all the chances. Can White win?

There are a couple things happening here. First, both pawn majorities seem frozen by a single enemy pawn. Second, even if White achieves a Chicken Coup infiltration, he'll be left with a rook-pawn.

However, it turns out that White can easily create a passed pawn, while Black can't. Once that is done, the race is on, with White winning by one move.

1.c5+!

A nice idea. It seems that White's losing a pawn, but that turns out to be an illusion.

1...bxc5+ 2.Kc4 Kc7

There's no hope in 2...g5 3.hxg6 e.p.

3.Kxc5 Kb7

Now the footrace begins. White needs to rush to the kingside, eat all the black pawns, and move his King to g7 before black's King can reach f8, f7, or f6.

4.Kd6

Actually, White doesn't need to test his "foot speed" at all. An alternative way to victory is 4.b6 Kb8 5.Kc6 Kc8 6.b7+ Kb8 7.Kb6 g5 8.hxg6 e.p. h5 9.g7 h4 10.g8=Q mate.

4...Kb6 5.Ke6 Kxb5 6.Kf7 Kc6 7.Kxg7 Kd7 8.Kxh6 Ke7 9.Kg7, 1-0.

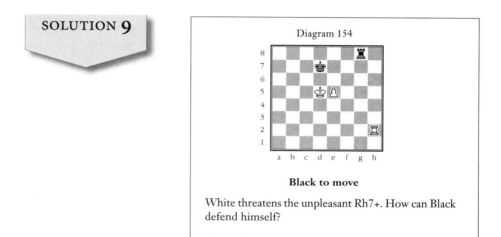

SOLUTION 9

Diagram 154

Black to move

White threatens the unpleasant Rh7+. How can Black defend himself?

If you thought passively stopping White's check was the way to go, you're wrong: 1...Rg7 2.Rh6! (Preventing Black from setting up a Philidor with ...Rg6.) 2...Ke7 3.Ra6! when the threat of Ra7+ is quite annoying. Instead, Black can effortlessly hold a half point by using the classic Philidor formula.

1...Rg6! 2.Rh7+ Ke8

Now white's King can't advance onto the 6th rank. Since Black can endlessly tread water by moving his Rook back and forth along that rank, White must eventually push his e-pawn.

3.e6

Threatening to win by 4.Kd6.

3...Rg1! and the coming cascade of Rook-checks will make it clear that White has no chance whatsoever of winning.

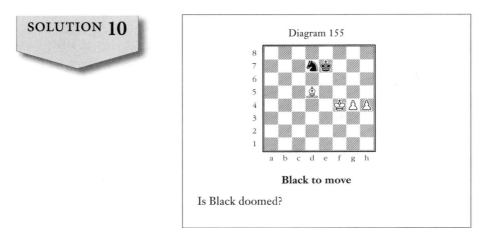

SOLUTION **10**

Diagram 155

Black to move

Is Black doomed?

Black can draw by giving up his Knight for the g-pawn and creating a miracle-save rook-pawn and wrong colored Bishop vs. lone King draw.

1...Nf6! 2.Bf3 Nxg4!

Taking it before g4-g5 can be played!

3.Bxg4 Kf6 4.h5 Kg7, ½-½.

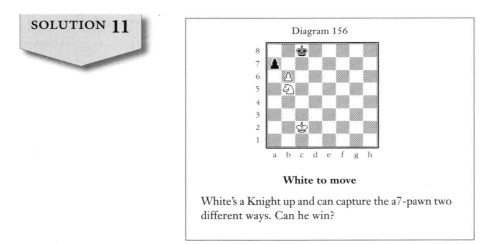

SOLUTION **11**

Diagram 156

White to move

White's a Knight up and can capture the a7-pawn two different ways. Can he win?

This is an easy position to blow. For example, 1.Nxa7+?? Kb7 leads to the loss of the b-pawn. Most tempting is 1.bxa7??, but if you had studied the earlier material you would know that the position after 1...Kb7 is dead drawn.

1.Nd6+!

The only way to secure victory.

1...Kb8 2.b7 Kc7 3.Kb3, 1-0. White wins by marching his King down the board: 3...Kb8 4.Kb4 Kc7 5.Kb5 Kb8 6.Ka6 Kc7 7.Kxa7, etc.

SOLUTION **12**

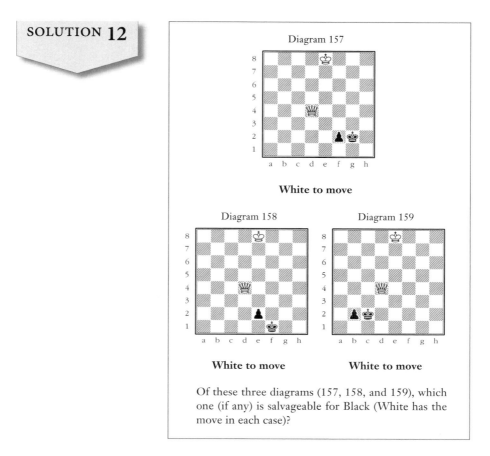

Diagram 157

White to move

Diagram 158

White to move

Diagram 159

White to move

Of these three diagrams (157, 158, and 159), which one (if any) is salvageable for Black (White has the move in each case)?

Position one (diagram 157) is a forced draw, while the others are resignable. Look over the material in Part Four again if you didn't get this right.

SOLUTION **13**

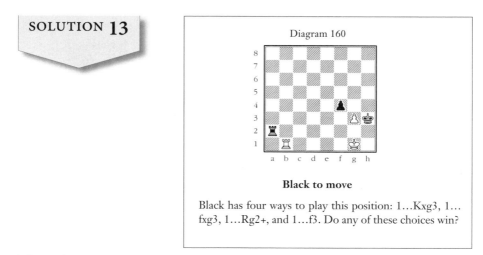

Diagram 160

Black to move

Black has four ways to play this position: 1...Kxg3, 1...fxg3, 1...Rg2+, and 1...f3. Do any of these choices win?

The only correct move is ...

1...Kxg3!

The other moves don't get the job done:

■———➤ 1...fxg3?? is a basic draw—a g-pawn can't win, even though white's Rook is passive.

■———➤ 1...Rg2+?? 2.Kf1 Kxg3 3.Rb3+ f3 4.Rb8 drawing since Black can't deal with the avalanche of checks to come.

■———➤ 1...f3?? 2.Rb8 and the upcoming long distance checks will assure White of the draw.

After 1...Kxg3, White can't activate his Rook (2.Rb8 Ra1+ mates) and also can't prevent Black from following up with 2...f3 with an easy theoretical win thanks to the passive state of white's Rook. An example:

2.Rb3+ (2.Kh1 f3 3.Rg1+ Kf2 is also easy for Black) **2...f3 3.Rb1 Rg2+ 4.Kf1 Rh2 5.Kg1 f2+ 6.Kf1 Rh1+**, 0-1.

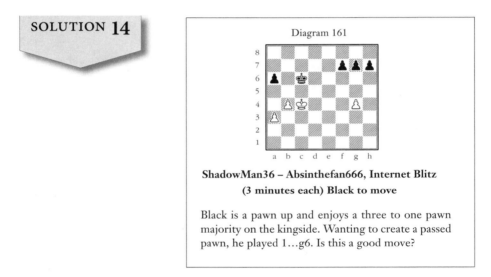

SOLUTION **14**

Diagram 161

ShadowMan36 – Absinthefan666, Internet Blitz
(3 minutes each) Black to move

Black is a pawn up and enjoys a three to one pawn majority on the kingside. Wanting to create a passed pawn, he played 1...g6. Is this a good move?

This example, which deserves careful study, is a mix of several things we've already learned (or should have already learned!): Opposition, Chicken Coup, Trébuchet, freezing a pawn majority, Square of the Pawn, and Outside Passed Pawns.

A student of mine, who had the black pieces, showed me this game because he was very curious about the resulting King and pawn ending. He's a pawn up and doing well, but the move he chose left me clutching my heart in convulsive agony.

1...g6??

Turning a win into a loss in one move! Instead, 1...h6 followed by 2...g6, 3...f6, and eventually ...h6-h5, would have won.

2.g5!

A super Deep Freeze! We looked at this idea in Part Three, where one pawn killed two. Here, though, we see one pawn killing three! Now White wins by:

➤ Turning his queenside majority into a passed pawn.

➤ Rushing his King to the kingside with drooling Chicken Coup desires.

➤ Eating black's kingside pawns while black's King deals with white's Outside Passer on the opposite wing.

2...Kb6 3.a4

The immediate 3.Kd5?? allows 3...Kb5 with a draw: 4.Kd4 Ka4 5.Kc4 Kxa3 6.Kc3 Ka2 7.Kc2 Ka3 8.Kc3 Ka4 9.Kc4 when black's King is permanently trapped on the a-file.

3...Kc6 4.a5!

Also sufficient is 4.b5+ axb5+ 5.axb5+ Kb6 6.Kb4 Kb7 7.Kc5 (Back to the old Fox in the Chicken Coup routine!) 7...Kc7 8.Kd5 Kb6 9.Ke5 Kxb5 10.Kf6 Kc5 11.Kxf7 Kd6 12.Kg7 Ke5 (or 12...Ke7 13.Kxh7 Kf7 14.Kh6 Kf8 15.Kxg6 Kg8 16.Kh6 Kh8 17.g6 Kg8 18.g7 Kf7 19.Kh7, 1-0.) 13.Kxh7 Kf5 14.Kh6 and White wins thanks to the wonders of Trébuchet!

With 4.a5, White creates an Outside Passed Pawn that's even further from the action than the one that would result from 4.b5+. Ultimately it doesn't make a difference in this particular game, but often a little detail like this (i.e., dragging the black King even farther from the action on the kingside) can be the only way to win.

4...Kd6

On 4...Kb7 5.Kd5 (taking the Diagonal Opposition) 5...Kc7 6.Kc5 Kb7 7.Kd6 White can win by going after a6, or continue with his Chicken Coup strategy and ravage black's kingside pawns: 7...Kb8 (Though Black takes the Opposition, it has no effect since it can't prevent his a-pawn from falling.) 8.Kc6 (8.Ke7 also ices the game) 8...Ka7 (Keeping the Opposition by 8...Kc8 is futile due to 9.Kb6 and 10.Kxa6) 9.Kc7 (retaking the Opposition and forcing black's King away from the protection of a6) 9...Ka8 10.Kb6 and it's all over.

5.b5

Wisely avoiding 5.Kd4 Kc6 6.Ke5?? (White could still win by 6.Kc4) 6...Kb5 7.Kf6 Kxb4 8.Kxf7 Kxa5 9.Kg7 Kb4 10.Kxh7 a5 11.Kxg6 a4 12.Kh7 a3 13.g6 a2 14.g7 a1=Q 15.g8=Q with a draw.

5...axb5+ 6.Kxb5 Kc7 7.Kc5

Time to go back to our "Chicken Coup" mentality!

7...Kb7 8.Kd6 Ka6 9.Ke7 Kxa5 10.Kxf7 Kb6 11.Kg7 Kc6 12.Kxh7 Kd7 13.Kxg6 Ke8 14.Kh7, 1-0. Black can't do anything about g5-g6-g7-g8=Q.

Final Thoughts

Wow! That was a lot of material! However, you now have an extremely solid endgame base that puts you far ahead of most of your competition, and even ahead of players a few hundred rating points higher than you that *should* have mastered these endgames long ago, but never got around to it.

Trust me when I tell you that the time you've spent learning everything in Part Four will likely prove to be the most rewarding study time of your chess life. You'll see the effects both in your newfound confidence, and in the results you gain against people who were once your equals, but now are not in your league once an endgame is reached.

Even if you decide that you have no desire to ever go past Part Four, do yourself a favor: if you don't view King and pawn vs. King positions as kid stuff, if any mention of the Square of the pawn and Outside Passed Pawns makes your eyes roll up into your head, if you have even a shred of doubt about how to handle the Lucena and Philidor positions, if the winning procedure in a Queen vs. pawn on the 7th situation is something you have to ponder, please go back and read Part Four again. Do so over and over until everything in it is muscle memory—your mind might go blank, but your hand will reach out and play these positions perfectly.

Part Five

Endgames for Class "B" (1600-1799)

Contents

After slogging through the seemingly endless expanse of Part Four, you should suddenly possess more endgame knowledge than you might have thought possible. Now, as a "B" player, we're ready to finish up the "basics" and leave you lording it over the unschooled masses—the fact is, few other non-Russian "B" players will know what you know (they should have learned this information, but they didn't).

I must admit that when I scaled the rating list and finally hit 1600, I ignorantly thought I knew all the endgames that I would ever need. The reality was that I only knew about forty percent of the material that encompasses the first five parts of this book. Now that I have a lifetime of teaching experience, it's become clear to me that most players under 1800 know even less, as proved by their many unnecessary defeats—losses that often occur as soon as an endgame appears.

Why throw away games in this fashion when the easy task of learning the material through Part Five will allow you to dominate others in your new ("B") rating class in most endgame situations? Not only that, but if you have a goal of reaching class "A" or Expert, knowing this material is an absolute must.

Compared to the ocean of information in Part Four, the lessons here will seem "a walk in the park!" In fact, most of Part Five's lessons are merely tune-ups and add-ons to the endgame skills you've already assimilated.

King and Pawn Endgames

At this point you have a wealth of knowledge about King and pawn endgames. You know the importance of using your King, all forms of Opposition, the Square of the Pawn, the strength of Outside Passed Pawns, Fox in the Chicken Coup, all aspects of King and pawn vs. King situations, the drawish tendencies of rook-pawns, the ins and outs of Trébuchet, and quite a bit more. It's now time to solidify your grasp of King and pawn basics.

The following material will enable you to play most King and pawn endgames with some real skill, and set you up for the more detailed knowledge that's required of players in the "A," Expert, and Master categories.

King and Two Healthy Pawns vs. Lone King

We've already seen (in Part Four) that a King and two safe doubled pawns (non rook-pawns!) win against a lone King. With that in mind, it's logical to assume that two non-doubled pawns should be even more decisive. Indeed, such situations are usually trivial wins, but there are two cases that might pose problems to the uninitiated:

▶ Split pawns

▶ Connected pawns

When you are two pawns up, the only way your opponent will survive is if you blunder into a stalemate, or if one of your pawns is lost. This "lost pawn" scenario usually occurs when the stronger side's King is far from the action, leaving the poor pawns to fend for themselves.

Diagram 162

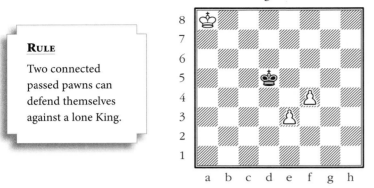

Black to move

RULE

Two connected passed pawns can defend themselves against a lone King.

The white King isn't participating, but he has nothing to worry about since connected pawns always defend themselves.

1...Ke4 2.Kb7 and white's King can approach the embattled area at its leisure since 2...Kxe3 3.f5 leads to the quick promotion of the f-pawn.

RULE

Two passed pawns, on the same rank but separated by one file, have the ability to defend themselves from attacks by the enemy King. When the King attacks one, push the other and the attacked pawn suddenly becomes poison!

Diagram 163

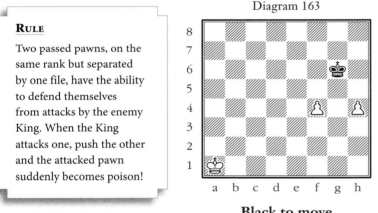

Black to move

White's King is, once again, light-years away, and it looks like his pawns might be vulnerable. However, it turns out that the two disconnected pawns do a great job protecting themselves!

1...Kh5

1...Kf5 is met by 2.h5!

2.f5!

Suddenly it becomes clear that 2...Kxh4 fails to 3.f6 when the pawn promotes.

2...Kh6 3.Kb2

White's King begins its winning journey. If Black can't pick up one of the white pawns, he's doomed!

3...Kg7

Naturally, 3...Kh5 4.Kc3 is easy for White since the h-pawn is still immune from capture.

4.h5!

An important move. Bringing the King up by 4.Kc3 loses the f-pawn and allows a draw after 4...Kf6 followed by 5...Kxf5.

4...Kf6 5.h6!

More punishment for Black. Now 5...Kxf5 loses to 6.h7.

5...Kf7 6.Kc3 Kg8 7.f6

Actually, White could also win by 7.Kd4 Kh7 8.Ke5 Kxh6 9.Kf6. The advance of the f-pawn, though, is even stronger and forces a new Queen without the King's help.

> **RULE**
>
> Two passed pawns, on the 6th rank but separated by one file, can force the creation of a new Queen even without help from their King.

7...Kh7 8.f7, 1-0.

Diagram 164

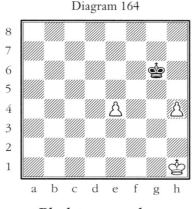

Black to move draws

Black can force a draw since one of the pawns will fall.

1...Kh5 2.e5

Giving up the h-pawn doesn't change the result: 2.Kg2 Kxh4 3.Kf3 Kg5 4.Ke3 Kf6 4.Kd4 Ke6 with a basic draw.

2...Kg6!

The big difference between this position and the previous one where the pawns were only one file apart is now clear. In that case, the advance of the f-pawn covered the g6-square and forced the black King to step straight backwards (when it poses no threat to the advanced pawn). In the present example, though, the King move to g6 threatens to pick off the e-pawn by ...Kf5.

3.Kg2

No better is 3.h5+ Kxh5 4.e6 Kg6 5.e7 Kf7, ½-½.

3...Kf5 4.Kf3 Kxe5 5.Kg4 Kf6 with a basic draw.

Nevertheless, in our last example Black drew because White ended up with a rook-pawn. If we slightly tweak that example, things might well have been different.

Diagram 165

RULE

The result of King and two pawns on the same rank two files apart vs. lone King usually depends on whether or not the stronger side can sacrifice one of his pawns, using the time gained to bring his King into the game and create a winning King and pawn vs. King position.

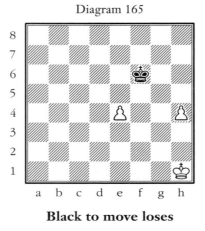

Black to move loses

This is the same position as the previous one, except now the black King stands on f6 instead of g6. This is enough to turn the position into a win for White because now he will be left with a center pawn instead of an h-pawn and, as a result, can create a winning King and pawn vs. King position.

1...Ke5 2.h5 Kf6 3.Kg2 Kg5 4.Kf3 Kxh5 5.Kf4 Kg6 6.Ke5 Kf7 7.Kd6, 1-0.

If the pawns get to the 5th rank, then (unless the defending King can immediately capture one of them) black's cause is hopeless.

Diagram 166

RULE

King and two pawns on the fifth rank two files apart vs. lone King is an easy win for the pawns.

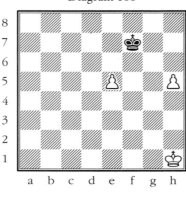

Black loses

1...Ke6 2.h6 Kf7 3.e6+ and one of the pawns will turn into a Queen.

Diagram 167

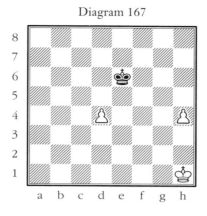

Black to move

Black's a goner.

1...Kd5 2.h5 Ke6

Alas, 2...Kxd4 3.h6 is clear sailing for White.

3.d5+ Kf6

Again, 3...Kxd5 4.h6 is finis.

4.d6 Ke6 5.h6, 1-0. Too easy!

> **RULE**
>
> If the pawns are three or more files apart (and not yet on the 5th rank), the defender loses unless he can immediately capture one of the pawns.

To sum up our observations about self-defending (Kingless) pawns:

➤ Connected pawns always defend each other.

➤ Pawns that are one file apart on any rank can usually defend themselves until the King arrives to shuttle one of them down the board.

➤ The defender has his best survival chances if the pawns are two files apart. However, if those pawns are on the 5th rank or farther then the game is resignable unless one of the pawns can be instantly captured.

➤ Pawns that are three files or more apart (on any rank) are too much for the defending King to handle.

Two connected passed pawns vs. a lone King almost always wins easily. The only time connected pawns pose a problem is if one of them is a rook-pawn.

Diagram 168

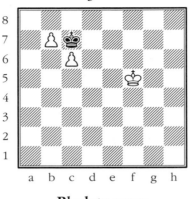

Black to move

No rook-pawn here! Black should resign but, evidently, he still has to be shown.

1...Kb8

As usual, the pawns defend themselves. 1...Kxc6 2.b8=Q.

2.Ke6 Kc7 3.Ke7

Also good is 3.b8=Q+ Kxb8 4.Kd7, 1-0.

3...Kb8 4.Kd7, 1-0.

As mentioned before, the difficulty level goes way, way up if we make one of the pawns a rook-pawn.

Diagram 169

Black to move

White still wins, but now he must earn the point by showing a bit of skill.

1...Kb7 2.Kd5 Ka8 3.Kc5

The first chance to go wrong was 3.Kc6?? stalemate! Many players give 3.Kd6 a try here, but watch out for 3...Kb7 4.Kd7 Ka8 5.Kc7?? stalemate.

3...Kb7 4.a8=Q+!

The key to this endgame and many other King and pawn endgames as well. By giving up the a-pawn White does two things:

➤ He ends most stalemating tricks.

➤ He forces Black to give White the Opposition, which in this position will prove decisive.

In effect, we have this situation:

Diagram 170

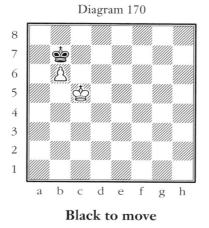

Black to move

If Black follows the advice from earlier parts of this book and steps straight back with 1...Kb8, the game is a draw. However, if he plays 1...Ka8?? or 1...Kc8??, the game is lost because White gets the Opposition and forces the black King away from the front of the pawn.

In our example of two vs. one (diagram 169), the move 4.a8=Q+! forces Black to make that losing move and enter a lost King and pawn vs. King endgame.

4...Kxa8 5.Kc6

Taking the Opposition and icing the win.

5...Kb8 6.b7 Ka7 7.Kc7, 1-0.

Tactical Bombs

In King and pawn endgames, there are quite a few tactical breaks—some pretty cool—that one must be aware of. We'll only look at a couple basic examples here, but more complex tactical ideas are available in Part Nine, Tactics.

Diagram 171

White to move

Black feels pretty confident since he has a passed a-pawn and his one kingside pawn appears to stop white's two. However, this is shown to be an illusion.

1.g5!

Turning his two vs. one pawn majority into an unstoppable passed pawn. Of course, waiting around with 1.Kb1 Kc4 2.Ka2?? (2.g5! would still do the trick) 2...Kd5 wins for Black thanks to the good old Chicken Coup routine.

1...fxg5 2.f6 g4 3.f7 g3 4.f8=Q g2 and now both 5.Qg8+ and 5.Qf3+ followed by Qxg2 end the game in white's favor.

Diagram 172

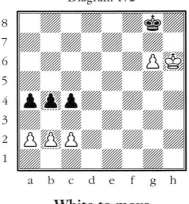

White to move

White is a pawn up and should win the game by using our favorite Chicken Coup technique (i.e., running over to the queenside and feasting on black pawns while the enemy King deals with the g-pawn).

1.Kg5??

White follows his Chicken Coup plan, certain of victory. He's hoping for 1...Kg7 2.Kf5 a3?? 3.bxa3 bxa3 4.c3 Kg8 5.Ke5 when black's queenside pawns are toast. Sadly, he's in for a painful surprise.

Other losing moves for White are 1.a3?? c3! and 1.c3?? a3! when Black makes a new Queen.

1...b3!

A very important tactical motif that will save you grief if you avoid it, and bring you points if you make use of it. White is suddenly dead lost!

2.axb3

If White had tried 2.cxb3 then Black ends things with 2...a3!! 3.bxa3 c3 when the c-pawn will promote to a Queen.

2...c3!!

> **REMEMBER**
>
> Shocking pawn breaks are common in King and pawn endgames. Being conversant with such themes means you can make use of them in some situations, and avoid them in others.

Diagram 173

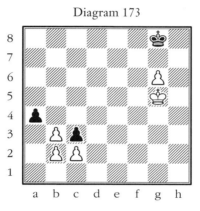

White to move, Black wins

The point. White clears away the b2-pawn which allows the black a-pawn to make a dash for the back rank.

3.bxc3 a3, 0-1.

So what did White do wrong from our initial position?

Diagram 174

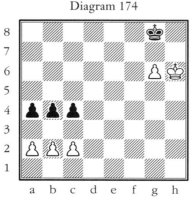

White to move and win

Obviously, White can't allow the tactical explosion we just witnessed. That means he must block it.

1.b3! axb3

Naturally, 1...cxb3 is answered by 2.cxb3 when Black isn't allowed a passed pawn.

2.axb3

Suicide was still possible by 2.cxb3?? c3, 0-1.

2...cxb3

A quicker death results from 2...c3 3.g7 Kf7 4.Kh7, 1-0.

3.cxb3 Kh8 4.Kg5

Correctly making use of the Chicken Coup idea, and avoiding 4.g7+?? Kg8 5.Kg6 stalemate. Note that after 4.g7+?? Kg8 it was already too late for White to undo the harm: 5.Kg5 Kxg7 6.Kf5 Kf7 7.Ke5 Ke7 8.Kd5 Kd7 9.Kc5 Kc7 10.Kxb4 Kb6, ½-½.

4...Kg7 5.Kf5 Kg8

Avoiding 5...Kf8 6.Kf6 Kg8 7.g7, 1-0.

6.Ke5

Feeding time!

6...Kg7 7.Kd5 Kxg6 8.Kc5 Kf6 9.Kxb4 Ke7 10.Kc5 Kd8 11.Kb6 Kc8 12.b4 Kb8 13.b5 Ka8 14.Kc7 Ka7 15.b6+, 1-0.

Triangulation

Triangulation is a seemingly complicated term that makes a chess player seem intellectually superior to everyone else when he says, "I won because I Triangulated my King, gained the Opposition, and ultimately left my opponent in zugzwang." Very impressive indeed!

The fact of the matter is that Triangulation's the name of a very small, often uncomplicated maneuver designed to give your opponent the move and, as a result, you the Opposition. But don't pass this on to the non-chess playing public—why not let them continue to think that chess players are geniuses?

The position in diagram 175 is our first realistic multi-pawn King endgame. And it looks complicated too! But the result really boils down to two questions:

➤ Can White win black's e-pawn?

Diagram 175

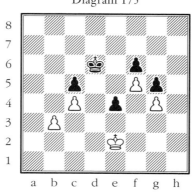

Does having the move make a difference?

➤ Can Black successfully penetrate with his King to f4 (where it will eat white's pawns on g4 and f5)?

First, let's see what happens if Black has the move.

1...Ke5

On 1...Kc6 White plays 2.Ke3 and wins the e4-pawn: 2...Kb6 3.Kxe4 Ka5 4.Kd5 Kb4 5.Kd6 and Black has to give up c5, and with it the game.

2.Ke3

Taking the Opposition and forcing black's King backwards.

2...Kd6 3.Kxe4 Kc6 4.Kd3

White's plan is to exchange his b-pawn for black's c-pawn, creating a passed pawn on c4. He'll then make use of the Chicken Coup idea to pick off black's remaining pawns on f6 and g5.

4...Kb6 5.Kc3 Ka5

Diagram 176

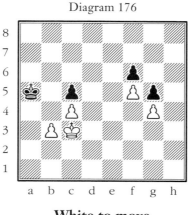

White to move

Has Black stopped white's plans?

6.b4+!

No, this instructive idea makes it clear that Black has no chance whatsoever of saving the game.

6...cxb4+ 7.Kb3 Kb6 8.Kxb4 Kc6 9.c5 Kc7 10.Kb5 Kb7 11.c6+ Kc7 12.Kc5 Kc8 13.Kd6 Kd8 14.Ke6, 1-0.

Okay, that was simple enough. But now let's see if we get the same result if White moves first.

Diagram 177

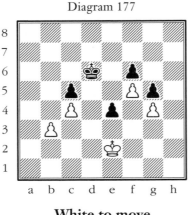

White to move

Many people would play 1.Ke3?? here, but after 1...Ke5 Black takes the Opposition and forces White backwards: 2.Ke2 Kf4 and white's pawns fall like ducks in hunting season.

Clearly, the direct approach is a horrible failure in our diagrammed position. However, White can turn the tables by playing 1.Kd2 or 1.Kf2, when 1...Ke5 2.Ke3 leaves White in possession of the Opposition. Both Kd2 and Kf2 are Triangulation maneuvers—White steps to the side, then moves diagonally forward to create a small triangle. Believe it or not, that's what Triangulation (in its most basic form) is all about.

So let's see White, with correct play, win from diagram 177:

1.Kf2!

By the way, this move also takes the Indirect Opposition, while 1.Kd2! would take Distant Opposition.

1...e3+!

The best try. As stated earlier, 1...Ke5 2.Ke3 is an easy win for White.

2.Ke2!

Not falling for 2.Kxe3?? Ke5! when Black once again takes the Opposition and manages to penetrate with his King to d4 or f4. White's 2.Ke2 is yet another example of Triangulation.

I should add that 2.Kf3! also does the job, since 2...e2 3.Kxe2 Ke5 4.Ke3 gives White the Opposition.

2...Ke5 3.Kxe3, 1-0.

> **RULE**
>
> Basic Triangulation is a maneuver where the King steps to the side and then moves forward diagonally, thus losing a move and gaining the Opposition.

Outflanking

Outflanking is a simple but useful tool to know. With it a player can make inroads into a position that were not otherwise possible. Admittedly, this often costs the Opposition, but it must be remembered that the Opposition is only a means to an end, not the end itself!

> **RULE**
>
> Outflanking is a maneuver where the stronger side's King moves to the side, placing a file between the Kings (sometimes even giving the opponent the Opposition while doing so!). This allows the Outflanking King to march forward towards the target, without allowing the enemy monarch to step in front of it and take Direct Opposition.

Diagram 178

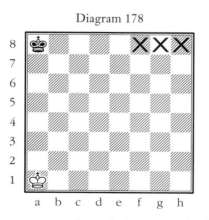

White to move and reach f8, g8, or h8 by force!

Believe it or not, a close study of this position and its correct handling will teach the student the finer points of Opposition, Outflanking, and Triangulation. White to play has the Opposition. His goal is to reach f8, g8 or h8 in at most seventeen moves. Black will constantly try to stop this, using Opposition (i.e., the threat to retake the Opposition) as a defensive device.

Once you've mastered this position and the techniques involved, we'll say that you have earned your "King diploma."

1.Ka2!

The only way to take the Opposition. The more direct path fails because it allows Black to take the Opposition: 1.Kb2?? Kb8! (It is already impossible to reach the target squares.) 2.Kc3 Kc7 3.Kd4 Kd6 4.Ke4 Ke6 and White will not get close to his targets.

1...Kb8!

A fine defensive move! Now 2.Ka3? loses the Opposition since Black has his choice of two squares on the a-file and thus can make it either odd or even (2...Ka7!). White will also fail to reach his goals after 2.Kb3? Kb7.

> **REMEMBER**
>
> Direct Opposition occurs when you create an odd number of squares between the Kings with the opponent to move.

2.Kb2

Heading over to the target side of the board.

2...Kc8

Still keeping white's options to a minimum. The seemingly more active 2...Kc7 3.Kc3 only aids White.

3.Kc2

Still heading for the kingside. Instead White could try to Outflank Black, but at the moment this would fail to achieve the set goal. Let's look at an example of Outflanking by having White play 3.Ka3 instead of the superior 3.Kc2:

Diagram 179

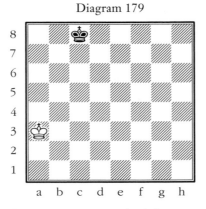

White plays 3.Ka3 instead of the correct 3.Kc2

By putting a file between the Kings, White prevents Black from taking Direct Opposition while simultaneously making forward progress. This process is called Outflanking. After 3.Ka3 Black can take the Opposition with 3...Kc7 (forming connecting points on c7, c3, a3 and a7) but White will be able to move forward: 4.Ka4 Kc6 5.Ka5 Kc5 6.Ka6 Kc6. White has managed to make inroads into black's position, but he will never be able to get over to the kingside.

To solve the problem posed in diagram 178, White must first go to the target side of board (kingside) and only then Outflank his opponent. The logic for this is easy to understand: when you are on the kingside, any forward motion will allow White to land on his goal squares.

Back to the position after 3.Kc2:

Diagram 180

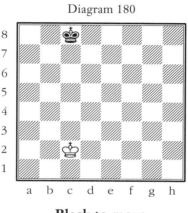

Black to move

3...Kd8 4.Kd2 Ke8 5.Ke2 Kf8 6.Kf2 Kg8 7.Kg2

White is now on the optimum file since his King stands right in the middle of the target squares.

7...Kh8

Or 7...Kf8 8.Kh3.

8.Kf3

The Outflanking process finally takes place.

8...Kg7

Black could take the Opposition by 8...Kh7 but after 9.Kf4 Kh6 10.Kf5 Kh5 11.Kf6 White would be able to conquer the target square on f8. This idea of giving up the Opposition for a higher prize is a major part of Outflanking.

9.Kg3!

Satisfied that he has advanced one rank, White retakes the Opposition. Blunders would be 9.Kf4? Kf6 and 9.Kg4? Kg6. In both cases White will never reach his goal.

9...Kf7

9...Kh7 10.Kf4 leads to the same type of play.

10.Kh4!

Another Outflanking maneuver. White once again offers Black the Opposition.

10...Kg6

And Black once again refused to take it! After 10...Kf6 11.Kh5 Kf5 Black would clearly have the Opposition, but White would dance forward with 12.Kh6 and claim h8 for himself.

11.Kg4

Once more grabbing the Opposition.

11...Kh6

Or 11...Kf7 12.Kf5 Kg7 13.Kg5 Kh7 14.Kf6, etc.

12.Kf5 Kg7 13.Kg5 Kf7 14.Kh6 Kg8 15.Kg6 Kf8 16.Kh7 and White cannot be prevented from achieving his goal by 17.Kh8.

Please study the information on the Opposition and Outflanking carefully. Don't let the scientific names or the strange Xs in diagram 178 scare you away from learning something that is both easy to understand and highly useful! I should add that the position in diagram 178 is a fun one to show friends. They will not be able to solve it and will be amazed when you demonstrate how one King can actually be stronger than another just by understanding the basics of the Opposition and Outflanking.

Rook Endings

Ready to take another step in deepening your understanding of Rook endgame basics? Here we'll look at how one goes about winning with a Rook and two connected passed pawns vs. a lone Rook. We'll settle for this one position because, though it sounds easy, it's actually quite a pain to win!

Rook and Two Connected Pawns vs. Rook

A Rook endgame where one side is up two connected passed pawns is usually, as you might imagine, a clear win. Surprisingly, it can be quite time consuming and success is often dependent on you knowing the key ideas, and on you avoiding the many stalemate tricks that are lurking in the shadows. This endgame occurs quite a lot, and therefore the ideas involved in herding your pawns safely down the board must be mastered.

A word of warning: You'll find this to be the most complicated situation in the book thus far, so look over the information slowly, and don't get frustrated. It will take you a bit of time before you fully master it!

Diagram 181

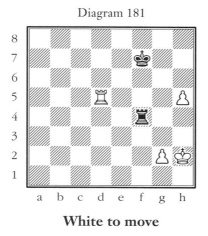

White to move

Connected rook-pawns and knight-pawns is the hardest case. So if you learn to handle this, you'll have no problem icing connected central pawns.

In the present position, white's h-pawn is ahead of the rest of its forces. Thus white's first order of business is to patiently move his King and g-pawn forward so they join the h-pawn and form one connected whole.

1.Kh3

The King steps up so it can support its pawns.

1...Kf6

There is little Black can do, so he brings his King closer to the white pawns and then waits to see how White will improve his position.

2.g3

Also good was 2.g4, but 2.g3 gives white's King access to the g4-square in some lines.

2...Rf1

Preparing to unleash some checks from the back rank. Also possible was 2... Ra4 3.g4 Kg7 4.Kh4 (4.g5, which also wins, leaves white's King cut off from its pawns. In general, you should avoid this kind of thing like the plague! 4.Kh4 is the proper way to handle these positions: always keep your King and pawns together!) 4...Kh6 5.Rd6+ Kh7 6.h6 Rb4 (or 6...Ra1 7.Kh5 Rh1+ 8.Kg5) 7.Kh5 Rb5+ 8.g5 with the same kind of play as that which occurs in the game.

Diagram 182

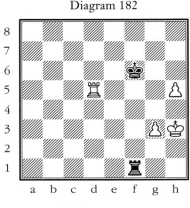

White to move

3.Kg4!

Preparing to push the black King back.

3...Rf2

More active ideas don't change anything: 3...Ra1 4.Rd6+ Kg7 5.Kg5 Ra5+ 6.Kh4 Ra4+ 7.g4, etc.

4.Rd6+

Forcing Black to relinquish control of the g5-square.

4...Ke7

Moving back to g7 is met by 5.Kg5, while 4...Ke5 5.Ra6 puts black's King on the side (instead of in front) of white's pawns.

5.Ra6

> **REMEMBER**
>
> In Rook endings it is always a good idea to put your Rook as far away from the enemy King as possible. This is called "Checking Distance."

5...Rb2 6.Kh4

Preparing to push the g-pawn. Note that White can use his pawns to shield his King from checks: 6...Rb4+ 7.g4 or 6...Rh2+ 7.Kg5.

6...Kf7 7.g4

Following our rule that the pawns must stay close together.

> **REMEMBER**
>
> Make sure that your pawns can shield your King from checks!

7...Kg7 8.h6+

As usual, White leads with his rook-pawn. 8.g5? would allow 8...Rb4+ when white's King is without a good hiding place.

An excellent alternative to 8.h6+ would be 8.Ra7+ when 8...Kh6?? 9.g5 is mate, while 8...Kf6? 9.g5+ Kf5 (9...Ke6 10.h6 is also easy) 10.Rf7+ Ke6 11.Rf6+ Ke7 12.h6 and Black can resign since his King is cut off from the battlefield on the kingside, and 12...Rh2+ is met by 13.Kg4 Rg2+ 14.Kh5 followed by Kg6. After 8.Ra7+ Black would do best to play 8...Kh8 with likely transposition into our main line analysis.

8...Kh7 9.Kh5

Hopefully you're becoming familiar with the pattern of allowing the g-pawn to guard the King against checks—in this position the pawn guards against checks along the rank in the case of 9...Rb5+ 10.g5 and along the file in the case of 9...Rh2+ 10.Kg5.

9...Rb5+ 10.g5 Rc5

Keeping the pawn pinned is the best chance. Worse is 10...Rb7? 11.g6+ Kg8 12.Ra8+ which leads to immediate defeat.

11.Ra7+ Kh8

Black sticks his King in the corner and sets up possible stalemates. One of the best examples of such a stalemate can occur after 11...Kg8 12.h7+?? Kh8 13.Kh6

Diagram 183

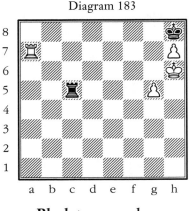

Black to move draws

13...Rc6+ 14.g6 Rxg6+! 15.Kxg6 stalemate. An important idea to be aware of!

After 11...Kg8, White should play 12.Rg7+ Kh8 (12...Kf8? 13.Kg6 Rc6+ 14.Kh7 is easy for White since black's King is now deprived of access to g8 and h8—in general, the defender needs to keep his King in front of the enemy pawns. Allowing the stronger side's King to get in front of its own pawns is a recipe for disaster!) 13.Re7 (and not 13.Kg6?? Rxg5+! 14.Kxg5 stalemate) transposing back into our main line analysis.

12.Re7!

Diagram 184

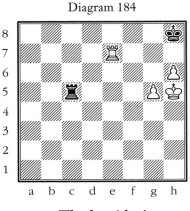

The key idea!

What are the points of this odd move?

➤ White would like to bring his King to f7 when enemy checks along the 7th rank would be blocked.

➤ Sometimes white's King will march to f6 when a black check along the 6th rank can be met by Re6.

➤ Once white's g-pawn gets to g6, a back rank mate will be threatened. To stop this, Black will have to pull his Rook to its 1st rank. White then wins by marching his King to f7 or d7 and trading Rooks by Re8+. The resulting King and two pawns vs. King endgame would then give Black every reason to resign.

Don't panic if this sounds too complicated! Look over the solution several times and the winning plans will soon become remarkably easy to execute.

12...Rc8

Another try is 12...Kg8 13.Kg6 Rc6+ 14.Kf5 Rc5+ 15.Kf6 Rc6+ 16.Re6 (this is our first clear illustration of one of the virtues of 12.Re7) 16...Rc8 17.g6 Rb8 18.Rd6 Ra8 (of course, 18...Rf8+ 19.Ke7 helps White) 19.Ke7 takes us back to the winning idea in our main line.

Oddly, there is a more accurate win on move 18, namely 18.h7+ (instead of 18.Rd6): 18...Kh8 19.Kg5 when Kh6 will follow, with a quick mate. Just be careful about pushing your pawn to h7 in this fashion! Take a look at the two diagrams below and you'll see why I'm putting up red flags.

Diagram 185

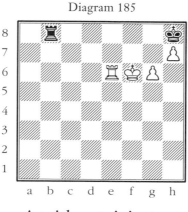

A quick mate is in store

RULE

King, Rook, knight-pawn, and rook-pawn on the same side of the board vs. King and Rook give the defender some stalemate tricks thanks to the rook-pawn's eternal "pain-in-the-ass" factor.

Diagram 186

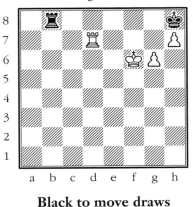

Black to move draws

In diagram 185, Black can't stop White from playing Kg5 and Kh6 when it's all over. Note that the tricky 1...Rb6, hoping for 2.Rxb6?? stalemate, fails to 2.g7+ (giving black's King some freedom so he can safely capture the Rook) 2...Kxh7 3.Rxb6.

In diagram 186, black's King has no legal moves—as in diagram 185. However, due to white's Rook being on the 7th rank instead of on the 6th (where it stopped 6th rank checks), Black can force a draw by "sacrificially throwing his Rook into the volcano": 1...Rb6+ (White to move would have won by 1.Rd6 followed by Kg5 and Kh6) 2.Kf5 (2.Kg5 Rxg6+! 3.Kxg6 stalemate) 2...Rf6+! ("Take my Rook!") 3.Kg5 Rxg6+ ("Take it! I insist!") 4.Kxg6 stalemate.

13.g6

Diagam 187

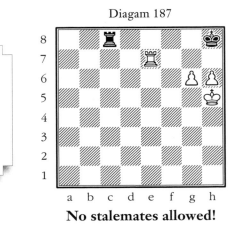

No stalemates allowed!

> **USEFUL ADVICE**
>
> In this endgame, only push the pawn to h7 if you're 100% sure you've avoided the sacrificial stalemate tricks.

Once again, White must be very certain that pushing the h-pawn to h7 doesn't create stalemate difficulties. In this case, 13.h7?? throws away the win after 13...Rc7! when moving the Rook away allows ...Kxh7 with a draw, while 14.Rxc7 is a stalemate.

13...Rc5+ 14.Kg4 Rc4+ 15.Kf5 Rc8

More checks just force white's King to where it wants to go: 15...Rc5+ 16.Kf6 Rc6+ 17.Kf7.

16.Ke6

Threatening 17.Kd7 Ra8 18.Re8+ trading Rooks (which would/should be enough to make Black immediately resign).

16...Ra8 17.Rd7

Intending Ke7 and Rd8+, exchanging Rooks. The tempting 17.Kf7 leaves black's King without a legal move (which we don't want to do!) and allows 17...Rf8+! when 18.Kxf8?? is a draw by stalemate. Fortunately, after 17...Rf8+ White could backtrack by 18.Ke6.

17...Re8+

Attacking the g-pawn by 17...Rg8 runs into the annoying 18.Rh7 mate.

18.Kf7 Rg8

Of course, 18...Rf8+ 19.Ke7! allows White to set up his Rook exchange by 20.Rd8.

19.g7+

White avoids 19.Re7 Rf8+! since 20.Ke6 would take a bit longer to win the game. However, another easy way to end things is 19.Rd5! ("Wasting" a move so that black's Rook has to give up its attack against g6. This allows white's King to then move to e7 since it no longer has to defend the pawn.) 19...Ra8 (19...Rf8+ 20.Ke7) 20.Ke7 Ra7+ 21.Rd7 Ra8 22.Rd8+, etc.

19...Kh7 20.Re7 Ra8

Or 20...Kxh6 21.Kxg8, 1-0.

21.Re8 Ra7+ 22.Kf8, 1-0.

Okay, a first look at this example might horrify you, but calm down and let's take another look at the step-by-step winning process:

➤ Advance your pawns together so your King has shelter, your pawns can defend one another, and blockades can be avoided—don't allow one pawn to madly charge down the board on its own!

➤ Make sure your King and pawns are in close contact. As in most chess situations, a team effort is needed for a successful result.

➤ Make sure that your pawns can shield your King from checks!

► Be patient! Push the enemy King back slowly, always making sure the above conditions have been met.

► Once you have forced the enemy King to the back rank, move your Rook (which should be on the 7th rank) a couple files to the side of your pawns.

Your plan now is to:

► Place both your pawns on the 6th rank (forcing black's Rook to guard against back rank mates).

► Bring your King to the 7th rank—your Rook on the 7th will prevent checks along that rank.

► Give check by moving your Rook (protected by your King on the 7th rank!) to the 8th rank, forcing an exchange. The resulting King and two pawns vs. lone King endgame should be baby stuff for you at this point.

WARNING

Only move your h-pawn to h7 if you are 100% sure you have prevented the many stalemate tricks that are so commonly found in these positions! Don't forget the need for (yes, I'm repeating myself) *patience*!

With all this in mind, go back, play through the endgame again, and it will make more sense.

All Hail the 7th Rank!

Everyone has heard that "Rooks belong on the 7th rank." However, can you explain why a Rook isn't equally delighted to be on the 6th rank or even the 8th?

The appeal of the 7th rank is twofold:

► Usually the enemy has many pawns on his 2nd rank, so placing a Rook on the 7th targets them for extermination.

► The defender's King is often on its 1st rank. A Rook on the 7th freezes the King, preventing it from becoming active and—in some instances—setting up possible back rank mating threats.

Diagram 188

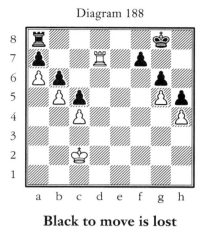

Black to move is lost

This position shows us the domination that a simple Rook jump to the 7th bestows. Black's Rook is doomed to stay on a8 so it can defend a7, while black's King can't leave the safety of e8, f8, g7, or g8 for fear of hanging f7. Though Black is a pawn ahead, he's completely lost.

1...Kf8

Naturally, 1...f5 would be met by 2.gxf6 e.p.

2.Rb7 Ke8 3.Kc3!

White avoids 3.Kd3 Rd8+ 4.Ke4 Rd7 5.Ke5 Ke7. The text (3.Kc3) places Black in zugzwang—any move he makes worsens his position.

3...Kf8 4.Kd3 Rd8+

Seeing that 4...Ke8 5.Ke4 gives him no chance at all (unless White falls for 5...Kf8 6.Ke5 Re8+ 7.Kf6?? Re6 mate!), Black makes a bid for counterplay.

5.Ke4 Re8+

More challenging is 5...Rd4+, but White still wins: 6.Ke5 Rxc4 7.Rxa7 Rxh4 (7...Rb4 8.Rb7 Rxb5 9.a7 Ra5 10.Rb8+ Kg7 11.a8=Q) 8.Rd7! (Far stronger than 8.Rb7 Ra4 followed by 9...h4) 8...Ra4 9.a7 Kg7 10.Kd5

Diagram 189

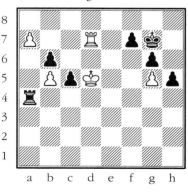

Black loses

Though two pawns down, two things guarantee white's victory: 1) His King is going to play a major part in the action, compared to black's which is sitting on the sidelines (it's nice to be a King ahead!); 2) White's passed pawns are more advanced than black's. 10...h4 11.Kc6 h3 12.Kxb6 h2 13.Rd1, 1-0.

6.Kd5 Re7 7.Kd6 Re6+

Also unattractive are both 7...Rxb7 8.axb7, and 7...Re4 8.Rxa7 Rxc4 9.Rc7.

8.Kc7 Re7+ 9.Kb8, 1-0.

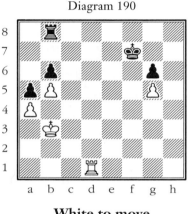

Diagram 190

White to move

1.Rd6!

Instead, 1.Rd7+? would be a mistake since it neither attacks the enemy pawns nor traps the enemy King. After 1...Ke6, black's King is free to roam.

1.Rd6, on the other hand, stops the defending King from ever moving past its 3rd rank, while also eyeing both b6 and g6. In other words, in our diagrammed position a Rook on the 6th rank has all the advantages that a Rook on the 7th usually possesses.

1...Re8

Desperation, but passive defense is hopeless: 1...Rb7 2.Kc4 Rb8 3.Kd5 with Kc6 to follow.

Another stab at active counterplay is 1...Ke7 (Black is trying to swing his King over to the queenside where it will defend b6. Though he will sacrifice his g-pawn, he hopes to get his Rook active and create threats against white's pawn on a4.), but White easily prevails after 2.Rxg6 Kd7 3.Kc4 (don't forget to use your King!) 3...Rf8 (or 3...Kc7 4.Rc6+ Kb7 5.g6 when Black can resign) 4.Rf6! (Simplest. black's Rook is chased to a square that allows the white King to successfully penetrate. Also possible is 4.Rxb6, but why allow the complications of 4...Rf4+ and 5...Rxa4 when the text leaves Black without counterplay or hope?)

Diagram 191

No counterplay!

> **USEFUL ADVICE**
>
> In Rook endgames, it's always a good idea to deprive your opponent of counterplay by keeping his Rook and/or King caged and inactive whenever possible.

4...Rh8 (4...Re8 5.Kd5 or 4...Rg8 5.g6 are no better, while 4...Rxf6 5.gxf6 Ke6 6.f7 Kxf7 7.Kd5 followed by Kc6 and Kxb6 is resignable) 5.Kd5 Rh4 6.Rxb6 Rxa4 7.Rb7+ Kc8 8.Rf7 Rg4 9.Kc6! (threatening a "tiny" back rank mate) 9...Kd8 10.b6 Rxg5 11.Rd7+ Ke8 (11...Kc8 12.b7+ Kb8 13.Rd8+ leads to a quick mate) 12.b7 Rg6+ 13.Rd6, 1-0.

2.Rf6+!

This move forces Black to step to g7, thus pushing it farther away from the war zone on the queenside.

2...Kg7 3.Rxb6 Re3+ 4.Kc4 Re4+ 5.Kc5 Rxa4 6.Rb7+ Kf8 7.b6 Rg4 8.Rc7 Rxg5+ 9.Kc6 Rg1 10.b7 Rb1 11.Rc8+ Kf7 12.b8=Q Rxb8 13.Rxb8 Kf6 14.Kd5

White will win the a-pawn as his leisure, but first he lets his King personally deal with the g-pawn.

14...Kf5

Or 14...a4 15.Ke4 a3 16.Ra8.

15.Rf8+ Kg4 16.Ke4 g5 17.Ra8 Kg3 18.Rxa5 g4 19.Rg5 Kh3 20.Kf4 winning black's final pawn.

Minor Piece Endgames

We took our first tentative steps into the world of minor piece endgames in Part Four. Here I'll continue to gently introduce you to basic endgame positions that involve Bishops and/or Knights—we'll ingest a bit more about Bishops of opposite colors, we'll tackle very basic two pawns vs. one on the same side of the board, and we'll even address two Bishops vs. lone King, which is far easier than you might imagine.

Two Bishops vs. Lone King

Some of you might be wondering when I'm going to teach you Bishop and Knight vs. lone King. The shocking (almost heretical!) answer is, "Never!" My reasoning is very simple: I personally have had this position once in my whole career. That's right, just once! My good friend (and well known chess author) IM John Watson has never had it at all! On top of that, Bishop and Knight vs. King is not at all easy to learn, and mastering it would take a significant chunk of time. Should the chess hopeful really spend many of the precious hours he's put aside for chess study learning an endgame that he'll achieve (at most) only once or twice in his lifetime?

In general, every position I give in this book will happen fairly often, or understanding it will allow you to solve other positions with similar themes. I don't feel Bishop and Knight vs. King falls into this category, but then, two Bishops vs. King is also a rare bird in tournament play. So why should I insist you learn two Bishops vs. lone King? There are three reasons for its inclusion:

➤ I find the need to use all three of your pieces in a balanced team effort to be quite instructive.

➤ Seeing how powerful two Bishops are when working together can be enlightening.

➤ It's very easy to learn and only involves a small expenditure of time to fully understand.

188

Diagram 192

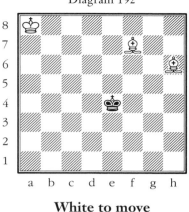

White to move

The keys to this endgame:

▶ Use the Bishops to cut off two "connected" diagonals at the same time. This traps the defending King in one sector of the board.

▶ The Bishops will be able to take away other important squares while also making whole diagonals impassable.

▶ You will need your own King to win, so bring it up so it can directly challenge its counterpart.

▶ Bit by bit, shrink the "diagonal Box," in much the same way we shrink the Box in Rook vs. King or Queen vs. King.

▶ You will need to chase the defending King to a corner. Once there, you'll easily deliver mate.

1.Bg6+ Ke5 2.Kb7

The King heads for the embattled area. Also note that white's Bishops control the b1-h7 and c1-h6 diagonals. Black's King can't pass through this "fence"—a fence White intends to shrink when the time is right.

Diagram 193

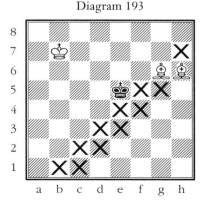

A thick, impenetrable fence

2...Kf6 3.Bh7

Watch out! Don't fall asleep and let the desperate enemy King snap off one of your Bishops! Now the Bishops can't be approached.

3...Ke5 4.Kc6 Kd4 5.Bf4

Depriving black's King of the e5-square.

5...Kc4

Even easier for White is 5...Kc3 6.Kc5.

6.Be5

The diagonal Box has shrunk. Now White controls a1-h8 and b1-h7.

6...Kb4 7.Bg8

Diagram 194

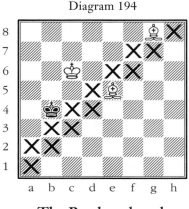

The Box has shrunk

Once again shrinking the Box by laying claim to the a2-g8 diagonal.

7...Ka3 8.Kc5 Ka4 9.Bb2

The final phase: White takes away the a3-square and herds black's King to-wards the a8-corner.

9...Ka5 10.Bb3

There goes the a4-square!

10...Ka6 11.Kc6 Ka7

Or 11...Ka5 12.Bc3+ Ka6 13.Bc4+ Ka7 14.Kc7 Ka8 15.Bd2 (Wasting a tempo so that a check can be given when the black King goes to a7) 15...Ka7 16.Be3+ Ka8 17.Bd5 mate.

12.Be5

It's as if the Bishop is saying, "Sorry, but I can't allow you to run out of the corner via the b8-square."

12...Ka6

12...Ka8 13.Kc7 Ka7 14.Bc4 Ka8 15.Bf4 Ka7 16.Be3+ Ka8 17.Bd5 mate.

13.Bc7

Now both a5 and b8 are off limits.

13...Ka7 14.Bc4

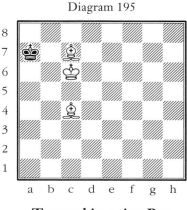

Diagram 195

Trapped in a tiny Box

And now only a7 and a8 are available to Black.

14...Ka8 15.Be5

Having done its job, the dark-squared Bishop now puts some Checking Distance between it and black's King. As always, watch out for stalemates! 15.Kb6 stalemate would be a disaster.

15...Ka7 16.Kc7

White's King frees the dark-squared Bishop of b8 guard duty.

16...Ka8 17.Bf4

Wasting a move and waiting for ...Ka7, when a check-cascade and mate will follow.

If the player of the Black pieces is your spouse and you fear later retribution, you may wish to play 17.Bd4?? stalemate, thus drawing the game and keeping marital harmony intact.

> **REMEMBER**
>
> Watch out for stalemates!

17...Ka7 18.Be3+ Ka8 19.Bd5 mate.

Bishops of Opposite Colors (Two Pawns Down and Loving it!)

In Part Four, we saw that a one-pawn advantage is often not enough to guarantee victory. At times, a two-pawn advantage (with no other pawns on the board) isn't enough when there is only one file between them. The reason? White's King and Bishop can team up to blockade both pawns.

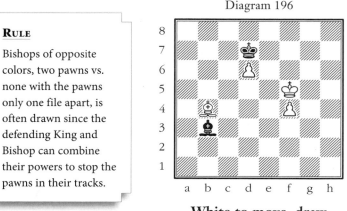

Diagram 196

RULE

Bishops of opposite colors, two pawns vs. none with the pawns only one file apart, is often drawn since the defending King and Bishop can combine their powers to stop the pawns in their tracks.

White to move, draw

With the pawn on d6 firmly blocked, the result hinges on whether or not White can force Black to give up his Bishop for white's f-pawn.

1.Kg6

Taking control over f7 and getting out of the way of the f-pawn. Is Black doomed?

1...Ba2

He seems unconcerned.

2.f5 Bb3 3.f6 Ke8

Now we can see why one file between the pawns isn't enough: black's King can eye both key squares on d7 and f7 and thus create a blockade. Yes, White can win the Bishop with 4.d7+ Kxd7 5.f7 Bxf7+ but, since no other pawns exist, that would be an immediate draw.

Since Black can now do the old Bishop shuffle (...Bb3-a2-b3-a2, etc.), White marches his King to the other side in one last effort.

4.Kf5 Ba2 5.Ke5 Bb3 6.Kd4 Ba2

And not 6...Kf7?? 7.d7 when White makes a new Queen.

7.Kc5 Kd7 and, since White isn't getting anywhere, ½-½.

Of course, if each side had one extra pawn, the result would be different:

Diagram 197

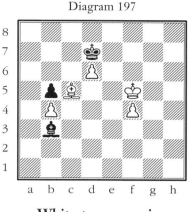

White to move wins

White now plays as he did in the previous example, but the addition of those b-pawns is enough to bring him victory.

1.Kg6 Ba2 2.f5 Bb3 3.f6 Ke8

The same moves that we saw from diagram 196, but the addition of one set of pawns proves decisive for White.

4.d7+ Kxd7 5.f7 Bxf7+ 6.Kxf7 Kc6 7.Ke6 Kc7 8.Kd5 Kb7 9.Kd6 Ka6 10.Bd4

Not falling for the hasty 10.Kc6?? stalemate!

10...Kb7 11.Kc5 Ka6 12.Be5

Again, 12.Kc6?? is a draw by stalemate.

12...Kb7 13.Kxb5, 1-0.

As we've seen, a two-pawn advantage with the pawns only being one file apart isn't always decisive. However, when the pawns are two or more files from each other the stronger side's winning chances go way up.

There are many cases of White winning when the pawns are two files apart, but the defender does have drawing chances if his Bishop can freeze both pawns at the same time.

In diagram 198 it's clear that neither pawn is going anywhere without help from its King. Since 1.Kd4 (threatening 2.e4) is stymied by 1...Kf5! 2.Kc5 Ke6 when the Bishop is still stopping both pawns in their tracks, White comes up with the idea of bringing his King to a6 in an effort to help escort the b-pawn to the Promised Land.

Diagram 198

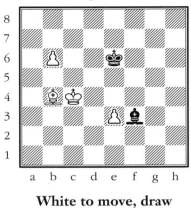

White to move, draw

1.Kb5 Kd7! 2.Ka6

On 2.Kc5 Black would play 2...Ke6! so as to meet Kd4 with ...Kf5.

2...Kc8

Now Black has stopped both pawns again, and any Bishop moves by White will be met with the same back and forth wandering (along the h1-a8 diagonal) by Black.

3.Kb5 Kd7 4.Kc5 Ke6! 5.Bc3 Bg2

The Bishop moves are tossed in merely to show that both players can waste infinite amounts of time without changing the nature of the position.

6.Kd4

Trying to play e3-e4.

6...Kf5!, ½-½.

What allowed Black to draw this position? Here are the key defensive elements:

> Both pawns can only advance to light-colored squares, thus, white's Bishop wasn't able to take part in the fight to move forward.

> Black's Bishop covered the squares in front of both pawns at the same time.

> Black's King was able to shadow white's King whenever it moved to the aid of either pawn. The blockading combination of black King and Bishop is enough to stop any progress by White.

Diagram 199

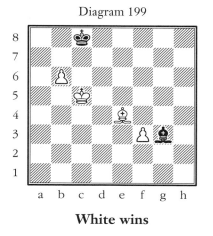

White wins

1.Bd5

White isn't in any hurry, so he frees the e4-square for his King since he knows that it eventually has to march over to the kingside and escort the f-pawn down the board.

1...Kb8 2.Kc4

And not 2.Kd4?? Bf2+ followed by 3...Bxb6.

2...Bf2 3.b7 Bg3 4.Kd4 Bd6 5.Ke4 Kc7

Doing nothing allows White to ultimately win black's Bishop for the f-pawn. Thus, black's King will rush to the kingside and try and stave off the inevitable.

6.Kf5 Kd8 7.f4

Playing 7.Kf6 or 7.Kg6 makes it impossible to safely push the f-pawn to f4.

7...Ke7 8.Kg5 Bc7 9.f5 Be5 10.Kg6

Diagram 200

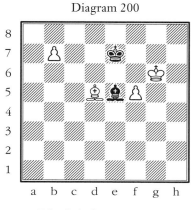

Black is in zugzwang

If Black could retain this defensive position, he would draw. Unfortunately, any Bishop move would give up control over b8 or f6, while a King move allows the f-pawn to plow through f6.

10...Bb8

Of course, 10...Kd6 allows 11.b8=Q+.

11.f6+ Kf8

No better is 11...Kd6 12.f7 Ke7 13.Kg7 and the f-pawn promotes.

12.f7 Be5

Also easy for White is 12...Bd6 13.Kf6 followed by Ke6. Note that 12...Ke7 13.Kg7 wins immediately.

13.Kf5 Bb8 14.Ke6 Bg3 15.Kd7 Bf4 16.Kc8 followed by b8=Q, winning a piece and the game.

The only time Black can draw split pawns that are three or more files apart is when one of them is a rook-pawn of the wrong color.

Diagram 201

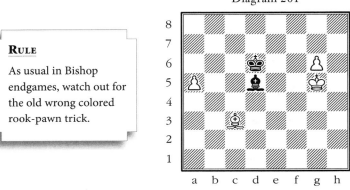

> **RULE**
>
> As usual in Bishop endgames, watch out for the old wrong colored rook-pawn trick.

Black draws

Black draws easily by rushing over to b7 and allowing White to win a piece for his g-pawn.

1.Kh6 Kc6 2.Kh7 Kb7 3.g7 Ka8 4.g8=Q+ Bxg8+ 5.Kxg8 and we have the classic Bishop and rook-pawn of the wrong color draw.

In a nutshell, when one side is two pawns up (vs. lone King and Bishop) in a Bishop of opposite color endgame, here are some rules to chew on:

- ► Positions where the pawns are separated by one file are often drawn since the defending Bishop and King are close enough to work together in creating a blockade against both pawns.

- ► Positions where the pawns are separated by two files offer some drawing chances, particularly if the defending Bishop eyes the advance squares of both pawns at the same time.

- ► Positions where the pawns are separated by three or more files offer few defensive chances. However, a draw is likely if one of the pawns is a rook-pawn of the wrong color.

Summing Up

King and Pawn Endgames

➤ King and two connected pawns vs. lone King always wins.

➤ King and two split pawns vs. lone King:

- Pawns that are one file apart on any rank can usually defend themselves until the King arrives to shuttle one of them down the board.

- Pawns that are several files apart (on any rank) are too much for the defending King to handle.

- The defender has his best survival chances if the pawns are two files apart. However, if those pawns are on the 5th rank or farther then the game is resignable.

➤ Triangulation is the name of a very small, often uncomplicated maneuver designed to give your opponent the move and, as a result, you the Opposition.

➤ Outflanking is a maneuver where the stronger side's King moves to the side, placing a file between the Kings (sometimes even giving the opponent the Opposition while doing so!). This allows the Outflanking King to march forward towards the target, without allowing the enemy monarch to step in front of it and take Direct Opposition.

Rook Endgames

➤ Rook and two connected passed pawns (knight-pawn and rook-pawn, which is the hardest case) vs. lone Rook. Here is the step-by-step winning process:

- Advance your pawns together so your King has shelter, your pawns can defend one another, and blockades can be avoided—don't allow one pawn to madly charge down the board on its own!

- Make sure your King and pawns are in close contact. As in most chess situations, a team effort is needed for a successful result.

- Make sure that your pawns can shield your King from checks!

- Be patient! Push the enemy King back slowly, always making sure the above conditions have been met.

- Once you have forced the enemy King to the back rank, move your Rook (which should be on the 7th rank) a couple files to the side of your pawns.

- Place both your pawns on the 6th rank (forcing your opponent's Rook to guard against back rank mates).

- Bring your King to the 7th rank—your Rook on the 7th will prevent checks along that rank.

- Give check by moving your Rook (protected by your King on the 7th rank!) to the 8th rank, forcing an exchange. The resulting King and two pawns vs. lone King endgame should be baby stuff for you at this point.

▸ Rooks belong on the 7th rank, but only if the Rook inconveniences the enemy King (usually by trapping it on the back rank) and/or attacks one or more enemy pawns.

Minor Piece Endgames

▸ Two Bishops vs. Lone King. The keys to this endgame are:

- Use the Bishops to cut off two "connected" diagonals at the same time. This traps the defending King in one sector of the board.

- The Bishops will be able to take away other important squares while also making whole diagonals impassable.

- You will need to use your King to win, so bring it up so it can directly challenge its counterpart.

- Bit by bit, shrink the "diagonal Box", in much the same way we shrink the Box in Rook vs. King or Queen vs. King.

- You will need to chase the defending King to a corner. Once there, you'll easily deliver mate.

▸ Bishop and two split pawns vs. Bishop of the opposite color:

- Positions where the pawns are separated by one file are often drawn since the defending Bishop and King are close enough to work together in creating a blockade against both pawns.

- Positions where the pawns are separated by two files offer some drawing chances, particularly if the defending Bishop eyes the advance squares of both pawns at the same time.

- Positions where the pawns are separated by three or more files offer few defensive chances. However, a draw is likely if one of the pawns is a rook-pawn of the wrong color.

Tests and Solutions

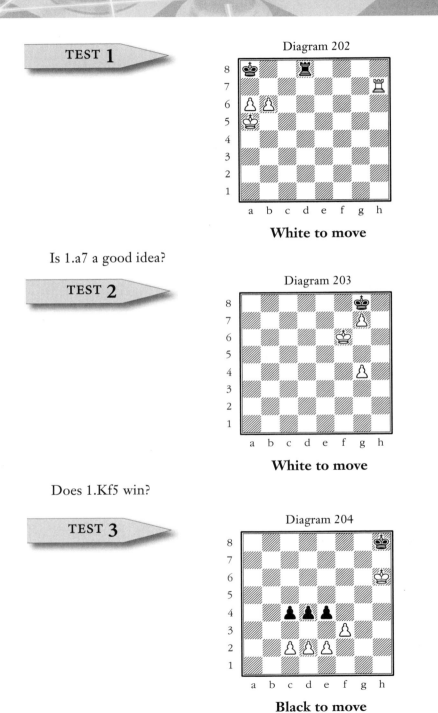

TEST **1**

Diagram 202

White to move

Is 1.a7 a good idea?

TEST **2**

Diagram 203

White to move

Does 1.Kf5 win?

TEST **3**

Diagram 204

Black to move

Is Black doomed?

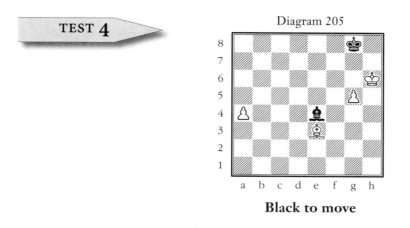

TEST 4

Diagram 205

Black to move

Can Black draw?

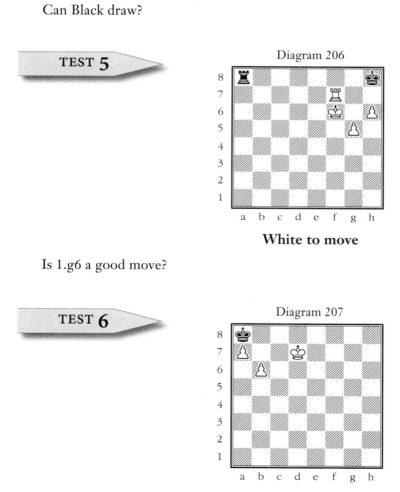

TEST 5

Diagram 206

White to move

Is 1.g6 a good move?

TEST 6

Diagram 207

White to move

Look at 1.Kc8, 1.Kc7, 1.Kc6, and 1.b7+. Which one wins for White?

TEST **7**

Diagram 208

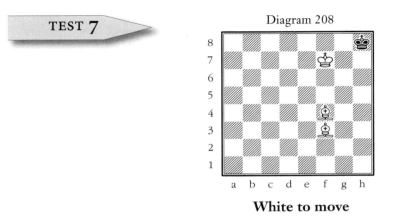

White to move

Is 1.Be4 a good move?

TEST **8**

Diagram 209

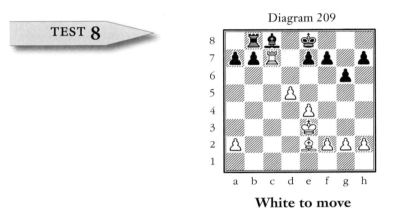

White to move

White has two strong moves at his disposal that both make use of a similar theme. If you see the position's theme, you'll find the moves.

TEST **9**

Diagram 210

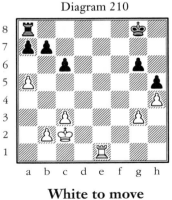

White to move

Does White have winning chances?

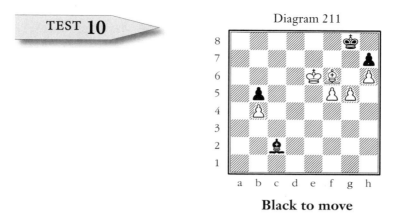

TEST **10**

Diagram 211

Black to move

White is two pawns up. Can Black save himself?

* * * * *

SOLUTION **1**

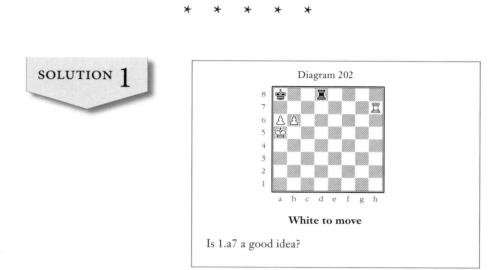

Diagram 202

White to move

Is 1.a7 a good idea?

No! By taking away all of the black King's legal moves, you've allowed Black to force a draw by playing directly for a stalemate.

1.a7?? Rd5+ 2.Ka4

2.Ka6 Ra5+! 3.Kxa5 stalemate.

2...Ra5+!

"Take my Rook!"

3.Kb4 Rb5+

"Take it!"

4.Kc4 Rb4+

Also good is 4...Rxb6. 4...Rb4+, trying to make white's King run to the other side of the board before taking on b6, is more melodramatic!

5.Kd3 Rb3+ 6.Ke4 Rb4+

Again, …Rxb6 is still an instant draw.

7.Kd5 Rb5+ 8.Kc6 Rxb6+! 9.Kxb6 stalemate.

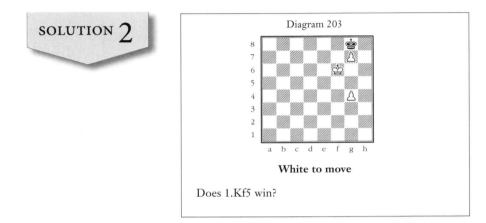

SOLUTION 2

Diagram 203

White to move

Does 1.Kf5 win?

It's clear that 1.Kg6?? creates a draw by stalemate, and that 1.Kg5?? Kxg7 also draws since Black would have the Opposition. One obvious way to win from our initial position is 1.g5 Kh7 2.g8=Q+! (avoiding 2.Kf7?? stalemate, and 2.g6+?? Kg8 with a draw) 2…Kxg8 3.Kg6 Kh8 4.Kf7 Kh7 5.g6+ and the pawn turns into a Queen.

The question, though, was whether White could win by the odd looking 1.Kf5. The answer is yes:

1…Kf7!

A good try. The more mundane 1…Kxg7 2.Kg5 takes the Opposition and is an easy win.

2.g8=Q+!

Not falling for 2.Kg5?? Kxg7 when Black has the Opposition and draws, while 2.g5?? Kxg7 3.g6 Kg8 is a basic draw.

2…Kxg8 3.Kg6! and the Opposition will prove decisive (3…Kh8 4.Kh6 Kg8 5.g5 Kh8 6.g6 Kg8 7.g7, 1-0).

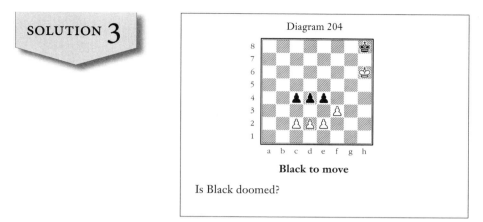

SOLUTION 3

Diagram 204

Black to move

Is Black doomed?

Black wins by using a typical "tactical bomb" trick: **1...d3!! 2.cxd3 e3!! 3.dxe3 c3** and black's last remaining pawn promotes.

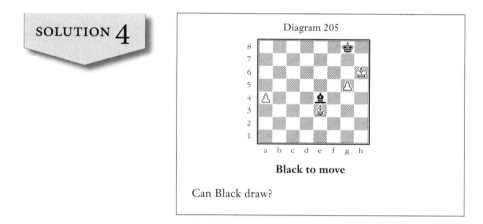

SOLUTION 4

Diagram 205

Black to move

Can Black draw?

The defender usually loses when the pawns are this far apart (black's two pieces can't work together against both enemy pawns, and this ensures that his Bishop will eventually be lost.), but in this case it's a draw because the rook-pawn is of the wrong color.

1...Kf7

Heading for the queenside. Black knows he will ultimately lose his Bishop, but this won't matter if he can get his King to b7.

2.a5 Ke7 3.g6

No better is 3.a6 Kd7 4.a7 Kc7 5.g6 Kb7 6.g7 Bd5, 1/2-1/2.

3...Kd7 4.g7 Bd5 5.a6 Kc7

And not 5...Kc8?? 6.Bf4! and White wins since black's King won't get to b7 or a8.

6.Kh7 Kb8 7.g8=Q+ Bxg8+ 8.Kxg8 Ka8, $^{1}/_{2}$-$^{1}/_{2}$.

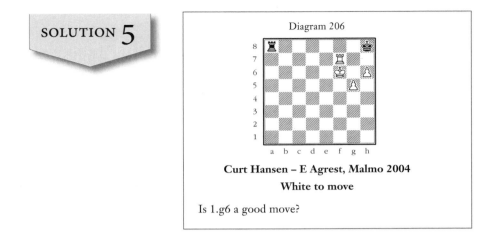

SOLUTION 5

Diagram 206

Curt Hansen – E Agrest, Malmo 2004

White to move

Is 1.g6 a good move?

Yes, 1.g6 is excellent since it creates back rank mate possibilities if black's Rook moves off its 1st rank. All White has to do is avoid stalemate tricks and victory will be his:

1.g6 Kg8

No better is 1...Ra6+ 2.Kg5 (threatening 3.Rf8 mate) 2...Ra5+ 3.Rf5 Ra8 4.Rd5 and White wins since he'll follow by moving the King to e7 and exchanging Rooks by Rd8+.

2.Rg7+ Kh8 3.Rd7

An important move, since leaving the Rook on g7 stalemates the black King—something you don't want to do in this endgame!

After 3.Rd7, White threatens to trade Rooks by Ke7 followed by Rd8+.

3...Re8

Momentarily stopping Ke7.

4.Kf7 Rg8

Again stopping Ke7.

5.Rd6

Defending g6 and finally threatening to end things with 6.Ke7 and 7.Rd8.

5...Rf8+

A last bit of desperation. Of course, 6.Kxf8?? would draw by stalemate.

6.Ke7, 1-0.

SOLUTION 6

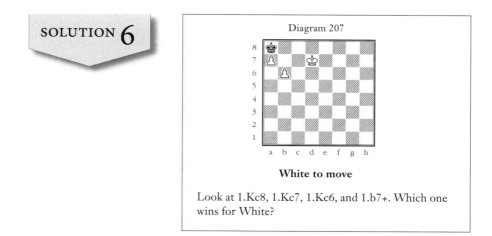

Diagram 207

White to move

Look at 1.Kc8, 1.Kc7, 1.Kc6, and 1.b7+. Which one wins for White?

All four of these moves are blunders that throw away the win. It's clear that 1.Kc8, 1.Kc7, and 1.Kc6 all lead to stalemate and an immediate draw. 1.b7+ is tricky, but also leads to a draw after 1...Kxb7! (and not 1...Kxa7?? 2.Kc7 when White promotes his b-pawn).

The correct way to ice this position is

1.Kd6 Kb7 2.a8=Q+!

Giving up this pawn allows white's King to move to c6—taking the Opposition!—without a stalemate occurring.

2...Kxa8 3.Kc6!

Deftly avoiding 3.Kc7?? stalemate.

3...Kb8 4.b7 Ka7 5.Kc7 Ka6 6.b8=Q Ka5 7.Qb3!

Fastest. This forces Black to step towards white's King.

7...Ka6 8.Qb6 mate.

SOLUTION 7

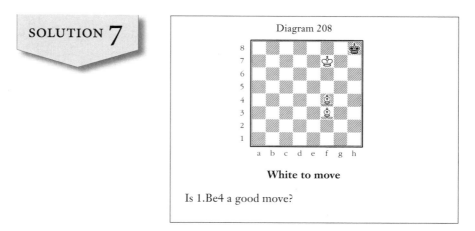

Diagram 208

White to move

Is 1.Be4 a good move?

It's a great move if you want a draw (since it creates an immediate stalemate), but if victory tastes sweeter, then waste a move and only play your Bishop to e4 when it's a check:

1.Be3

Keeping this Bishop on the c1-h6 diagonal stops the black King from running out of the corner since h6 is now untouchable. Also, don't chase black's King out of the corner by 1.Be5+ Kh7 2.Be4+ Kh6, and don't stalemate by 1.Be5+ Kh7 2.Bg7??, $\frac{1}{2}$-$\frac{1}{2}$.

1...Kh7 2.Be4+ Kh8 3.Bd4 mate.

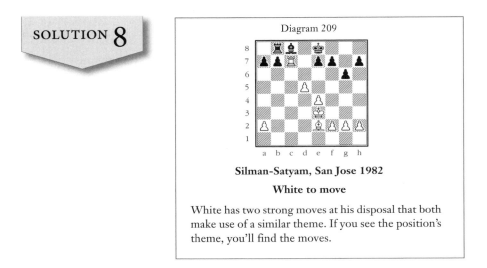

Diagram 209

Silman-Satyam, San Jose 1982

White to move

White has two strong moves at his disposal that both make use of a similar theme. If you see the position's theme, you'll find the moves.

The theme is to give white's Rook control of the absolute 7th rank and, as a result, leave black's pieces passive and helpless (in other words, no counterplay for Black!). Since Black threatens to chase the Rook away with ...Kd8, White needs to give his Rook some breathing room on the 7th.

1.d6!

Creating absolute 7th rank. The other way of doing this is 1.Bb5!+ Kd8 (or 1...Kf8 2.Bc4 with the threat of d6) 2.d6!.

Very good for White, but not as strong, is 1.e5 Kd8 2.d6 Bd7.

1...exd6

1...Bd7 2.dxe7 is bad for Black since 2...Kxe7 is met by 3.Bb5 Rd8 4.Rxb7, while 2...a6 3.Bc4 Kxe7 4.Bxf7 Kd6 5.Rc2 is an easy win for White.

2.Bb5+ Kf8 3.Bc4 Be6 4.Bxe6 fxe6 5.Rxh7

White's Rook now rules the 7th. Black won't be able to avoid material losses.

5...Kg8

Preventing Rh8+, when White picks up black's Rook.

6.Re7 e5 7.Re6 Kf7 8.Rxd6 Rc8 9.Rd7+ Kf6 10.Rxb7

With two healthy extra pawns, White is assured of victory. All he has to do is patiently improve his position.

10…Rc3+ 11.Kd2 Ra3 12.Rb2 Kg5 13.Ke2 Kf4 14.f3 Kg5 15.g3 Ra5 16.Kf2 Kf6 17.g4 Rc5 18.Rd2 Ra5 19.Kg3 Ra3 20.h4 a5 21.Rd7 Ke6 22.Rg7 Kf6 23.Ra7 g5 24.hxg5+ Kxg5 25.Rf7 Kg6 26.Rf5 Rxa2 27.Rxe5 Ra1 28.Kf4 a4 29.Ra5 a3 30.Ra6+ Kf7 31.Kf5 a2 32.Ra7+ Kf8 33.f4, 1-0.

SOLUTION **9**

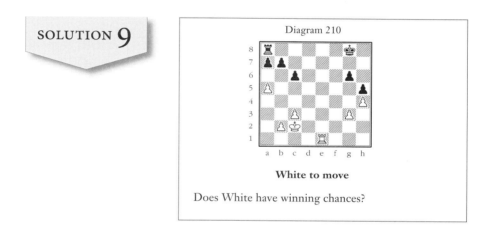

Diagram 210

White to move

Does White have winning chances?

White has a winning position after …

1.Re7 Rb8

1…b6 2.a6 fixes the target on a7 and only makes things worse for Black.

2.Kd3 a6

This prevents White from answering …b7-b6 with a5-a6.

3.Rc7! Kf8

Or 3…b6 4.Rxc6 bxa5 5.Rxg6+ Kf7 6.Rg5 with an easy win.

4.b4

White takes his time and continues to fix the enemy pawns, while also placing his own pawns on protected squares.

4…Ke8 5.Kc4

Stopping ideas based on …Rd8+ followed by …Rd7.

5…Kd8 6.Rg7, 1-0. Black wasn't able to do more than whimper!

SOLUTION 10

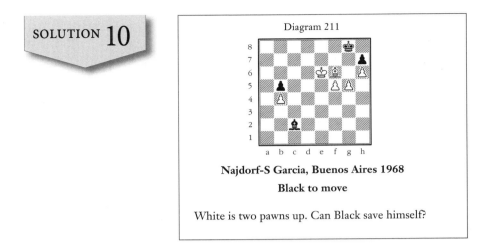

Diagram 211

Najdorf-S Garcia, Buenos Aires 1968

Black to move

White is two pawns up. Can Black save himself?

The game would be drawn if the b-pawns didn't exist. But with them on the board, White will easily score the full point. He has two ways of doing this:

Plan 1: Exchange his g-pawn for black's h-pawn. Then force the win of black's Bishop for white's two kingside pawns. Once this is done, white's King will march over to the queenside and eat the b5-pawn, ending the game.

Plan 2: Exchange his f- and g-pawns for black's b-pawn and h-pawn. White's two passed pawns would then be too far from each other for Black to deal with.

1...Bb3+

Even easier for White is 1...Kf8 2.g6 Kg8 (2...hxg6 3.h7 promotes the h-pawn) 3.gxh7+ Kxh7 4.Bg5 Kg8 5.f6 Bb3+ (5...Kf8 6.h7 Bxh7 7.Bh6+ Ke8 8.f7+ promotes the f-pawn) 6.Ke7 Bc4 7.h7+ Kxh7 8.f7 Bxf7 9.Kxf7, 1-0. This is a good illustration of white's first plan.

2.Kd6 Bc2 3.Kc5

Najdorf decides to take his time and torture his opponent. He's hoping for 3...Bxf5 4.Kxb5 when Black would draw if he could get his King to b7, but that's clearly not possible here: 4...Kf7 5.Kc6 Be4+ 6.Kb6 Ke8 (Keeping the King on the kingside is also hopeless: 6...Kg8 7.b5 Kf7 8.Kc7 Kg8 9.b6 Kf7 10.b7 Bxb7 11.Kxb7 Kg8 12.Kc7 Kf7 13.Kd6 Kg8 14.Ke6 Kf8 5.Kf5 Kf7 16.g6+ hxg6+ 17.Kg5 Kg8 18.Kxg6 and White promotes his pawn because it queens on the same color as his Bishop) 7.b5 Kd7 (7...Bd3 8.Kc6 Be4+ 9.Kc7) 8.Ka7 Kc7 9.b6+ Kc8 10.g6! when the poor Bishop can't defend b7 and g6 at once. Since 10...hxg6 is killed by 11.h7, Black would have to resign.

Nevertheless, instead of 3.Kc5, it was faster to go for victory by plan one: 3.Ke5 Bd3 4.Be7 Bc2 (4...Kf7 5.g6+ hxg6 7.h7 Kg7 7.f6+ Kxh7 8.f7, etc.)

5.Bd6 Bd3 6.Kf6 Be4 7.g6 Bc2 8.gxh7+ Kxh7 9.Bf4 Bd3 10.Ke6 Bc4+ 11.Ke7 Kg8 12.f6 Bb3 13.h7+ Kxh7 14.f7 when White wins black's Bishop and the game.

3...Bd3 4.Kb6 Kf7 5.g6+ Kg8

Not falling for 5...hxg6 6.h7.

6.Bg7 Bc4 7.Be5 Bd3 8.Bf4

Still hoping for 8...Bxf5 when 9.gxh7+ Kxh7 10.Kxb5 is easy for White. However, Black refuses to bite.

8...Bf1 9.Kc6 Bd3 10.Kc5 Bf1

Black's King can't move: 10...Kh8 fails to 11.f6! Bxg6 12.Kxb5, while 10...Kf8 11.gxh7 makes a new Queen.

11.Kd4

Finally, after torturing both his opponent and us, Najdorf goes back to the kingside and Plan 1.

11...Bc4 12.Ke5 Bd3 13.gxh7+ Kxh7 14.Ke6 Kg8 15.f6 Bg6 16.Ke7, 1-0.

Final Thoughts

Triangulation? Outflanking? Have I gone berserk? For those that felt panic when they eyed the contents of Part Five, I would guess that you've now calmed down a bit—the material might have been a bit ponderous to go over, but far from difficult to learn.

So what's your reward for slogging through topics like Rook and two connected passers vs. lone Rook? How about an extremely tight understanding of basic endgames that will give you a lifetime of confidence every time the final phase of the game is reached.

Make no mistake about it: you *can* make do (even with an "A" or Expert rating) with the material through Part Five (plus the bits and pieces you pick up from experience) for the rest of your life. Your endgame foundation is *that* good!

So, if you feel that you've now put more than enough effort into the endgame, you can put this book aside without guilt or misgivings. You worked hard and have come a long way, and that's very impressive! However, for these "I never want to see another endgame book for the rest of my life" people, may I suggest that you spend a bit of time with the three chapters in Endgames for Pure Pleasure (Part Nine). I think that material will send you off in style, and with a smile on your face.

For those that have serious aspirations towards Class "A" or even Expert, and who want to know more about the endgame than others in those classes, things will get a bit difficult in Parts Six and Seven. Are you going to tough it out? If so, I'll see you there.

Part Six

Endgames for Class "A" (1800–1999)

Contents

Y ou've come a long way and *finally* enjoy an elite rating. As you've moved up the ladder, you might have noticed that more and more games reach endings, and often they prove to be rather complex. Now, more than ever, you'll need to have mastered all the endgame material in past sections and assimilate the new material here.

Believe it or not, if you completely master everything through Part Six, you will have an understanding of endgame basics that far surpasses 75% of those in the Expert (2000-2199) category. And it's that lack of general endgame knowledge among tournament players who pride themselves on being "good" that will give you a huge advantage over them during the course of your chess career.

Of course, absorbing this new information won't be easy. Everything here is far more difficult than anything we've looked at thus far. But I wouldn't present it if I didn't think it was very learnable and well within the grasp of an "A" class player. So, since you're here and since you seem determined to go to that next level, fasten your seatbelt and let's begin!

King and Pawn Endgames

You should already be well versed in King and pawn basics, but now it's time to learn a new idea or two that will prepare you for the more expansive, and complicated, examples in Part Seven.

Strange Races

Many King and pawn endgames are decided by simple races that center on whose pawn promotes first. When one side queens and the other can't, it's usually game over. And, when both sides promote, one after the other, it's usually a draw. Much of the beauty of chess, though, lies in the exceptions. And there are several "race exceptions" that are must knows.

Diagram 212

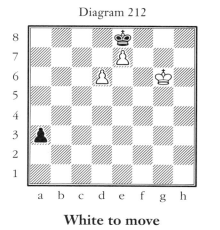

White to move

> **USEFUL ADVICE**
>
> Pawn mates are something you must be familiar with. They form the basis of many (sometimes surprising) victories in more complex pawn endgames.

Black's pawn has a clear, and quick, path to a1, while black's King is trying to hold off the White hoards on d6 and e7. Nevertheless, White wins because mate trumps the queening of a pawn.

1.Kf6 a2

Black could also play 1...Kd7 but then White wins because his pawn promotes with check: 2.Kf7 a2 3.e8=Q+ and Black loses the race.

2.Ke6 a1=Q 3.d7 mate. Black won the race but lost the war!

Success in many races depends on the knowledge gleaned in past sections. Our next position is an excellent example of this.

Diagram 213

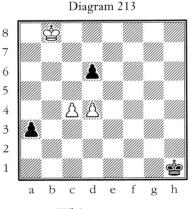

White to move

This position is lost for White since his opponent is clearly ahead in the race. Nevertheless, Black needs to be aware of a little trick or he'll end up botching it.

1.c5 dxc5??

Such an innocent and natural move, but it throws the victory out the window! Correct was 1...a2!, which we'll explore after we finish up with 1...dxc5.

> **REMEMBER**
>
> Even the most innocent move can have life and death ramifications in a King and pawn endgame.

2.dxc5 a2

Isn't Black winning this race? Yes he is, but if you remember your lessons from Part Four, you'll know that White is going to save the game.

3.c6 a1=Q 4.c7 and we have a basic draw—lone Queen vs. pawn on the 7th with the stronger side's King being far out of play can't win against either rook-pawn or bishop-pawn. The end could be: 4...Qe5 5.Kb7 Qb5+ 6.Ka8 Qc6+ 7.Kb8 Qb6+ 8.Ka8! Qxc7 stalemate.

Now let's take a look at the position after...

1.c5 a2 2.c6

Also hopeless is 2.cxd6 a1=Q 3.d7 Qxd4 4.Kc7 Qc5+ 5.Kb7 Qd6 6.Kc8 Qc6+ 7.Kd8 Kg2 and black's King slowly but surely makes its way to the embattled area and wins the game.

2...a1=Q 3.c7

Diagram 214

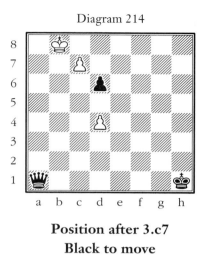

Position after 3.c7
Black to move

White has a c-pawn, so why can't he draw? Two reasons:

➤ White's stalemate save (after a later Ka8 …Qxc7) isn't stalemate anymore due to the existence of the d4-pawn.

➤ In some lines Black can capture the d4-pawn then give up his Queen for white's remaining pawn on c7. Then it's off to the races for black's pawn on d6!

3…Qb2+ 4.Ka8

Not 4.Ka7? Qxd4+.

4…Qa3+ 5.Kb7 Qb4+ 6.Ka8 Qa5+ 7.Kb7 Qb5+ 8.Ka8 Qc6+ 9.Kb8 Qb6+, 0-1 since 10.Ka8 Qxc7 is no longer stalemate, while 10.Kc8 Qxd4 is no better.

Diagram 215

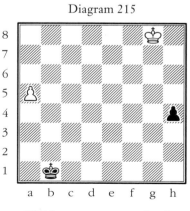

White to move and win

> **REMEMBER**
>
> Complex positions can't be solved unless you are firmly trained in endgame basics!

Even though the race seems to be even, the fact that there are two rook-pawns means that both queening squares connect on the long diagonal. This can easily have decisive ramifications.

1.a6 h3 2.a7 h2 3.a8=Q, 1-0, since 3…h1=Q 4.Qxh1 isn't pleasant.

However, a slight adjustment in King position can change a position from lost to drawn.

Diagram 216

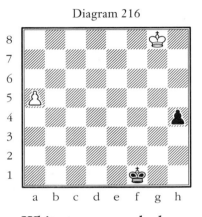

White to move only draws

1.a6 h3 2.a7 h2 3.a8=Q Kg1!, ½-½ (as shown in Part Four).

Thus far we've seen that the result of some races depends on prior knowledge of other endgames, on King position, and/or on whether or not a pawn queens with check. Our next position (a study by the great Réti in 1921) seems completely lost for White—so much so that resignation might be in order!

Diagram 217

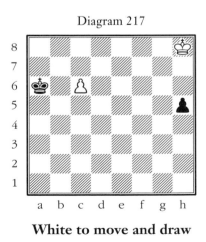

White to move and draw

How can White possibly save himself? It's clear that Black is going to win this race hands down, and to make matters worse, the black King is only two moves away from eating white's pawn! However, White makes use of a solid understanding of the Square of the pawn, good King footwork, and the fact that his pawn queens with check to make the miracle complete.

1.Kg7 h4

Another try is 1...Kb6 2.Kf6 (threatening Kg5) 2...h4 3.Ke5 and the double threat of Kf4 (winning black's pawn) and Kd6 (queening his own pawn) saves the day: 3...h3 4.Kd6 h2 5.c7 Kb7 6.Kd7, ½-½.

2.Kf6

White's King does a tightrope act—on one hand threatening to escort his pawn to c8, and on the other hand trying to enter the square of black's pawn.

2...h3

Of course, 2...Kb6 3.Ke5! transposes into the note to move one.

3.Ke7!

3.Ke6 amounts to the same thing.

3...h2 4.c7 Kb7 5.Kd7, ½-½. Magic!

Réti's discovery created quite a stir back in 1921, and other problem composers rushed to emulate him. The following example is one such attempt.

Diagram 218

Adamson 1922
White to move and draw

1.Kg6 a4 2.Kf5 a3

On 2...Kb6 White uses the Réti device: 3.Ke5! (getting ready to step into the Square of the a-pawn) when 3...Kxc6 4.Kd4 and 3...a3 4.Kd6 are both drawn.

3.Ke6 and white's pawn promotes.

USEFUL ADVICE

King and pawn endgames are always tricky. If you enter one—even one that seems hopeless—take a long think and try to grasp the position's true meaning. This involves taking into account promotion with checks, the Square of a passed pawn, Opposition, Triangulation, Outflanking, and a King's ability to escort its pawn to the 8th rank.

King and Pawn vs. King and Pawn

All versions of this endgame have already been addressed (or indirectly addressed) via Strange Races, via Trébuchet (in Part Four), or in any of the King and pawn vs. King positions that can so easily occur. Here are a few more examples that should firm up the knowledge you already possess.

Diagram 219

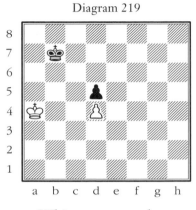

White to move, draw

White will force the win of black's pawn on d5, but the resulting position (if Black responds properly!) is a basic draw:

1.Kb5 Kc7 2.Kc5 Kd8!

Wisely avoiding 2…Kd7?? 3.Kxd5 when White wins since he has the Opposition. You should be thoroughly familiar with the position after 3.Kxd5.

I should add that 2…Kc8! achieves the same result.

3.Kxd5 Kd7, ½-½ since Black now has the Opposition.

Diagram 220

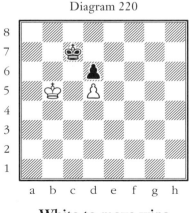

White to move wins

1.Ka6

This forces the win of black's pawn.

1...Kd8 2.Kb6 Kd7 3.Kb7 Kd8 4.Kc6 Ke7 5.Kc7 Ke8 6.Kxd6 Kd8

Black has the Opposition, but it won't help him since his inability to move straight back (he's out of board!) will prevent him from achieving a drawn setup. You should already know this position, but I'll give the rest anyway.

7.Ke6 Ke8 8.d6

Taking the Opposition.

8...Kd8 9.d7 Kc7 10.Ke7, 1-0.

These two examples were nothing more than glorified versions of basic King and pawn vs. lone King theory. But knowledge of them allows us to solve positions that would be unintelligible otherwise. The last several examples made it clear that, aside from simple race considerations (brought about by both pawns being passed), the real question surrounding King and pawn vs. King and pawn theory is whether or not a pawn can be won. If a pawn does indeed drop, the assessment of the resulting position (which has suddenly transposed into one of our already mastered King and pawn vs. lone King situations) is made by who owns the Opposition. Diagram 219 saw the defender safely take the Opposition (thus gaining a draw). The position after that (diagram 220) had white's pawn on the 5th rank—a decisive advantage *if* the white King can crash through and pick off the enemy pawn.

The position in diagram 221 takes things a bit further. To fully understand it, you have to use the tools from diagrams 219 and 220, plus all your Opposition skills.

Diagram 221

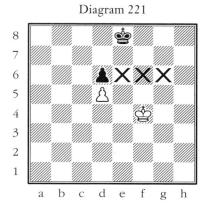

> **RULE**
>
> This kind of situation, where the defender must give up his pawn but can take the Opposition, is always drawn *unless* white's pawn is on the 5th rank.

White to move wins, Black to move draws

Since white's pawn is on the 5th rank, he knows he'll win if he can pick off black's pawn. Black's only hope is to keep the white King from penetrating to e6, f6, or g6, since the d6-pawn will be lost if white's King reaches any of those squares.

White to move wins by **1.Kg5** when 1...Kf7 2.Kf5 and 1...Ke7 2.Kg6 leads to the loss of d6 and the game.

> ### USEFUL ADVICE (IF YOU ARE THE DEFENDER)
>
> Before allowing a position of this nature to occur, make sure the opponent can't penetrate with his King! If he can penetrate, make sure his pawn isn't on the 5th, and that you can take the Opposition when he captures your pawn.

Black to move draws by **1...Kf8!** This takes the Distant Opposition and allows Black to successfully meet 2.Kg5 with 2...Kg7, and 2.Kf5 with 2...Kf7 when white's King can't get in.

The next position is full of interest, and very instructive.

Diagram 222

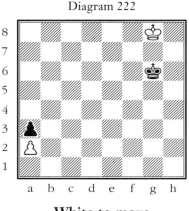

White to move

It's clear that Black will win the pawn on a2. This means that White can only draw if he can reach the c2-square. Again, solving this position is only possible with a firm grasp of basic King and pawn vs. King theory.

1.Kh8!!

Visually this seems very odd. However, it makes perfect sense when looked at in the cold light of reason: Moving to f8 allows 1...Kf6 when Black has gotten closer to his goal on a3, but White hasn't gotten closer to his goal on c2 (note how the black King would block white's King from stepping forward). After 1.Kf8?? Kf6, black's win is illustrated by the following obvious moves: 2.Ke8 Ke5 3.Ke7 Kd4 4.Ke6 Kc3 5.Kd5 Kb2 6.Kc4 Kxa2 7.Kc3 Kb1 and the pawn promotes.

On the other hand, 1.Kh8 Kh6 takes Black farther away from his a3-goal. That only leaves ...

1...Kf5

Or 1...Kf6 2.Kh7, which amounts to the same thing.

2.Kg7 Ke5 3.Kg6 Kd4 4.Kf5 Kc3 5.Ke4 Kb2 6.Kd3 Kxa2 7.Kc2, ½-½.

Rook Endings

The *practical* study of King and pawn endgames is finite—truly complex/impractical King and pawn endgames become the stuff of theorists or very strong players with a fetish for such things. However, the study of Rook endgames—no matter how complex—always remains eminently useful simply because they occur so often and in so many different forms.

Though the student might think that the first five parts of this book has left him with a sizeable amount of Rook endgame skill, the daunting fact is that you are still in Rook endgame infancy and will continue to be long after you make master. Nevertheless, don't be depressed by this news. The material presented here in Part Six will leave you with a very solid base of Rook endgame understanding and—on a competitive level—this knowledge will far outgun that which most of your opposition will ever possess.

"Lucena" with a Rook-Pawn

We've learned that achieving a Lucena Position guarantees a win, *unless* the extra pawn is a rook-pawn. The rule with a "Lucena" rook-pawn—I'm using the word "Lucena" loosely here, since a real Lucena Position only occurs with a knight-pawn, bishop-pawn, or center pawn—is that black's King needs to be cut off by *four or more files* for White to win (one file is sufficient in a real Lucena).

> **RULE**
>
> If you're into memory prompts, and numbers such as "four or more files" don't do the job for you, another way of stating this rule is, *"It's a win if the enemy King is cut off on or beyond the farthest bishop-file."*

Diagram 223

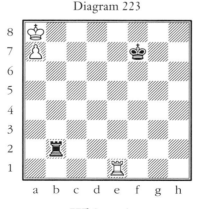

White wins

White's only plan is to get a Rook to b8 and escape with the King. Thanks to the fact that black's King is four files away from the pawn, White can force a win. However, the technique for achieving this is far more difficult than one might imagine!

1.Rc1 Ke7 2.Rc8 Kd6!

2...Kd7 3.Rb8 Ra2 4.Kb7 (and not 4.Rb7+?? Kc8, =) 4...Rb2+ 5.Ka6 Ra2+ 6.Kb6 Rb2+ 7.Kc5 and the King walks towards the Rook and soon forces resignation.

3.Rb8 Ra2 4.Kb7

Escaping from the pit. Leading to nothing is 4.Rb7 (threatening Kb8) 4...Rh2 when 5.Kb8?? Rh8 mate is embarrassing, 5.Rg7 Rb2 6.Rb7 Rh2 just repeats the position, and 5.Rb1 Kc7 is a dead draw.

Diagram 224

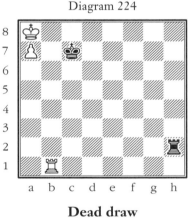

Dead draw

Let's spend a moment explaining why this is so drawn. First, Black to move (from diagram 224) would play 1...Rc2 when White can't even dream of winning: 2.Rh1 (or 2.Rb7+ Kc8 3.Rb8+ Kc7 and white's King will never escape from the corner) 2...Rc3 3.Rh7+ Kc8 4.Rh8+ Kc7 and it should now be clear that white's King is forever entombed on a8.

White to move (from diagram 224): 1.Rc1+ Kd7 2.Kb7 (no choice, since 2.Rd1+ Kc7 only helps Black, 2.Rb1 Kc7 gets nowhere fast, and trying to build a Lucena bridge by 3.Rc4 fails to 3...Rb2) 2...Rb2+ 3.Ka6 Ra2+ 4.Kb6 Rb2+ 5.Kc5 Ra2, ½-½.

4...Rb2+ 5.Kc8

The only good move. 5.Ka6 Ra2+ 6.Kb6 Rb2+ is nothing, and White would have to repeat with 7.Ka6 Ra2+ 8.Kb7 Rb2+ 9.Kc8 in order to get back on the right path.

5...Rc2+ 6.Kd8 Rh2! 7.Rb6+

Of course, 7.a8=Q?? allows 7...Rh8 mate, while 7.Ke8?? fails to 7...Rh8+ 8.Kf7 Rh7+ followed by 9...Rxa7 with a draw.

7...Kc5

7...Ke5 makes things easy for White after 8.Ra6 Rh8+ 9.Kc7 Ra8 10.Kb7, etc.

Diagram 225

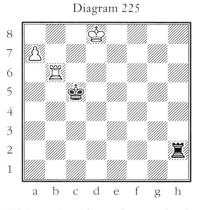

White wins if you know the key!

8.Rc6+!

The key to this endgame. 8.Ra6 fails to 8...Rh8+ 9.Ke7 Rh7+ 10.Kf8 (10.Kf6?? Rh6+) 10...Rh8+ 11.Kg7 Ra8 followed by ...Kb5 when the pawn is lost.

Now, after 8.Rc6+!, Black realizes that taking the Rook allows the white pawn to promote to a Queen with check—not a happy thing for Black to face, but 8...Kb5 (8...Kd5 9.Ra6) 9.Rc8 Rh8+ 10.Kc7 Rh7+ 11.Kb8, 1-0, is even worse!

8...Kxc6 9.a8=Q+

Diagram 226

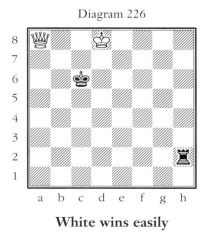

White wins easily

I can imagine some of you looking on in horror and thinking, "I'm not sure if I know how to win Queen vs. Rook!" To make matters worse, a glance in our Contents shows that I don't even cover that endgame! What's going on? First, calm down, you don't need to understand the ins and outs of Queen vs. Rook theory (which I feel is too rare and too hard for this book) to easily win this position. You see, Queen vs. Rook is only difficult if the Rook is fairly close to its King or, at the very least, on the same side of the board (saving it from a Rook-winning fork by white's Queen). In our present position, the Rook and King are far away from each other, and a simple series of checks will pick up the Rook and end the game.

9...Kc5

9...Kb5 (9...Kd6 10.Qb8+ and 11.Qxh2) 10.Qb8+ and 11.Qxh2 is even more abrupt!

10.Qc8+

White wants to swing his Queen over to the kingside (placing his Queen between the black King and its Rook!) when just about any combination of checks will lead to the Rook's demise.

10...Kd4

10...Kd5 11.Qf5+ amounts to the same thing as our main line.

11.Qg4+ Kd5

Black would love to get closer to his Rook, but 11...Kc3/11...Kd3/11...Ke3 all drop the Rook immediately to 12.Qg3+. Note that 11...Ke5 12.Qg3+ and 11...Kc5 12.Qg1+ also lead to instant resignation.

12.Qf5+ Kc6

The only way to stretch things out a bit. 12...Kc4/12...Kd4/12...Kd6 all hang the Rook to 13.Qf4+.

13.Qe6+ Kb7

Again, there's no choice. 13...Kb5/13...Kc5 14.Qe5+ is game over.

14.Qc8+ Ka7 15.Qc7+, 1-0 since 16.Qxh2 follows.

> **RULE**
>
> If you possess the "Lucena" rook-pawn (King in front of its pawn and enemy Rook trapping it there), you can only win if the enemy King is trapped four or more files away/cut off on or beyond the further bishop-file.

As mentioned in the last example, it's a draw if the defending King is three files away (or closer) from the pawn. Much of this was explained in the note to white's 4th move in the previous example (diagram 224), but let's start from scratch just to ram the point home.

Diagram 227

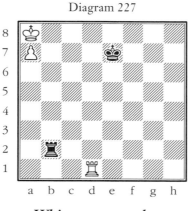

White to move, draw

Black's King is close enough to trap white's monarch in the corner.

1.Rh1 Kd7 2.Rh8

Of course, 2.Rh7+ Kc8 only helps Black.

2...Kc7 3.Rb8 Rh2 4.Rb7+ Kc8! 5.Rb1 White's last chance to get his King out is to play Rc1+ (though even that would lead to a draw, as illustrated in diagram 224), so Black ends this hope by 5...Rc2! when White can't dream of progress here as long as Black has c7 and c8 available to the King.

> **REMEMBER**
>
> Rook-pawns tend to be a bother for the attacker and a joy for the defender!

Rook in Front of its 7th Rank Pawn

When a Rook is trying to shepherd a pawn down the board, it usually dreams of being *behind* the pawn.

Diagram 228

Black is busted

Note how white's Rook is a tower of strength that is helping to push the pawn home. In comparison, black's Rook is passively stopping the inevitable. White wins by Kd4-c5-b6-b7.

> **RULE**
>
> Both sides should try to get their Rook behind a passed pawn.

This means that defensively, having one's Rook behind the enemy passed pawn is of enormous importance. To illustrate, let's take the previous diagram—quite hopeless for Black when white's Rook is behind its pawn—and reverse the position of the Rooks.

Diagram 229

Draw

White can't win because Black now has an ideal defensive stance with his Rook, while white's Rook is stuck in a corner guarding its pawn. White's only chance is to defend the pawn with his King, then bring his Rook out. But this fails:

1.Kc5 Ra2

Many moves are fine. For example, 1...Kg7 also does the job, while 1...Rc1+ 2.Kb6 Rb1+ 3.Kc5 Rc1+ is quite sufficient, though Black can't get too overzealous with his checks: 4.Kb4 Rb1+ 5.Kc3 Rc1+?? (5...Ra1, draw) 6.Kb2 when suddenly black's Rook isn't able to get back behind the passed pawn! White wins after 6...Rc7 7.Rh8+ Kxh8 8.a8=Q+ with a theoretical win that's a bit too complex for our present course of study.

I should point out that another way to lose after 1.Kc5 is 1...Ra5+?? since this lets White attack the Rook and guard his pawn at the same time by 2.Kb6. The continuation might then be: 2...Ra1 3.Rb8 (Freedom at last! This Rook can finally take an active part in the battle to promote the pawn.) 3...Rb1+ 4.Kc7 Rc1+ 5.Kb7 Rb1+ 6.Ka8 Rg1 7.Rb7+ Kh6 8.Kb8 (threatening a8=Q) 8...Rg8+ 9.Kc7 (threatening Rb8) 9...Rg7+ (or 9...Ra8 10.Kb6 followed by 11.Rb8)

10.Kb6 Rg6+ 11.Ka5 Rg1 (A last trick. No better is 11...Rg5+ 12.Ka6 Rg6+ 13.Rb6, 1-0) 12.Rb6+ (And not 12.a8=Q?? Ra1+ and 13...Rxa8, =) 12...Kh7 13.Ka6, 1-0, since 13...Ra1+ 14.Kb7 and 13...Rg8 14.Rb7+ Kh6 15.Rb8 Rg6+ 16.Rb6 are both game over.

2.Kb6 Rb2+

> **RULE**
>
> In these positions, whenever the King touches its pawn (trying to free its Rook), the defender should smack it away immediately with a check!

3.Kc7 Ra2

> **REMEMBER**
>
> The defending Rook needs to be behind the enemy passed pawn. Failing to do so will allow the stronger side's Rook to get out of its cage!

4.Kb7 Rb2+ 5.Kc6 Ra2

White's insurmountable problem is now clear: Black will check white's King whenever it touches its pawn. Then, when that King/pawn contact is lost, the Rook will leap in back of the pawn and leave White with no constructive ideas.

After 5...Ra2, White should just shake hands and accept a draw.

> **USEFUL ADVICE**
>
> It's often critically important to get your Rook behind a passed pawn (be it your passed pawn or your opponent's).

Diagram 230

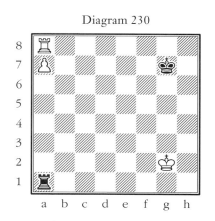

Draw, but watch out for the trap!

Here Black should just move his Rook back and forth along the a-file, and/or he can break the monotony by doing a little jig with his King via ...Kg7-h7-g7-h7 when White has to accept the draw. But what if White whispers (in evil fashion), "Hey, can't you just walk over to the queenside with your King and win my pawn?"

Obviously, the voice of greed has dragged many a good man and woman to their doom, so let's demonstrate what happens if such a queenside trek is attempted:

1...Kf7??

It's clear that 1...Kf6?? 2.Rf8+ followed by 3.a8=Q is a disaster!

2.Rh8!

Diagram 231

A key tactical idea

And the trap is sprung! White threatens 3.a8=Q, and since 2...Rxa7 loses to 3.Rh7+, Black must resign. This tactical idea is extremely important in this kind of endgame, and its influence drastically effects many more complex situations.

> **REMEMBER**
>
> Many class "A" players have fallen victim to this trap, so always be on the lookout for it!

As we can see, having a pawn on the 7th rank, with your Rook in front, is a doubled edged sword. On one hand it dooms your Rook to passivity. On the other, it forces the black King to everlasting imprisonment on h7 and g7 (otherwise the above tactic ends matters quickly). This brings up an important question: If Black gets his Rook behind your pawn (with your Rook in front of it), but the pawn is only on the 6th rank, should you push it to the 7th or leave it where it is?

(See diagram 232)

Pushing the pawn to a7 creates an instant draw (the previous examples should have convinced you of this!) because white's Rook would remain forever passive and any attempt to defend the pawn with the white King would fail because black's Rook would just check it away and then return to its defensive position behind the passed pawn.

Diagram 232

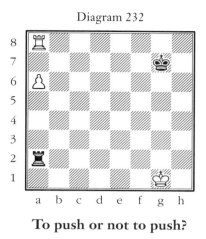

To push or not to push?

The real question here is, how can White try to win? It turns out that White has many advantages:

➤ His King can easily break black's "block" on the 2nd rank (by scuttling over to b1) and then march up the board to its pawn.

➤ When the pawn is on the 7th rank, white's King would have nowhere to hide. With the pawn on the 6th, the King can hide in front of it (on a7). This finally frees the a8-Rook.

➤ Black's King is forever stuck on h7 and g7 since any attempt to rush over to the queenside fails to a well-timed a6-a7 when the poor King would be stuck in no-man's land.

All these facts make it sound as if White should prevail, and if Black tries to maintain his Rook's position behind the passed pawn White will indeed be able to claim victory:

1.Kf1 Kh7

Note that black's King can't participate in the defense: 1...Kf7 2.Ke1 (2.a7 Kg7! is our basic draw) 2...Ke7?? (Making a dash for the queenside, but this backfires horribly!) 3.a7! and suddenly black's King can't get back to the safe squares on g7 and h7. Both 3...Kd7 and 3...Kf7 lose to 4.Rh8 Rxa7 5.Rh7+.

2.Ke1 Kg7 3.Kd1 Kh7 4.Kc1 Kg7 5.Kb1

Finally breaking black's 2nd rank blockade.

5...Ra5 6.Kb2 Ra4 7.Kb3 Ra1 8.Kb4 Kf7

Black doesn't intend to go too far—he sees that the immediate 9.a7 is safely answered by 9...Kg7! with a draw.

9.Kb5

Defending the pawn and threatening to free the a8-Rook.

9...Rb1+ 10.Kc6 Rc1+ 11.Kb7 Rb1+ 12.Ka7

White's King has reached the safe haven on a7. The white Rook is finally ready to emerge.

12...Ke7 13.Rb8 Ra1 14.Rb6 Kd7 15.Kb7 and, since a6-a7-a8 can't be prevented, Black must resign.

> **RULE**
>
> When defending these positions, the normally successful "passive defense" (i.e., moving the King back and forth, and giving a check when the stronger side's King touches its pawn)—which works so well with the stronger side's pawn on the 7th rank and his Rook in front of it—doesn't succeed if the pawn is only on the 6th rank.

Is this a win after all? No, Black can save the game if he's familiar with the surprisingly little known (though extremely important!) *Vancura Position*.

Diagram 233

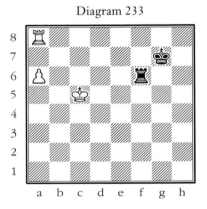

Either side to move, Black draws

Just as the pawn on the 7th deprived white's King of any cover, the flexible position of the defensive Rook (and the unfortunate position of the stronger side's Rook) effectively does the same thing since:

➤ Black can check along the f-file.

➤ His Rook attacks a6 and thus keeps the white Rook cornered.

➤ White's King has nowhere to hide (if White had a b-pawn instead of an a-pawn, this would no longer be the case since white's King could hide on a6).

1.Kb5

Defending the pawn and threatening to free the a8-Rook. Of course, 1.a7 Ra6! 2.Kb5 Ra1 is an easy draw, and 1.Ra7+ Kg6 is also nothing for White.

1...Rf5+ 2.Kc6 Rf6+ 3.Kd5

There are no gains for White after 3.Kb7 Rf7+.

3...Rb6

This important move keeps contact with the a6-pawn and continues to force white's Rook to act as a permanent babysitter.

4.Ke5 Rc6

Black could also draw with 4...Kh7 (the King on h7 and Rook on g6 is as fully adequate as the King on g7 and Rook on f6). However, some care must be given since 4...Rf6?? instantly drops the game to 5.Rg8+ Kxg8 6.Kxf6, 1-0.

5.Ra7+

White is running out of ideas since he's already tried moving his King to the queenside, while 5.a7 Ra6 is a mindlessly simple draw.

5...Kg6 6.Kd5 Rf6 7.Kc5 Rf5+ 8.Kb6 Rf6+ 9.Kb7 Rf7+ 10.Ka8 Rf8+, ½-½. White can't make any progress.

Diagram 234

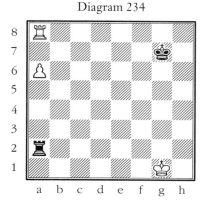

Black finds the correct path to a draw

Diagram 234 takes us back to the position (seen earlier in diagram 232) we didn't quite solve. Now we should have the knowledge to find black's draw. Since staying behind the pawn doesn't work, his correct defensive strategy is to set up a Vancura Position.

1.Kf1 Ra5! 2.Ke2 Re5+

This doesn't give white's Rook a chance to escape from its prison on a8.

3.Kd3 Re6! 4.Kc4 Rf6 5.Kb5 Rf5+, ½-½.

Diagram 235

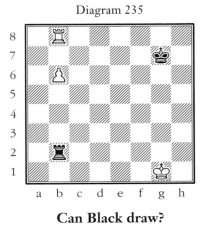

Can Black draw?

As was the case with the a-pawn, White wants to rush his King to the front of his pawn (b7) with a won game. Now the Vancura Position doesn't work since white's King has access to a6:

1.Kf1

Of course, 1.b7? Kh7 is still a total draw.

1...Rb5 2.Ke2 Re5+ 3.Kd3 Re6 4.Kc4 Rf6 5.Kb5 Rf5+ 6.Ka6, 1-0.

However, the pawn on b6 is closer to black's King, so a more straightforward drawing idea is possible, this time keeping the black Rook behind the passed pawn.

Diagram 236

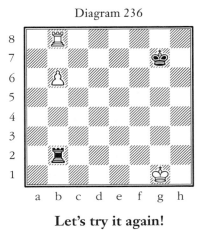

Let's try it again!

1.Kf1 Kf7! 2.Ke1

1.b7 Kg7!, =.

2...Ke7!

Bravely entering no-man's land. Though this fails with the a-pawn, it does the trick with the closer b-pawn.

3.b7

Else …Kd7 and …Kc6 picks up the b-pawn. Now White threatens to win by 4.Rh8.

3…Kd7 4.Rh8 Rxb7 5.Rh7+ Kc8, ½-½.

Thus, we have two important rules:

> **RULES**
>
> When combating a rook-pawn on the 6th (with the stronger side's Rook in front of its pawn and the stronger side's King off in the hinterlands), the Vancura Position is the defender's road to salvation.
>
> When combating a knight-pawn on the 6th (with the stronger side's Rook in front of its pawn and the stronger side's King off in the hinterlands), the Vancura Position is no longer sufficient for a draw. However, keeping the Rook behind the pawn and rushing the King towards the embattled area should pick up the pawn and draw the game.

Rook and Pawn (on 4th or 5th) vs. Rook

We've already determined that the game is easily drawn if the defending King can get in front of the pawn (i.e., using the Philidor Position, as shown in Part Four). However, what happens if the defending King is trapped one or more files to the side of the pawn?

The result of this endgame depends on whether or not the stronger side can reach a Lucena position, and this is determined by the following specific rules (as usual, rook-pawns form exceptions, so we'll only explore positions with a knight-pawn, bishop-pawn, or center pawn):

> **RULES**
>
> A pawn on the 5th rank or beyond wins if the defending King is cut off by one file on the Long Side of the board!
>
> A pawn on the 4th rank wins if the defending King is cut off by two files. A knight-pawn is an exception and takes three files.

Diagram 237

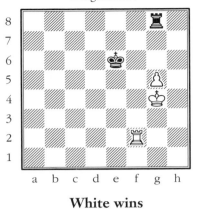

White wins

The position in diagram 237 is a good illustration of our 5th rank rule—a pawn on the 5th rank or beyond wins if the defending King is cut off by one file on the **Long Side** of the board. White easily achieves a Lucena Position because black's King is on the Long Side of the board.

Now it's time to address the Long Side and **Short Side** of the pawn: The Short Side is the side with the least amount of squares from the pawn to the side of the board. In general, the defender should always move his King to the Short Side of the pawn. Placing the defending King on the Short Side is extremely important! The point is that the defending Rook can use the Long Side for long distance checking (known as **Checking Distance**) without having to worry about his King getting in the way of those checks! By blasting the enemy King with long distance checks, the beleaguered King won't be able to find shelter since approaching the nasty Rook would entail a long trek that completely abandons the battle zone.

1.Kh5

Preparing to advance the pawn. If Black does nothing, White will win easily by 2.g6, 3.Kh6, etc.

1...Rh8+ 2.Kg6

Threatening to play 3.Kg7 and 4.g6.

2...Rg8+ 3.Kh6 Rh8+ 4.Kg7 Rh1 5.g6 Rg1

Else White would play 6.Kg8 and 7.g7.

6.Kh7 Ke7 7.g7 Rh1+ 8.Kg8 and White has a basic Lucena Position which, as you know, is an easy win.

> **RULE**
>
> In a pawn down Rook endgame where the defending King can no longer stay in front of the enemy pawn, the defender should always move his King to the Short Side of the board so that his Rook will have Checking Distance.

That was easy! But be careful that the defending King really is cut off.

Diagram 238

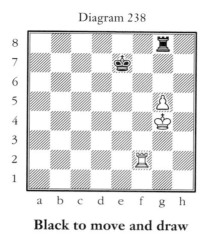

Black to move and draw

This is almost identical to our previous position, which was won for White. However, the "almost" proves to be very important—instead of being on e6, black's King resides on e7. Also, Black has the move. This allows **1...Rf8!**. Suddenly it's clear that black's King wasn't cut off at all! Now 2.Rxf8 Kxf8 is a dead draw, while 2.Ra2 Kf7! gets the King to the front of the pawn, achieving a drawn position.

Our next example shows how the defender can draw against a pawn on the 5th if his King is correctly placed on the Short Side of the board.

Diagram 239

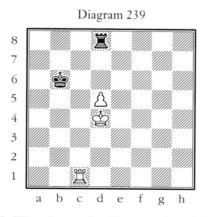

Black's King is on the Short Side of the pawn

Black draws by giving his Rook Checking Distance on the Long Side of the board.

1...Rh8!

Suddenly Black threatens a cascade of checks along the distant h-file. Incredibly, White has no answer to this!

2.d6

The attempt to block the checks with the white Rook via 2.Re1 fails to 2...Kc7 when black's King gets in front of the pawn with a drawn position. Counting on the King to do the job also doesn't work: 2.Ke5 Rh5+ 3.Ke6 Rh6+ 4.Kd7 Rh7+ 5.Kc8 Rh8+ 6.Kd7 Rh7+ 7.Ke6 Rh6+ 8.Kf7 Rh7+ (8...Rd6 is also fine) 9.Kg6 Rd7 (Now that white's King is far from its pawn, Black is able to pile up on the abandoned unit and win it.) 10.Rd1 Kc5, ½-½.

2...Rh4+ 3.Ke5 Rh5+ 4.Kf6

Or 4.Kf4 Rd5 and the pawn is lost.

4...Rh6+ 5.Ke7 Rh7+ 6.Kf8 Rd7, ½-½.

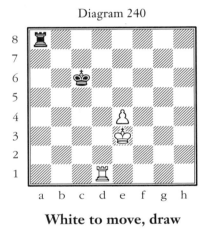

Diagram 240

White to move, draw

Earlier we stated that a pawn on the 4th rank wins if the defending King is cut off by two files. The position in diagram 240 is drawn because the defending king is only cut off by one file.

1.Kf4

The tempting 1.e5 seems strong, since 1...Re8?? 2.Ke4 takes us to our first rule: *A pawn on the 5th rank or beyond wins if the enemy King is cut off by one file on the Long Side of the board.* However, instead of the compliant 1...Re8, Black can answer 1.e5 with 1...Ra4! when white's King is cut off from its pawn! Now moves that take the white Rook off the d-file allow ...Kd7 with an immediate draw, 2.Rd6+ Kc7 also leaves White without a good follow-up, and 2.Rd4 Rxd4 is a drawn King and pawn vs. King endgame. Thus: 1.e5 Ra4 2.e6. Now White threatens to win by 3.e7 Ra8 4.Rd8, but 2...Kc7! (stopping the aforementioned possibility of e7 followed by Rd8) holds the draw: 3.Rd7+ (3.e7 Ra8 followed by ...Re8, =) 3...Kc8 4.Rh7 (4.Kd3 or 4.Rd1 run into 4...Ra6, =) 4...Kd8, ½-½.

1...Rf8+

This frontal check defense is quite effective against a pawn on the 4th rank.

2.Kg5

Note that 2.Ke5 Re8+ 3.Kf5 Rf8+ 4.Ke6 Re8+ gets White absolutely nowhere due to the vulnerability of the pawn.

2...Re8!

And not 2...Rg8+?? 3.Kf6 when 3...Rf8+ 4.Ke7 and 3...Re8 4.e5 both lose for Black. Also note that 3...Rh8 doesn't give Black enough Checking Distance because black's King is on the Long Side: 4.e5 Rh6+ 5.Kg5 Re6 (5...Rh8 6.e6) 6.Kf5 Re8 7.e6, winning.

The annoying attack against e4 (2...Re8) freezes the pawn in its tracks and forces White to lose time defending the pawn.

3.Kf5 Rf8+ 4.Kg6 Re8! 5.Rd4

White's last shot (which threatens 6.Kf7 Re5 7.Kf6 Re8 8.e5), since 5.Re1 Kd6 is completely drawn.

5...Kc5!

A *very important* resource! Note that if our original position had started with black's King on c7 instead of c6, this move wouldn't be possible and the result would be very different:

Diagram 241

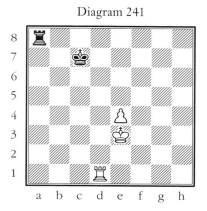

Black to move draws, White to move wins

Black to move draws in two different ways: 1...Kc6 (which takes us back to diagram 240) or 1...Rd8 2.Rxd8 Kxd8 3.Kf4 Ke8!, ½-½.

White to move wins because he can take advantage of the fact that Black no longer has the ...Kc5 defensive idea at his disposal: 1.Kf4 Rf8+ 2.Kg5 Re8 3.Kf5 Rf8+ 4.Kg6 Re8! 5.Rd4 Kc6 6.Kf7 Re5 (6...Kc5 7.Rd5+, 1-0) 7.Kf6 Re8 8.e5, 1-0.

6.Rd5+ Kc6 7.Kf5 Rf8+

Diagram 242

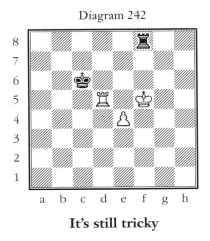

It's still tricky

8.Ke5

The alternative, 8.Kg4, also forces Black to use some care: 8...Re8 9.Kf4 Rf8+ 10.Rf5 Ra8 11.Rf7 (11.e5 Kd7 will achieve an easily drawn Philidor Position) 11...Kd6 12.Kf5 Ra5+ 13.Kf6 Re5 14.Rd7+ Kxd7 15.Kxe5 Ke7 and, since Black has the Opposition, the game is drawn.

8...Re8+ 9.Kd4 Re7 10.e5 Rd7!

An idea that we've already seen. The Rook move allows the black King to make its way to the front of the pawn.

11.Rxd7 Kxd7 12.Kd5 Ke7 13.e6 Ke8 14.Kd6 Kd8 15.e7+ Ke8 16.Ke6 stalemate.

Diagram 243

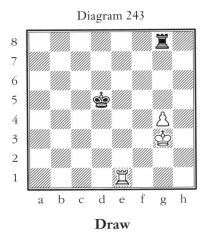

Draw

Though the stronger side wins with a bishop-pawn or center-pawn on the 4th rank if the defending King is trapped two files away, a knight-pawn on the 4th is more problematic. In this case the stronger side usually wins if the defending King is trapped three files away.

The position in diagram 243 is drawn since the defending King is only two files away.

1.Re2

White can't improve his position so he "passes" in the hope that Black will make a mistake.

1...Kd6!

Oddly, this is the only way to draw! Let's look at the alternatives and see why:

> ▶ 1...Rg7?? destroys the Rook's Checking Distance. Black is toast after 2.Kh4 Rh7+ 3.Kg5 Rg7+ 4.Kh5 Rh7+ 5.Kg6.

> ▶ 1...Ra8?? 2.g5 is hopeless.

> ▶ 1...Kd4?? is the most interesting blunder since it allows White to cut the black King off on a rank by 2.Re6! Kd5 3.Rh6.

Diagram 244

Black is lost!

Suddenly black's game is lost! His King can't get back into the fight since the 6th rank is a no-pass zone, and the white Rook blocks all checks along the h-file which allows the King to calmly march up to h5. A sample of what could occur: 3...Ke5 4.Kh4 Rg7 5.Kh5 Rg8 6.g5 Kf5 7.Rf6+ Ke5 8.Kh6 Rh8+ 9.Kg7 Rh1 10.Rf2 Ke6 11.g6 and White will achieve the desired Lucena Position.

> **USEFUL ADVICE**
>
> Sometimes cutting the defending King off along a rank is as good as cutting it off along a file.

2.Re4

Otherwise Black just moves his King back and forth between d6 and d5. By defending his pawn with the Rook, White hopes to relieve his King of guard duty which will allow it to march triumphantly down the board.

2...Kd5!

Chasing the Rook away from its good position. A major mistake would be 2...Kd7?? 3.Kh4 Rh8+ 4.Kg5 Rg8+ 5.Kf6 Rf8+ (or 6.g5 would have followed) 6.Kg7 and White wins.

3.Re1

Black draws easily after 3.Ra4 Ke6.

3...Kd6 and White must agree to a draw since he can't make any progress.

Minor Piece Endgames

Bishops of Opposite Colors (Bishop and Two Connected Passers vs. Lone Bishop and King)

One would think that this endgame would be an easy win for the two connected passed pawns. However, this simply isn't the case. To illustrate my point, allow me to indulge in a little story.

The year was 1978, the city was London, and I was playing my second game with the white pieces in the span of a few months against Jonathan Speelman. I had won the first and now my opponent was after blood. The opening promised a sharp struggle:

1.e4 c5 2.Nf3 d6 3.d4 cxd4 4.Nxd4 Nf6 5.Nc3 a6 6.Bg5 Nc6 7.Qd2 e6 8.0–0–0 Bd7 9.f4 b5 10.Nxc6 Bxc6 11.Qe3 Be7 12.Bxf6 Bxf6 13.e5 Be7 14.exd6 Bxd6 15.Ne4 Bxe4 16.Qxe4 0–0

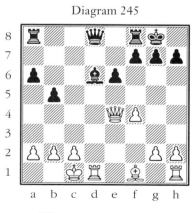

Diagram 245

How not to prepare

I had prepared this system a year before, and whatever theory I had access to at that time had promised me good chances with 17.Bd3 g6 18.h4. Indeed, it looks dangerous for Black, but as I sat there wondering why my opponent exuded an air of confidence, I decided to take a deep look at the position for the first time (Mindlessly memorizing book, and exploring a variation seriously, are two very different things!). Sure enough, after pondering the situation for a long while I realized that White didn't have anything at all! It occurred to me that after 18...Qf6 19.Rdf1 Rfd8 20.h5 Bf8 21.hxg6 hxg6 22.g4 Bg7 my opponent's Bishop would be very happy on g7 where it would defend the black King while simultaneously eyeing my monarch in a lecherous state of rut.

Diagram 246

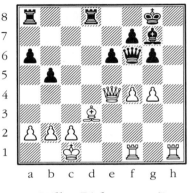

Killer Bishop on g7

(Years later the position after 21.hxg6 hxg6 22.g4 Bg7 did indeed occur, with this result: 23.c3 b4 24.f5 exf5 25.gxf5 g5, 0-1, Santo Roman - Palac, Cannes 2000).

> **RULE**
>
> Opposite colored Bishops are wonderful attacking weapons in the middlegame (or in endgames with many pieces remaining) since one Bishop can attack something that the other can't defend.

Whatever the truth about this line might be, during the game I began to panic, and this led to a "cowardly" act on my part (from diagram 245):

17.Qd4 Bc7 18.Qxd8 Raxd8 19.Rxd8 Rxd8 20.g3

Yes, I renounced my manhood and shamelessly played for a draw!

20...h5 21.Be2 h4 22.Rd1

Since leaving too many pieces on would actually make the Bishops of opposite colors useful to Black, I made sure to exchange everything that wasn't nailed down.

> **RULE**
>
> Bishops of opposite colors often give the defender serious drawing chances in the endgame even if he's one or two pawns behind!

22...Rxd1+ 23.Kxd1 g5 24.fxg5 hxg3 25.hxg3 we arrived at the following situation.

Diagram 247

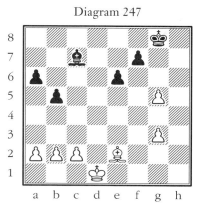

Is Black getting something?

My opponent was getting a bit excited, no doubt due to the fact that both my g-pawns were in bad shape. Losing them would lead to two black connected passed pawns marching down the board. Was it time for me to get hysterical? Not at all! Why? Because I knew that the following position (a true worst case scenario) was dead drawn.

Diagram 248

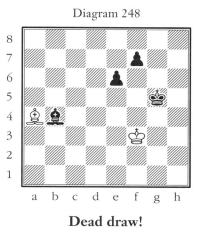

Dead draw!

That's right. If White loses both g-pawns *and* his three queenside pawns for black's two, the game is still a draw!

The extreme position in the last diagram didn't occur though, and the actual game ended without any adventures:

25...Kg7 26.a4 bxa4 27.Bxa6 Kg6 28.Bb5 Bxg3 29.Bxa4 Kxg5 30.Ke2 f5 31.Kf3 Bd6 32.c3 e5 33.Bc2, ½-½.

Okay, after seeing me label diagram 248 a dead draw, many of you might be thinking, "Someone let Silman loose in the pharmaceuticals again!" So, just in case you doubt this humble writer, let me try and prove my point of view.

We'll explore two different methods for Black.

Diagram 249

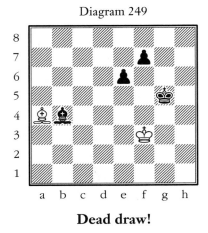

Dead draw!

| Method 1 |

Black tries to bring his King to d4 without pushing his pawns.

1...Kf5 2.Be8!

So that the f7-pawn won't be defending the e6-pawn anymore.

2...f6 3.Bd7!

Now the black King is stuck defending the e6-pawn. He has to give up his plan and try

3...Ke5 4.Bc8 Kd6 5.Ke4

But now Black will have to push his pawns if he wants to win, and that will be examined next. However, we've discovered an important idea (brought to light by the moves 2.Be8! and 3.Bd7!) when defending this kind of opposite colored Bishop endgame: The defender can tie his opponent's King down by using his Bishop to attack the pawns.

We'll see many examples of this rule in action.

| Method 2 |

Black shoves his pawns forward!
(From diagram 249)

1...f5 2.Bb3!

RULE

The defender must attack an enemy pawn with his Bishop in order to tie down the enemy King.

This fine move gives Black two choices: he can play …Kf6 and simply guard the pawn for the rest of the game (which means he'll make no progress whatsoever), or he can push the pawn to e5, which is clearly what Black was aiming for anyway. However, once this pawn moves to e5, White can then demonstrate his key defensive plan.

2...e5

Now Black threatens (after something hideous such as 3.Ba4??) 3...e4+ 4.Ke3 Bc5+ 5.Ke2 f4 when the pawns will soon make their way to the 6th rank: 6.Bc2 f3+ 7.Ke1 Kf4 8.Bb1 e3 9.Bd3 Bb4+ 10.Kf1 Ke5 (Black will march his King around to d2 so he can play …e3-e2+ without letting White sacrifice his Bishop for both enemy pawns. White can't do anything to prevent this plan.) 11.Ba6 Kd4 12.Bb5 Kc3 13.Ke1 Kc2+ 14.Kf1 Kd2, 0-1.

> **RULE**
>
> In this kind of endgame, two connected passed pawns on the sixth are winning. The defender must not allow the pawns to get that far!

3.Bc2!

Believe it or not, this simple move, which stops …e4+ due to Bxe4, ends the game. Black is no longer able to generate any kind of threat whatsoever.

3...Kf6 4.Bd3 Ke6 5.Bc2

Black would have chances if he could get his King to d4 (which would help the e-pawn safely advance to e4), but white's attack on f5 freezes the enemy King in its tracks. Since white's defensive plan now calls for nothing more than Bc2-b1-c2-b1, the game should be declared drawn.

Let's now compare two positions that seem to be very similar, yet their result turns out to be vastly different!

Diagram 250

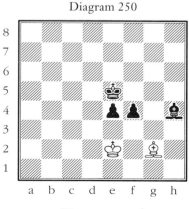

Draw agreed

This position is literally over (White didn't let the Black pawns get to the sixth, as mentioned earlier), and should be agreed drawn. White will simply play Bg2-h1-g2-h1 and Black can't make progress since ...f4-f3+ is always met by Bxf3. Note how the Bishop ties the black King to the defense of its e-pawn.

However, our next position is won for Black.

Diagram 251

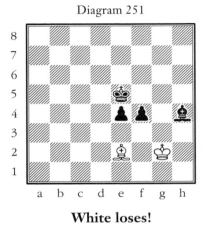

White loses!

Ah, the lovely sound of chess players mumbling in confusion! Why is diagram 250 a dead draw while this one is dead lost? Understanding the difference will give you the true key to this whole endgame!

In the drawn version of this position (diagram 250), black's King is forever doomed to baby-sit the e4-pawn. That means he can't get the King to g3 (which would allow a winning ...f4-f3 push) because the e-pawn would hang. Of course, if Black tries ...e4-e3, then White just moves his Bishop mindlessly (and end-lessly!) along the h1-a8 diagonal, forming a perfect block to both enemy pawns.

In the losing version (diagram 251), the e4-pawn is not attacked by the white Bishop. Now the black King is indeed free to roam, and after ...Kd4-e3, the ...f4-f3 advance will seal the deal.

REMEMBER

The correct defensive stance calls for the defender's Bishop to tie the enemy King down to the defense of its pawn.

Some of you might now be wondering what happens if Black leaves his pawns back a bit and instead strives to improve the position of his King (in an effort to avoid the drawn position we have just seen). If you glance back to Method 1 (it probably didn't make much sense earlier!), you'll finally understand what I was trying to do—the defender will answer this strategy by attacking the pawns with his Bishop and force their advance!

Let's look at a simple example of this:

Diagram 252

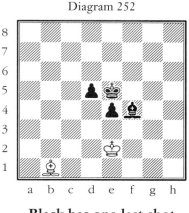

Black has one last shot

In this position, we're familiar with 1...d4 2.Bc2 when we have our basic dead drawn defensive posture. But suppose Black refuses to take the bait and instead tries to activate his King by **1...Kd4**. Here's a quick white suicide that will serve as an example of what Black has in mind: 2.Bc2 Kc3 3.Bb1?? (3.Kd1!) 3...Kb2 when the Bishop, and the game, are lost!

Fortunately, after **1...Kd4** White can easily draw if he remembers to always restrict the enemy King's movements by forcing it to defend its pawns. Thus **2.Ba2!** stops the King's march in its tracks! After **2...Bg5** (Hoping White will move his Bishop off the d5-pawn.) **3.Bb3** (Nope. White can go Bb3-a2-b3 all day!) **3...Kc5 4.Ba2 d4 5.Bb1! Kd5 6.Bc2** and we once again have our ideal drawing posture.

Fortresses in Bishop-up Endgames

The idea of a defensive fortress is an important one. In general, you're *not* expected to memorize lots of fortress examples. Instead, seeing a few patterns and keeping the possibility in mind will serve you well.

Fortresses in Bishop-up endgames are fairly common due to the Bishop's inability to control a whole color complex. These usually occur when the stronger side's rook-pawn or knight-pawn get down to the sixth and/or 7th rank, or if a rook-pawn of the wrong color is lurking on the board. Here are a few examples that don't need much explanation.

> **RULE**
>
> There are *no* fortresses for bishop-pawn, queen-pawn or king-pawn!

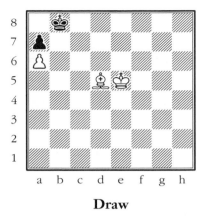

Draw

White reaches a dead end if Black shuffles his King between b8 and c8. Allowing black's King access to a8 also doesn't get the job done: **1.Be6 Ka8 2.Kd6 Kb8**, ½-½.

Diagram 254

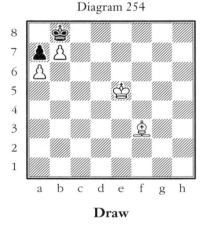

Draw

White is up a Bishop and pawn, yet the game's a draw since white's King can't approach without delivering stalemate. Note that sacrificing the b-pawn (in the hope of giving black's King more wiggle room) leads to the previous diagram after **1.Bd5 Kc7 2.b8=Q+ Kxb8**.

Diagram 255

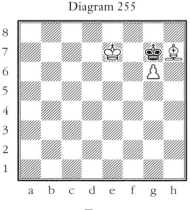

Draw

The dreadful position of white's Bishop allows Black to draw. His mindless plan of …Kg7-h8-g7, etc. is unbreakable. Oddly, if white's Bishop where to turn into a pawn, then White would win by 1.h8=Q+ Kxh8 2.Kf6. In other words, the Bishop on h7 is *worse* than a pawn!

Diagram 256

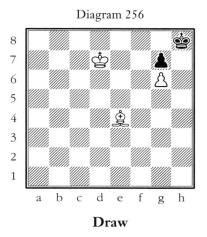

Draw

Black happily dances between g8 and h8 until White finally gives up and stalemates his opponent.

Diagram 257

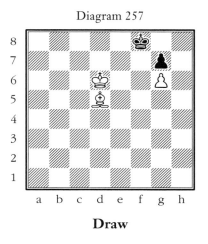

Draw

We've seen that White has no chance of winning if black's King gets to g8/h8. That means that white's Bishop must prevent this by staying on the a2-g8 diagonal. However, now Black skips between e8 and f8 and, again, White must eventually tip his hat to the draw.

As stated earlier, c/f-, d-, and e-pawns prevent such blockades, as shown by the following example:

Diagram 258

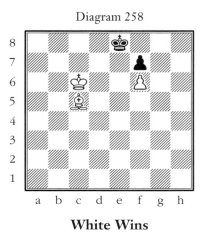

White Wins

1.Bb6 Kf8 2.Kd7 Kg8 3.Ke7, 1-0. It doesn't get too much easier than that!

Queen Endgames
(A Trick Win in Queen vs. Rook-Pawn and Queen vs. Bishop-Pawn on the 7th)

Diagram 259

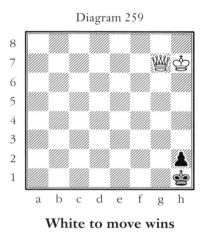

White to move wins

Usually a rook-pawn will draw in a Queen vs. King and pawn on the 7th rank endgame. However, the position in the diagram is an exception, and the technique White makes use of is important. It shows how, in some endgames, you can allow one side to promote his pawn to a Queen and still win by weaving a back rank mating net.

1.Kg6

Not 1.Kh6?? since that would stalemate the black King! By 1.Kg6, White moves his King closer to the enemy pawn and simultaneously blocks the Queen's control over the g-file, thus preventing an unpleasant stalemate.

1...Kg2 2.Kf5+

In this kind of endgame, White wins if he can get his King into the box shown in diagram 260. The reason for this will be clear in a moment.

Diagram 260

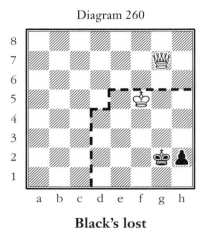

Black's lost

2...Kf2

Black realizes that 2...Kh1 3.Kg4! just helps White get closer with his King.

3.Qb2+ Kg1

Black loses immediately after 3...Kg3 4.Qb7 when the pawn is permanently frozen.

4.Kg4!

White lets Black make a Queen!

4...h1=Q 5.Kg3 and Black must resign since he can't stop Qf2 mate or a back rank mate unless he gives away his Queen.

As you can see, in the case of a rook-pawn vs. a Queen and close King (diagrams 259 and 260), the Queen can easily create this mate from any position along its 2nd rank (the moves after diagram 260 had White's Queen settling on b2). Thus, if the white King gets in the box shown in diagram 260 (with White having the move or Black being in check), he always wins.

Note that this idea is sometimes possible against a bishop-pawn—whether it does or doesn't work against the other pawns is of no consequence since the Queen easily beats a knight-pawn or center pawn no matter where the Kings might stand. In a situation where Black turns his bishop-pawn into a new Queen *and* has the move, the white King has to be on its third rank in front of the enemy King, and the white Queen must be on a2 or e2 in the case of a c-pawn/h2 or d2 in the case of an f-pawn. Diagrams 261 and 262 clearly illustrate both situations.

From diagram 261: **1.Qh2!** (the best possible square) **1...Ke1 2.Kf4 f1=Q+ 3.Ke3** and Black can't stop mate since white's Queen prevents all black checks by covering e2, f2, g1, and h3 (White's King defends against the other checks on its own).

Diagram 261

White to move and win

White won (in diagram 261) because the Queen on h2 keeps the Black King out of the corner and doesn't allow him any stalemate tricks.

Diagram 262

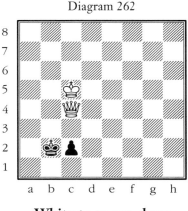

White to move, draw

The position in diagram 262 looks promising for White since his King is quite close: 1.Qe2 Kb1?? 2.Kc4 c1=Q+ 3.Kb3 mates. Sadly, **1.Qe2 Ka1!** is a huge improvement which forces a draw: **2.Qd2** (2.Qxc2 stalemate) **2...Kb1 3.Kb4 c1=Q** and White can't win.

In the case of a bishop-pawn, mate is only possible if White has the move immediately after Black promotes his pawn to a Queen, or if the Queen can safely reach one of the specified squares (i.e., c-pawn = a2 or e2, while the f-pawn = h2 or d2). As we've seen (in diagram 262), the Queen on e2 doesn't always ice the win, but getting the Queen to h2 (as in diagram 261) grabs the brass ring and doesn't let go.

Summing Up

Overview

➤ Complex positions can't be solved unless you are firmly trained in endgame basics!

King and Pawn endgames

➤ In a King and pawn vs. King and pawn situation, when the defending side can give up his pawn but take the Opposition, the game is drawn unless the stronger side's pawn is on the 5th rank.

➤ It's clear that, aside from simple race considerations (brought about by both pawns being passed), the real question surrounding King and pawn vs. King and pawn theory is whether or not a pawn can be won. If a pawn does indeed drop, the assessment of the resulting position (which has suddenly transposed into one of our already mastered King and pawn vs. lone King situations) is made by who owns the Opposition.

Rook Endgames

➤ In a Rook and pawn endgame, a "Lucena" with a rook-pawn is only won if the defending King is cut off by four or more files. Another way of putting it is: It's a win if the enemy King is cut off on or beyond the farthest bishop-file.

➤ In general, both sides should strive to get their Rooks behind a passed pawn.

➤ In the case of a passed rook-pawn on the 6th with the defending Rook behind it, the stronger sides King must try and wend its way down the board and find shelter in front of its pawn. When this is going to happen, having the defending Rook behind the passed pawn doesn't quite hold up, so a knowledge of the Vancura Position is necessary.

➤ The Vancura Position doesn't suffice if it's facing any pawn other than a rook-pawn.

⮞ In the case of a Rook and pawn vs. Rook endgame where the defending King is trapped one or more files to the side of the pawn, the result depends on whether or not the stronger side can achieve a Lucena Position. This is determined by the following rules:

- A pawn on the 5th rank or beyond wins if the enemy King is cut off by one file on the Long Side of the board!

- A pawn on the 4th rank wins if the enemy King is cut off by two files. A knight-pawn is an exception and takes three files.

Bishops of Opposite Colors Endgames

⮞ Bishop and two conected pawns vs. Bishop

- Two connected pawns on the 6th rank are winning.

- The correct defensive stance (only valid if both pawns don't make it to the 6th) calls for the defender's King to be in front of the pawns, while the Bishop ties the enemy King down to the defense of its pawn. Ideally, this freezes the pawns since one push allows a total blockade, while the other allows the defender to sacrifice his Bishop for the two remaining pawns.

Fortresses in Bishop Endgames

⮞ Fortresses in Bishop-up endgames are fairly common due to the Bishop's inability to control a whole color complex. These usually occur when the stronger side's rook-pawn or knight-pawn get down to the 6th and/or 7th rank, or if a rook-pawn of the wrong color is lurking on the board. There are *no* fortresses for a bishop-pawn, queen-pawn or king-pawn!

Tests and Solutions

Diagram 263

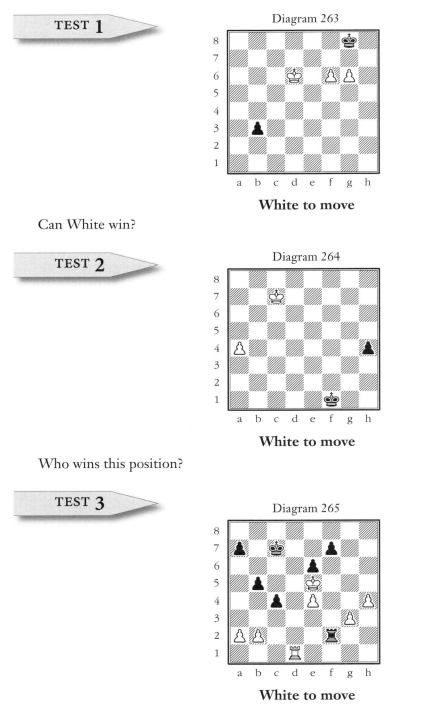

White to move

Can White win?

Diagram 264

White to move

Who wins this position?

Diagram 265

White to move

What's going on?

TEST **4**

Diagram 266

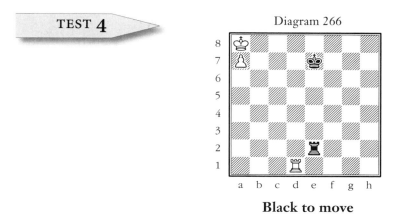

Black to move

Can White win or is this a draw?

TEST **5**

Diagram 267

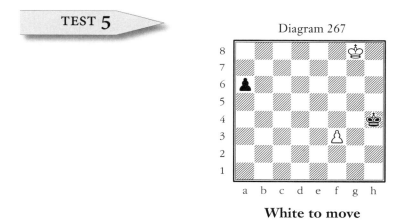

White to move

White appears to be lost. How can he save himself?

TEST **6**

Diagram 268

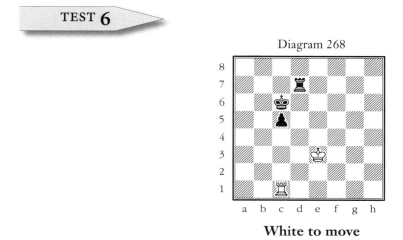

White to move

Consider both 1.Ke2 and 1.Ke4, which is correct?

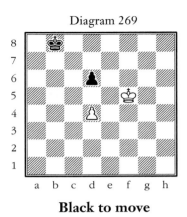

Diagram 269

Black to move

Can Black save himself?

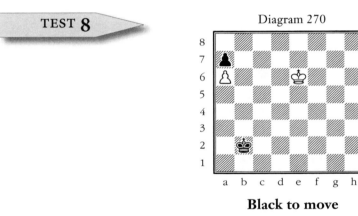

Diagram 270

Black to move

White is targeting the a7-pawn. Can Black save himself?

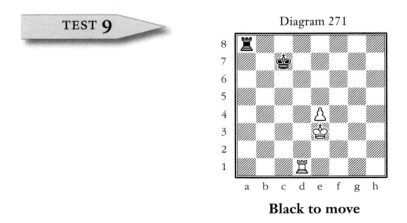

Diagram 271

Black to move

Black has two ways to draw this position. What's the easiest one?

TEST **10**

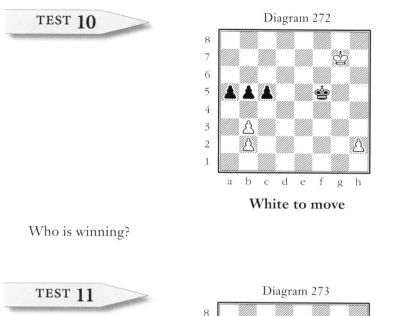

Diagram 272

White to move

Who is winning?

TEST **11**

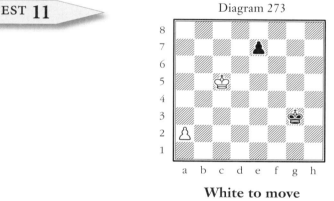

Diagram 273

White to move

How do you assess this position?

TEST **12**

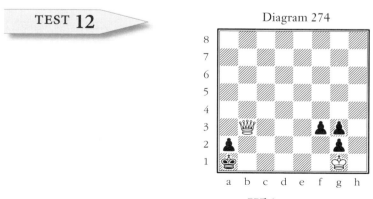

Diagram 274

White to move

What in the world is going on here?

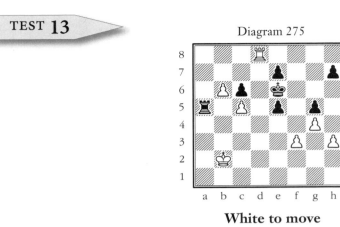

TEST **13**

Diagram 275

White to move

White's clearly better, but can he win?

* * * * *

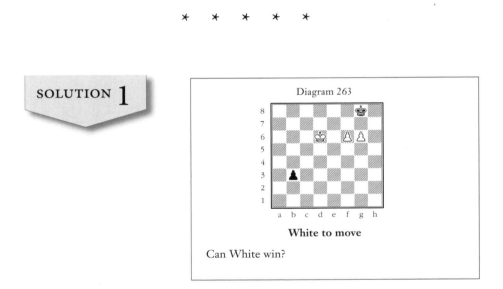

SOLUTION **1**

Diagram 263

White to move

Can White win?

White wins easily after …

1.f7+ Kf8

1…Kg7 2.Ke7 b2 3.f8=Q+.

2.Ke6! b2 3.Kf6 b1=Q 4.g7 mate.

SOLUTION 2

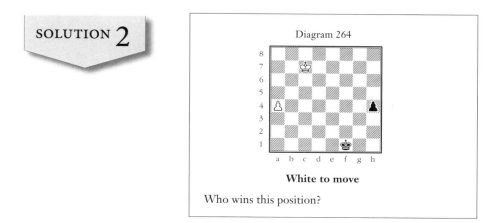

Diagram 264

White to move

Who wins this position?

White can draw: **1.a5 h3 2.a6 h2 3.a7 h1=Q 4.Kb8!**, =.

SOLUTION 3

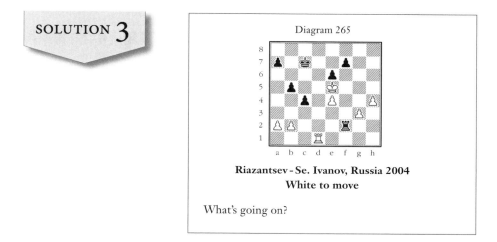

Diagram 265

Riazantsev - Se. Ivanov, Russia 2004
White to move

What's going on?

White has a forced win.

1.Rh1!

By leaping behind the passed pawn ("Rooks belong behind passed pawns."), White turns it into a run away train that will ultimately force the win of the enemy Rook.

1...Rxb2 2.h5 Rd2

2...Rxa2 3.h6 Rd2 4.h7 Rd8 5.h8=Q Rxh8 6.Rxh8 a5 7.Kd4 wins. Anaylsis by Riazantsev.

3.h6 Rd8 4.h7 Rh8 5.Kf6 a5 6.Kxf7

An important move that turns the g-pawn into a passer.

6...b4 7.Kg7 Rd8 8.h8=Q Rxh8 9.Kxh8 b3 10.axb3 cxb3 11.g4 a4 12.Rb1!, 1-0.

SOLUTION 4

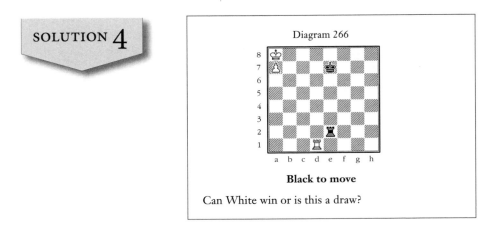

Diagram 266

Black to move

Can White win or is this a draw?

Black draws because his King is only cut off three files from the pawn. To win, White needs to cut the black King off by four or more files!

1...Rb2! (Trapping the white King on a8) **2.Rh1 Kd7 3.Rh8 Kc7 4.Rb8 Rc2 5.Rb7+ Kc8** and White can't free his King. Thus, ½-½.

SOLUTION 5

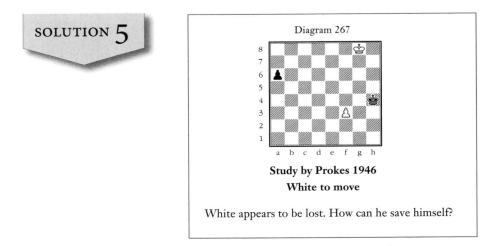

Diagram 267

Study by Prokes 1946
White to move

White appears to be lost. How can he save himself?

1.Kf7

An obvious move that threatens to enter the Square of the a6-pawn (thus stopping it) by Ke6.

1...a5 2.f4!

Not 2.Ke6?? a4 3.f4 a3 4.f5 a2 5.f6 a1=Q 6.f7 Qa3 followed by 7...Qf8.

2...a4

Black also fails to secure victory with 2...Kg4 due to 3.Ke6! Kxf4 (3...a4 4.f5 is a draw since both sides promote) 4.Kd5 and White has entered the a-pawn's square.

3.f5 a3 4.f6 a2 5.Kg8!

An important move since 5.Ke7?? a1=Q 6.f7 Qe5+ 7.Kd7 Qf6 8.Ke8 Qe6+ 9.Kf8 Kg5 lets the black King get too close: 10.Kg7 Qe7 11.Kg8 (11.Kh8 loses to 11...Qf8+, and not 11...Qxf7 stalemate) 11...Kg6 12.f8=N+ (Note that 12.f8=Q fails to 12...Qh7 mate) 12...Kh6, 0-1.

5...a1=Q 6.f7, ½-½.

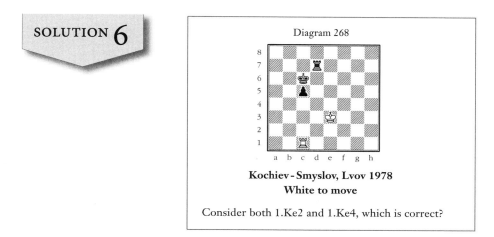

Diagram 268

Kochiev - Smyslov, Lvov 1978
White to move

Consider both 1.Ke2 and 1.Ke4, which is correct?

In the actual game, Kochiev played 1.Ke2?, which loses: 1...Kb5 2.Rb1+ Ka4 3.Rc1 Kb4 4.Rb1+ Ka3 5.Rc1 Rd5! 6.Ke3 Kb2 7.Rc4 Kb3, 0-1. It's interesting to see how even grandmasters sometimes botch these basic theoretical positions!

1.Ke4 is a draw since 1...Rd4+ 2.Ke3 Kb5 3.Rh1 Kb4 4.Rb1+ Ka3 5.Rc1 Rd5 and now 6.Ke4! saves the day. Compare this with the actual game continuation where Ke4 wasn't available.

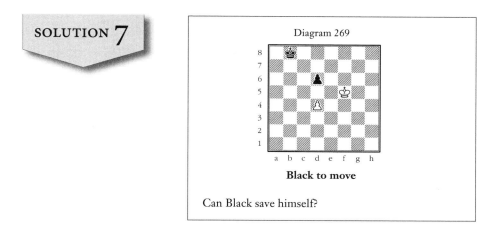

Diagram 269

Black to move

Can Black save himself?

White will win if he is allowed to push his pawn to d5: 1...Kc7?? 2.d5 Kb6 (2...Kd7 3.Kf6 Kd8 4.Ke6 Kc7 5.Ke7 Kc8 6.Kxd6 is also winning) 3.Kf6! (And not 3.Ke6?? Kc5 with a winning Trébuchet for Black!) 3...Kb5 4.Ke7! Kc5 5.Ke6, 1-0.

To prevent white's pawn from reaching the 5th rank, Black must play:

1...d5!

He knows he's losing his pawn, but he also knows he will be able to take the Opposition and make a draw.

2.Ke6 Kc7 3.Kxd5 Kd7, ½-½.

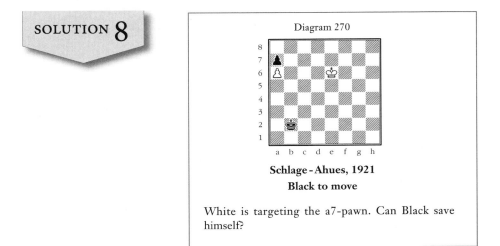

SOLUTION 8

Diagram 270

Schlage - Ahues, 1921
Black to move

White is targeting the a7-pawn. Can Black save himself?

No, Black is quite lost.

1...Kc3 2.Kd5!! wins. (This move was discovered by Maizelis.)

In the actual game, White blundered with 2.Kd6?? and drew after 2...Kd4 3.Kc6 Ke5 4.Kb7 Kd6 5.Kxa7 Kc7, ½-½.

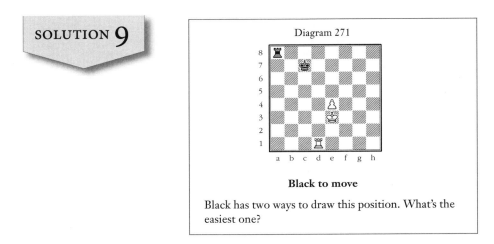

SOLUTION 9

Diagram 271

Black to move

Black has two ways to draw this position. What's the easiest one?

White to move wins by 1.Kf4. Fortunately, Black has the move and is able to improve the position of his King in two fundamentally different ways.

1...Rd8!

Simplest. Black also draws with 1...Kc6 intending to meet 2.Kf4 with 2...Rf8+ 3.Kg5 Re8 4.Kf5 Rf8+ 5.Kg6 Re8 6.Rd4 Kc5!

2.Rxd8

Naturally, 2.Rh1 Kd7 poses no problems for Black, who will get his King in front of the pawn and draw by making use of Philidor's Position.

2...Kxd8 3.Kf4 Ke8!

The only move! Now Black can take the Opposition on any advance by white's King. Losing choices are 3...Kd7?? 4.Kf5 Ke7 5.Ke5, and 3...Kc7 4.Ke5 Kd7 5.Kf6.

4.Kf5

Obviously 4.Ke5 Ke7 and 4.Kg5 Ke7 also give Black the Opposition, while 4.Kg4 Ke7 (and not 4...Kd7?? 5.Kf5) 5.Kf5 Kf7, is equal.

4...Kf7, =.

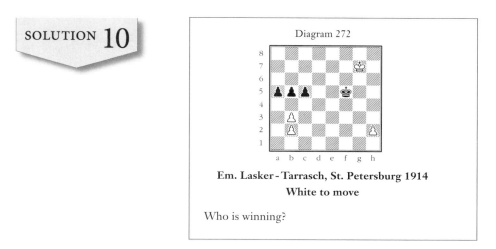

SOLUTION 10

Diagram 272

Em. Lasker - Tarrasch, St. Petersburg 1914

White to move

Who is winning?

A glance might convince us that White is losing, but Lasker found a nice idea that, up to that time, had never been seen before.

1.h4! Kg4 2.Kg6!

This is it! White threatens to promote his pawn, but if it's taken the white King has a faster road to the queenside than black's.

2...Kxh4 3.Kf5

Suddenly it's Black who is fighting for a draw!

3...Kg3 4.Ke4 Kf2 5.Kd5 Ke3 6.Kxc5 Kd3 7.Kxb5 Kc2 8.Kxa5 Kxb3, $\frac{1}{2}$-$\frac{1}{2}$.

SOLUTION 11

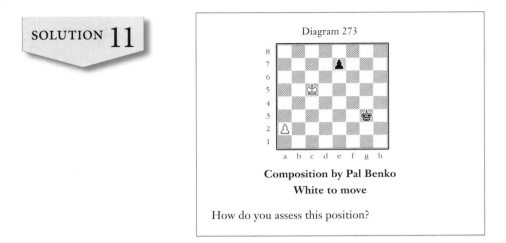

Diagram 273

Composition by Pal Benko

White to move

How do you assess this position?

White wins by forcing the black King on to a square that will allow the a-pawn to promote with check.

1.a4

Not 1.Kd4? Kf4 2.a4 e5+ 3.Kc3 e4 4.a5 e3 5.a6 Kg3! 6.Kd3 Kf2, =.

1...e5 2.a5 e4 3.Kd4 Kf4 4.a6 e3 5.Kd3 Kf3 6.a7 e2 7.a8=Q+, 1-0.

SOLUTION 12

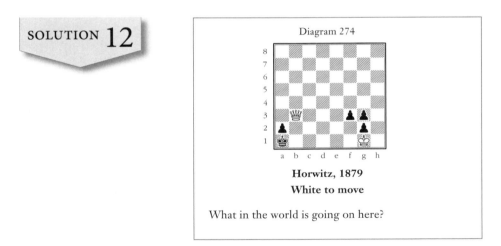

Diagram 274

Horwitz, 1879

White to move

What in the world is going on here?

The problem White faces is not so much his opponent's three kingside pawns, but rather the fact that his King is far from the queenside. This means that if we removed all the kingside pawns, the resulting position is drawn.

The solution is to use the movements of the kingside pawns to get white's King a bit closer, then employ the idea we learned in "A Trick Win in Queen vs. rook-pawn on 7th" (diagram 259) which allows Black to promote his a-pawn, only to find himself in a mating net.

1.Qb6 f2+ 2.Kxg2 f1=Q+ 3.Kxf1 g2+ 4.Ke2 g1=Q 5.Qxg1+ Kb2 6.Kd2 a1=Q 7.Qb6+ Ka3 8.Qa5+ Kb2 9.Qb4+ Ka2 10.Kc2 and mates. Personally I would now give 10…Qc3+ a go, since 11.Qxc3 is stalemate! Of course, 10…Qc3+ 11.Kxc3 forces mate next move.

SOLUTION 13

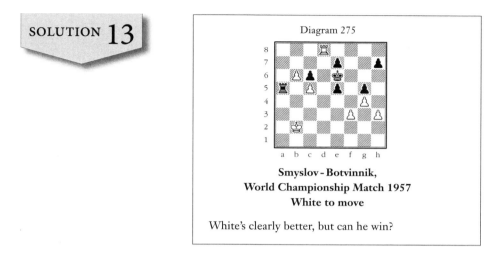

Diagram 275

**Smyslov - Botvinnik,
World Championship Match 1957
White to move**

White's clearly better, but can he win?

White wins by placing his Rook behind his passed pawn. Once he freezes black's Rook on b8, he can then decisively penetrate into black's helpless kingside with his King.

1.Rd3 Ra8 2.Kb3 Ra5 and Black resigned without waiting for a reply. Why? Because black's kingside pawns fall like ripe fruit after 3.Kb4 Rb5+ 4.Kc4 Rb1 5.Rb3 Rc1+ 6.Kd3 Rd1+ 7.Ke3 Rd8 8.b7 Rb8 9.Ke4 Kd7 10.Kf5! Analysis by Botvinnik.

Final Thoughts

Complex Rook endgames are the main focus of this section, and it takes a certain amount of chess strength (i.e., tactical clarity and the ability to absorb complicated patterns) and work ethic to absorb the advanced material presented here. Apparently, you've succeeded in doing so. This not only verifies that you belong in the "A" class, but it also speaks volumes about your dedication to climbing up the rating ladder.

At this point, you could easily rest on your endgame laurels for the rest of your life and never have to back-down to anyone when the final phase of a game is reached. However, why stop here? You've done the vast majority of "grunt-work" and will be surprised to find that the Expert section concentrates more on concepts and making use of the material you already possess than the memorization of alien ideas and rules.

So, when you've recovered from the effort you've just made and feel that it's time to leave the "A" class behind and become an Expert, feel free to open yourself up to the mysteries of Part Seven.

Part Seven

Endgames for Experts (2000–2199)

Contents

Rook Endgames

The Flowchart—Taking a Simple Position Into
  Deeper Water
Rook and Two Connected Passed Pawns vs. Rook
  and Pawn
When a Philidor Goes Bad
Pawns on One Side of the Board
  Rook and Two vs. Rook and One
  Rook and Three vs. Rook and Two
  Rook and Four vs. Rook and Three
**Bishop Endgames (Bishop and Pawn[s] vs. Lone
Bishop of the Same Color)**
Queen Endgames
  Blockade—Queen vs. Rook and Pawn
  Blockade—Queen and Pawn vs. Rook and Two Pawns
Summing Up
Tests and Solutions
Final Thoughts

PART SEVEN—ENDGAMES FOR EXPERTS (2000-2199)

At this point you know enough basics to change your general mode of study. Instead of looking at isolated positions, we will look at more complex situations that are made easy by being firmly schooled in all the foundation endgames. Here you'll be introduced to the concept of solving complicated positions by beginning with a very simple idea (i.e., your previously acquired knowledge), then adding a bit more complexity to it, and adding to it again. This "flow" of information, in essence a *Flowchart*, can be used to deconstruct a surprising amount of endings, no matter how advanced they might appear to be at first glance.

Rook Endgames

Rook endgames are a mystery to most players. The fact is, if you don't know the building blocks of Rook endgames, you won't be able to play any Rook endgame properly. In other words, knowledge is a *must*. Since you're reading this Expert section, you should be well acquainted with the ins-and-outs of basic Rook endgame theory. This will allow you to understand the more complex situations that we'll be addressing here, and also make the concept of the Flowchart rather easy to grasp.

The Flowchart—Taking a Simple Position Into Deeper Water

We will now take a leap into Flowchart mentality—a simple technique that will enable you to turn many complex positions, which at first glance will appear unintelligible, into simple situations that you have already mastered.

The Flowchart mentality is, in reality, a form of transition where you take the game from one situation to another and, perhaps, to yet another! This can mean maneuvering a complex Rook endgame into a basic, well known situation, or it can mean going from one specific kind of endgame to a completely different situation (for example, a Rook and minor piece can turn into a favorable Rook endgame if you exchange the minor pieces, and this can turn into a winning King and pawn endgame if you later exchange the Rooks).

Let's start with the following "confusing" position.

Diagram 276

> **REMEMBER**
>
> A Flowchart is nothing more than a way of using basic knowledge to solve positions that seem extremely complex.

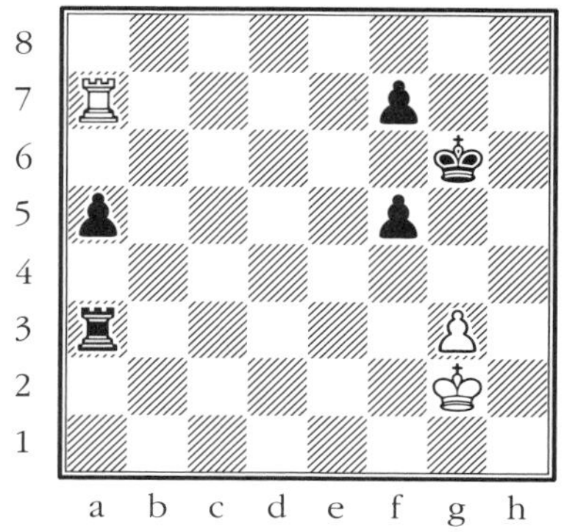

Black to move, can he win?

Compare it with this next one.

Diagram 277

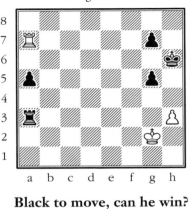

Black to move, can he win?

The average Expert or Master would hazard a guess, but would not be able to definitively figure out either of these positions. We'll return to them when you have the tools to make some educated deductions. And what are these "tools?" Basic building blocks, of course! By this time, you should have dozens of building block positions stored in your head, though we'll add a few more in the pages to come.

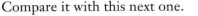

Building Block 1

Diagram 278

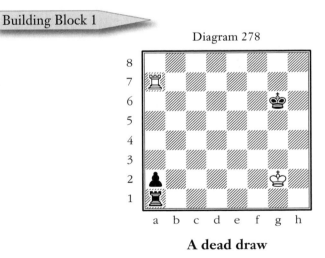

A dead draw

This is a position you already have in your internal "basics" database. As long as white's King stays on h2 or g2, and as long as the Rook remains on the a-file and checks the black King every time it touches its pawn, the game can't be won.

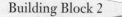

Building Block 2

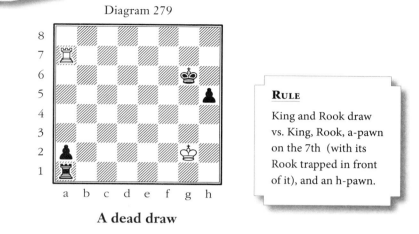

Diagram 279

RULE

King and Rook draw vs. King, Rook, a-pawn on the 7th (with its Rook trapped in front of it), and an h-pawn.

A dead draw

This is new, and should be added to your rapidly growing store of memorized basic positions. Black can't win because the h-pawn isn't able to deprive the white King of both critical squares (it can take away g2, but not h2). Thus:

1...h4 2.Kh2 h3 3.Ra8

And not 3.Kxh3?? Rh1+ followed by a1=Q.

3...Kf5 4.Ra7 Ke4 5.Ra8 Kd3 6.Ra7 Kc2 7.Ra8 Kb3 8.Rb8+ Kc3 9.Ra8, ½-½. Black's King can wander the Earth like Cain, but it can't bother white's King, nor can it help extricate its Rook from the prison on a1.

Building Block 3

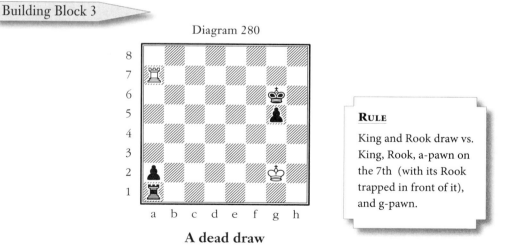

Diagram 280

RULE

King and Rook draw vs. King, Rook, a-pawn on the 7th (with its Rook trapped in front of it), and g-pawn.

A dead draw

Another new position. This is also drawn because the pawn can take the h2-square away from white's King, but not g2.

1...g4 2.Ra8 g3 3.Ra7

Naturally, moves like 3.Ra6+ are also more than sufficient to split the point.

3...Kf5 4.Ra8 Kf4 5.Ra7, ½-½. Black can't come close to winning.

Building Block 4

Diagram 281

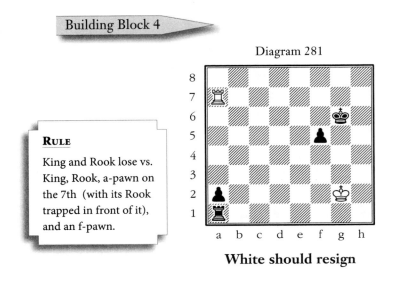

RULE

King and Rook lose vs. King, Rook, a-pawn on the 7th (with its Rook trapped in front of it), and an f-pawn.

White should resign

New and very important! The win is suddenly effortless since the f-pawn will successfully pull white's King off of both critical squares on h2 and g2. In fact, Black doesn't even need to use his King to claim to full point.

1...f4 2.Ra8

Checking by 2.Ra6+ doesn't accomplish anything since black's King would just march towards the Rook (e.g., 2...Kf7 3.Ra7+ Ke6 4.Ra6+ Kd7 5.Ra7+ Kc6 6.Ra6+ Kb7 and the checks are history) and then continue pushing the f-pawn once the checks ended.

2...f3+!, 0-1. White's choices are 3.Kh2 f2 when f1=Q can't be prevented, 3.Kxf3 Rf1+ 4.Kg2 a1=Q, or 3.Kf2 Rh1! 4.Rxa2 Rh2+ 5.Kxf3 Rxa2.

Building Block 5

Diagram 282

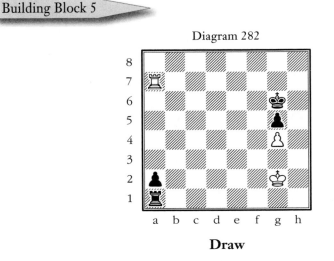

Draw

This must be a draw since even if Black manages to win the g4-pawn, it takes us back to the dead drawn position in Building Block 3.

Building Block 6

Diagram 283

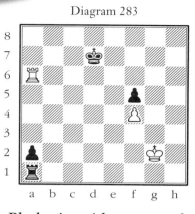

Black wins with accurate play

Since building block four was an easy win for Black, it's clear that the same holds true here *if* Black can win the f4-pawn. The winning method is simple and instructive.

1...Kc7

If Black wants to make contact with the f4-pawn, he must break through the 6th rank.

2.Kh2 Kb7 3.Ra3 Kb6 4.Kg2 Kb5 5.Ra8 Kb4 6.Ra7 Kc3 7.Ra5 Kd3

Of course, Black has no fear of 8.Rxf5 since that allows the black Rook to safely leave its prison on a1: 8...Rb1 and 9...a1=Q.

8.Ra8 Ke4!

Avoiding 8...Ke3 9.Ra4 when a key position has occurred:

Diagram 284

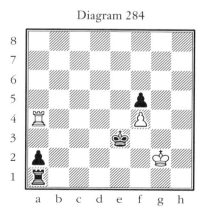

Black wants White to move here!

Black to move can't force White to implode, so he would have to dance around a bit until this same position is reached with White to move: 9...Kd3 10.Kh2 (10.Ra8 Ke4! transposes to our main line) 10...Ke2 (threatens 11...Kf2 and/or

11...Kf3) 11.Kg2 Ke3 reaching the diagrammed position with White to move and winning due to zugszwang, as explained in our main line.

9.Ra4+ Ke3

Zugzwang! White is forced to drop his pawn or move his King to a poor square.

10.Kh2 Kf3 and White must give up the pawn since 11.Kh3?? Rh1 is mate. After 11.Ra8 Kxf4 we are back to building block four.

These six building block positions should give you enough Flowchart knowledge to make solving our original two "problems" possible. So let's take another look.

Diagram 285

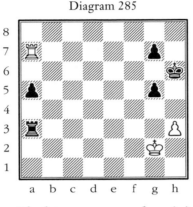

Black to move, can he win?

A quick guess would tell us that Black can't win because if he pushes his a-pawn to a2 and trades the g5-pawn for white's h3-pawn, the resulting two extra pawn position is drawn, as shown in building block three.

Diagram 286

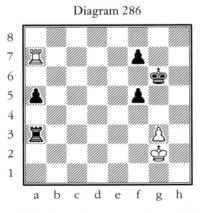

Black to move, can he win?

This position, though, seems very winnable because we can see a clear "light at the end of the tunnel." Using building block four as our guidepost, we know that pushing the a-pawn to a2 (which freezes the white King) and then exchanging the f5-pawn for the g3-pawn would be game over.

Furthermore, building block six showed us that we would win the position even if we got the a-pawn to a2 and dragged white's g-pawn to f4. Once we have a goal position in mind, coming up with the actual moves that allow us to reach our dream position is rather easy:

1...a4

Black immediately rushes his pawn to a2, knowing that this will leave the white King shackled to the h2- and g2-squares.

2.Kf2 Ra1 3.Kf3 a3 4.Kg2

And not 4.Kf4?? a2 when White can't stop a back rank check followed by the promotion of the a-pawn.

4...a2

Black's first goal is accomplished! White's King is now stuck on h2 and g2. If you are not completely familiar with this, the material in Part Six should refresh your memory.

5.Kh2 f4! 6.gxf4 f5! and we've reached building block six, which we should now know is a basic win for Black.

We'll be looking at other complex situations in Part Seven where Flowcharts prove useful, but all of them are only comprehensible if you've retained the lessons learned in the first six parts of this book.

Rook and Two Connected Passed Pawns vs. Rook and Pawn

Positions featuring two passed pawns vs. one enemy passed pawn are usually winning for the two pawns. Previous knowledge is important here, too, since many positions are won by following basic rules, and by exchanging a pair of pawns and creating a winning Rook and one vs. Rook position.

Diagram 287

White wins

1.Kf2

The King *must* take part in this battle!

1...Kf5 2.Kf3 g5 3.Re8

White's Rook prepares to place itself behind the enemy passed pawn (as discussed in Part Six).

3...Rb1 4.Rf8+ Ke6 5.Ke4

White isn't too concerned with black's pawn. Instead, he continues to bring his own King up so it can support his two passers.

5...Re1+ 6.Kd3 Rd1+

The immediate 6...g4 loses to 7.Re8+ followed by 8.Rxe1.

7.Kc4 g4 8.Kc5

Optimizing the position of white's King. He's finally ready to start moving his own pawns forward. Please note: he will only do so *after* the King gets into a position to support them.

8...g3 9.Rg8

Placing the Rook behind black's passed pawn and stopping it from dashing to g1.

9...Rg1 10.c4

At last!

10...g2 11.d5+ Kd7 12.Rg7+ Ke8

Diagram 288

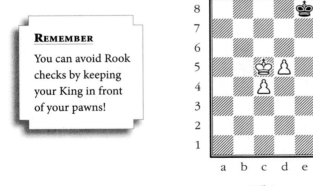

White to move

13.Kd6

White heads for a winning Rook and pawn vs. Rook endgame. Even stronger is 13.d6 Kf8 18.Rg4 Kf7 15.Kc6 Rc1 16.d7, 1-0. However, the play after 13.Kd6 is more instructive.

13...Rc1

13...Kf8 14.Rg4 Rc1 15.Rxg2 Rxc4 16.Kd7 would transpose into our main line.

14.Rg8+

This check forces black's King away from e8 and thus gives white's King access to the d7-square.

14...Kf7 15.Rxg2 Rxc4 16.Kd7

White is heading for a Lucena Position (explored in Part Four). Black tries to resist, but his position is too far gone.

16...Ra4 17.Rf2+

Trapping black's King away from the action (see Part Four).

17...Kg7 18.d6 Ra7+

Poor Black doesn't even have Checking Distance (explained in Part Six).

19.Kc6 Ra6+ 20.Kc7 Ra7+ 21.Kb6 Rd7 22.Kc6, 1-0.

When a Philidor Goes Bad

In Part Four we explored one of the most important Rook endgames one can know: the Philidor Position. We saw that it offers the key to defending a pawn down Rook and pawn versus Rook endgame. However, what if a Philidor goes bad and one isn't allowed to use the main "dominate the rank and stop the enemy King from advancing" idea?

Diagram 289

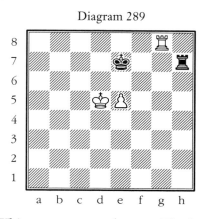

White to move and cause Black pain

We used this same diagram in Part Four, though in that case we gave Black the move. This allowed him to end things right away by 1...Rh6 when White can't make any progress. However, what if White has the move? In that case

1.Rg6! prevents the key defensive maneuver and forces Black to adopt a "plan B." Of course, if you don't know "plan B" off the top of your head, and if you don't remember our lessons about the Philidor Position (Part Four), the Lucena Position (Part Four), Checking Distance (Part Six) and the Short and Long Side of the board (Part Six), then you are, to put it mildly, up the creek without a paddle.

Let's play a few moves so you can see how knowledge of the Rook endgame basics (as listed above), and the Flowchart they allow you to create, will make your life easy.

1.Rg6! Kd7

Black seems unimpressed. Isn't his King safe?

2.Ra6!

So black's King wasn't safe after all. Now the threat of Ra7+ forces a reaction.

2...Rh1

Best.

REMEMBER

If you intend to check the enemy King, try to put as much distance between your Rook and his King as possible (i.e., Checking Distance).

We'll soon see why this is important.

3.Ra7+ Ke8 4.Kd6!

Diagram 290

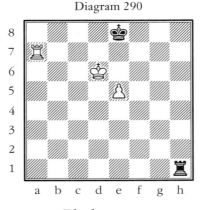

Black to move
The start of a multi-question "test"

Our key position. This is where you must have a preexisting knowledge of the saving idea and/or a firm understanding of the basics that enable you to make sense of it, or you'll almost certainly go down in flames. Since 4...Rh6+?

5.e6 is clearly horrible, and 4...Rd1+? 5.Ke6 Kf8 (in Part Four, we saw that laying passively on the back rank via 5...Rd8 fails to 6.Rh7) 6.Ra8+ Kg7 7.Ke7 has White rushing towards the creation of a Lucena, Black is forced to pass a multi-question test to survive!

> **REMEMBER**
>
> White is trying to create a Lucena Position (which would win).
> Black is trying to create a Philidor (which would draw).

4...Re1!

Question one: correct! What does this do? 4...Re1 makes it hard for White to advance his pawn, as you'll see in a moment.

5.Ra8+ Kf7

The point of 4...Re1 is now clear: White can't play 6.e6+ due to 6...Rxe6+. Since Black now threatens to make an immediate draw via 6...Rd1+, White must step back and move to the previous position.

6.Ra7+ Ke8 7.Ke6

Diagram 291

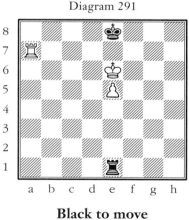

Black to move
Part two of the "test"

The threat isn't subtle—Black must take immediate measures against Ra8 mate.

7...Kf8!

This is known as going to the Short Side (explored in Part Six). The idea is that Black is leaving far more distance on the left for future lateral checks with his Rook (without his King getting in the way). Remember: when you check a King with your Rook, you always like to have as much distance between your Rook and the enemy King as possible.

8.Ra8+ Kg7 9.Kd6

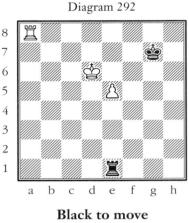

Diagram 292

Black to move
Part three of the "test"

9...Kf7!

Again showing the strength of 4...Re1. Now the e-pawn is again stuck and ...Rd1+ is threatened, chasing the white King away from the action. Far worse was 9...Rd1+? 10.Ke7 when White is again getting perilously close to setting up a Lucena Position (the defender must avoid this at all costs!).

10.Ra7+

White repeats the position again and sets up a completely different kind of test for his opponent.

10...Ke8 11.Ke6 Kf8 12.Ra8+ Kg7

We've been here before, but now White tries a different idea.

13.Re8

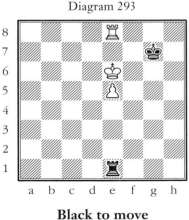

Diagram 293

Black to move
Part four of the "test"

Now "passing" doesn't work: 13...Re2? 14.Kd7! when 14...Kf7 fails to the simple 15.e6+, while 14...Rd2+ 15.Ke7 has allowed White to make progress. How can Black defend?

13...Ra1!

After 13...Ra1 we can see long distance checking at work. Black threatens to set up a pure, easily drawn Philidor Position by 14...Ra6+ 15.Kf5 Kf7 and the game is as good as over.

14.Rd8

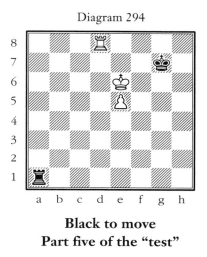

Diagram 294

Black to move
Part five of the "test"

White is hoping for 14...Ra6+ 15.Rd6. But Black doesn't have to be so accommodating.

14...Re1!

Back to our key idea! White can't make progress and, since Black has demonstrated his understanding of this endgame, the game can be agreed drawn.

Pawns on One Side of the Board

In the vast majority of endgames, the defender's drawing chances are improved with every pawn trade. This is certainly the case of a Rook endgame where one side has an extra pawn, but all the pawns are situated on the same side of the board. The defensive ideas are based on:

➤ Trade as many pawns as possible (unless striving for a particular pawn exchange severely weakens your pawn formation).

➤ Keep the Rook as active as possible (preferably tying the defender's King down to the defense of its pawns).

➤ Keep trading down until you end up with a Philidor position, which we know from experience is a simple draw.

Rook and Two vs. Rook and One

In positions where the two vs. one pawn difference is on one side of the board, *the game is usually drawn if the stronger side doesn't have a passed pawn*. Nevertheless, even in non-passed pawn situations, like e- and f- vs. f-pawn, the defense can still be difficult in over-the-board practice (just because something is a theoretical draw doesn't mean it's easy to achieve!). The simplest two vs. one situation to draw is King, Rook, and h- and g-pawns vs. King, Rook, and g-pawn. However, even here good players have been known to botch the defense and go down in flames.

Unfortunately, in cases where one side *does* have a passed pawn, these endgames often prove far more complex than one might imagine. For example, if one side has a passed pawn, as in e- & f- vs. g-pawn, the stronger side has serious winning chances. There are several reasons for this:

➤ The stronger side's King will enjoy more cover than its counterpart.

➤ The stronger side can use his greater force to push the opponent back and, ideally, win the defender's remaining pawn.

➤ The stronger side can push his pawns to the 5th and/or 6th rank, exchange a pair of pawns, and end up with a favorable King, Rook and pawn vs. King and Rook situation where the weaker side hasn't been allowed to create his ideal defensive setup.

➤ The passed pawn will always be threatening to "go somewhere," forcing the defender to deal with that on top of everything else.

Personally, I've met very few players under 2400 who have mastered these different two vs. one on the same side of the board situations. And why should they? The defensive technique is hard to quantify, and I find that most of the positions need heaping doses of common sense, care, accurate calculation, and a good knowledge of more basic positions to draw. As a result, I'll leave it to the reader to study these complex situations if and when he feels the need to do so—personally, I strongly feel that such in-depth study of complex specifics is a waste of time for players in the Expert and even low Master class.

Having said that, we can still acquire a basic understanding of many two vs. one situations by making use of a simple defensive Flowchart:

- Don't allow a losing Rook and one vs. Rook position to occur. This usually means that the defending King gets trapped on the side and can no longer prevent a Lucena from materializing, or it can mean that the defending Rook is passively placed.

- Trade a pawn and get a Philidor Position.

- King and pawn endgames might occur. You'll need to make occasional use of your of knowledge of Trébuchet (Part Four) if you're going to do well in cases like this.

- You'll need to know the drawing technique for failed Philidor positions (found in Part Seven).

Let's take the following position and let it show us how all these things might occur from a "simple" Rook and two vs. Rook and one endgame.

Diagram 295

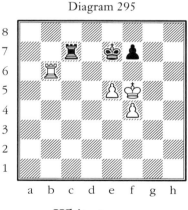

White to move

1.Kg5

This frees the f4-pawn and allows it to advance. Once it gets to f5, it will put the big squeeze on black's King.

1...Rc5

An important move that intends to chop off e5 if the f4-pawn advances! Trying to activate this Rook so it can check from a distance doesn't work: 1...Rc1?? (This position occurred in Hanisch - Steibl, 1996 when White showed his confusion with 2.Ra6?, failing to take advantage of black's error. Instead, White can force a win.) 2.Rb7+ Ke8 3.f5 Rh1 (Also hopeless is 3…Rc5 4.Kf6 Rc6+ 5.e6 fxe6 6.fxe6 when 6…Rc8 7.Rh7 wins thanks to black's passive Rook—you can find a study of this concept in Part Four) 4.Rb8+ Ke7 5.f6+ Kd7 6.Rf8 Rh7 (This is one ugly Rook, but how else can Black defend the f7-pawn? 6…Ke6 7.Re8+ Kd5 8.e6! is certainly no improvement) 7.Kg4! (This creates a zugzwang since any black Rook move allows Rxf7 while any black King move allows Re8 followed by Re7) 7…Kc7 8.Re8 when Re7 followed by e6 is completely decisive.

2.Rb7+

In Markus – Lenhardt, Poland 1993, White gave Black a chance to move off the rank by 2.Ra6 and only checked after 2…Rb5 3.Ra7+, when the game was agreed drawn. Evidently, White didn't realize that there was still a lot of tricky chess to be played, though perhaps the fact that it was already move 91 and rigor mortis was beginning to set in had something to do with the somewhat hasty peace offering.

2…Kf8!

2…Ke6?? 3.f5+! Kxe5 4.Re7+ Kd6 5.Rxf7 leads to a winning Rook and pawn vs. Rook position since black's King can no longer get in front of the pawn.

3.f5

3.Kh6 Rc6+ 4.Kh7 f6 lets Black trade a pawn in favorable circumstances (i.e., white's King is pathetically off to the side) and draws easily.

3…Rxe5 4.Kf6 Re1

Diagram 296

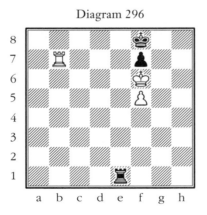

We're about to enter familiar territory

5.Rxf7+

The King and pawn endgame after 5.Rb8+ Re8 6.Rxe8+ is nothing for White: 6…Kxe8 7.Kg7 (7.Ke5 Ke7 8.f6+ Kd7 9.Kd5 Kc7, =) 7…Ke7 8.f6+?? (Suicide. The sane 8.Kg8 Kf6 9.Kf8 draws) 8…Ke6 and suddenly Black finds himself with a winning Trébuchet (Part Four).

5...Kg8 6.Rg7+ Kh8 7.Rb7 Rf1!

This key idea (it ties the white King to the defense of its pawn and also prevents the pawn's advance after 8.Rb8+ Kh7) in the "Philidor gone bad" situation was looked at earlier in Part Seven.

Though I would expect the reader to know this position (since it was explored earlier in this section), I will give the remaining moves to push the defensive technique home.

8.Ke6

Threatening 9.f6. Note that 8.Kg6 Rg1+ 9.Kf6 (9.Kf7?? Rg7+) 9...Rf1! gets White nowhere.

8...Kg8 9.Kf6

9.f6 Re1+ ends white's hopes.

9...Rf2 10.Rb8+ Kh7 11.Rf8

Threatening 12.Ke7 when 12...Kg7 13.f6+ and 12...Re2+ 13.Kf7 would both make White happy.

11...Ra2!

Creating lots of Checking Distance and threatening to enter a dead drawn Philidor Position by 12...Ra6+ 13.Kg5 Kg7.

12.Re8

Intending to meet 12...Ra6+ with 13.Re6.

12...Rf2!, ½-½. White can't make any progress.

We've seen that the stronger side's chances (in a Rook and two vs. Rook and one) are based on pushing his pawns to the 5th rank, which creates a squeeze against the defending King and pressure against the weaker side's final pawn.

With that in mind, the defender can't wait passively for his opponent to tighten the screws. The next position is a very basic example of this.

Diagram 297

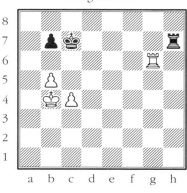

Black to move and draw

Waiting around by 1...Rf7?? runs into 2.c5 when Black begins to get that, "I'm being squeezed" feeling. Fortunately, after the correct **1...b6** White has no winning chances at all (2.Rc6+ Kb7).

Another hopelessly drawn position can be seen in diagram 298.

Diagram 298

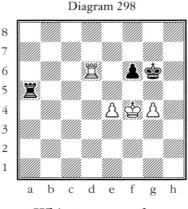

White to move, draw

The problem White faces is that even if he succeeds in pushing his g-pawn and exchanging it for black's f-pawn, a drawn Philidor Position would result. Nevertheless, that's the only plan White has.

1.Rd5

Otherwise Black just moves his Rook back and forth along the 5th rank.

1...Ra4

You should know that trading Rooks would lead to an easily won King and pawn vs. King position for White thanks to the lessons in Parts Three and Four: 1...Rxd5?? 2.exd5 Kf7 3.Kf5 Ke7 4.d6+! (sacrificing the outside passed pawn for the unit on f6) 4...Kf7 5.d7 (White insists!) 5...Ke7 6.d8=Q+ Kxd8 7.Kxf6 Ke8 8.Kg7, 1-0.

The move 1...Ra4 pins the e-pawn and leaves White with no useful way to improve his position.

2.g5 fxg5+ 3.Rxg5+ Kf6 and Black will get a Philidor Position (Part Four) or, if things get out of hand, a Philidor Gone Bad (Part Seven), either of which are easy draws.

Rook and Three vs. Rook and Two

This common endgame is also a draw if Black has prevented white's pawns from eating up too much space (the space-gaining pawns would result in black's King being pushed back and his pawns becoming vulnerable).

Diagram 299

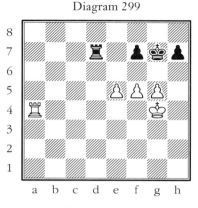

White to move
Black's worst nightmare

Black is doomed because white's pawns are far too strong. Usually this kind of debacle is caused by passive defensive play.

1.Kh5

Preventing …Kg6 when f5-f6 is played.

1…Rd8

White threatened a back rank mate after f5-f6, so Black was compelled to prevent this with his Rook.

2.f6+ Kg8 3.Kh6 Rb8

Black is helpless since any Rook move off the back rank allows mate by Ra8.

4.Ra7

Threatening 5.e6! fxe6 6.Rxh7 when Black should quietly resign.

4…Re8

"I stopped it," thinks Black. Alas, he's wrong.

5.e6!, 1-0. Black had no wish to experience 5…Rxe6 6.Ra8+, nor 5…fxe6 6.f7+, which picks up black's Rook.

> **USEFUL ADVICE**
>
> Don't play passively and let the superior side's pawns march down the board and eat up every bit of space!

Diagram 300

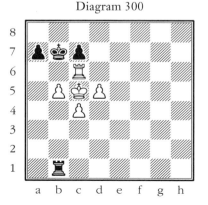

White wins thanks to the power of his pawns

White has achieved (in diagram 300) a dominant pawn position and can now force a win by mixing two plans:

➤ Moving the King and Rook out of the way and then playing for c4-c5-c6.

➤ Placing the Rook on the 7th rank, threatening to take advantage of the pinned c-pawn by d5-d6.

1.Re6

It's important to move to the e-file since in some lines when White plays Kc6, a check along the 6th rank can be met by the white Rook returning to e6 (where it's defended by the d-pawn).

1...Rc1

Forced, since something like 1...Rb2 runs into 2.Re7 (threatening d6) 2...Kb8 3.Kc6 when it's all over.

2.Re8!

This forces the black Rook to step up to c2 or c3 when there won't be suffi-cient Checking Distance (explained in Part Six) to bother the white King when it moves off of the c5-square.

2...Rc2

And not 2...Rg1 3.Re7 (threatening d6) 3...Kb8 4.Kc6 Rg6+ 5.Re6 Rg8 6.c5 (Once again, the pawns roll Black off the board) 6...Rd8 (On 6...Rh8, White wins by 7.Kd7—the idea is to trade Rooks by Re8—7...Rh7+ 8.Re7 Rh5 9.Re8+ Kb7 10.c6+ Kb6 11.Rb8+ followed by Kxc7) 7.Re7 Rc8 8.Rh7 and Black loses the c-pawn.

Also of importance is 2...a6 (Trying to exchange pawns, but it's too late for this to help!) 3.bxa6+ Kxa6 4.Rb8 (trapping the enemy King away from the ac-tion) when the threat of Rb4 followed by Kc6 is decisive.

3.Re1!

Preparing to pull the white King away from c5. Now the black Rook doesn't have access to the 1st rank, which means it won't be able to gain serious Check-ing Distance.

3...Rc3

We've already seen that moves like 3...Rh2 fail to 4.Re7.

4.Kd4 Rc2 5.Kd3

Avoiding the annoyance of 5.f5 Rd2+.

5...Rh2

5...Rb2 doesn't help due to 6.Kc3.

6.c5

Diagram 301

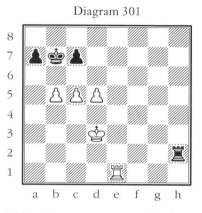

White's pawns eat up the board

Success! White's pawns have achieved their dream positions.

6...Rh3+

Black doesn't fare any better with 6...Rb2 7.Re7 Rxb5 8.Kc4 Rb1 9.d6 Rc1+ 10.Kd5 Rd1+ 11.Ke6 Re1+ 12.Kf7 Rf1+ 13.Ke8, 1-0.

7.Kd4 Rh4+ 8.Re4 Rh7 9.Re8 Rh4+ 10.Kc3 Rh5

10...Rh3+ 11.Kb4 Rh4+ 12.Ka5 only helps White.

11.Kb4!

11.Rd8 a6 is less forcing.

11...a5+!

11...Rxd5?? 12.c6+ Kb6 13.Rb8 mate.

12.Kxa5 Rxd5 13.c6+ Ka7 14.Re7!

Giving black's King a bit of room and avoiding 14.Rc8?? Rxb5+! 15.Kxb5 stalemate.

14...Kb8 15.Ka6 Rd8 16.b6! Rc8

No better is 16...cxb6 17.c7+.

After 16...Rc8 both 17.b7 and 17.Rd7 cxb6 18.Kxb6 win easily (this position with Black having a passive Rook was examined in Part Four).

Clearly, the defender can't allow his opponent to march his pawns down the board in this fashion. However, *by strategically placing the black pawns so that any white advance leads to soothing exchanges*, the game can usually be saved without too much difficulty.

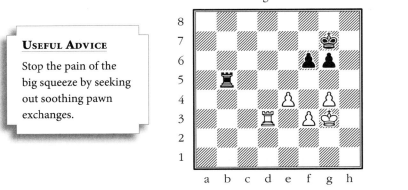

Diagram 302

Black to move

White hopes to play f3-f4, gaining space and putting his pawns into aggressive motion. Black's simplest response to this threat is:

1...g5!

Now any pawn advance leads to a trade and an easily drawn 2 vs. 1 position.

2.Rd5

Trying to coax Black into the exchange.

2...Rb3

Refusing to bite. Instead Black follows the usual formula: *Keep the Rook active by using it to pin and tie down white's King to its pawns.*

3.e5 fxe5 4.Rxe5 Kf6 5.Ra5 Kg6 6.Ra6+ Kg7 and white's position can't be improved since any swap of the f-pawn for black's g-pawn leads to a dead drawn Philidor Position.

Rook and Four vs. Rook and Three

In this endgame the defender has the following fears:

▶ The stronger side's pawns will create the kind of big squeeze we've seen in our Rook and Three vs. Rook and Two examples.

▶ A transposition to a poor Rook and Three vs. Rook and Two or Rook and Two vs. Rook and one will occur.

Fortunately, being forewarned is being forearmed—it's clear that the defender must favorably exchange pawns whenever possible, while also being careful to prevent the stronger side's pawns from swarming down the board. This "swarming" should be stopped in two ways:

- Use your own pawns to stop the enemy's.

- Use your Rook to tie the enemy King to the defense of its pawns.

Diagram 303

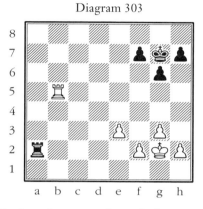

Having the move here is important!

This is a typical basic starting position for Rook and Four vs. Rook and Three. One might think that having the move wouldn't be that important, but this isn't the case. Black to move would rush to play 1...h5!. This key move stops white's pawns from expanding (no big squeeze!) since h3 followed by g4 would allow a well-received pawn trade.

With this in mind, it's clear that, if White had the move, he would play 1.g4!, stopping ...h5 and ...f5 (White would capture and leave Black with a shattered pawn formation) and preparing the squeeze by Kg3, h4 and perhaps h5. This doesn't mean that White is winning after 1.g4, but black's defensive chore would be considerably more difficult.

Diagram 304

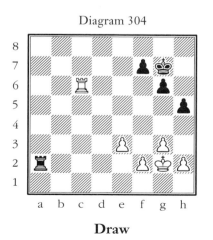

RULE

In this kind of 4 vs. 3 Rook endgame ...h7-h5, whch stops White from playing the space gaining/ weakness fixing g3-g4, is a huge accomplishment!

Draw

Black has managed to get in the extremely useful …h7-h5 advance. He should now draw easily by following our basic formula:

▶ Exchange pawns.

▶ Use the Rook to tie white's King down to the defense of its pawns.

One possible continuation might be:

1.h3 Rb2

The Rook is happy to stay on the f2-pawn, where it keeps the white King under control.

2.g4 hxg4

And trading a pair of pawns is definitely a part of black's plans!

3.hxg4 g5!

Telling White that any future advance of the f-pawn will lead to even more pawn exchanges. Play now enters areas we've already explored. Rook and Three vs. Rook and Two, Rook and Two vs. Rook and One, and even Philidor and "Philidor gone bad" situations. For example:

4.Rc3

Black would meet 4.Kg3 with 4…Rb3, continuing to annoy White with pins. Seeing that he has to allow another exchange of pawns after f2-f4, White hopes to recapture on f4 with his e-pawn since split e- and g- vs. f-pawn offers no chances at all.

4…f6 5.Kg3 Kg6 6.f4 gxf4+ 7.exf4

As stated earlier, accepting split pawns by 7.Kxf4 doesn't give White any hope of victory.

7…Rb1

It's a good idea to keep the Rook as active as possible. This move creates a bit of Checking Distance, and sets up some checks on the 1st rank.

8.Rc7

Preparing the advanced of the f5-pawn. The immediate 8.f5+ Kg5 is clearly a bad idea, while 8.Kh4 gets nowhere fast after 8…Rh1+.

8…Rg1+ 9.Kh3 Rh1+ 10.Kg2 Ra1

Intending to incarcerate white's King by 11…Ra3.

11.f5+ Kg5 13.Rg7+ Kf4, ½-½.

That was easy, but even if White manages to trick Black into a worse case scenario, knowledge of the trusty "Philidor gone bad" drawing formula should still save the day.

Diagram 305

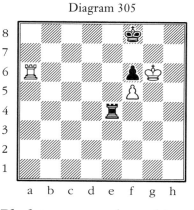

Black to move and save himself

If you imagine this coming from a four vs. three situation (chopped down to a three vs. two and finally two vs. one), it's clear that White has made real progress. In fact, one can imagine Black panicking here and going down in multi-colored flames: 1...Re8?? 2.Kxf6 Kg8 3.Kg6 Rc8 4.f6 with an easy win thanks to the passive black Rook as seen in Part Four.

Fortunately, if you studiously learned the lessons in the order given, you'll be aware of the "Philidor gone bad" formula and, without hesitation, toss your Rook behind white's (soon to be) passed f-pawn.

1...Rf4!

This isn't ideal since we'd prefer the Rook on f1 (Checking Distance). However, it turns out that this still allows Black to draw via his usual "Philidor gone bad" techniques.

2.Kxf6

Clearly, 2.Ra8+ Ke7 only helps Black. Also ineffective is 2.Ra7 Rf1 with a position explored earlier in Part Seven. In case of 2.Rxf6+ Kg8 3.Ra6 Rg4+ 4.Kf6 Rf4, we end up in the same position that occurs after 2.Kxf6.

2...Kg8!

Going to the Short Side of the board so, in some lines, black's Rook can have Checking Distance on the side.

3.Ra8+

Nothing is changed by 3.Ra7 Rf1, while 3.Ke6 Re4+ 4.Kf6 Rf4 and 3.Kg6 Rg4+ 4.Kf6 Rf4 also achieve nothing.

3...Kh7 4.Ke6

Or 3.Rf8 Ra4! (Here's that Checking Distance I mentioned a moment ago) 4.Re8 Rf4!, =.

4...Kg7 and White can't make progress.

We've seen that, in a Rook and four vs. Rook and three, exchanging pawns is something the defender loves to see. That leaves the stronger side with only one other idea: he needs to avoid trades and try and gain some space by pushing his center pawn up the board. This is by far the more dangerous plan and, even though it is still a draw, it's worth avoiding by making use of the following defensive setup.

Diagram 306

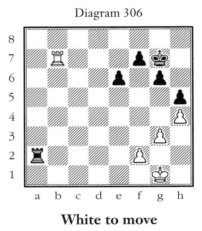

White to move

Black threatens to make things difficult for White with 1...e5 when White can draw by 2.Rb6 (keeping black's King at bay) but it's complicated and far beyond what the student needs to know at this stage of his endgame training.

However, knowing that such positions are dangerous is important, and this knowledge should frighten the defender so much that he goes out of his way to avoid the advance of the e-pawn. Thus the move 1.f4! and the resulting defensive posture has proven remarkably effective.

Diagram 307

Uncrackable

The f-pawn stops black's e-pawn in its tracks while the white Rook ties black's King to its pawn on f7. Since an attack on g3 via 1...Ra3 can be comfortably met by 2.Kf2, Black is forced to "go for the gusto" with:

1...Kf6 2.Rc7 Kf5

Otherwise White would continue to shuffle his Rook back and forth along the 7th rank.

3.Rxf7+ Kg4 4.Rf6 Kxg3 5.Rxg6+ Kxf4 6.Rxe6 Kg3 7.Re3+ with a hope-lessly drawn position.

Bishop Endgames
(Bishop and Pawn[s] vs. Lone Bishop of the Same Color)

We've looked at Bishop of opposite color endgames, but what happens if the Bishops are of the same color? Where the presence of opposite colored Bishops gives the defender hope of drawing, same-colored Bishops usually guarantee the side with the extra pawn(s) serious winning chances.

Diagram 308

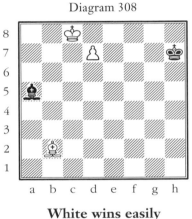

White wins easily

When up a pawn (with no other pawns remaining), the stronger side has winning chances if the pawn is advanced and if the defending King isn't able to get in front of it. In general, a situation will often be reached where the defending Bishop is preventing the pawn from advancing (an immediate draw will result if it can sacrifice itself for the last pawn). The stronger side can only win if his own Bishop can block the diagonal of the defending Bishop. Diagram 308 offers a simplistic example of this.

1.Be5 Kg6 2.Bc7, 1-0.

Even if the weaker side's Bishop is on the longer diagonal (d8-h4 instead of d8-a5, as in the following position) the game is still "in the bag."

In diagram 309 the black Bishop's control of the h4-d8 diagonal makes things a bit harder for White, but black's cause is still hopeless.

Diagram 309

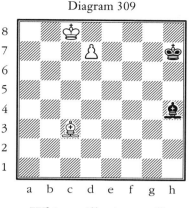

White still wins easily

1.Ba5 Kg6 2.Bd8

Ending black's domination of this long diagonal.

2...Be1 3.Be7 Ba5 4.Bd6, 1-0 since Black can't prevent 5.Bc7.

To have any drawing chances, the defending King must be directly in front of its counterpart.

Diagram 310

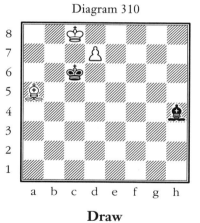

Draw

> **RULE**
>
> In this kind of endgame, center pawns only win if the defending King isn't on top of the action.

Here white's normal winning idea of chasing black's Bishop to the a5-d8 diagonal and then maneuvering his own Bishop to c7 is no longer viable since black's King controls the c7-square: 1.Bd8 Be1 2.Bg5 (2.Bb6 Bh4) 2...Ba5 3.Bd2 Bb6 4.Bf4 Ba5 fails to make progress for White. Note that Black didn't face any problems here because:

 The c7-square is covered by black's Bishop and King.

 White's King is frozen since it needs to defend the d-pawn.

 Black will never run out of tempo moves since he can shuffle his Bishop to g5, f6, and/or e7 at will, while he also has access to three squares on the a5-d8 diagonal if his Bishop is chased there.

This "shuffle defense" isn't possible if the pawn is a bishop-pawn—then the side diagonal is shortened and zugzwangs appear.

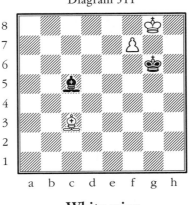

Diagram 311

White wins

White's first order of business is to chase the black Bishop off the a3-f8 diagonal and onto the fatally short h6-f8 line.

1.Bg7 Bb4 2.Bf8 Bd2 3.Bc5 Bh6

Our first goal has been reached, and black's Bishop is now stuck on the uncomfortably short h6-f8 diagonal. Next stop, zugzwang!

4.Bd4!

Suddenly, Black has no good move! Moving the Bishop off the h6-f8 diagonal lets White make a new Queen, while moves like 4…Bg7 or 4…Bf8 both hang the Bishop. Since 4…Kf6 isn't possible, and since 4…Kg5 runs into 5.Be3+, Black is left with either 4…Kf5 or 4…Kh5. Sadly, White would then end matters with 5.Bg7, ensuring the successful promotion of the pawn.

RULE

This idea of a shortened defensive diagonal means that one's winning chances improve when the pawn is a bishop-pawn or knight-pawn.

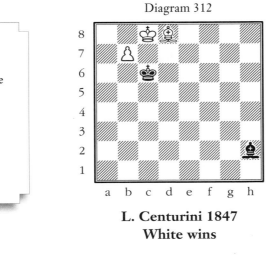

Diagram 312

L. Centurini 1847
White wins

White wins by chasing the black Bishop off the h2-b8 diagonal and onto the pathetically short a7-b8 complex. Then a timely Bishop move/sacrifice along the g1-a7 diagonal forces the black Bishop off the queening square and allows the pawn to successfully promote.

1.Bh4 Bf4 2.Bf2 Bh2 3.Ba7 Bg3 4.Bb8 Bf2 5.Bf4 Ba7

Black is now undone due to the lack of diagonal length.

6.Be3!, 1-0.

This seemed easy, but Black can improve and put up some annoying resistance:

1...Kb5! (Far better than the lemming-like 1...Bf4) **2.Bf2 Ka6**

Suddenly Black has prevented Ba7. Can White still win?

Diagram 313

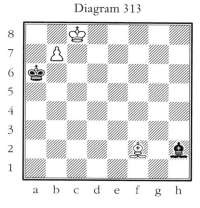

White has only one good move

3.Bc5!

Getting ready to swing back to c7.

3...Be5

Black will rush his King back to c6, but he can't do it yet since 3...Kb5 is met by 4.Ba7.

4.Be7 Kb5

Else White wins by Bd8 followed by Bc7.

5.Bd8 Kc6

It seems like Black has stopped White again, but now a nice maneuver shows that the game is, in fact, over.

6.Bf6! Bf4 7.Bd4 when Black can no longer keep white's Bishop off of a7. The rest: **7...Bg3 8.Ba7 Bf4 9.Bb8 Be3 10.Bg3 Ba7 11.Bf2**, 1-0.

This leaves us with one question: from our last diagram, why was 3.Bc5 the only way to win? Wouldn't 3.Be3 be just as effective? It's important that you understand the answer to this question: **3.Be3 Bd6 4.Bg5 Kb5 5.Bd8 Kc6 6.Be7 Bh2** and 7.Bc5 isn't possible due to 7...Kxc5. Therefore, 3.Bc5! was very important since it stopped Black from moving his Bishop to d6, which in turn allows White to successfully swing his Bishop with tempo to the g1-a7 diagonal and avoid contact with black's King.

Let's repeat this in a slight different way: 3.Bc5! prevents ...Bd6 and forces the black Bishop to move to g3, f4, or e5. When White ultimately challenges that Bishop via Bh4, Bg5, or Bf6, white's Bishop will then be out of reach of the enemy King (now on c6) when it moves to f2, e3, or d4.

Centurini, in the middle of the nineteenth century, postulated that a zugzwang isn't possible if two free squares along the crucial diagonal remain open to the defending Bishop. If the defending Bishop has less than two, then the stronger side will usually win (there are a couple of exceptions, but since we're after concept and not brute memorization, we'll let these pass by—if you wish to make an in-depth study of this kind of Bishop endgame, you can find the exceptions in any detailed endgame tome).

Centurini's Rule

A zugzwang isn't possible if two free squares along the crucial diagonal remain open to the defending Bishop. If the defending Bishop has less than two, then the stronger side will usually win.

The following example illustrates this rule rather nicely, while also showing the student how these ideas can often allow you to successfully advance a pawn that's as far back as the 5th rank.

Diagram 314

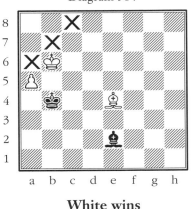

White wins

If White can safely push his pawn to a6, the game will be won. White's first order of business is to chase the black Bishop off the f1-a6 diagonal (easily done by moving the Bishop to a6). This will force black's Bishop to the a6-c8 diagonal, but he will find it impossible to remain there due to the diagonal's shortness (only one free square will be available which, according to Centurini's Rule, means that black's defense will break down).

1.Bb7 Bd3 2.Ba6 Be4 3.Bb5!

Phase one is accomplished. Now Black has to try and set up a block along the shorter, and thus less stable, a6-c8 diagonal.

3...Bb7 4.Bd7!

Naturally, 4.Kxb7?? Kxa5 must be avoided. After 4.Bd7, we have Centurini's rule: "If the defending Bishop has less than two free squares along the crucial diagonal, zugszwang will occur and the stronger side will win."

Indeed, this position is zugszwang since black's Bishop only has one free square along the a6-c8 diagonal. Thus, any black King move will allow Kxb7, and any black Bishop move along the h1-a8 diagonal will allow the pawn to safely make its way up the board.

4...Bg2 5.a6 Bf3 6.a7, 1-0 since 7.Bc6 follows.

Two extra split pawns usually win since in most cases the stronger side can play to promote one pawn, secure in the knowledge that the defender can no longer draw by sacrificing his Bishop since the remaining pawn will eventually promote.

Diagram 315

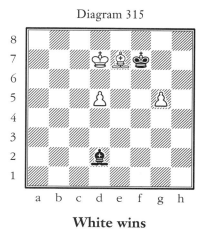

White wins

1.d6 Ba5 (1...Bb4 2.Bf6 followed by Kc7) **2.Bf6**, 1-0 since Black has no way to deal with 3.Kc8, 4.d7, and 5.d8=Q.

As always, one must be mindful of cases where one of the pawns is a rook-pawn of the wrong color.

Diagram 316

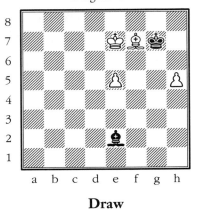

Draw

Black draws by giving up his Bishop for the e-pawn, which leaves him with a basic Bishop and wrong colored h-pawn vs. King.

1.Bg6

1.e6 Bc4 followed by 2...Bxe6, =.

1...Bg4 and White can't make progress.

Two extra protected passed pawns usually assure the stronger side of the full point.

Diagram 317

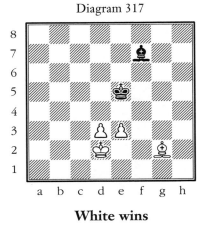

White wins

1.d4+

An important idea: pushing the d-pawn takes control of the dark squares (c5 and e5) while the Bishop keeps an eye on the light squares. This team control over the key squares forces the enemy King back.

White must be careful to avoid letting the enemy King create a blockade. This would occur after 1.e4?? Kd4 when the game is drawn since White can't march his King to f3 and f4 due to …Kxd3, while 2.Bf1 (preparing for the King march to f4) runs headlong into …Bg6 followed by …Bxe4.

1…Kd6 2.e4 Bg6 3.Ke3

It's very important to support the pawns with the King!

3…Bh7 4.e5+

Again, 4.d5?? (losing control over the dark squares) allows Black to create a blockade with 4…Ke5.

4…Ke6 5.Kf4 Bc2 6.d5+ Kd7 7.Bh3+ Ke7 8.d6+ Kd8 9.e6 Ba4 10.Ke5

Of course, there's nothing wrong with 10.e7+ either. But I like the idea of making sure every piece participates in the execution.

10…Bb5 11.Kf6 Ba4 11.e7+ Ke8 12.Bg4 Bb5 13.d7+!

Naturally, 13.Bh5+ Kd7 14.e8=Q+ nukes Black, but why not force mate.

13…Bxd7 14.Bh5 mate.

Pretty easy, as long as you don't allow one of two things:

▶ Don't let the defender give up his Bishop for both pawns.

▶ Don't let the defender achieve a blockade by creating a hole (which the defender's King would live on) on the opposite color of your Bishop.

Queen Endgames

In general, the study of Queen endgames is not something a non-professional should waste his time on. I recall playing a five-minute game against Fritz where I ended up on the happy side of a Queen and pawn vs. Queen position. I had no idea if it was a theoretical win for me or not, but that didn't matter—it was clear that I could torture the computer for a long, long time. Suddenly Fritz "lit up" and announced that I could mate it in 83 moves! Horrified, I did something that seemed logical and Fritz said, "Mate in 87!" I then turned Fritz off—who needed the humiliation?

The rarified air of Queen endgame theory shouldn't be inhaled until you're a senior master (2400 and up), but the following situations deserve a "first taste" right now.

Blockade—Queen vs. Rook and Pawn

In general, any pawn on the 2nd rank other than a rook-pawn will give the defender a draw unless the stronger side's King has managed to break through to the 6th rank. A knight-pawn almost always draws.

Diagram 318

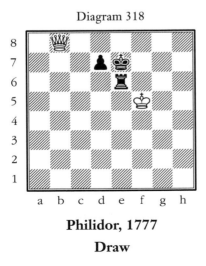

Philidor, 1777

Draw

Black has all the key bases covered:

308

➤ His Rook is stopping white's King from penetrating to the 6th and/or 7th ranks.

➤ His Rook can mark time by going to two safe posts (c6 and e6). A rook-pawn only allows the defender one safe post.

➤ White's Queen isn't able to get behind the pawn and it will never be able to chase black's King away from e7, e8, or c7, c8.

Thus, after **1.Qh8 Rc6 2.Qg7+ Ke8** White can't improve his position.

Such Queen vs. pawn endgames can be very complicated and rule dependent (and these rules change as the pawn advances), and are far beyond anything a non-professional needs to study. Suffice it to say that if you keep in mind our one example and its rules, you'll have something to grasp onto if you're down material and this kind of defensive situation happens to arise.

Blockade—Queen and Pawn vs. Rook and Two Pawns

The weaker side can often draw by creating the same kind of blockade as we saw in Queen vs. Rook and Pawn.

Diagram 319

Draw

White draws easily by shuffling his Rook between e4 and g4. Black might eventually try to sacrifice his Queen for the Rook (on e4 or g4) and a pawn, but the resulting King and pawn vs. King and pawn endgame is easily drawn.

It's important that the student is aware of this kind of blockade since it can occur from many positions that might, at first glance, appear hopeless. The following position shows a simple example of this.

Diagram 320

White to Move

Black seems to be on his way to victory since his Queen and pawn would normally run roughshod over a Rook and Bishop. However, White can sacrifice his Bishop and create a successful blockade.

1.Bxd4+!

1.Re4 is playing with fire: 1...Qc5 2.Bg3 d3 3.Rxe5? Qxe5 4.Bxe5 d2 and Black wins.

1...exd4 2.Rxd4

Since White threatens to safely plant his Rook on e4 or g4, Black must start checking in the hope of taking advantage of white's loose Rook.

2...Qc7+ 3.Kh1

And not 3.Kg1?? Qc5, picking up the Rook.

3...Qh7+ 4.Kg1 Qb1+ 5.Kh2 and Black isn't getting anywhere.

Summing Up

The Flowchart

➤ Complex positions can't be solved unless you have a firm foundation of knowledge behind you. The Flowchart method, which is really nothing more than the recognition of previously absorbed patterns, is dependent on the student having thoroughly mastered the material in earlier sections.

Rook Endgames

➤ A Rook and rook-pawn or knight-pawn on the 7th, with the stronger side's Rook in front of its pawn and the defending Rook behind the pawn, is drawn even if an extra knight-pawn or rook-pawn exist on the other side of the board.

➤ A Rook and rook-pawn or knight-pawn on the 7th, with the stronger side's Rook in front of its pawn and the defending Rook behind the pawn, is easily won if an extra bishop-pawn exists on the other side of the board.

➤ Positions featuring Rook and two passed pawns vs. Rook and one passed pawn are usually winning for the two pawns.

➤ In a Rook and pawn vs. Rook endgame, an inability to achieve a perfect Philidor defensive setup doesn't necessarily mean doom for the defender if his King is in front of the pawn and his Rook is actively placed behind it.

➤ In a Rook and four vs. Rook and three, or Rook and three vs. Rook and two, or Rook and two vs. Rook and one with all the pawns on one side of the board, the defender's goals are to:

- Trade as many pawns as possible (unless striving for a particular pawn exchange severely weakens your pawn formation).

- Keep the Rook as active as possible (preferably tying the defender's King down to the defense of its pawns).

- Keep trading down until you end up with a Philidor position, which we know from experience is a simple draw.

Bishops of the Same Color Endgames

➤ Where the presence of opposite colored Bishops gives the defender hope of drawing, same-colored Bishops usually guarantee the side with the extra pawn(s) serious winning chances.

➤ Bishop and pawn vs. Bishop: When up a pawn (with no other pawns remaining), the stronger side has winning chances if the pawn is advanced and if the defending King isn't able to get in front of it.

➤ Centurini's Rule (for Bishop and advanced pawn vs. Bishop): If the defending Bishop has fewer than two free squares along the crucial diagonal, zugszwang will occur and the stronger side will win.

Queen Endgames

➤ Queen vs. Rook and pawn or Queen and pawn vs. Rook and two pawns: The defender's main hope is the creation of a successful blockade that keeps the stronger side's King from approaching the defender's pawn(s).

Tests and Solutions

TEST 1

Diagram 321

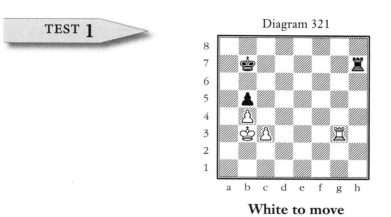

White to move

Does White have any realistic winning chances?

TEST 2

Diagram 322

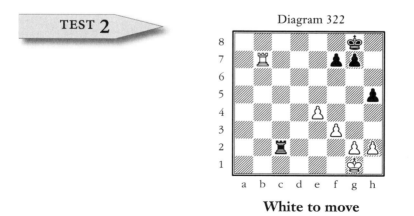

White to move

Is black's pawn on h5 a weakness? If so, would it be more comfortable on h6? Finally, should White win this position?

313

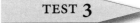

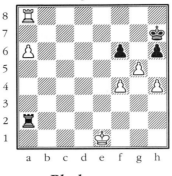

Diagram 323

Black to move

Assess the position.

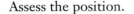

Diagram 324

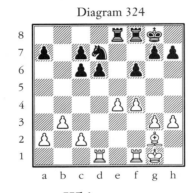

White to move

Another seemingly ungraspable position is really just a prelude to yet another Flowchart puzzle. See if you can ascertain (or guess!) what basic concept will appear on the board.

Diagram 325

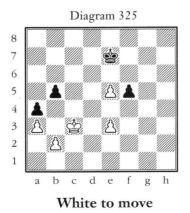

White to move

This is a surprise quiz in that it dredges up an important lesson from Part Five (Which you should know! You didn't think I was going to let you get away with a haphazard understanding of past material, did you?). Can White win, or is the game a draw?

TEST **6**

Diagram 326

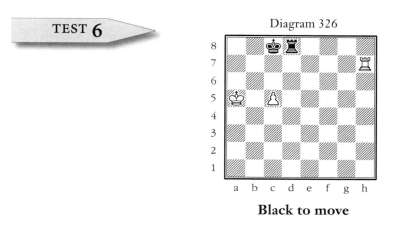

Black to move

Is Black doomed?

TEST **7**

Diagram 327

White to move

Can White win?

TEST **8**

Diagram 328

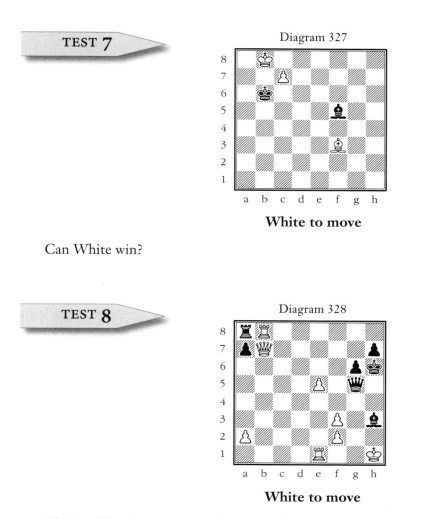

White to move

This is a Flowchart exercise. Try to turn this insane position into something we can understand from our basic endgame foundation.

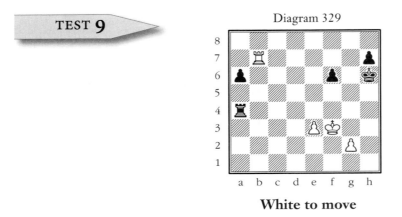

Diagram 329

White to move

As White, what defensive ideas come to mind? These ideas should be word and concept based and not dependent on streams of variations.

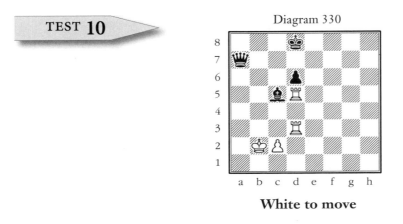

Diagram 330

White to move

Black appears to be headed towards victory. Is this true?

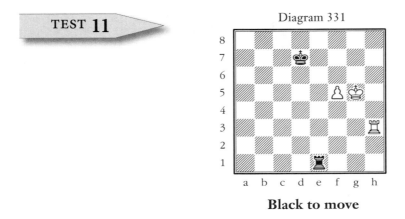

Diagram 331

Black to move

Can Black save the game?

TEST **12**

Diagram 332

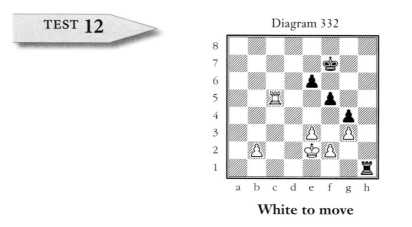

White to move

This seems to be a complex position that has nothing to do with the basics we've studied thus far. Try and see how some of these basics might prove useful in this position. Remember, I'm looking for ideas, not moves.

TEST **13**

Diagram 333

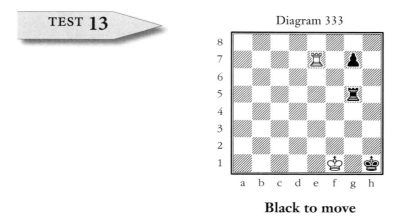

Black to move

What kind of basic situation is Black trying to achieve? Can he win?

TEST **14**

Diagram 334

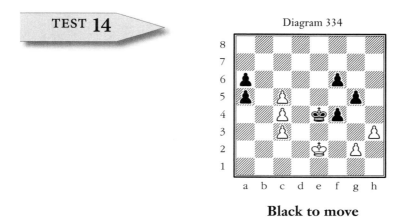

Black to move

Who stands better in this extremely strange position?

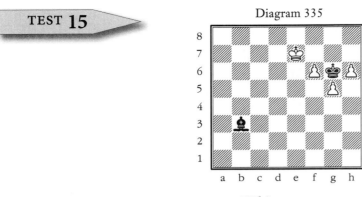

TEST **15**

Diagram 335

White to move

Does 1.f7 win the game, or does the resulting King and pawn endgame hide stalemate tricks?

TEST **16**

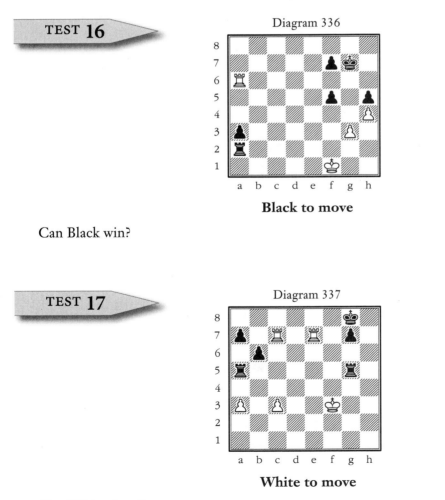

Diagram 336

Black to move

Can Black win?

TEST **17**

Diagram 337

White to move

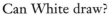

Can White draw?

TEST 18

Diagram 338

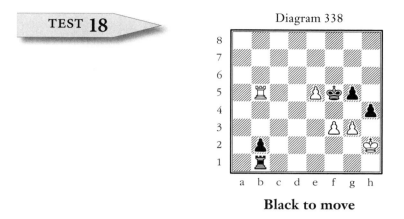

Black to move

White just moved his pawn to g3. Is he going to lose?

TEST 19

Diagram 339

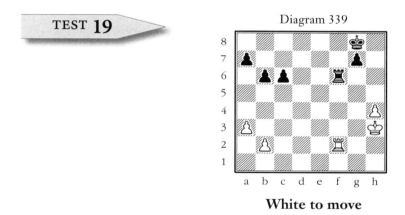

White to move

Should White keep the Rooks on or exchange by Rxf6?

TEST 20

Diagram 340

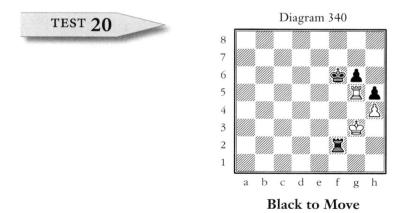

Black to Move

Black now played 55...Rf5. Was this wise?

TEST **21**

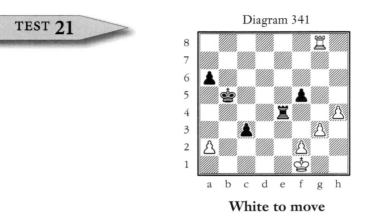

Diagram 341

White to move

Is 1.Rc8 a good move?

TEST **22**

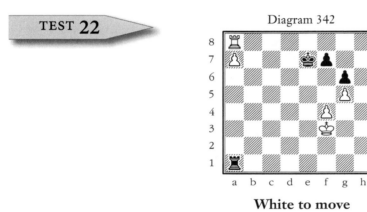

Diagram 342

White to move

Can White win this position?

TEST **23**

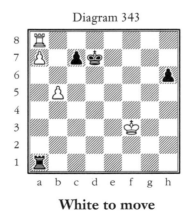

Diagram 343

White to move

Is White winning?

TEST 24

Diagram 344

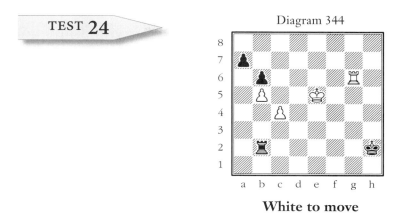

White to move

Can Black save the game?

TEST 25

Diagram 345

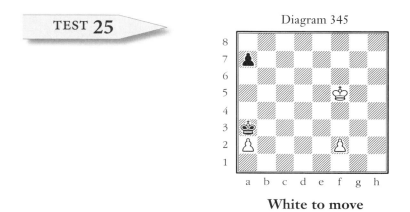

White to move

Does White have any realistic winning chances?

TEST 26

Diagram 346

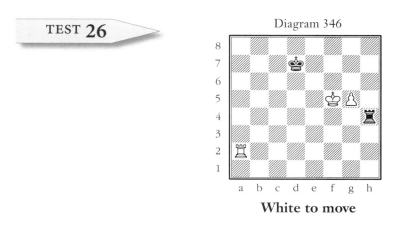

White to move

Can White win?

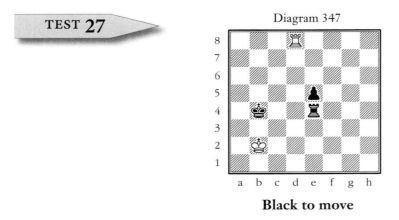

Diagram 347

Black to move

Does 1...Rc4 give Black any realistic winning chances?

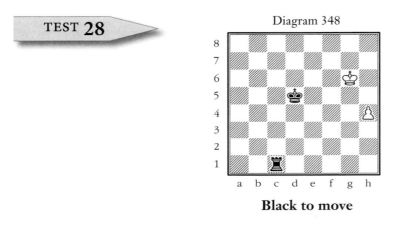

Diagram 348

Black to move

Does White have any chance of saving this game?

Diagram 349

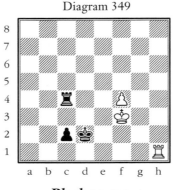

Black to move

Does promoting the pawn win?

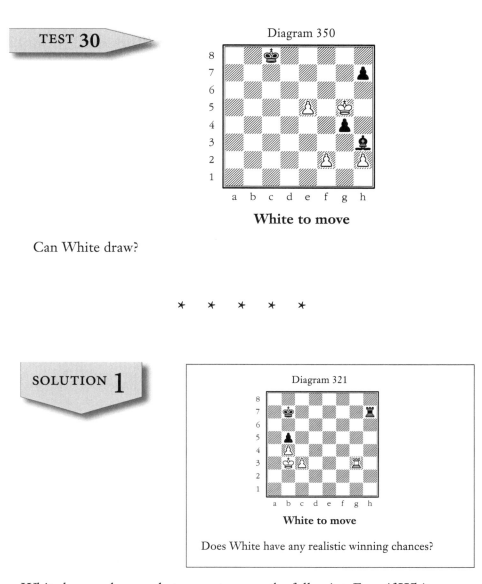

TEST **30**

Diagram 350

White to move

Can White draw?

＊　＊　＊　＊　＊

SOLUTION **1**

Diagram 321

White to move

Does White have any realistic winning chances?

White has no chance whatsoever to score the full point. Even if White swaps his c-pawn for black's b-pawn, the game would still be completely drawn. Why? Because a Philidor could be set up, which is an easy draw, while the fact that White would be left with a knight-pawn means that even a passive Rook position would be drawn.

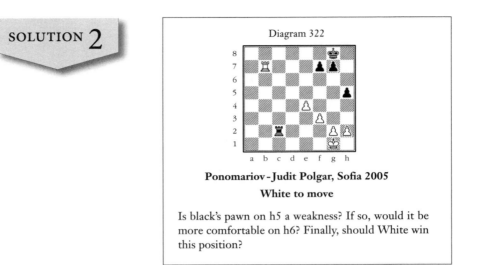

SOLUTION 2

Diagram 322

Ponomariov–Judit Polgar, Sofia 2005

White to move

Is black's pawn on h5 a weakness? If so, would it be more comfortable on h6? Finally, should White win this position?

Having the pawn on h5 is an important defensive idea for Black! It stops the white pawns from taking over too much kingside space, and happily seeks exchanges if White ever plays his g-pawn to g4. Though the defense of such positions is long and tedious, Black should be able to comfortably make a draw.

1.h4 g6 2.Kh2 Kg7 3.Kg3 Re2

Black's Rook is tying white's King to the defense of g2.

4.Rb6 Kf8 5.Rb1 Kg7 6.Rg1

Freeing the King, but this doesn't mean that White can make any real progress.

6...Ra2 7.Kf4 Rb2 8.g3 Rb4 9.Rd1 Ra4 10.Ke3 Ra2 11.Rd4 Rg2

It turns out that white's King is still tied down to its g-pawn!

12.Kf4 Rg1 13.e5 Re1 14.Re4 Rg1 15.Re3 Rg2 16.Re1 Rf2 17.g4

White didn't want to exchange pawns, but he wasn't able to make any progress. Black's pressure against the e- and g-pawns kept White off balance.

17...hxg4 18.Kxg4 Rg2+ 19.Kh3 Rf2 20.Kg3 Ra2 21.Rd1 Re2 22.Rd5 Re1 23.Kf2 Rh1

With white's g-pawn gone, Black turns her attention to the pawn on h4!

24.Rd4 Rh2+ 25.Kg3 Re2 26.Re4 Ra2 27.Re3 Ra1 28.Rd3 Re1 29.f4 Rg1+ 30.Kf3 Rh1 31.Kg4 f5+ 32.Kg3

Of course, 32.Kg5?? Rg1+ 33.Rg3 Rxg3 mate is something that only happens in nightmares (or in dreams, if you're Black!).

32...Rg1+ 33.Kf3 Rh1 34.Rd7+

34.Kg3 Rg1+ 35.Kh2 Rf4 was also an easy draw.

34...Kg8 35.Ke3 Rxh4 36.e6 Kf8 37.Kd4 g5 38.Ke5 gxf4 39.Rf7+ Ke8 40.Rxf5 Rh1 41.Rxf4 Ke7 42.Rf2 Re1+ 43.Kd5 Rxe6, ½-½.

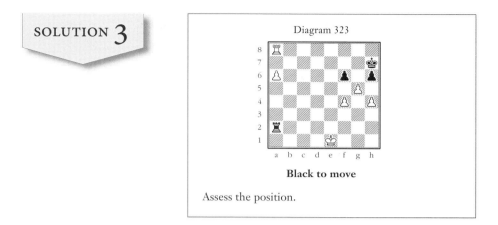

SOLUTION 3

Diagram 323

Black to move

Assess the position.

Your past knowledge (Flowcharting a seemingly complex situation) should make it clear that White is winning if he avoids the many pitfalls that are lurking. The key elements here are:

- White must not allow a Vancura Position.

- White must not allow a two pawn up position where his a-pawn is on the 7th and his other pawn is a g-pawn.

- White must be aware that the win is easy in a two pawn up position where the a-pawn is on the 7th and his other pawn is an f-pawn.

The following moves might occur:

1...hxg5

1...fxg5 2.hxg5 will transpose to our main line.

2.hxg5 fxg5

The position after 2...f5 is an easy win for White, even if he doesn't have the g-pawn!

3.f5!

Not falling into a drawn Vancura Position after 3.fxg5?? Ra5! 4.Kd2 (4.g6+ Kxg6 5.a7 Kg7, =) 4...Rxg5 5.Kc3 Rg6 (entering Vancura's safe waters) 6.Kd4 Kg7 7.Ke5 (of course, 7.a7 Ra6 is an instant draw) 7...Rb6 (not 7...Rf6?? 8.Rg8+!) 8.Kd5 (White's Rook is stuck to its pawn, and a7 allows ...Ra6, so White brings his King to the queenside. However, the Vancura holds firm.) 8...Rf6 9.Kc5 Kh7 10.Kb5 Rf5+ 11.Kc6 Rf6+ 12.Kb7 (or 12.Kd5 Kg7, =) 12...Rf7+, =.

3...g4

No better was 3...Kg7 4.a7! g4 5.f6+ Kh7 6.f7, 1-0, or 3...Ra5 4.a7 when the threat of f6 is decisive and 4...Rxf5 doesn't help since 5.Rb8 will leave White with an extra Rook.

4.a7

Freezing black's King and Rook.

4...g3

Threatening to win by 5...g2.

5.Kf1! Kg7

Nothing works, since 5...Rf2+ 6.Kg1 Rxf5 7.Rb8 forces the win of black's Rook (or creates a new Queen), while 5...g2+ 6.Kg1 leaves Black unable to deal with the threat of f6-f7-f8.

6.f6+! Kh7!

A last try. Hopeless is 6...Kxf6 7.Rf8+ Kg7 8.a8=Q, and 6...Kf7 7.Rh8 Rxa7 8.Rh7+.

7.Kg1!

White also wins after 7.f7 Rf2+ 8.Kg1 Rxf7 9.Rh8+ Kxh8 10.a8=Q+, but why rush into a complex Queen vs. Rook position when the text move makes things easy?

After 7.Kg1 Black must resign since he has no answer to the threat of f7 and f8=Q.

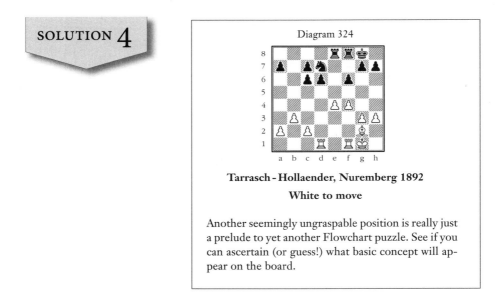

SOLUTION 4

Diagram 324

Tarrasch - Hollaender, Nuremberg 1892

White to move

Another seemingly ungraspable position is really just a prelude to yet another Flowchart puzzle. See if you can ascertain (or guess!) what basic concept will appear on the board.

Believe it or not, a King and pawn endgame featuring Fox in the Chicken Coup will soon appear!

Optically White seems a bit better: his Bishop has possibilities along the h1-a8 diagonal, he possesses more central space, black's doubled c-pawns create a certain lack of flexibility, and black's a-pawn is weak.

Tactically though, things are even worse—the c6-pawn and the Knight are unprotected. White makes immediate use of these factors to either win a pawn or transition the game into an easily won King and pawn endgame.

1.e5!

Blasting open the h1-a8 diagonal.

1...fxe5

1...d5 2.c4! leads to a very unpleasant position for Black after 2...fxe5 3.cxd5 c5 4.d6! cxd6 5.Bd5+ Kh8 6.Bc6 Rd8 7.Rxd6. For example 7...Nb8 8.Rxd8 Rxd8 9.Bb5 a6 10.Bc4 exf4 11.Rxf4 g6 12.Rf6 Kg7 13.Rb6 and Black, whose pawns are weak and whose Knight is dominated, is completely lost.

2.Bxc6

Not only threatening the Knight, but also pinning it to the e8-Rook.

2...Re7

And not 2...Rf7? 3.Bd5, winning the Exchange.

3.Bxd7

Why exchange this nice Bishop for black's Knight? Because it forces the black Rook onto an unprotected square.

3...Rxd7 4.fxe5 Rxf1+ 5.Kxf1 Rf7+?

This prevents the loss of a pawn, but allows a resignable King and pawn end-game to arise. Instead, Black should have kept the Rooks on the board (It's still bad, but at least he can fight!) by 5...d5 when 6.c4 (6.e6 Rd6 7.e7 Kf7 8.Re1 Ke8) 6...d4 7.Ke2 Kf7 8.Kd3 Ke6 9.Ke4 c5 10.Rf1 (stronger is 10.b4! cxb4 11.Rxd4) 10...Rd8 (not allowing White to penetrate to f8) when Black can battle on (ideas like ...Rb8 followed by ...a5 and ...a4 are screaming to be tried).

6.Kg2

And not 6.Ke2?? Re7 when Black is suddenly okay.

6...dxe5 7.Rd8+

This final transition, taking the game into a King and pawn ending, is deci-sive since white's queenside majority will ultimately leave him with a Fox in the Chicken Coup situation.

7...Rf8 8.Rxf8+ Kxf8 9.Kf3 Ke7 10.Ke4 Kd6 11.b4!

A very important move which leaves white's queenside pawns free to roam. Badly mistaken is 11.c4? c5 12.a3 a5 with a situation where two black pawns are stopping three white pawns.

11...a6 12.a4 g6 13.c4 a5

13...c6 14.b5 axb5 (14...cxb5 15.cxb5) 15.axb5 cxb5 16.cxb5 Kc5 17.Kxe5 Kxb5 18.Kf6 is a classic Fox in the Chicken Coup. Also hopeless is 13...Ke6 14.b5 a5 (14...axb5 15.cxb5) 15.c5.

14.bxa5 Kc5 15.Kxe5, 1-0.

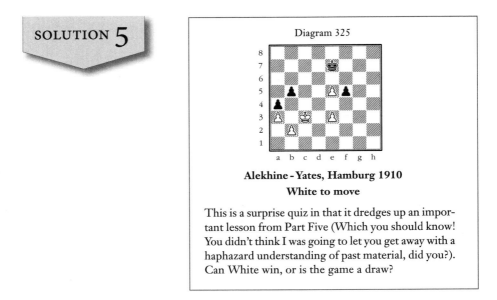

Diagram 325

Alekhine - Yates, Hamburg 1910
White to move

This is a surprise quiz in that it dredges up an important lesson from Part Five (Which you should know! You didn't think I was going to let you get away with a haphazard understanding of past material, did you?). Can White win, or is the game a draw?

White wins by making use of Opposition and Triangulation.

1.Kd3!

1.Kd4?? Ke6 gives Black the Opposition, loses the e5-pawn, and allows Black to enter a very difficult Queen endgame after 2.Kc5 Kxe5 3.Kxb5 Ke4 4.Kxa4 Kxe3 5.b4 f4 6.b5 f3 7.b6 f2 8.b7 f1=Q 9.b8=Q that White would really prefer to avoid.

1...Kd7!

Taking Distant Opposition and avoiding 1...Ke6? 2.Kd4.

2.e4! f4

2...fxe4+ 3.Kxe4 is resignable for Black.

3.Ke2

Threatening Kf3 followed by Kxf4. Black's reply is forced.

3...Ke6 4.Kf2!, 1-0. White wisely avoided 4.Kf3?? Kxe5 when Black wins! After 4.Kf2 Kxe5 5.Kf3 White takes the Opposition, wins the f-pawn, and wins the game. If this was too difficult, go back to Part Five and review the material there!

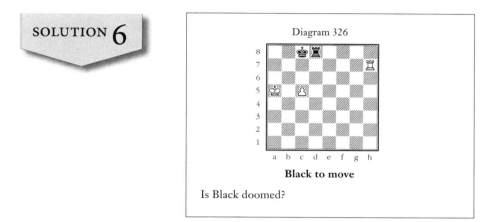

SOLUTION 6

Diagram 326

Black to move

Is Black doomed?

It's too late to set up a Philidor Position, but he can still save himself by using our "Philidor gone bad" formula:

➤ Activate the Rook

➤ Place it behind the pawn

➤ Run the King to the Short Side of the board.

➤ Make sure you create Checking Distance for your Rook.

1...Rd1

Creating maximum Checking Distance! Note that the pawn endgame after 1...Rd7?? 2.Rxd7 Kxd7 3.Kb6 Kc8 4.Kc6 is completely lost.

2.Kb6 Rc1!!

And not 2...Rb1+? 3.Kc6.

3.Kc6

Of course, White can't make any progress after 3.Rh8+ Kd7 since black's Rook and King make c6 impossible.

3...Kb8!

Going to the Short Side of the board so the Rook can have Checking Distance on the kingside.

4.Rh8+ Ka7 5.Rc8

No better is 5.Kd6 Kb7!, =.

5...Rh1!

Creating optimum Checking Distance and threatening to slide back into a perfect Philidor with 6...Rh6+.

6.Rd8

Now White can meet 6...Rh6+ with 7.Kc7 Rh7+ 8.Rd7.

6...Rc1!, ½-½ since White can't make any progress.

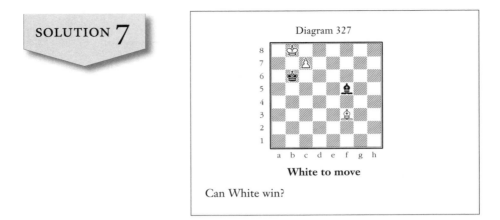

SOLUTION 7

Diagram 327

White to move

Can White win?

White would not win an analogous position with a center pawn (with the Kings facing off), but here the shortened second diagonal (a6-c8) allows White to claim victory:

1.Bb7 Bg4 2.Bc8 Be2 3.Bf5 Ba6 4.Be4! and Black must resign since any King move allows Bb7, while a Bishop move either hangs the Bishop or allows White to make a Queen.

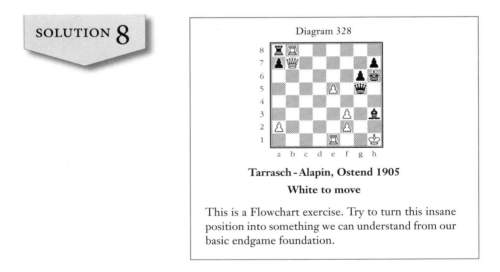

SOLUTION 8

Diagram 328

Tarrasch - Alapin, Ostend 1905

White to move

This is a Flowchart exercise. Try to turn this insane position into something we can understand from our basic endgame foundation.

It seems odd to mention endgame transitions and Flowcharts when we're faced with a very sharp, complex middlegame position. Yet it's quite proper to do so since White has the opportunity to end black's attack and reach a winning Rook endgame by sacrificing some of his excess material.

1.f4!

The winning move. White hits the enemy Queen and allows his own Queen to stop black's threatened ...Qg2 mate.

1...Qg2+

Even easier for White is 1...Qh5 2.Qxa8! (Pure greed in chess is a lovely sight!) 2...Bg4+ 3.Kg1 Bf3 4.Qxf3! Qxf3 5.Rb3 Qg4+ 6.Rg3 Qxf4 7.e6 and white's two Rooks and passed e-pawn will pick up the full point.

2.Qxg2 Bxg2+ 3.Kxg2 Rxb8

The first transition has been achieved: the complex middlegame is gone and a pawn up Rook endgame has "miraculously" appeared in which white's Rook is resting happily behind its passed pawn.

4.Kf3 Kg7 5.Rd1

It turns out that pushing the e-pawn would now be a mistake, so White activates his Rook in search of new weaknesses to conquer.

5...Rb7 6.f5!

An excellent move that takes us to our second transition (in fine Flowchart fashion). White temporarily gives up his doubled f-pawn so that:

➤ He creates a target on f5.

➤ After winning it he reaches known territory: the resulting connected passed e- and f-pawns vs. lone passed h-pawn is an easy win.

6...gxf5 7.Kf4 Kf8

Black can't hold onto his pawn since 7...Kg6 is met by 8.Rg1+, while 7...Rf7 8.Rg1+ followed by 9.Rg5 and 10.Rxf5 is also easy for White.

8.f3

The f5-pawn can't be held, so why rush things and allow 8.Kxf5 Rc2, attacking both a2 and f2 at the same time?

8...Rf7 9.e6 Rc7

9...Rf6 10.Ke5 is hopeless for Black.

10.Kxf5 Ke7 11.Rd5!

This stops 5th rank Rook checks and kills the opponent's counterplay since black's Rook can't leave its 2nd rank due to Rd7+. Now that everything is safe, White will calmly advance his f-pawn.

11...h5 12.f4 h4 13.Ke5 h3 14.f5 h2 15.f6+ Ke8 16.Rb5!, 1-0. Black had no desire to experience 16...Rc8 (to stop back rank mate) 17.f7+ Ke7 18.Rb7+ Kf8 19.Kf6 h1=Q 20.e7 mate.

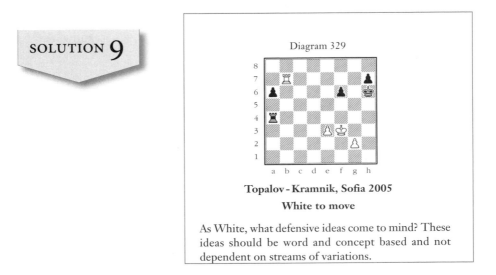

SOLUTION 9

Diagram 329

Topalov - Kramnik, Sofia 2005

White to move

As White, what defensive ideas come to mind? These ideas should be word and concept based and not dependent on streams of variations.

Don't fail to make use of your basic knowledge! Most players just calculate in these situations, without getting a grip on various defensive possibilities first. However, you can't find good moves if you don't have a verbal goal in mind.

Bravo if you thought of some of the following things:

- ➤ It's an easy draw if White can exchange all the kingside pawns.

- ➤ If Black ends up with his pawn on a2 and Rook on a1 (white's Rook behind the pawn on a7), it's a draw if White can trade his two pawns on e3 and g2 for black's f-pawn.

- ➤ If Black ends up with his pawn on a2 and Rook on a1 (white's Rook behind the pawn on a7), White loses if he trades his two pawns on e3 and g2 for black's h-pawn.

- ➤ If black's pawn gets to a2, white's King must be on h2 or g2, or be in front of one of its pawns so a Rook check isn't possible.

- ➤ Black's kingside pawns are vulnerable. Attacking them will prove very annoying.

It turns out that attacking black's kingside pawns is very annoying indeed!

1.e4 Kg6 2.g4 Ra1 3.Kf4

White intends to attack black's pawns by Rb6 followed by e5 (taking advantage of the pin along the rank). Black has no good answer to this plan.

3...a5

No better is 3...Rf1+ 4.Kg3 a5 5.Rb6 a4 (5...Kf7 6.Rb7+ Ke6 7.Rxh7 a4 8.Ra7, =) 6.Ra6 Ra1 7.e5 a3 8.Rxf6+ Kg7 9.Ra6 a2 10.Kg2 is a draw even if White doesn't have his e- and g-pawns!

4.Rb6 a4

4...Kf7 5.Rb7+ Kg6 6.Rb6 doesn't get Black anywhere, so he has no choice but to slog on with his pawn.

5.e5 a3 6.Rxf6+ Kg7 7.Kg5!

The only good move. 7.Ra6?? loses because white's King can't get back to g2 or h2 in time, while moving to g5 now encounters a problem: 7.Ra6?? a2 (threatening ...Rf1+) 8.Kg5 (8.Ra7+ Kg6 9.Ra6+ Kf7 10.Ra7+ Ke6 11.Kg5 h5! destroys the white King's cover.) 8...h6+! 9.Rxh6 (9.Kf5 Rf1+ followed by ...a1=Q) 9...Rb1 10.Ra6 a1=Q 11.Rxa1 Rxa1 and it's all over.

7...a2

7...h5 leads to more interesting positions, though they also end in draws: 8.Rf2 Re1 9.Kf5 h4 (9...hxg4 10.Ra2 Re3 11.Kxg4 Kf7 12.Kf4, =) 10.g5 h3 11.Ra2 Kf7 12.g6+ Kg7 13.e6 Re3 14.Kf4, =, intending to meet 14...Rc3 with 15.e7, =.

8.Rf2!

Avoiding 8.Ra6?? h6+ when white's King loses its protective cover.

8...Re1 9.Rxa2 Rxe5+, ½-½.

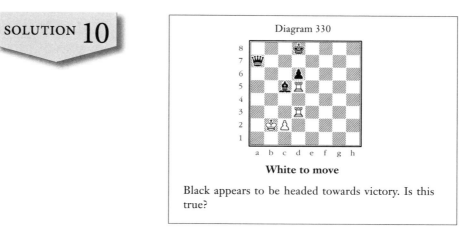

Diagram 330

White to move

Black appears to be headed towards victory. Is this true?

White can draw by **1.Rxd6+! Bxd6 2.Rxd6+ Kc7 3.Rd3** with a blockade.

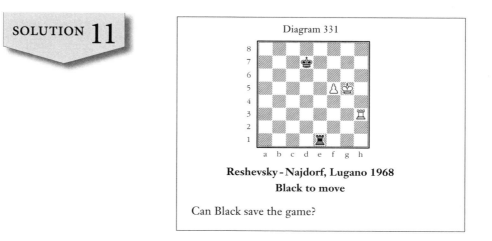

Diagram 331

Reshevsky - Najdorf, Lugano 1968

Black to move

Can Black save the game?

Black can draw, but his King needs to reach the Short Side of the board. In the actual game, Black dismally fails in this goal: 1...Ke8? 2.Kf6 Kd7 3.Rh7+ Ke8 4.Rh8+ Kd7 5.Rf8 Rh1 6.Kg7 Rg1+ 7.Kf7 Rf1 8.f6, 1-0.

Instead, he could have saved himself by **1...Ke7 2.Rh7+ Kf8 3.Kf6 Kg8 4.Ra7 Rf1!** and White can't win.

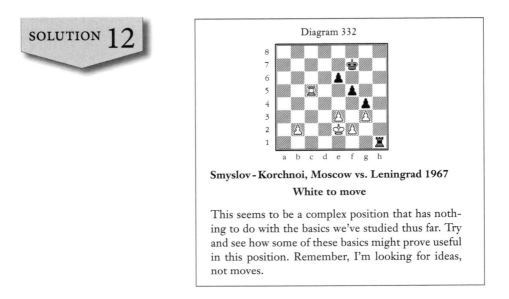

SOLUTION 12

Diagram 332

Smyslov–Korchnoi, Moscow vs. Leningrad 1967

White to move

This seems to be a complex position that has nothing to do with the basics we've studied thus far. Try and see how some of these basics might prove useful in this position. Remember, I'm looking for ideas, not moves.

This position seems complicated and hard to define in terms of the basic lessons we've learned in this book. However, there are some key ideas we can grasp onto. We've seen many instances of weak pawns being attacked, so White would like to make black's pawn mass on the kingside as vulnerable as possible (you should always try to create new weaknesses in the enemy camp!). And, since White has a passed b-pawn, he should be aiming to advance it and force black's King and Rook to the queenside so they can deal with it.

The idea of using the outside passed pawn should dredge up two more concepts: placing the Rook behind its passed pawn and Fox in the Chicken Coup. You might find it odd to think of Fox in the Chicken Coup in the context of a Rook and pawn endgame, but it makes good sense and brings to mind two different scenarios:

➤ White's Rook gets behind the passed pawn, pushes it as far as possible, and if Black wins the pawn by taking it with his Rook (leading to a Rook exchange and black's King sitting somewhere on the b-file), White wins the resulting King and pawn endgame because his King is on the kingside, ready to eat black's pawns.

➤ White sacrifices his b-pawn so that he can win a kingside pawn. The resulting Rook and kingside pawn vs. Rook endgame will be winning due to the AWOL black King.

1.Rc2!

By defending the only two attackable points in white's camp (i.e., b2 and f2), white's King is relieved of guard duty and is thus free to march up to d4 or c4.

1...Ke7

After 1...e5, White would have moved his King to c4 and then pushed the b-pawn.

2.e4

This pawn advance, and the ultimate exchange of pawns that it leads to, will leave black's kingside pawns far more vulnerable than they were in the initial diagram. I'll discuss this move once the position crystallizes.

2...Ra1

2...fxe4 3.Ke3 Re1+ 4.Re2 picks up e4 (trading Rooks is an easy win for White) and leaves Black with two very weak pawns on e6 and g4.

3.Kd3 Kd6 4.exf5 exf5

Black's kingside pawns are now vulnerable to attack if the white King can reach f4 or e5 (clearly f5 is far easier for White to attack than e6 was).

5.Kc4

White would prefer to move his King to f4, but this isn't so easy to achieve since Ke3 is met by ...Ra4. Due to this, White will calmly prepare to advance his b-pawn. Once that pawn gets moving, it will demand the attention of black's Rook and King which, hopefully, will allow white's King to attack black's kingside pawns.

5...Kc6 6.Kd4+ Kd6 7.b3 Re1 8.Kc4 Kc6 9.Kd3+ Kd5 10.b4 Rb1

Logically placing his Rook behind white's passed pawn.

11.Kc3 Kc6

Black would prefer to play more aggressively via 11...Ke4. Unfortunately that would allow 12.Rb2 when 12...Rxb2 13.Kxb2 Kf3 14.b5 wins. As a result of this, black's King has to prepare to block the b-pawn.

12.Kd4+ Kd6 13.Kc4 Kc6

Refusing to let white's King penetrate into his position. It's time for white's Rook to play a more dynamic role in the proceedings.

14.Re2!

This creates a real problem for Black! Re6+ is threatened, and stopping this by ...Kd6 allows Kb5. That leaves 14...Rc1+, which has flaws of its own.

14...Rc1+ 15.Kd4

And now Black is facing the double threat of 16.Ke5 and 16.Rb2.

15...Kd6 16.Rb2 Ra1 17.b5 Ra4+ 18.Ke3 Kc7 19.b6+ Kb7 20.Rb5!

Threatening to jettison the b-pawn by 21.Rxf5 Kxb6 22.Rf4 with an easy win for White.

20...Re4+

Both 20...Kc6 21.b7! and 20...Ra3+ 21.Kf4 Rf3+ 22.Kg5 Rxf2 23.Rxf5 are also hopeless.

21.Kd3 Re8 22.Rxf5 Kxb6 23.Rg5

White's Fox in the Chicken Coup plan has been realized. The battle is raging on the kingside while black's King is napping on the other wing.

23...Rd8+ 24.Ke4 Re8+ 25.Kf5 Rf8+ 26.Ke6 Rxf2 27.Rxg4

It's all over. Black's King needs to be in front of white's passed pawn or at least close by.

27...Re2+ 28.Kf5 Kc5 29.Re4 Rf2+ 30.Rf4 Rd2 31.g4 Rd5+ 32.Kg6, 1-0.

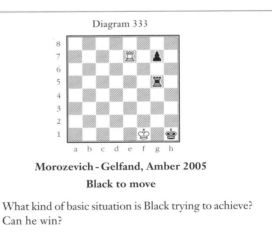

Diagram 333

Morozevich - Gelfand, Amber 2005

Black to move

What kind of basic situation is Black trying to achieve? Can he win?

Black's dream is to create a Lucena Position. The first step towards this goal is to trap the white King away from the action. The advance of the pawn will follow.

1...Rf5+ 2.Ke2 g5 3.Ke3 Kg2 4.Ke4 Rf4+ 5.Ke3 Rf3+ 6.Ke2 g4 7.Re4 g3 8.Rb4 Rf8 9.Rh4 Re8+ 10.Kd3 Kf2 11.Rf4+ Kg1 12.Kd2 g2 13.Rf7 Rh8 14.Ke2 Kh1, 0–1.

SOLUTION 14

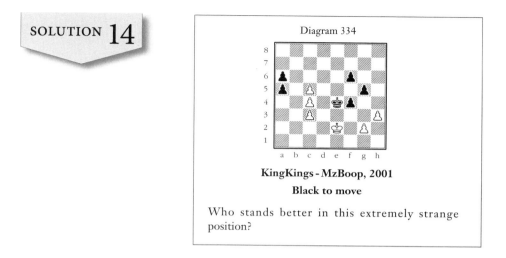

Diagram 334

KingKings - MzBoop, 2001

Black to move

Who stands better in this extremely strange position?

This amazing position occurred in a one-minute bullet game (with two-second increment). Black wins easily because his a-pawns are outside passed pawns.

1...Ke5 2.Kd3 Ke6 3.Kc2 Kd7 4.Kb3 Kc6 and Black won. He can either play ...f5, ...g4, and ... f3, or do a Fox in the Chicken Coup by chopping off all the c-pawns and then dashing over the kingside and eating g2.

SOLUTION 15

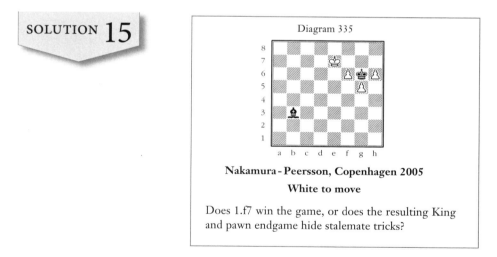

Diagram 335

Nakamura - Peersson, Copenhagen 2005

White to move

Does 1.f7 win the game, or does the resulting King and pawn endgame hide stalemate tricks?

1.f7 wins, and black's one stalemating trick is easily dealt with: **1.f7 Bxf7 2.h7 Kxh7 3.Kxf7 Kh8 4.Kg6!** (Avoiding 4.g6?? stalemate), 1–0. If you didn't get this, reread Part Two through Part Four.

SOLUTION 16

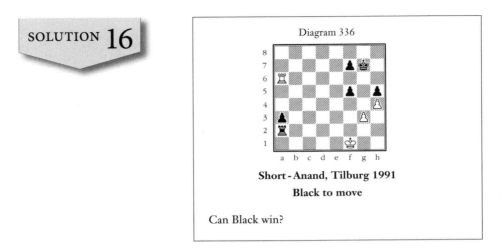

Diagram 336

Short - Anand, Tilburg 1991

Black to move

Can Black win?

The material in Part Seven should have made this one easy to solve: **1...Ra1+ 2.Kg2 a2 3.Kh2 Kf8 4.Ra7 Ke8 5.Kg2 Kd8 6.Kh2 Kc8 7.Kg2 Kb8 8.Ra4 Kb7 9.Ra3 Kb6 10.Ra8 f4 11.gxf4 f5 12.Ra3 Kc5 13.Ra8 Kc4 14.Ra3 Kd4 15.Ra8 Ke4 16.Ra4+ Ke3**, 0–1.

SOLUTION 17

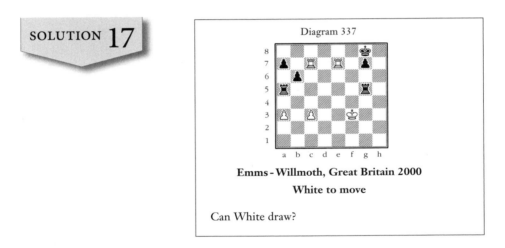

Diagram 337

Emms - Willmoth, Great Britain 2000

White to move

Can White draw?

White draws by trading off all the queenside pawns and one pair of Rooks: **1.Rxa7 Rxa7 2.Rxa7 Rc5 3.a4 Rxc3+ 4.Kg2 Rb3 5.a5 Rb5**, ½-½.

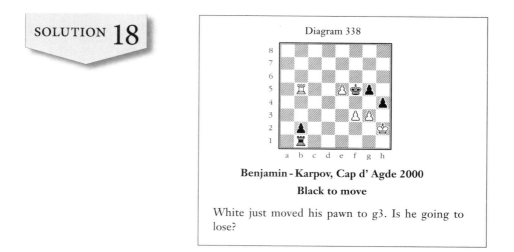

Diagram 338

Benjamin - Karpov, Cap d' Agde 2000

Black to move

White just moved his pawn to g3. Is he going to lose?

White draws because he knows that it's unwinnable even if he ends up two pawns down: **1...hxg3+ 2.Kg2!** (Avoiding 2.Kxg3?? Rg1+) **2...Ke6 3.Rb8 Kxe5 4.Rb7 Kd6 5.Rb8 g4 6.fxg4 Ke5 7.Rb4 Kf6 8.Rb5 Kg6 9.Rb8 Kg5 10.Rg8+ Kf4 11.Rf8+ Kxg4 12.Rg8+ Kf5 13.Rf8+ Ke6 14.Re8+,** ½-½.

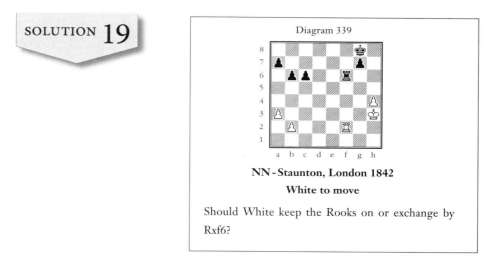

Diagram 339

NN - Staunton, London 1842

White to move

Should White keep the Rooks on or exchange by Rxf6?

White feared the King and pawn endgame that would occur after 1.Rxf6, so he tried 1.Rd2 and went on to lose: 1...a5 2.Kg4 Kh7 3.h5 b5 4.Kg5 Re6 5.Kf5 Re1 6.Rc2 Rh1 7.Kg4 Rb1 8.Kf4 a4 9.Kf5 c5 10.Ke4 Kh6 11.Kf5 b4 12.axb4 cxb4 13.Rg2 a3 14.bxa3 bxa3 15.Ra2 Rb3 16.Kg4 Rb4+ 17.Kf5 Rb5+ 18.Kf4 Ra5 19.Kg4 Ra4+ 20.Kf5 Kxh5 21.Rh2+ Rh4 22.Rg2 g6+ 23.Kf6 Rf4+, 0–1.

However, taking on f6 by 1.Rxf6 would have given White an outside passed pawn, and this would have allowed him to save the game: **1.Rxf6! gxf6 2.Kg4 Kf7 3.h5 c5 4.Kf5 b5 5.h6 c4** (No better is 5...a5 6.h7 Kg7 7.h8=Q+ Kxh8 8.Kxf6 b4 9.axb4 cxb4 10.Ke5 a4 11.Kd4, ½-½) **6.h7 Kg7 7.h8=Q+ Kxh8 8.Kxf6 a5 9.Ke5 b4 10.axb4 axb4 11.Kd4,** ½-½.

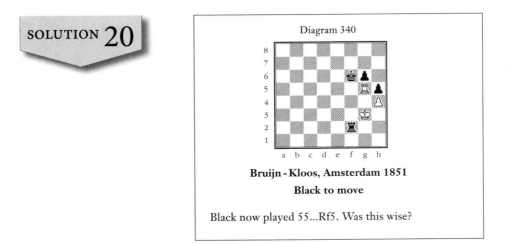

SOLUTION 20

Diagram 340

Bruijn - Kloos, Amsterdam 1851

Black to move

Black now played 55...Rf5. Was this wise?

Yes, this forced transposition into a King and pawn ending wins an otherwise drawn Rook endgame:

1...Rf5! 2.Rxf5+ gxf5

The actual game saw 2...Kxf5?? 3.Kf3 Ke5 4.Ke3 Kf5 5.Kf3 g5 6.hxg5 Kxg5, ½-½.

3.Kf4 Ke6 4.Kg5 Ke5 5.Kxh5 f4

The ever alert Fritz points out that 5...Kf6! 6.Kh6 f4 7.Kh5 f3 is even easier.

6.Kg4 Ke4 7.h5 f3 8.Kg3 Ke3 9.h6 f2 10.h7 f1=Q 11.h8=Q Qg1+ 12.Kh4 Qh2+, 0-1.

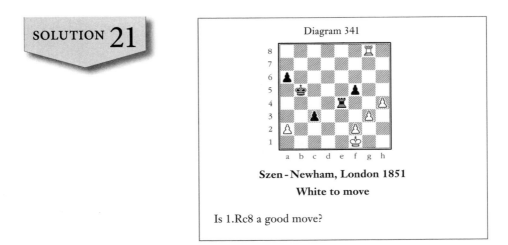

SOLUTION 21

Diagram 341

Szen - Newham, London 1851

White to move

Is 1.Rc8 a good move?

Placing a Rook behind a passed pawn is often important, and that rule holds true here since Black threatened to win with 1...c2. By stopping the pawn with 1.Rc8, white's material advantage will ultimately prevail.

1.Rc8 Kb4

1...Rc4 2.Rxc4 Kxc4 3.Ke2 is easy for White.

2.h5 Re6 3.f3 a5 4.g4 fxg4 5.fxg4 Rh6

Also hopeless is 5...Re4 6.h6 Rxg4 7.h7 Rh4 8.h8=Q Rxh8 9.Rxh8 Ka3 10.Ke2.

6.Ke2 Ka3 7.Rxc3+ Kxa2 8.Rc5 a4 9.Rb5 a3 10.Kf3 Ka1 11.Ra5

White makes sure he doesn't stalemate the black King by 11.Kf4 a2 12.Kg5 Rxh5+ 13.Kxh5 stalemate.

11...a2 12.Kg3 Kb2 13.Kh4 a1=Q

A better defense was 13…Rc6, but after 14.Rxa2+ Kxa2 15.g5 White still wins because black's King is too far away from the pawns.

14.Rxa1 Kxa1 15.g5 Ra6 16.h6 Ra7 17.g6 Ra4+ 18.Kg5 Ra5+ 19.Kf4 Ra4+ 20.Ke5 Ra5+ 21.Kd4 Ra4+ 22.Kc5, 1–0. An impressive performance by the legendary Szen. Hard to believe they were playing such fine endgames way back in 1851!

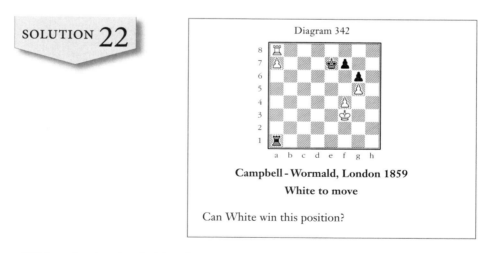

SOLUTION 22

Diagram 342

Campbell - Wormald, London 1859

White to move

Can White win this position?

White wins in nice fashion by

1.f5! gxf5 2.g6

Clearing off the 7th rank so White can make use of the old Rh8-h7+ trick.

2...Ra3+ 3.Kf4 Ra4+ 4.Kxf5 Ra5+ 5.Kg4 Ra4+ 6.Kg5 Ra5+ 7.Kh6 Ra6 8.Kh7 Ra1

It's also over after 8...fxg6 9.Rg8 Rxa7 10.Rg7+ Kf6 11.Rxa7 g5 12.Ra5 g4 13.Kh6 g3 14.Ra3 g2 15.Rg3.

9.g7, 1–0 since 9...Rh1+ 10.Kg8 Ra1 11.Rf8 is game over.

SOLUTION 23

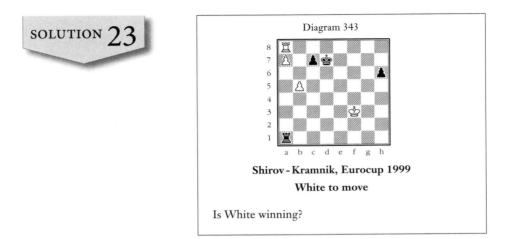

Diagram 343

Shirov - Kramnik, Eurocup 1999

White to move

Is White winning?

White employs a simpler version of the idea used in Test 22 to force a quick kill: **1.b6! cxb6 2.Rh8**, 1–0.

SOLUTION 24

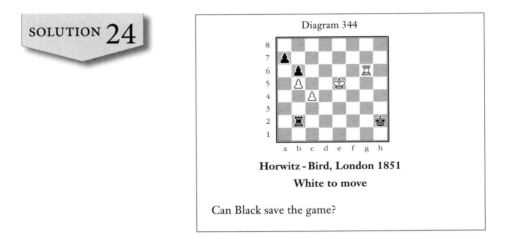

Diagram 344

Horwitz - Bird, London 1851

White to move

Can Black save the game?

White wins because black's King is too far away from the queenside action: **1.Kd5 Rd2+ 2.Kc6 Rd4 3.Kb7 Rd7+ 4.Ka6 Kh3 5.Rg8 Rc7 6.Ra8 Kg4 7.Rxa7 Rxc4 8.Rf7 Kg5 9.Kxb6 Rc2 10.Kb7 Rc5 11.b6 Rc3 12.Kb8**, 1–0.

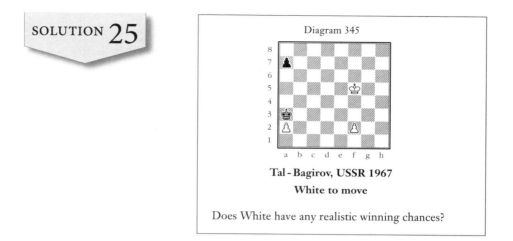

SOLUTION 25

Diagram 345

Tal - Bagirov, USSR 1967

White to move

Does White have any realistic winning chances?

White wins by force because he promotes first and his King gets close to the enemy monarch: **1.Ke4! Kxa2 2.f4 a5 3.f5 a4 4.f6 a3 5.f7**, 1–0. Black didn't need to be shown 57...Kb2 58.f8=Q a2 59.Qb4+ Ka1 60.Qd2 Kb1 61.Kd3 a1=Q 62.Qc2 mate.

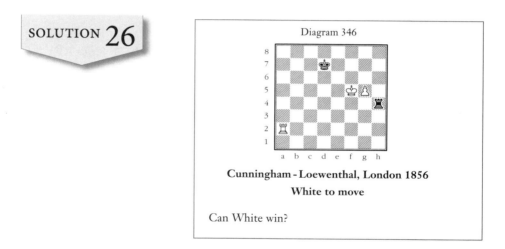

SOLUTION 26

Diagram 346

Cunningham - Loewenthal, London 1856

White to move

Can White win?

White wins by cutting the black King off from the kingside: **1.Re2! Rh1 2.Kf6 Rf1+ 3.Kg7 Rg1 4.g6 Rg3 5.Kh7 Rh3+ 6.Kg8 Rg3 7.g7 Rg1 8.Re4 Rg2 9.Kh7 Rh2+ 10.Kg6 Rg2+ 11.Kh6 Rh2+ 12.Kg5**, 1–0.

SOLUTION 27

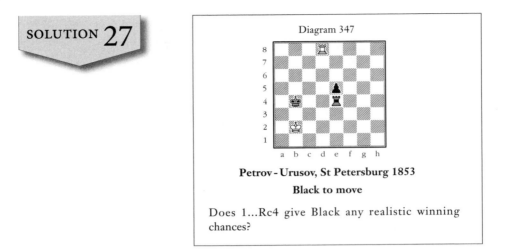

Diagram 347

Petrov - Urusov, St Petersburg 1853

Black to move

Does 1...Rc4 give Black any realistic winning chances?

No, the game was dead drawn no matter what Black had played:

1...Rc4

The game continuation was 1...Re2+ 2.Kc1 Kc3 3.Kd1 Re4 4.Ra8 Re3 5.Ra3+ Kd4 6.Ra4+ Kd3 7.Rb4 e4 8.Ra4 Rf3 9.Ke1 Ke3 10.Ra8 Rf7 11.Ra3+ Kf4 12.Kf2 Rc7 13.Ra2 Rh7 14.Kg2, ½-½.

2.Rb8+ Kc5 3.Rc8+ Kd4 4.Rxc4+ Kxc4 5.Kc2 e4 6.Kd2 Kd4 7.Ke2 e3 8.Ke1, ½-½.

SOLUTION 28

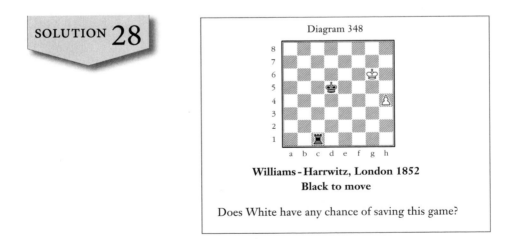

Diagram 348

Williams - Harrwitz, London 1852

Black to move

Does White have any chance of saving this game?

White's dead: **1...Ke6 2.h5 Rg1+ 3.Kh7 Kf7**, 0–1.

SOLUTION **29**

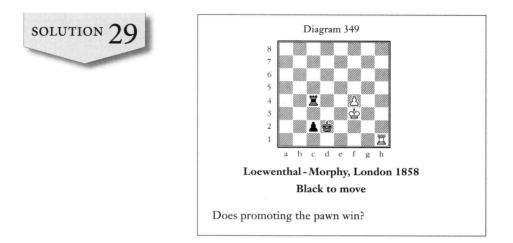

Diagram 349

Loewenthal - Morphy, London 1858

Black to move

Does promoting the pawn win?

Promoting the pawn (which wins white's Rook) is decisive, since the black King is able to get back in time to stop white's pawn: **1...c1=Q 2.Rxc1 Rxc1 3.Ke4 Re1+ 4.Kd4 Ke2 5.f5 Kf3 6.Kd5 Kf4 7.f6 Kg5 8.f7 Rf1 9.Ke6 Kg6**, 0–1.

SOLUTION **30**

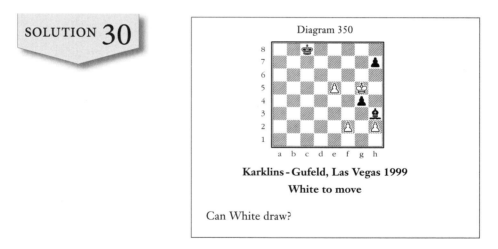

Diagram 350

Karklins - Gufeld, Las Vegas 1999

White to move

Can White draw?

The defender is usually happy to trade off pawns, and in this case a draw can be achieved if he can exchange his three remaining pawns for black's two.

1.Kh4

In the actual game, White lost quickly after 1.Kf6 Kd8 2.Kf7 Bf1 3.e6 Bc4 4.Kg7 Ke7 5.Kxh7 Kxe6 6.Kg6 Ke5 7.Kg5 Be6, 0–1.

1...Kd7 2.f3 h5 3.f4

And not 51.fxg4?? Bxg4.

3...Ke6 4.Kxh5

Also fine is 4.Kg5 Bg2 5.Kxh5 Kf5 6.e6 Bc6 7.Kh4 Kxf4 8.e7 Kf3 9.Kg5 Bd7 10.Kh4 with a positional draw: Black can't improve his position since ...Kf4 leads to the stalemate in our main line, while moves like ...Ke4 or ...Kg2 allow White to win black's final pawn.

4...Kf5 5.Kh4 Kxf4 6.e6 Bg2 7.e7 Bc6 8.h3 g3 9.e8=Q Bxe8, ½-½. A beautiful stalemate, discovered by IM Jack Peters.

Final Thoughts

This section tightened up the material you already know, and showed you how to make use of your acquired knowledge to figure out positions that appear to be extremely complex. Having done this, you're more than ready for one final step.

Where in past sections I only wanted you to move on if you felt you had serious aspirations towards that next rating group, now I highly recommend you study Part Eight (Endgames for Masters) and Part Nine (Endgames for Pure Pleasure). Why the change of heart? Because these final two parts of the book are concept driven—anyone who has mastered the material through Part Seven should find Parts Eight and Nine enlightening, easy to understand, and enjoyable.

Let me extend my congratulations for your efforts thus far. You've come a long way, and now possess an impressive internal "endgame database." You're almost at the top of the mountain—there are only a few easy steps left to take.

Part Eight

Endgames for Masters (2200–2399)

Contents

You've finished Part Seven, and now you should have a rich foundation in *all* endgame basics. Of course, you will add to that knowledge by experience and any extra study you feel like doing.

Though there is always a place for mastering complex positions—Rook and pawn, Queen and pawn, and King and pawn endgames have unlimited depths—the need to shore up one's openings and add to one's middlegame skills forces the 2200 player to take a more practical approach. At this point "concept" (memorization finally takes a back seat to simple understanding) is the thing one needs to round out the endgame skills taught in this book's earlier parts. Here we'll focus on six concepts that will enable the master to play many kinds of endgames with depth and flair.

Cat and Mouse

or
The Art of Doing Very Little as Slowly as Possible
or
The Chess Sadist at Work

Weak players usually deal with one-move threats, while players who reach 2000 to 2200 try to imbue every move with a deeper, more expansive purpose. In a normal position, where the opponent is trying hard to show that his ideas and plans trump yours, every move *should* be filled with carefully crafted design.

However, from time to time a player is blessed with a position where his opponent is helpless—doomed to passively wait while the stronger side prepares the decisive break/thrust/maneuver/tactic. In such situations it's often a good idea to take your time, make small improvements in your position, and let the horror of the defender's seemingly endless defensive task slowly seep into his blown out, exhausted brain. This kind of "water torture" punishment is known in chess circles as ***Cat and Mouse***.

A strange rule of thumb is, "Do in ten what you can do in two." Lest you think I'm joking, consider this: taking your time and torturing an opponent is fun, but being the object of this torture is painful, depressing, and leads to a form of lobotomy that can linger for weeks afterwards. The ideas behind "do in ten what you can do in two" are:

> ➤ If you make some pointed move right away, your opponent will be expecting it and will take appropriate measures. However, if you dither about for a while before employing your grand scheme, he will be lulled into the aforementioned lobotomized state and miss anything and everything you are intending.

> ➤ Since your opponent is helpless, you have nothing to lose by showing your almost preternatural patience.

➤ Optimizing your position before undertaking a decisive move forward has to be useful. Usually one doesn't have the luxury of wasting time in this fashion, but if you have carte blanche to tidy up every imperfection, why not take advantage of it?

➤ You might find that you're burning up too much time on the clock in an effort to find the final, winning maneuver. If another time control can be painlessly reached by treading water (thus giving added time in a safe fashion), grab the gift of free minutes with both hands!

Our first example features two famous endgame aficionados—Grandmasters Pal Benko and Yuri Averbakh—going head to head, with Benko relishing his ability to inflict long, slow torture on his esteemed foe.

Diagram 351

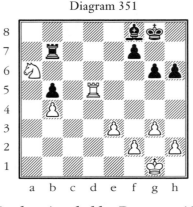

Benko - Averbakh, Portoroz 1958
White to move

Benko had this to say about the position: "Black's dream is to trade the b-pawns and the minor pieces and play a Rook ending with four vs. three on the kingside. Such an endgame is usually drawn. Dreams are one thing, though, and reality is quite another. I would never allow such a situation to come to pass."

1.Nc5 Ra7

1...Bxc5 2.Rxc5 is winning for White because he has two advantages: his Rook is more active than its black counterpart (due to the need to defend b5), and he's a solid pawn up on the kingside.

2.Nd3 Ra1+ 3.Kg2 Rd1 4.Kf3

White's winning plan is very simple: he intends to slowly improve his position on the kingside (e3-e4, gaining space and defending the Rook, is a useful prelude), defend the Knight with his King (the immediate threat is Ke2), and then win the pawn on b5.

4...Rd2

This stops Ke2.

5.e4

Preparing Ke3.

5...h5

This move not only prepares ...h5-h4, but also intends to meet 6.Ke3 with 6...Bh6+.

6.e5

Gains space and gives white's King access to e4.

6...h4

Let's borrow a bit more from Benko: "Another pawn is about to fall so Black tries one last idea: if he can trade as many pawns as possible, he might be able to sacrifice a piece for white's remaining pawns."

7.gxh4 Rd1 8.Ke2

The pin is finally broken and White will get to eat the b-pawn, giving him a powerful passer.

8...Rh1 9.Rxb5 Rxh2 10.Rb8 Rxh4 11.b5 Kg7 12.b6 Rh1 13.Rb7 Rb1 14.f4

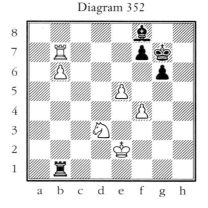

Diagram 352

Benko is happy to solidify his position and keep black's counterplay to almost zero. The very tempting 14.e6 Kg8 15.e7 (15.exf7+ Kg7) 15...Bxe7 16.Rxe7 Rxb6 would have left White with only one pawn. Why deal with such a hard technical task when you can torture your opponent at your leisure?

14...Kg8 15.Kd2 Ba3 16.Kc2 Rb5 17.Kc3 Bf8 18.Kc4 Rb1 19.Rb8

White's King is now near its passed pawn. With all his pieces so well placed, the win must be just a few moves away.

19...g5

Desperation, but 19...Kg7 runs afoul of 20.Rxf8! Kxf8 21.Nb4 Rc1+ 22.Kb5.

20.fxg5 Kg7 21.Rxf8! Rxb6

Black wasn't happy about this, but 21...Kxf8 22.Nb4 Rc1+ 23.Kb5 Rc8 24.Nc6 is hopeless.

22.Rd8 Rg6 23.Rd7 Kf8 24.Kd5 Rxg5 25.Ke4

Diagram 353

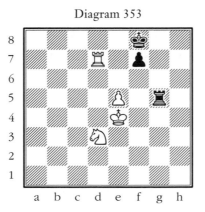

The game is clearly won, but Benko goes about it with extreme patience. Obviously he can't allow the exchange of the last pair of pawns, but other than that his goal is clear: make use of the power of the 7th rank Rook combined with the free-range King and Knight to attack f7 or create potential mating nets.

25...Rg1 26.Nf4 Re1+ 27.Kf5 Rf1 28.Ra7 Ke8 29.Rb7

Cat and Mouse. In a way, White is asking his opponent, "Are you enjoying this? I certainly am!"

29...Kf8 30.Kg5 Ke8 31.Nd5 Rg1+ 32.Kf5 Rf1+ 33.Ke4 Kf8 34.Ne3 Rf2 35.Nf5 Ke8 36.Nd6+ Kf8 37.Rc7 Rf1 38.Kd5

Benko finally decides to put his opponent out of his misery. The King will march down the board and prepare to create a winning King and pawn vs. King position by sacrificing his Rook and Knight for black's Rook and pawn.

38...Rd1+ 39.Kc6 Rc1+ 40.Kb7 Rxc7+

40...Rb1+ 41.Kc8 Rf1 42.Rxf7+ Rxf7 43.Nxf7 Kxf7 44.Kd7 amounts to the same thing.

41.Kxc7 Ke7 42.Nxf7!, 1-0. The pawn promotes after 42...Kxf7 (or 42...Ke6 43.Kc6) 43.Kd7.

If you thought that game showed patience, let's let Benko take us even deeper into the world of Cat and Mouse against another great endgame player—the legendary Victor Korchnoi!

Diagram 354

Benko - Korchnoi, Curacao 1962

White to move

1.Nd4

Benko: "I was willing to trade my Bishop for the Knight because I felt that, ultimately, my Knight would prove itself to be more useful than the enemy Bishop."

1...Nc4+ 2.Bxc4 Bxc4 3.Rc2 Ba6 4.Rhc1 Rxc2 5.Rxc2 Kd7 6.e5

Diagram 355

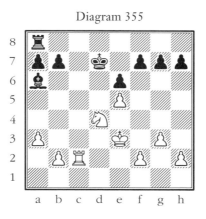

Benko: "In such positions, little things make all the difference. Here I'm gaining central space, getting my pawns off the color of black's bishop, and (by preventing an eventual ...e6-e5) making sure the d4-square will be permanently available for use by my Knight or King."

6...Rc8 7.Rxc8 Kxc8

Benko: "The Rooks are traded and, to the uninitiated, the game appears to be headed for a draw. However, the position is actually very pleasant for White because only he can play for a win while Black will be defending for a long time to come. Why is White better? The flexibility of the Knight is one huge factor (the d6-square in particular is calling to it!), and my central space advantage and superior King also combine to make black's life unpleasant."

Note how Benko is raving about the superiority of his Knight over black's Bishop. We'll delve far deeper in this "Knight worship" in the section The Pleasures of a Knight.

8.Nf3 h6 9.Nd2 Kd7 10.Ne4 b6 11.f4 Bf1 12.Kd4 Bg2 13.Nd6 f5

Benko: "White's position has improved, but Black has everything covered. Now starts a long game of Cat and Mouse: I make little jabs at his weak points and torment him endlessly."

14.Nb5 Bf1 15.Nd6

Benko points out that 15.Nxa7 Kc7 16.a4 Kb7 17.Nb5 Bxb5 18.axb5 would be drawn because his King would not be able to penetrate into the enemy camp.

15...a5 16.b4 axb4 17.axb4 Bh3 18.Nc4 Kc6 19.Nd6 Kd7 20.Nc4 Kc6 21.Ne3 Kb5 22.Kc3 g5 23.Nc4 gxf4 24.gxf4 Kc6 25.Kd4 h5 26.Nd6 h4 27.Nc8 Bg2 28.Ne7+ Kb5 29.Kc3 h3 30.Ng8 Kc6 31.Nf6 Bf3 32.Kd4 Kb5 33.Nd7 Bd5

Avoiding 33...Kxb4 34.Nxb6 Kb5 35.Nd7 Kc6 36.Nf8 Bd5 37.Nh7 Bg2 38.Ng5 Kd7 39.Ke3 when White wins a pawn by Kf2, Kg3, and Nxh3.

34.Kc3 Ba2 35.Nf8 Kc6 36.Nh7 Kd5 37.Nf6+ Kc6 38.Kd4 Kb5 39.Kc3 Kc6 40.Nh7 Kd5

Diagram 356

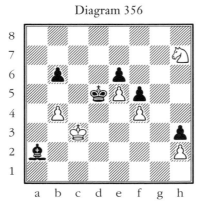

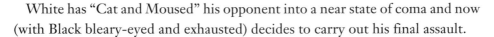

White has "Cat and Moused" his opponent into a near state of coma and now (with Black bleary-eyed and exhausted) decides to carry out his final assault.

41.Ng5 b5 42.Kd3

Benko: "Suddenly Black is facing some serious problems. White is willing to enter the race by giving up his b-pawn because the passed e-pawn or h-pawn (whichever one White creates) will prove faster. Note that the immediate 42.Nxh3? would have been an error due to 42...Ke4."

42...Bc4+ 43.Ke3 Bf1 44.Kf2 Bg2 45.Kg3??

Evidently Korchnoi wasn't the only one tired from the battle. Benko could have forced a win by 45.Ke2! (this allows the King to stop black's b-pawn in the key variation) 45...Kc4 46.Nxe6 Kxb4 47.Nd4 Kc5 48.Nxf5 b4 49.Kd2, etc.

45...Kc4 46.Nxe6 Kxb4 47.Nd4 Kc4??

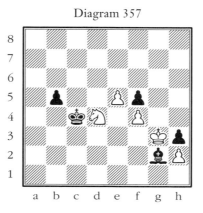

Diagram 357

Benko: "Korchnoi finally cracks. He had to try 47...Kc5! when the game would be drawn: 48.Nxf5 b4 49.Ne3 b3 50.Nd1 Kd4 51.e6 Bd5 52.e7 Bf7 53.Kxh3 Kd3 54.f5 Kd2 55.Nb2 Kc3, and a peaceful conclusion can't be avoided."—Benko.

48.Nxf5 b4 49.Ne3+ Kd3 50.Nxg2 hxg2 51.Kxg2 b3 52.e6 b2 53.e7 b1=Q 54.e8=Q

The rest is easy for White.

54...Qa2+ 55.Kg3 Qa7 56.Qb5+ Ke4 57.Qe5+ Kd3 58.f5 Qh7 59.h4 Qg8+ 60.Kf4 Qc4+ 61.Kg5 Qg8+ 62.Kh6 Qf8+ 63.Qg7 Qd8

63...Qxf5 64.Qg6 Ke4 65.h5 is also game over.

64.f6, 1-0.

Are you getting a feel for the power of Cat and Mouse yet? Remember, the concepts in this chapter are not things to be memorized, they are ideas that need to be embraced.

Since Benko is doing such a great job teaching us about the effectiveness of Cat and Mouse, I'll let him drive the message home by borrowing one more example from *Pal Benko: My Life, Games, and Compositions*. This time he Cat and Mouses one of the greatest endgame players of all time.

Diagram 358

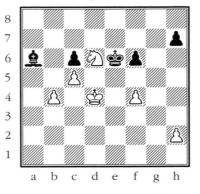

Benko - Smyslov, Zagreb 1959
White to move

White, with an extra pawn, a superior King, and a strong Knight vs. a Bishop should win. However, it won't be easy. This is what Benko had to say: "The game was adjourned here and after analyzing at leisure, I realized the win would take quite a long time. If victory is to be achieved, the white King will have to find a way to penetrate. Unfortunately, black's King and Bishop make this difficult. As a result, I decided that it was time for a bit of Cat and Mouse: I would patiently maneuver, hoping to make Smyslov less alert. I knew that such long-term torture from a passive position would be very hard for Black to deal with, so I sat down and resumed the game ready for a lengthy siege."

1.f5+

Benko: "The first order of business is to push back the black King. It isn't optimal to place my pawn on a vulnerable white square, but I had no choice in the matter."

I should add that, after 1.f5+, Black is completely passive and can't do anything but go back and forth and hope that White can't find a way to finish him off. Such positions virtually scream for Cat and Mouse treatment!

1...Kd7 2.Nc4 Bb5 3.Kc3 Ba6 4.Kb3 Bb5 5.Nd6 Be2 6.Kc3

Continuing his Cat and Mouse torture, but the more straightforward 6.Ka4 seems to win by force: 6...Bd3 7.Ka5 Kc7 8.h4 h6 9.h5 Be2 (9...Kd7 10.Kb6 Bc2 11.Kb7 Bd3 12.Nf7 Bxf5 13.Nxh6 Be6 14.Nf7 Bxf7 15.h6 Bg6 16.b5) 10.Ne8+ Kd8 11.Nxf6—analysis by Benko.

6...Ke7 7.Nc4 Kd7 8.Ne3 Ke7 9.Nc2 Kd7 10.Nd4 Bf1 11.Kd2 Bc4 12.Ke3 Bf7 13.Kf4 Bc4 14.Kg4 Bf7 15.Kh4 Kc7

Smyslov wrongly assumed that, after 15...Kc7, White wouldn't be able to win the h-pawn because the Knight gets trapped. However, Black was dead lost in any case: 15...Be8 16.b5 cxb5 17.Nxb5 and the threat of Nd6 or even Nc3-e4, mixed with ideas of pushing the c-pawn and/or advancing the King to h5 and h6, is overwhelming.

16.Ne6+ Kd7

16...Kc8 17.Nf8 Bg8 18.Kh5 is easy for White.

17.Nf8+! Ke7 18.Nxh7 Bg8 19.Ng5! fxg5+ 20.Kxg5

Diagram 359

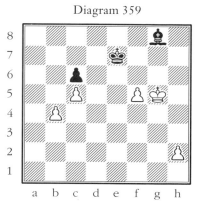

White's pawns are unstoppable since Black must also take a b4-b5 break into account.

20...Kf7 21.h4 Kg7 22.f6+ Kf8 23.h5 Bc4 24.Kf4 Kf7 25.Ke5 Bd3 26.h6 Kg6 27.Ke6 Bc4+ 28.Ke7 Bd5 29.f7 Bxf7 30.h7, 1-0.

Obviously, Cat and Mouse and patience go hand in hand. Our next example shows IM Jack Peters (who dominated Southern California chess for almost three decades!) picking his opponent apart in unhurried and impressive fashion.

Diagram 360

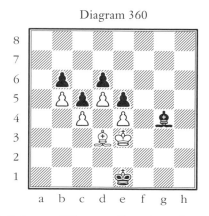

R Schutt - J Peters, Los Angeles 1989
White to move

Such bad Bishop positions are almost always lost—the fact that white's pawns are on light colored squares mean they are targets that will ultimately be picked off by black's pieces, while an exchange of Bishops usually leads to a lost King and pawn endgame since black's King is already deep in white's position.

In the present case the position seems resignable for White. Black has managed to penetrate with his King to e1 and an attack against white's pawn on c4 via ...Bd1 seems to ensure that material losses are impossible to avoid. However ...

1.Be2!

A shock! Taking the Bishop leads to immediate stalemate.

1...Bh3 2.Bf3

Black's King can't scamper over to the queenside due to the white Bishop's control over the d1-h5 diagonal, and black's Bishop isn't able to penetrate either, though he gives it one more shot.

2...Bf1 3.Be2!

Yes, I guess it's true! It really is stalemate! Has White managed to save the game?

3...Bg2 4.Bg4 Kf1

No, Black is still winning. Having accepted white's miracle defense (and that's an important emotional step, since a shock like white's stalemate defense can easily throw a player for a loop), Black calmly (and very, very patiently!) plans the following:

- ➤ He will swing his King around to g3 (which is where it came from earlier, by the way!). White's King would then be stuck keeping it out of the decisive f2- and f4-squares.

- ➤ He will force his Bishop into white's camp by leaping into d1.

- ➤ Once that is done, Black will make use of tempo moves and attacks against the white pawns to decisively penetrate with his King.

- ➤ If White tries to prevent this (i.e., black's Bishop reaching d1) by placing his Bishop on the d1-a4 diagonal, black's King will march to e1 and reach a position where the Be2 stalemate defense is no longer possible (it needs to be on the d1-h5 diagonal).

5.Bh5 Kg1 6.Be2

Forced. A move like 6.Bg4 would have lost immediately to 6...Bf1 7.Be2 Bxe2 8.Kxe2 Kg2 (This decisively takes the Opposition, though to be fair, the King and pawn endgame wins for Black in most instances here. White would have no defense, no matter who has the Opposition, if the black King reaches g4, h4, f3, g3, f2, or g2.) 9.Ke3 Kg3 10.Ke2 Kf4 11.Kd3 Kf3 and White loses all his pawns.

6...Kh2

Still patiently following the plan discussed on move four. Note that 6...Bf1?? fails to 7.Bxf1 Kxf1 8.Kf3 when White has reached one of the few positions where his King can successfully keep black's King away from his pawns.

7.Bd3 Kg3 8.Be2 Bh3

Diagram 361

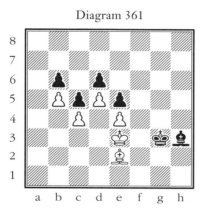

Black's King has reached g3. Next on the agenda is getting the Bishop to d1!

9.Bd3

No better is 9.Bd1 Bg4 when 10.Bxg4? Kxg4 is a winning King and pawn endgame for Black.

9...Bg4 10.Bc2 Bf3 11.Bd3

White allows the Bishop to reach d1 without a fight. Jack Peter's analysis (comments by Silman) shows that 11.Bb3 would not have changed the result: 11...Bg4 12.Bc2 Kg2 (Heading back to e1. Note that as long as white's Bishop is stuck on a4/b3/c2, the Be2 stalemate defense won't be possible.) 13.Bb3 (13.Bd3 Bd1 14.Kd2 Ba4 15.Ke3 Kg3 16.Bf1 Bc2 17.Be2 Kg2 18.Bh5 Kf1 19.Bg4 Ke1 20.Bf3 Bb3 21.Be2 Ba2 22.Bd3 Kd1 23.Bf1 Kc2 and white's pawns will soon fall from the board like [I'm quoting from dozens of old chess books] "ripe fruit.") 13...Kf1 14.Bc2 Ke1 15.Bb3 Be2! (Again, Black must avoid 15...Bd1?? since 16.Bxd1 Kxd1 17.Kd3 gives White the Opposition and a draw) 16.Ba2 Bd1 (Now that white's Bishop no longer controls the d1-square, black's King will be able to swing over to the queenside via d1 and c2) 17.Bb1 (Also easy for Black is 17.Kd3 Kf2 18.Kd2 Be2 19.Bb3 Kf3 20.Ba2 Bf1 and White loses material.) 17...Bb3 18.Bd3 (18.Kd3 Kf2) 18...Kd1 19.Bf1 Kc2 with ...Kc3 and ...Bxc4 to follow.

11...Bd1 12.Kd2 Ba4 13.Ke3 Bb3 14.Be2

Also losing are 14.Bf1 Bc2 15.Be2 Kg2 16.Bh5 Kf1 (when the black King will make decisive inroads into the white position) and 14.Ke2 Kf4 15.Kf2 Bd1, idea ...Bf3 and ...Bxe4.

14...Bc2 15.Bf3

This allows a pretty finish. However, 15.Bf1 wouldn't have made any difference: 15...Bb1 (forcing white's Bishop to give up control over g2) 16.Be2 Kg2 17.Bh5 Kf1 18.Bf3 Ke1

Diagram 362

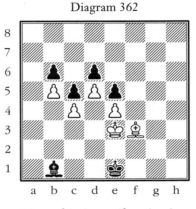

Now this is easily winning

Black wins this position (compared to our starting position) because his Bishop has already penetrated into the enemy camp! 19.Bg4 (Now 19.Be2 is blasted away by 19...Bxe4) 19...Ba2 20.Be2 Bb3 (Zugzwang! Either the Bishop must give up control over c4 or d1, or the King must hand Black access to f2 or d2.) 21.Bd3 (21.Kd3 Bxc4+; 21.Kf3 Kd2) 21...Kd1 22.Bf1 Kc2 when Black has finally achieved his dream penetration.

15...Bd3!, 0-1 since 16.Kxd3 Kxf3 leads to the loss of all the white pawns.

Diagram 363

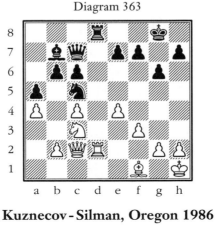

Kuznecov - Silman, Oregon 1986

Black to move

Black fixes white's pawns on light squares before stepping into the minor piece endgame. This shows how one can prepare a favorable endgame right in the middlegame.

1...e5!

A strong move that clamps down on d4, prepares ...Nc5-e6-d4, and also fixes white's e-pawn on the light-colored e4-square. White's position is now extremely uncomfortable.

2.Qd1 Rxd2 3.Qxd2 Ne6 4.Ne2 Qe7 5.Nc1 Kg7 6.Nb3 c5 7.Nc1 Bc6 8.Qd1 Qd7!

Simultaneously hitting a4 and d1 and forcing White to enter a very poor minor piece endgame.

9.Qxd7 Bxd7 10.b3

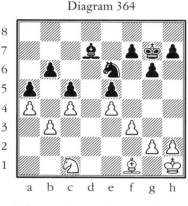

Diagram 364

A lost minor piece endgame

With so many of white's pawns on light squares, it's hard to imagine White saving the game. All Black needs is patience—slow improvements in pawn structure, kingside space, and piece position, followed by penetration into white's camp, should be enough to eventually claim the full point.

10...Nd4

Now white's Knight is stuck doing guard duty to the b3-pawn.

11.Kg1 f5

Adding to black's list of advantages by grabbing kingside space.

12.Bd3 Bc6

Putting pressure on e4 and letting White worry whether Black will leave the pawn on f5 or push to f4 with even more kingside territory.

13.exf5 gxf5 14.Kf2 Kf6 15.Ke3 Kg5 16.Bb1 h5 17.Bd3 h4

This threatens to undermine the f3-pawn by ...h3.

18.h3?

This is too much! Putting another pawn on a light square can't be healthy. He should have played 18.Be2 with the understanding that he was going to passively suffer for a long time to come.

18...Be8! 19.Be2 Bg6

Preparing ...f4+ followed by a Bishop penetration on the b1-h7 diagonal.

20.Bd1

Diagram 365

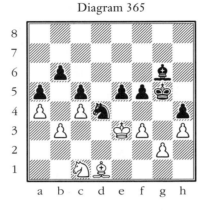

Also possible was the desperate 20.f4+ exf4+ 21.Kf2, though Black wins comfortably enough. One clear continuation is 21...Nxe2! 22.Nxe2 (22.Kxe2 Bh5+ 23.Kf2 Bd1 24.Ke1 Bc2 is completely hopeless) 22...Bh5 23.Ng1 (23.Nc3 Kf6 24.Nd5+ Ke5 25.Nxb6 Bd1 is resignable) 23...Bd1 24.Nf3+ Kf6 25.Nd2 Ke5 26.Ke1 Bc2 27.Nf3+ Kf6 28.Nd2 f3! 29.gxf3 Ke5 and it's time for White to shake hands.

20...f4+ 21.Kf2 Bb1 22.Ne2

Things end quickly after this, but even the more resilient 22.Ke1 couldn't hope to nullify the accumulated Black advantages. Both 22...e4 and 22...Bf5 23.Na2 Nc2+ would ultimately drag White down to defeat.

22...e4 23.fxe4

Of course, 23.Nxd4 e3+ followed by 24...cxd4 is horrific.

23...Nxe2! 24.Bxe2 Bxe4

The game is over. White can't stop ...Bc2 (winning material) and/or ...Kf6-e5-d4.

25.Bg4

25.Bd1 Kf6 is also easy for Black.

25...Bc2 26.Kf3 Bd1+ 27.Ke4 Bxg4 28.hxg4 Kxg4, 0-1.

I made Cat and Mouse the first topic in Part Eight since the idea of patience will overflow into many kinds of endgames.

The Principle of Two Weaknesses

In the middlegame, it's quite common to see a player saddling his opponent with as many weaknesses as possible. In general, it's hard to tear down a defensive position if there is only one weakness to attack. However, two or more weaknesses/unfavorable imbalances (these can be weak squares, weak pawns, material disadvantage or anything that causes a problem for the opponent) often spread the defense enough to allow breakthroughs to occur.

Here's a nice middlegame example that spills over into the endgame.

Diagram 366

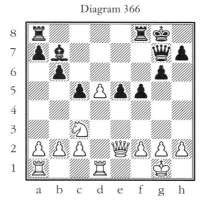

Unzicker - Donner, Goteborg 1955

White to move

White is clearly better thanks to his passed pawn (which can push to d6 at will) and the loosening of black's King position. However, the passed pawn alone won't win the game—another weakness will be needed to stretch black's defense to the breaking point.

1.a4!

Intending a5 followed by axb6, weakening the b6-pawn and the b5-square. In some lines the a-pawn might also march on to a6 where, with Nb5 to follow, it turns a7 into a target.

1...a5?!

Too panicky! Now White has a strong passed pawn to push, a weak b6-pawn to attack, and a juicy b5-square to live on. More than enough to force a win.

2.Qb5 Qc7 3.d6! Qc6

In the actual game, Black played 3…Qd8 and lost with hardly a whimper after 4.Nd5 Bxd5 5.Rxd5 e4 6.Rad1 Kg7 7.d7 Rf6 8.h3 Re6 9.Qc4 Re7 10.Rd6 Ra7 11.Qc3+ Kg8 12.Qf6 Ra8 13.Qxe7, 1-0 since 13…Qxe7 14.d8=Q+ Rxd8 15.Rxd8+ Kf7 16.R1d7 leaves White with an extra Rook.

The more aggressive looking 3…Qc6 allows us to see how an "innocent" weakening of the b6-pawn can have profound repercussions on a defender's position.

4.Qxc6 Bxc6 5.d7! Rfd8 6.Rd6 Bxd7 7.Rad1

The pin is killing Black.

7…Ra7 8.Nd5

Diagram 367

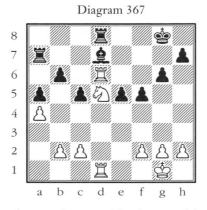

The weakness of b6 haunts black

The weakness of b6 has become extremely important since White threatens both Nf6+ (which can be defended by …Kf7) and Nxb6 (which can't be stopped).

8…Kf7 9.Nxb6 and now after **9…Ke7** White can torture his helpless (and quite lost) opponent in several ways (10.f3, 10.b3, and 10.R6d5 all leap to mind). Clearly, the creation of a second weakness/target in the enemy camp is a far from trivial accomplishment!

An untrained eye might consider things (in diagram 368) to be fairly balanced. However, White enjoys certain advantages that decisively tip the scales in his favor. Here's the short list:

➤ Superior King position.

➤ A passed c-pawn after a well timed c3-c4 push.

➤ Black's a6 pawn is a target that can be attacked if white's Rook is able to penetrate into the enemy position.

Diagram 368

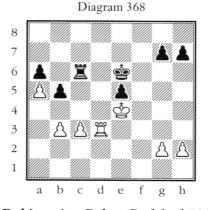

Rubinstein-Cohn, Carlsbad 1907
White to move

Two problems/questions must be addressed. One is whether black's e-pawn is a strength or weakness. The other is finding a way for White to infiltrate with his Rook.

1.Rh3!

This maneuver aims to turn black's kingside pawns into weaknesses. Defending the h- and g-pawns will force Black to make concessions which, when taking white's other plusses into account, should prove decisive (after all, there's only so much "bad news" a position can handle!).

1...h6

Mihail Marin, in his fantastic book, *Learn From the Legends—Chess Champions at Their Best*, gave a couple ways White can successfully deal with 1...g6. This is one of them: 2.Rxh7 Rxc3 3.Ra7 Rc6 (3...Rxb3 4.Rxa6+ Kf7 5.Rb6 also loses for Black) 4.Rg7 Kf6 5.Rb7 Rc3 6.Rb6+ Kg5 7.Rxa6 Rxb3 8.Re6 b4 9.Rxe5+ Kg4 10.Re6 g5 11.a6 Ra3 12.Kd4 Ra2 13.Kc4 Rxg2 14.a7 Ra2 15.Re7 Kh3 16.Kxb4 Kxh2 17.Kb3 Ra6 18.Re2+ Kg3 19.Ra2 Rxa7 20.Rxa7 Kf3 21.Rf7+ Ke3 22.Rg7 Kf4 23.Kc2 stopping black's pawn and winning the game.

2.Rg3

The two new weaknesses on g6 and g7 have placed Black under serious pressure to which there is no completely adequate response.

2...Kf6

2...g5 is met by the "obvious" 3.Rh3, a move low in subtlety but high in strength.

3.Kd5

White's vast superiority is now strikingly clear: White's King is completely dominant, while black's e-pawn has now been labeled as weak.

3...Re6 4.Rf3+ Ke7 5.g3!

A common "don't hurry" Rubinstein move. As discussed in the Cat and Mouse section, a player shouldn't hesitate to make quiet, "fixing moves" if his opponent is helpless. Placing the pawn on g3 gets a pawn off the 2nd rank in case black's Rook makes its way to d2 after ...Rd6+.

5...g6 6.Re3 Kf6 7.c4

Diagram 369

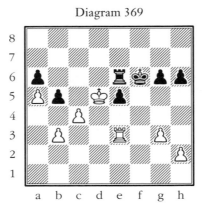

The c-pawn finally becomes a passed monster. Black's position has, as if by magic, become hopeless!

7...bxc4 8.bxc4 Re8 9.Rf3+ Kg5

Hoping to gain some counterplay by attacking white's kingside pawns.

10.c5 e4 11.h4+ Kg4 12.Rf4+ Kxg3 13.Rxe4 Ra8

This looks strange, but 13...Rd8+ 14.Kc6 Rc8+ 15.Kb6 was no picnic either.

14.c6 g5 15.hxg5 hxg5 16.c7 Kf3 17.Re1, 1-0. White will win black's Rook for the c-pawn, give up his own Rook for black's g-pawn, then finally have a meal on a6 and promote the a5-pawn.

Diagram 370

Smyslov-Simagin, Moscow 1966

White to move

White has an annoying edge. Aside from his superior kingside pawn structure, both his Rook and Knight are more active than their black counterparts. The main target is the b6-pawn, but before laying siege to it, White fixes black's kingside pawn weaknesses.

1.g4!

A huge move! Now the f6- and h7-pawns are long-term additions to black's "list of problems."

1...h5

Black can't wait for White to play Rc6 followed by Ke4-d3-c4-b5 with a total rout.

2.gxh5 Kh6 3.Kg4 f5+ 4.Kh4 f4

Trading off one of his potentially weak pawns makes good sense.

5. Rc8 fxe3 6.fxe3 Rd5 7.Rh8+ Kg7 8.Ra8 Nc3 9.Ra7

Threatening Nxe6+ but also preparing an attack against black's King by Nf3 and Ng5.

9...Re5

This stops Nxe6+ but gives White time for his kingside dreams.

10.Nf3 Re4+

And not 10...Rxe3 11.Ng5 when f7 can't be defended.

11.Kg5 Rxe3?

Black gets overwhelmed after this natural but poor move. Far better resistance was offered by 11...Nd5.

12.h6+ Kg8 13.h7+ Kxh7 14.Rxf7+ Kg8

Diagram 371

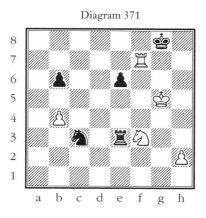

Both sides only have two pawns left, so one might expect Black to have real chances to survive. However, his King is in serious trouble and—by mixing threats to black's King and pawns—White can eventually pick up the bit on b6 and walk away with a won Rook endgame.

15.Kg6 Ne4

Black needs to have his Knight participate in the defense, but the jump to e4 doesn't get the job done. Sadly, neither does 15...Nd5 16.Ng5 e5 (Losing instantly is 16...Nxb4 17.Nh7 when the threat of Rf8 mate might prove a tad annoying) 17.Ne6 (the threat of Rf8 mate forces black's reply) 17...Nf4+ 18.Nxf4 exf4 19.Rxf4 Rh3 20.Kf5 Rxh2 21.Ke6 Rd2 22.Rf5 with a decisive advantage since White can eventually pick up black's b-pawn by Rd5, Kd6, b4-b5, and Kc7xb6.

16.h4 Nd6 17.Rd7 Rxf3 18.Rxd6 Kf8 19.Rxe6 Rg3+

As good as resignation is 19...Rf4 20.Rf6+.

20.Kf5 Rg1

20...Rh3 loses to 21.Kg5 (21.Kg4 is also good) 21...Rg3+ 22.Kh5 b5 23.Re5 with White owning two extra pawns.

21.Rxb6, 1-0.

Our final two examples show how "fishing for new weaknesses" is a common strategy even when material ahead. In the first, Alekhine turns what might be a complex technical task into something so smooth that it stuns the eye.

Diagram 372

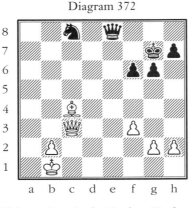

Alekhine - Samisch, Baden Baden 1925
White to move

White has an extra passed b-pawn but doesn't wish to push it right away since that would expose his King. Instead, he patiently plays to create a second weakness in black's position.

1.Qd4

Alekhine: "By this and his following move White selects the correct winning plan, which is the advance of his kingside pawns. The passed b-pawn must be advanced only later, when with the exchange of Queens the danger of perpetual check will be eliminated."

1...Qe7 2.Bd3! Qc7 3.g4 Kf7

Of course, 3...Qxh2?? loses the Knight to 4.Qd7+.

4.h4 Nb6 5.h5 gxh5 6.gxh5

A second weakness has been created—the h7-pawn.

6...Qc6 7.Be4!

White could have exchanged Queens with 7.Qe4 but decided to only do so when the h7-pawn was fixed, thus forcing the black King to stay on the kingside and baby-sit the weak h-pawn.

Note that White didn't fall for 7.Bxh7 Qxf3 8.Qxb6 Qd1+ 9.Ka2 Qa4+ with a draw by perpetual check.

7...Qb5 8.h6

Now the h7-pawn is stuck on a light square, where it will be forever vulnerable to the attentions of the Bishop.

8...Qb3

Also bad is 8...Qf1+ 9.Kc2 Qe2+ 10.Kc3 Qe1+ 11.Kb3 Qa5 12.Bxh7 Qb5+ 13.Qb4 Qd5+ 14.Kc2 Qc6+ 15.Qc3 and Black's done since 15...Qa4+ is killed by 16.Qb3+.

9.Bc2! Qb5

Diagram 373

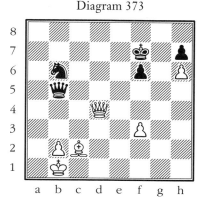

10.Qd3

Only now is White ready to force the trade of Queens. What's the difference between this position and the position after 6...Qc6 (when 7.Qe4 would have forced this exchange)? In the earlier position black's h-pawn could have advanced to the safe square on h6, which would have allowed black's King to rush over to the queenside and help stop the b-pawn. Now the h7-pawn is a permanent target and black's King is stuck doing guard duty in Siberia.

By the way, 10.Bxh7 also wins, but why allow Black to go bonkers with checks when you can trade Queens and win without any bother at all?

10...Qxd3 11.Bxd3

White has achieved the exchange of Queens in the most favorable circumstances: the black King is tied to the defense of the h-pawn and the Knight is quite unable to cope with the passed b-pawn supported by King and Bishop.

11...Nc8

Also hopeless was 11...Kg8 12.b4 when 12...Nd5 13.Bc4 picks up the pinned Knight, while 12...Nc8 13.b5 with Kb2-b3-b4-c5 to follow is not worth playing out.

12.Bxh7, 1-0.

Amazing what a second weakness in the opponent's position can do, isn't it?

Our last example is a very smooth victory by the 5th World Champion where we see simplification, a bit of Cat and Mouse, and the creation of more than one new weakness (the more the merrier!).

Diagram 374

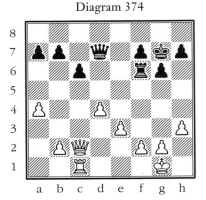

Euwe - van Doesburgh, Dutch Championship 1938
White to move

Before moving on, I can imagine some of you screaming, "Wait a second! White's a pawn up and should be winning easily. Why bother using such an example?"

This is a fair question, but I can answer it with a question of my own: "How often have you (meaning all of us) failed to convert such a decisive plus?"

The beauty of this game is that White doesn't rest on his laurels, nor lose his concentration. In fact, he does what we all should learn to do in such a situation: Don't give the opponent any counterplay whatsoever and constantly strive to make new positional gains in the form of multiple enemy weaknesses.

1.Qc5!

This more or less forces Black (who would love to retain the Queens and keep things as complicated as possible) to accept the trade of Queens, since both 1...a6 and 1...b6 run into 2.Qe5! when the Rook is pinned to its King.

1...Qf5 2.Qxf5 Rxf5 3.Kf1

Wisely bringing the King into the center. Absolutely horrible is 3.Rc5?? (What's the hurry?) 3...Rxc5 4.dxc5 Kf6 5.f4 (Trying to prevent ...Ke5/...Kd5/...Kxc5) 5...Kf5 (and not 5...Ke6? 6.e4) 6.Kf2 Ke4 when Black's the one in charge.

3...Kf8 4.Rc5

Now White is happy to transpose into a King and pawn endgame, but this time Black must avoid it since a pawn on c5 could now be supported.

4...Rf6

4...Rxc5 5.dxc5 Ke7 6.Ke2 Ke6 7.Kd3 Kd5 8.b4 a5 9.e4+ Ke5 10.bxa5 is winning for White.

5.Ra5!

A strong move that forces the creation of a hole on b6 that, after a4-a5, will freeze black's queenside pawns. Note that White isn't simply going to try and win by using his extra pawn. Instead, he wants to create as many weaknesses as possible in the enemy camp until the defense simply falls apart. *You can never give the opponent too many weaknesses!*

5...a6 6.Re5

Stopping the enemy King from coming towards the center. Note how patient White is, how he is slowly playing for new enemy weaknesses, and how he is going out of his way to prevent enemy counterplay.

6...Rd6

6...b6 7.a5 b5 leaves the c6- and a6-pawns very weak, and the c5-square ready to accept the white King as a squatter.

7.a5

Freezing black's pawns on a6 and b7. If Black plays passively, white's King will calmly walk all the way to b6.

7...f6 8.Rc5 Ke7 9.g4

Now that Black is more or less helpless, White begins a new plan: he intends to push this pawn to g5, exchange it for the f6-pawn, and create a passed e-pawn.

9...h6 10.Ke2 Re6 11.f4 Rd6 12.h4 Kf7 13.h5!

13.g5 hxg5 14.hxg5 f5 15.b4 is another way to win since his plan of marching the King all the way to b6 is hard to deal with, while a well-timed d4-d5 push is also in the air.

13...gxh5

No better is 13...g5 14.fxg5 fxg5 (14...hxg5 leaves White with a powerful passed h-pawn) 15.Rf5+ (Trapping the King on one side or the other.) 15...Ke7 16.Kd3 when e3-e4 gives Black few chances to resist.

14.Rxh5

Suddenly Black is not only a pawn down, but also must care for weaknesses on h6, f6, and b7!

14...Kg6 15.Kd3 Rd7 16.e4 Kh7

Things were looking grim, so Black allows a little sequence that leads to the exchange of a few pawns. However, this fails to ease black's pain.

17.g5 fxg5 18.fxg5 Kg6 19.Rxh6+ Kxg5

Black no doubt was happy that he has managed to trade off his weak pawns on f6 and h6; the defender is usually delighted to exchange pawns. Unfortunately, this position is, in reality, dead lost for Black.

20.Rh2!

Threatening Rf2, trapping the black King away from the action.

20...Kf6

No choice.

21.e5+ Ke6 22.Rh6+ Kd5

Again, there was no choice. 22...Ke7 23.Rh7+ trades Rooks and enters a won King and pawn endgame, while 22...Kf5 23.Rf6+ forces the black King to no-man's land.

23.b4

Diagram 375

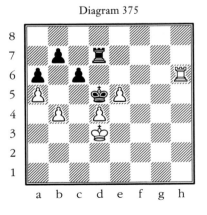

Another "No counterplay allowed!" move. Now that ...c6-c5 has been stopped, Black finds himself in zugzwang: any pawn move loses material, a King move is illegal, any move of the Rook away from the d-file allows Rd6 mate, and moving back to d8 (which is all he has) let's white's Rook target b7.

23...Rd8

Forced. The Rook must stay on the d-file since moving away allows Rd6 mate.

24.Rh7 Rb8 25.Re7!

Accurate to the end. Black must either give up his b-pawn or push it.

25...b6

25...Rh8 is met by 26.Rd7+ (Don't give Black counterplay after 26.Rxb7 Rh3+) 26...Ke6 27.Rxb7 when Black should resign.

26.Rd7+ Ke6 27.Rd6+, 1-0.

All King and Pawn Endgames are Confusing!

One would think that King and pawn endgames would be easy to master since all the pieces have been traded. Doesn't the lack of mutual armies make things far less complicated? The answer to this is a resounding "no!" In fact, many King and pawn endgames are so complex that they even boggle the minds of the world's elite players.

Due to this complexity, masters know that entering into any King and pawn endgame is an "all or nothing" decision. Leaping into one is perfectly okay (and often the only way to win or draw a game), but make sure you have a firm handle on the resulting position before doing so!

The following examples are meant to do two things:

 Teach you to appreciate their beauty.

 Act as a warning. Consider it a "Danger Will Robinson, danger!" kind of thing. Don't ever enter a King and pawn endgame unless you have no choice, or are sure that it leads to the desired result.

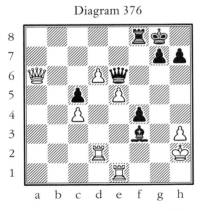

Diagram 376

Shirov – Grischuk, New Delhi 2000

Black to move

374

Okay, I can hear the outraged protests. This isn't even close to being a King and pawn endgame! True. But it turns out that one could occur by force after black's sacrificial move.

1...Bg4!? 2.hxg4

After pondering the upcoming King and pawn endgame, Shirov decided on 2.Qb7 in the actual game and ended up winning, though the Queen move didn't give him any advantage whatsoever. It turns out, though, that 2.hxg4 wins by force. But, as Shirov admits, it took him three years and computer assistance to finally prove this to himself!

2...Qxg4 3.Rf1 f3 4.Qa2 Qh4+ 5.Kg1 Qg3+ 6.Rg2 Qxg2+ 7.Qxg2 fxg2 8.Rxf8+ Kxf8 9.e6 g5 10.Kxg2 h5

Diagram 377

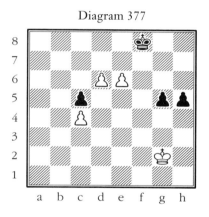

We've reached the position that Shirov couldn't quite solve during the game. It's clear that white's only hope of winning is to create a pawn mate, a concept we've already looked at in Strange Races in Part Six. To accomplish this, White needs to reach one of the following two positions:

Diagram 378

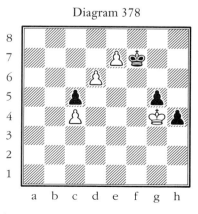

White wants Black to have the move

Diagram 379

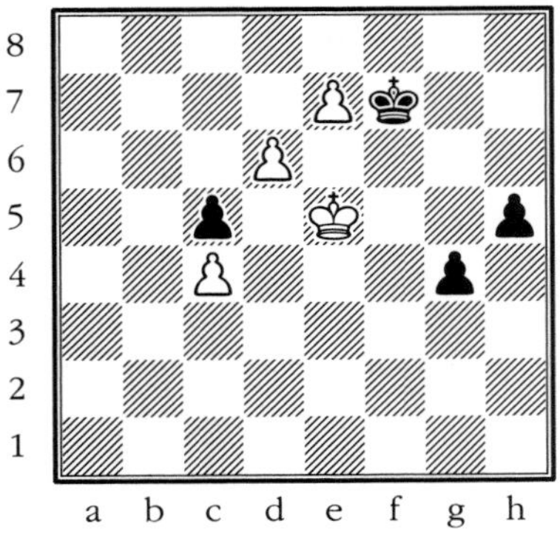

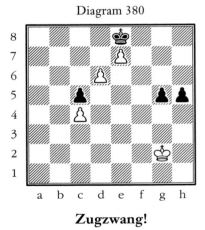

To win, White needs the move

The following tempo moves (from diagram 377) are all designed to make one of these two diagrammed positions occur.

11.e7+ Ke8 12.Kh2!

A key Triangulation maneuver. The straightforward 12.Kf3? h4 13.Kg4 Kf7 leads us to diagram 378, where White wins if Black has the move, but only draws if White has it (which is the unfortunate case here). The note to black's 12th move will demonstrate why this is so.

12...Kf7

12...h4 13.Kh3 Kf7 14.Kg4 gives White the position we labeled as winning in diagram 378. Black has the move and must step back to the fatal e8-square. 14...Ke8 15.Kxg5 h3 (else White would take the h-pawn) 16.Kf6 h2 (16...Kd7 17.Kf7 and white Queens with check) 17.Ke6 h1=Q 18.d7 mate.

13.Kg3 Ke8 14.Kg2!

Diagram 380

Zugzwang!

Incredibly, this seemingly innocuous move leaves Black in zugzwang! We've already seen that 14...h4 fails to 15.Kh3 Kf7 16.Kg4 when Black loses since he's left with the "fatal" move. However, a King move or pushing the pawn to g4 both allow White to create our second key diagram (379).

14...g4 15.Kg3 Kf7 16.Kf4 Ke8 17.Ke5 Kf7

Ke6 can't be allowed.

18.Kd5 g3 19.Kc6 g2

No choice. 19...Ke8 20.d7+ Kxe7 21.Kc7 g2 22.d8=Q+ is easy for White.

20.Kd7 g1=Q 21.e8=Q+ and White wins. Sure enough, after 21...Kg7 22.Qe5+! Kg6 3.Kc7 Black can't prevent White from promoting his d-pawn.

Though this game might seem unfathomable to some, at least the basic ideas (pawn mates and queening with check) are easy to grasp. Our next example is even more outrageous.

Diagram 381

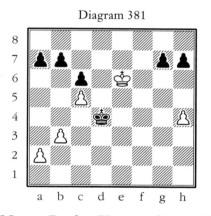

Martz - Benko, Torremolinos 1973
Black to move

Black is a pawn up *and* he has the move, so how hard can this be? Judge for yourself as we follow Benko's comments from his book, *Pal Benko: My Life, Games, and Compositions*:

"So we find ourselves in an interesting King and pawn endgame. This kind of ending rarely occurs in modern tournaments, so I was delighted to get the chance to play such a position.

"Here the game was adjourned and I had to seal my move. A quick calculation convinced me that 41...Kxc5 would be a blunder: 42.Kf7 b5 43.Kxg7 h5 44.Kg6 Kb4 45.Kxh5 c5 46.Kg6 c4 47.bxc4 bxc4 48.h5, with a draw. I must admit that, in the little time I had left, my first plan was 41...Ke4, when 42.Kf7 Kf5 43.Kxg7 h5 would be an easy win. Also winning for me is 41...Ke4 42.Kd6 a5 (or 42...h5 43.a3 Kd4) 43.Kc7 Kd5 44.Kb6 g6 45.a3 h6 46.b4 axb4 47.axb4

Kc4 48.Kxb7 Kb5!. Then I noticed that 41...Ke4 42.b4! created some difficulties for me: 42...h5! 43.a4! and now:

Diagram 382

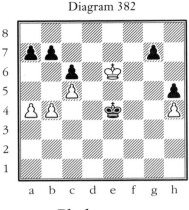

Black to move

> 43...Kd4 44.Kd6 (44.Kd7? a5!) 44...Kc4 45.Kc7 Kxb4
> 46.Kxb7 Kxc5 47.Kxa7 (47.a5? Kd6! 48.Kxa7 Kc7 49.Ka6 g6!
> wins) 47...Kb4 48.Kb6 Kxa4 49.Kxc6 is a draw.

> 43...Kf4 44.b5! g5 45.hxg5 Kxg5 46.b6! (46.a5!? a6!) 46...axb6
> 47.cxb6 h4 48.a5 isn't what Black wants. However, Black
> can improve his chances with 46...a5! (instead of 46...axb6)
> 47.Kd7 h4 48.Kc7 h3 49.Kxb7 h2 50.Ka8 h1=Q 51.b7 Qd5
> 52.b8=Q Qxc5, and now White can force a draw with 53.Qb6!
> Qc3 54.Kb7 c5 55.Kc6 c4 56.Qb5+ Kf4 47.Kc5, =.

> 43...a6! 44.a5! Kf4 45.Kd7 g5 46.hxg5 Kxg5 47.Kc7 h4
> 48.Kxb7 h3 49.Kxa6 h2 50.Kb7 h1=Q 51.a6 and a strange
> position has come about:

Diagram 383

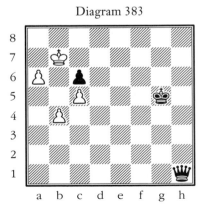

"White's pawn only stands on the 6th rank (which usually means that it's time to resign) but, despite this, Black has to show a bit of care if wants to reel in the point: 51...Qb1? (Correct is 51...Qh7+ 52.Kb8 Qg8+ 53.Kb7 Qf7+ 54.Kb8 Qf4+! and wins) 52.a7 Qxb4+ 53.Kc7 (not 53.Kxc6?? Qe4+ followed by 54...Qa8. Also bad is 53.Kc8?? Qxc5 54.a8=Q Qf8+ 55.Kb7 Qxa8+ 56.Kxa8 c5 and wins) 53...Qa5+ 54.Kb7 and Black doesn't have time to take the pawn on c5.

"The position after 43...a6 is full of interesting variations, e.g., 44.a5! Kd4 (instead of 44...Kf4) 45.Kf5 Kc4 46.Kg6 Kxb4 47.Kxg7! Kxc5! 48.Kg6 Kb4 49.Kxh5 c5 50.Kg4 c4 51.h5 c3 52.h6 c2 53.h7 c1=Q, and Black should win. After considering all of this, I came to the conclusion that I must find an easier solution. As it happens, there is one in the position."

The move Benko found was **41...g6!!** when there followed **42.Kf6 Ke4! 43.Kg7 Kf4 44.Kh6 Kg4 45.Kxh7 g5! 46.hxg5 Kxg5 47.Kg7 Kf5 48.Kf7 Ke5 49.Ke7 Kd5 50.Kd7 Kxc5 51.Kc7 b5 52.Kb7 a5 53.a3 b4 54.a4 Kd4 55.Kxc6 Kc3 56.Kb5 Kxb3 57.Kxa5 Ka3**, 0-1.

I don't know about you, but I have two thoughts whenever I look at this endgame. One is, "It's very beautiful." The other is, "My god! I would never have found any of that over the board!"

The message should be clear: *never enter a pawn endgame lightly!*

Transposition into a pawn ending often marks the final stage of the opponent's demise. However, masters have learned to be very wary of all King and pawn endgames since strange, often unforeseen, complications can turn an easy win into a draw or even a loss!

Diagram 384

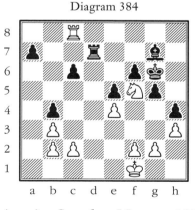

Aronin-Smyslov, Moscow 1951
White to move

Most experienced masters would note the possibility of entering an apparently winning King and pawn endgame with 1.Rg8. However, their spider sense would tingle and they would hold off on such mass exchanges. Why should they trade? Their Knight is a monster, their pawns are safe, and their Rook is active. Compare that with black's garbage Bishop, his passive Rook, and his vulnerable pawns.

One would expect such a strong player as Aronin to only go into a winning King and pawn endgame *after tidying up the position*. Thus, 1.Ke2, stopping black's Rook from penetrating into white's camp and also centralizing white's King, would easily win the game.

1.Rg8? Kh7 2.Rxg7+??

White completely missed black's brilliant defensive trap. It's easy to miss! But why go into something that might turn complex when simple moves keep the win safely in hand? For example: 2.Rb8 c5 3.Rc8 Kg6 4.Ke2 (the c-pawn isn't going anywhere) when Black will lose material without having any counterplay whatsoever.

2...Rxg7 3.Nxg7 Kxg7 4.g4

This was white's idea. It seems to end all kingside counterplay for Black since leaving the pawn on g4 results in a winning endgame for White, while taking en-passant gives White a "winning" outside passed pawn. It *is* winning, isn't it?

4...hxg3 e.p.

I guess it isn't! White had evidently hoped for 4...Kf7 5.Ke2 Ke6 6.Kd3 Kd6 7.Kc4 a5 8.c3 bxc3 (8...c5 9.Kb5 is no better) 9.bxc3 Kd7 10.Kc5 Kc7 11.c4 Kd7 12.Kb6 and wins.

5.fxg3 g4!! 6.h4

Diagram 385

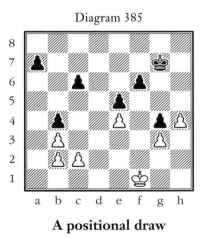

A positional draw

White has nothing after 6.hxg4 Kh6 7.Kf2 Kg5. However, it *does* seem that white's outside passed pawn should bring easy victory. Incredibly, this doesn't prove to be the case.

6...c5!

An important move that deprives white's King of the d4-square once the e5-pawn moves forward. Okay, this doesn't make sense now, but it will soon!

7.Ke2 Kh7! 8.Kd3 Kh6!

Black avoids the g6-square since, in the tactical lines that might follow, ...f6-f5 would allow an unfortunate check after exf5.

9.c3

9.Kc4?? actually loses to 9...f5! 10.exf5 (It's already too late to defend: 10.Kd3 f4 11.gxf4 exf4 12.Ke2 Kh5 13.e5 Kg6 wins) 10...e4! 11.c3 a5 12.f6 Kg6 when the e-pawn turns into a Queen.

9...a5 10.cxb4 axb4, ½-½. After 11.Ke2 Kh7 White can't make progress.

Are you convinced yet that almost any King and pawn endgame might turn out to be a minefield that you should think twice about before walking through? No? Yes? Let's look at a game won by IM Jack Peters. The transition into a King and pawn endgame was the perfect solution here, but the calculation necessary to prove this is far from easy in an over the board situation.

Diagram 386

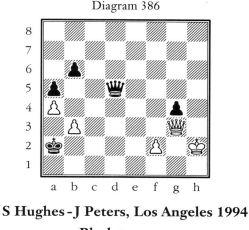

S Hughes - J Peters, Los Angeles 1994
Black to move

Queen and pawn endgames are notoriously difficult so, in the interest of making his life easier, Black must consider the very forcing 1...Qf3 when it's clear that, in the ensuing King and pawn endgame, both sides will eat each other's pawns. After a deep count it might seem that each side will promote with a resulting Queen and pawn vs. Queen endgame. Is that what Black wants, or is something else going on here?

1...Qf3!

It turns out that this is a dead win! But that decision can only be made if Black notices a subtle point at the end of a long, forcing sequence.

2.Qxf3

White doesn't have much choice. 2.Qh4 Kxb3 is hopeless, 2.Qc7 Qxf2+ is even worse, and 2.Qg1 Qh3 mate is the worst of all!

2...gxf3 3.Kg3 Kxb3 4.Kxf3 Kxa4 5.Kg4 Kb5!

Getting out of the way of the a-pawn and simultaneously preparing to stop white's pawn with the King.

6.f4 Kc6 7.Kg5 Kd7 8.Kg6 a4 9.f5 a3 10.f6 a2 11.f7 Ke7!, 0-1. This was seen by Black when he played 1...Qf3. White resigned since 12.Kg7 is met by 12...a1=Q+.

Such transitions from "messy" positions to the supposed serenity of a King and pawn endgame can be a blessing or a curse. In the following example White had to decide whether or not to leap into unknown King and pawn waters.

Diagram 387

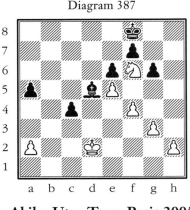

Akiko Uto - Tran, Paris 2005
White to move

In the game, White avoided the King and pawn endgame and took a walk down the wrong path with 1.Nd7+. The real questions concerning this position are:

➤ Is the King and pawn endgame worth considering after 1.Nxd5?

➤ If White retains the Knight, who is better and why?

The King and pawn endgame that arises after 1.Nxd5 exd5 2.g4 proves to be extremely interesting.

Diagram 388

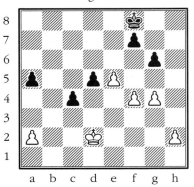

It seems that white's plan of creating a passed e- and h-pawn (which will be unstoppable due to their distance from each other) will give her the full point: 2...d4 3.h4 (and not 3.f5?? g5 when the g-pawn stops two white pawns) 3...Ke7 4.f5 followed by h5 when Black must resign.

Is it really that simple? Of course not! It's a pawn endgame and that means there are almost always surprising resources lurking behind the scenes. So let's try (after 2.g4) 2...g5. A bit of analysis makes it clear that this is a dismal failure: 3.fxg5 Ke7 (or 3...Kg7 4.h4 Kg6 5.Kc3 Kg7 6.h5 Kh7 7.g6+ fxg6 8.e6 Kg7 9.h6+ and a pawn will queen) 4.h4 d4 (4...Ke6 5.h5 Kxe5 6.h6 forces the promotion of the h-pawn) 5.h5 Kf8 6.h6 Kg8 7.g6! fxg6 8.e6, 1-0.

Can Black try ...f7-f6 at some point? Let's see: 2.g4 Ke7 3.h4 f6 4.h5! and we have a very pleasing pawn structure that guarantee's White success: 4...g5 5.h6 Kf7 6.e6+!, winning.

How about 2.g4 f6! (threatening to win by 3...fxe5 4.fxe5 g5!, fixing two pawns with one) when 3.e6 Ke7 4.f5 g5, =. Are we on to something? Suppose White chops off the pawn after 2...f6 3.exf6 Kf7 4.g5. This paints a nice visual picture, but it's only a draw after 4...d4 5.Ke2 c3 6.Kd3 Ke6—black's c- and d-pawns handcuff white's King, while white's four kingside pawns are stopped by black's King and pawn.

It seems we might have found a defense for Black, but one last calm look will give us the "answer": 2...f6 3.h4! fxe5 (3...Ke7 is met by 4.h5) 4.fxe5 Ke7 5.h5 and White's back in the win column.

At this point I can see White snapping off black's Bishop and rushing into this endgame, confident that victory will be hers. However, we've missed something! Take one final look at the position after 2...f6 3.h4

Diagram 389

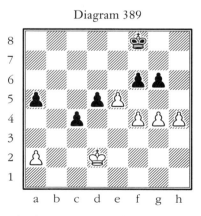

Black to move and save himself

It turns out that 3...g5!! saves the game:

➤ 4.hxg5 fxe5 5.fxe5 d4 6.a4 Kf7 7.Kc2 Kg6 8.e6 Kg7, =.

■──➤   4.exf6?? gxh4 and Black wins.

■──➤   4.h5 gxf4 (4...fxe5?? 5.fxe5 wins for White) 5.e6 f3 6.h6 c3+
7.Kc2! (This allows White to follow up with Qc8, an idea that isn't
possible after 7.Kxc3 f2 8.h7 f1=Q 9.h8=Q+ Ke7 10.Qc8?? [10.
Qg8 was correct] 10...Qc1+ picking up the Queen) 7...f2 8.h7
f1=Q 9.h8=Q+ Ke7 10.Qc8! Qe2+ when only Black has chances.

■──➤   4.fxg5 fxe5 and Black wins *if* he can reach the following key
position with White to move:

Diagram 390

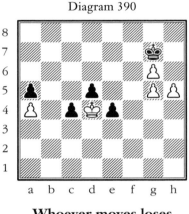

Whoever moves loses

White to move: 1.Kc3 e3 2.Kc2 d4 and black's pawns are like a tidal wave.

Black to move: 1...Kg8 2.h6 Kh8 3.g7+ Kh7 4.g6+ Kg8 5.Ke5 e3 6.Kf6 e2
7.h7 mate.

Returning to the arrowed analysis featuring 4.fxg5 fxe5 above, it turns out
that Black can indeed achieve the sunny side of diagram 390 after 5.Kc3 Kf7
6.h5 e4 7.Kd4 a4 8.g6+ Kg7! (and not 8...Kf6?? 9.g5+ Kg7 10.a3 and White
wins, as shown in the diagram above) 9.a3 Kf6! (Avoiding 9...Kh6?? 10.Ke5!
e3 11.Kf6 e2 12.g7 e1=Q 13.g8=Q) 10.g5+ Kg7 and White possesses the fatal
move and, as a result, loses.

So it turns out that White can't do more than draw the King and pawn endgame, once again confirming our adage that "all King and pawn endgames are
confusing!" Instead, returning to diagram 387, an experienced player would
quickly look over the mess we just explored and then refuse to make the exchange, even if he wasn't able to plumb the King and pawn endgame's depths.
Why would he make this decision? Because it should be obvious that the minor
piece endgame gives White a huge advantage with no risk whatsoever.

From diagram 387:

1.Kc3

White fixes the c-pawn on c4 and ties down black's Bishop to its defense.

1...Kg7

Moving towards the middle doesn't help: 1...Ke7 2.g4 Kf8 3.h4 Ke7 4.h5 gxh5 5.gxh5 Kf8 6.h6.

2.h4!

This not only gets white's kingside majority into motion, but also stops all ...g6-g5 based counterplay.

2...Kh6 3.g4 Kg7 and now White has many ways to win the game. She can take her time and play "fixer" moves like 4.a3, or she can go into a winning King and pawn endgame by 4.Nxd5 exd5 5.f5 (this is far superior to the King and pawn position we entered earlier—White will follow with h5 and promote one of her pawns), or White can go right for the win of material via 4.g5 Kf8 5.Nd7+ Ke7 6.Nb6 when Nxc4 can't be stopped.

After looking over this endgame, World Championship candidate Yasser Seirawan said: "My thought process would be that if the King and pawn ending was 'close,' White should start with 1.Kc3 in order to always get the King and pawn ending she wants by handcuffing the d5-Bishop to the c4-pawn. As Black 'passes,' White advances her kingside pawns to g4 and h4, getting a position where black's King is on g7 before playing f4-f5. Then she can transpose into the King and pawn ending."

Note that Seirawan made it clear that he would have no interest in entering a "close" position from a position of strength. In other words, why take risks when you can step into the King and pawn endgame on your own (highly favorable) terms?

We've seen players of all strengths having trouble correctly assessing some very complicated King and pawn endgames. However, it's not uncommon for even world-class players to botch positions that should be well within their range to solve. Our next game, between the legendary Miguel Najdorf and World Championship contender Henrique Mecking, is winning for Black, but he doesn't come close to winning it!

Diagram 391

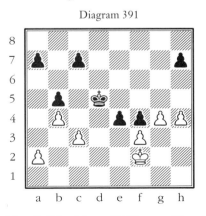

Najdorf-Mecking, Wijk aan Zee 1978

Black to move

In the actual game, Black tossed certain victory away by playing 1...e3+?? 2.Ke2 Kc4, but after 3.h5 and the game was drawn since 3...Kxc3 loses to 4.g5.

Instead, **1...exf3! 2.Kxf3 Ke5** wins for the following reasons:

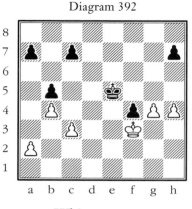

Diagram 392

White to move

━━━➤ At some point White will be forced to advance his kingside pawns, whereupon Black will be able to munch on them with his King.

━━━➤ Trying to hold Black off with King moves (such as Kf2) fails since ...Ke4 followed by ...f3 and ...Kf4 still picks off the kingside pawns.

━━━➤ Black has two tempo moves on the queenside to white's one. This is of critical importance!

3.Kf2 Ke4 4.h5

Lines like 4.g5? Kf5 5.Kf3 a6 6.a3 c6 7.Kf2 Kg4 and 4.Ke2? f3+ 5.Kf2 Kf4 6.g5 Kg4 and 4.Kf1? Kf3 5.g5 Kg4 are even easier for Black.

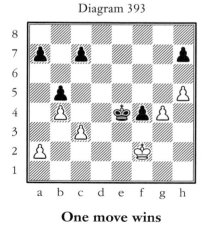

Diagram 393

One move wins

After 4.h5 we have a "Black to move and win" situation.

4...Ke5!

I can only guess that Mecking missed this move. Other tries don't get the job done:

▶ 4...h6?? 5.g5! wins for White!

▶ 4...f3 5.g5 Kf5 6.g6 hxg6 7.hxg6 (and not 7.h6?? Kf6 8.Kxf3 Kf7 9.Kf4 Kg8 10.Kg4 Kh7 11.Kg5 a6 12.a3 c6 and, thanks to that extra queenside tempo move, White has to drop his h-pawn and will lose the game) 7...Kxg6 8.Kxf3 Kf5 9.Ke3 Ke5 10.Kd3 Kd5 11.Kd2 when 11...Kc4 12.Kc2 and 11...c5 12.Kd3 both get nowhere for Black.

▶ 4...a6 5.Kf1! (5.Ke1 is the same thing since 5...Kf3 6.g5 Kg2 7.g6 hxg6 8.hxg6 f3 9.g7 f2+ 10.Kd2 f1=Q 11.g8=Q+ would make White happy) 5...Ke5 6.Kf2 and suddenly black's win is gone since he has tossed away one of his precious queenside tempo moves: 6...Kf6 7.Kf3 Kg5 8.h6! Kxh6 9.Kxf4, =.

5.Kf3

Nothing saves White: 5.g5 (or 5.Ke2 Kf6 6.Kf3 Kg5 7.a3 a6 8.h6 c6 and White loses all his kingside pawns.) 5...Kf5 6.g6 hxg6 7.h6 Kf6 8.Kf3 g5 and it's all over.

5...h6! 6.a3 a6 7.Kf2 Kf6 8.Ke2 Kg5 9.Kf3

Now, after black's quiet push with his c-pawn, we have a "whoever moves loses" situation. Thanks to that final queenside tempo move, Black gets the prize.

9...c6 and it's time for White to resign.

Diagram 394

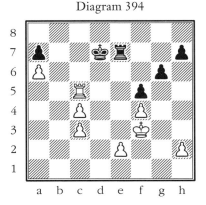

Bacrot - Kramnik, Dortmund 2005
White to move

White is two pawns up and is clearly winning, yet claiming a theoretical win and actually proving it are often two different things. In the present situation

White has many good moves (1.Rb5 and 1.h4 are good choices), but offering a Rook exchange by 1.Re5 is extremely tempting since, if the resulting King and pawn endgame is indeed a win, it would avoid the potential complications of a long, drawn out Rook endgame.

Thus we come face to face with a common question: does entry into the King endgame make life easier, or are we setting ourselves up for some strange King and pawn endgame pitfall?

1.Re5!

Best, but the two sets of doubled isolated pawns will demand some skill from White before he gains the full point.

> **USEFUL ADVICE**
>
> If you find yourself facing a decision like this and you have any doubts about the King and pawn endgame that results, avoid it like the plague!

1...Rxe5 2.fxe5 g5

Stopping white's King from penetrating and also gaining counterplay by setting his own pawn majority into motion. Completely hopeless is 2...Ke7 3.Kf4 Ke6 when both 4.h4 h6 5.c5 Kd5 6.h5 gxh5 7.Kxf5 Kxc5 8.e6 Kd6 9.Kf6 and 4.c5 Kd5 5.c4+ Kxc5 6.Kg5 win quickly.

3.c5

The material in Part Five should have already taught you that side-by-side passed pawns, separated by one file, guard themselves. For example, 3...Ke6 is met by 4.c6 when 4...Kxe5 5.c7 leads to a new Queen for White.

3...h6 4.c4

Diagram 395

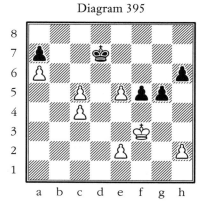

4...h5

Trying a waiting game by 4...Kd8 also fails: 5.Ke3 Ke7 (5...Kc7 6.e6 is easy while 5...Kd7 6.Kd4 intending Kd5 will shortly force Black to lay down his arms: 6...Ke6 7.c6 f4 8.c7 Kd7 9.e6+ Kxc7 10.Ke5 Kc6 11.e7 Kd7 12.Kf6 Ke8

13.Ke6 when the advance of the c-pawn leads to mate in six) 6.c6 Ke6 7.c5 Ke7 8.Kd4 g4 9.Kd5 f4 10.e6 (10.Ke4 g3 11.hxg3 fxg3 12.Kf3 is another way to go about it) 10...f3 11.exf3 gxf3 12.c7 f2 13.c8=Q f1=Q 14.Qd7+ Kf6 15.Qf7+ Kg5 16.Qxf1, 1-0.

5.h4 g4+

Black gets no hope at all from 5...gxh4 since 6.Kg2 followed by 7.Kh3 and Kxh4 is ridiculously easy.

6.Kf4 Ke6

Similar lines to the actual game occur after 6...Kd8 7.c6 Kc7 8.e6 Kxc6 9.c5 Kc7 10.e3 Kc6 (10...Kd8 11.c6) 11.Ke5.

7.c6 Ke7 8.c5 Ke6

Black has no choice since 8...Kd8 9.e6 forces a new Queen in a clear, simple manner.

9.c7!

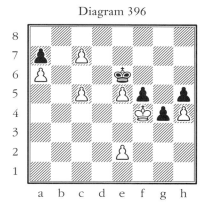

Diagram 396

The key to the position. White gives up this pawn so his e-pawn can march down the board with tempo.

9...Kd7 10.e6+ Kxc7 11.e3!

Most accurate. Since 11...Kd8 12.c6 loses immediately, Black must move his King to c6 where it will be in check if the pawn promotes on e8.

11...Kc6 12.Ke5!

This leads to a winning Queen endgame.

Though 12.e7?? Kd7 would win for Black, White could have played 12.Kxf5. He decided to leave that pawn on the board since, in some lines, it would block checks on the f-file by black's soon-to-be-born Queen.

12...g3 13.e7 Kd7 14.Kf6 g2 15.c6+ Kc7 16.e8=Q g1=Q 17.Qd7+ Kb6 18.c7, 1-0. Black would run out of checks after 18...Qa1+ (18...Qxe3 19.c8=Q Qh6+ 20.Kxf5) 19.Kg6 Qg1+ 20.Kh7.

Our final example shows me entering an extremely complex King and pawn endgame simply because it was my only chance for survival!

Diagram 397

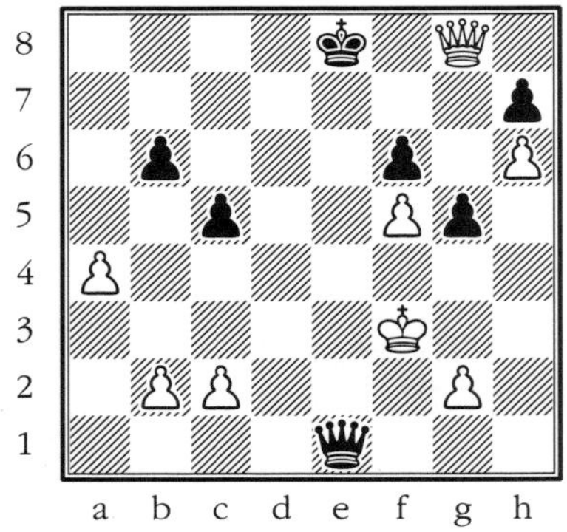

Milat - Silman, National Open 1998
Black to move

My opponent had been thrashing me for the whole game (White had missed at least one instant win), and the creation of various perpetual check themes was my last line of defense. After offering my opponent several bottles of free beer, which he refused (seemingly intent on winning the game), we reached the position in the diagram.

Black has a choice between two legal moves, 1...Kd7 and 1...Ke7. Only one is playable.

1...Ke7!

The only good move, and it shows how selection between seemingly similar choices can have an enormous impact on a game's result. When faced with this kind of decision, you can't take it lightly. It's very important to hunker down and try and discern what the differences are, and how those differences will ultimately affect your chances. In this case, 1...Kd7?? would have led to a lost King and pawn endgame after 2.Qe6+! Qxe6 3.fxe6+. Note that this move comes with check, meaning that Black must deal with the pawn immediately. Unfortunately, 3...Kxe6 allows 4.g4 when Black would have a very inferior version of the actual game since black's kingside pawn majority would be crippled.

2.Qe6+!?

At the time I was positive that this allowed me to save myself, though much of that view was based on ignorance. I was more worried about 2.Qxh7+ Kd6 3.Qb7 though I was pretty sure that 3...Qd1+ would give me sufficient play. I reasoned that my King was active, white's King was vulnerable, and the white Queen was out of play and unable to stop perpetual check. Whether this re-ally drew didn't matter at the time, the game had been going on for hours and my old, exhausted brain was willing to grab hold of any happy result, real or imagined, that it saw.

2...Qxe6 3.fxe6 f5!

Made possible by 1...Ke7 since his 3.fxe6 was no longer check. Now my kingside majority is mobile and keeps his King at bay.

4.b3 Kxe6 5.c3

Diagram 398

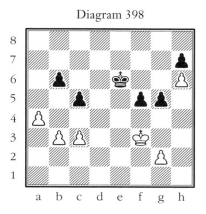

I began to think that I might even have winning chances! At this point a well-known grandmaster happened to stroll by. He glanced at the position for a couple of minutes and walked away. Later he confided that he also thought that I was on top (two minutes isn't time enough for anyone to figure things out, but it does show that even a world class player won't find these positions easy).

Now I began to think. I thought and thought and thought and became more and more depressed as the minutes ticked by. Finally I convinced myself that I was lost. White can create an annoying outside passed pawn on the queenside. True, black's King is more active than white's but, during the game, I couldn't see how this was going to save me against best play! Cursing my luck, I struggled to find some saving scheme and finally came up with something. Notice that I didn't say "something good."

5...Ke5

At the time I thought this was very important. The idea is to meet 6.Ke3 with 6...f4+. Unfortunately, it turns out that this check is a losing blunder. However, during the game I fully intended to play it! Embarrassing but true! Let's see why 6.Ke3 f4+ fails:

7.Kf3 (7.Kd3 Kd5 8.b4 c4+ 9.Ke2 g4 creates a drawing blockade. This is one of the important points of 5...Ke5) 7...Kf5 8.b4 g4+ 9.Ke2 Ke4 10.a5 bxa5 11.bxa5 Kd5.

Diagram 399

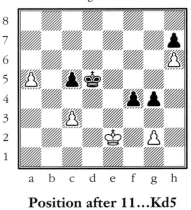

Position after 11...Kd5

I really believed I was drawing here since 12.Kd3?? is met by 12...c4+.

I happily rested in my fool's paradise until I got home. Setting up this position on a board, I immediately noticed that 12.c4+! wins: 12...Kc6 13.Kd3 Kb7 14.Ke4 f3 15.gxf3 gxf3 16.Kxf3 Ka6 17.Ke4 Kxa5 18.Ke5! Ka4 19.Kd6 Kb4 20.Kd5 and Black is toast since he's on the wrong end of a Trebuchet!

Fortunately, my opponent agreed with my incorrect assessment and tossed out:

6.g3

Now the game was eventually agreed drawn due to a line I'd worked out when I played 5...Ke5:

6...Kd5 7.Ke3 Kd6 8.Kd2 Kd5 9.Kc2

And not 9.Kd3?? c4+! when Black wins.

9...Kd6 10.Kd3 Kd5 11.b4 Kc6 12.Kc4 cxb4 13.cxb4 b5+! 14.axb5+ Kb6 15.Kd5 Kxb5 16.Ke5 f4 17.gxf4 gxf4 18.Kxf4 Kxb4 19.Kf5 Kc5 20.Kf6 Kd6 21.Kg7 Ke7 22.Kxh7 Kf7, ½-½.

At the time I was impressed with myself. As already pointed out, though, my elation turned to self-loathing when I returned home. It seemed (incorrectly, as it turns out) that I was indeed lost after 6.Ke3. In a way, I was lucky to have been deluded. Who knows what I would have done if I'd seen what was "really" going on? In this case, ignorance really was bliss.

Now other voices started to join in on this King and pawn endgame debate. First, IM Jack Peters offered up some new ideas from the position in diagram 400.

Diagram 400

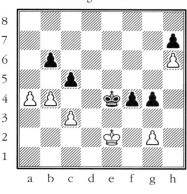

White to move and win

I have already pointed out that 10.a5 (10.bxc5 bxc5 11.c4 also does the trick) 10...bxa5 11.bxa5 Kd5 12.c4+ wins for White, but Jack noted, quite correctly, that Black can put up a better but ultimately hopeless defense after 12...Kc6 13.Kd3 Kb7 14.Ke4 with, instead of my 14...f3, 14...Ka6 15.Kxf4 Kxa5 16.Kxg4 Kb4 17.Kf3! Kxc4 18.g4 with four possibilities:

➤ 18...Kd5 19.g5 Ke6 20.g6, queening.

➤ 18...Kb3 19.g5 c4 20.g6 c3 21.g7!, when White queens with check.

➤ 18...Kd3 19.g5 c4 20.g6 c3 21.gxh7 c2 22.h8=Q c1=Q 23.Qd8+ Kc2 24.Qc8+ Kb1 25.Qxc1+ Kxc1 26.h7 and White wins.

➤ 18...Kb4 19.g5 c4 20.g6 c3 21.Ke2 Ka3 22.gxh7 c2 23.Kd2 Kb2 24.h8=Q+.

I wasn't too upset by these additions. They basically verified my own conclusions. Then I found a bombshell waiting in my e-mail. A strong grandmaster (who wishes to remain anonymous) claimed that my analysis was completely flawed and that Black was better after all (that makes two grandmasters who were off their rocker!), though a draw would ultimately be the correct result!

Shocked, I glanced at his e-mail "blindfolded" (as the years roll by, I get lazier and lazier and often don't bother looking at a chessboard) and took his word for it (yes, I too am influenced by a high rating!). Sending the analysis to IM John Watson, he lambasted me for listening to anyone (a very wise bit of criticism, by the way!). This prompted me to take a closer look and I immediately saw that the grandmaster was hallucinating.

Diagram 401

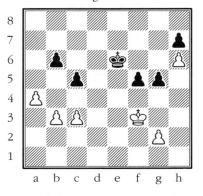

Black to move and demonstrate grandmaster dementia

5...Kd5

The "unknown grandmaster" considered 5...Ke5 (the actual game continuation) to be a mistake. As we shall eventually see, it turns out that, in reality, both 5...Kd5 and 5...Ke5 lead to a draw.

6.Ke3 Kc6

Black's idea is to play ...b6-b5. I must admit that I'd never considered such a plan.

7.Kd3

The grandmaster claimed a Black win after 7.b4 Kd5 8.Kd3 f4 9.a5 bxa5 (this analysis is horribly flawed. Here, 9...c4+ is the correct way for Black to ice the game) 10.bxa5 (and now 10.c4+ gives White the better game!) 10...c4+ 11.Ke2 g4, but IM John Watson and Patrick Hummel pointed out that he was a bit off since 9.c4+ wins easily for White. IM Ron Burnett came back with a challenge: "Just how does White win after 9.c4+?" Fortunately, Mr. Hummel had answered this several days earlier and saved me the trouble of doing any real work: 9.c4+ Kd6 (9...Ke5 10.bxc5 bxc5 11.a5 Kd6 12.Ke4 is easy for White) 10.b5 Ke5 11.Ke2! g4 (also hopeless is 11...Kf5 12.a5) 12.Kd3 and white's King will penetrate to e4 and enjoy a feast.

7...b5

I later discovered that this is a losing blunder but that Black could still draw with a correct seventh move, though I'm leaving that to the master or near master (don't forget, this *is* a master section!) who is reading this analysis to figure it out for himself.

After 7...b5, our mystery grandmaster claims a draw by: 8.axb5+ Kxb5 9.Ke2 Kc6 10.g3 Kd5 11.Ke3 Ke5 12.Kf3 Kd5. However, IM Watson once again points out that White wins easily with 8.a5 (instead of 8.axb5+??) 8...b4 9.cxb4 cxb4 10.Kd4 Kb5 11.Ke5 Kxa5 12.Kxf5 Kb5 13.Kf6 Kc5 14.Kg7 and it's time for Black to hang up his Rooks.

So what does this mean? Are international masters better endgame players than grandmasters? Was the grandmaster pulling my leg? Is there any meaning to unearth? I tend to think that the grandmasters in question were too lazy to give this position a serious look. But it does show that King and pawn endgames can be very tricky, and that anyone is capable of completely misjudging such a complicated situation.

We're done with the adventure. It's time to see what the truth is:

Diagram 402

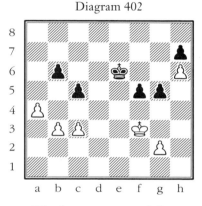

Black to move and draw

5...Ke5

As played in the actual game. At the last second, I also discovered that 5...Kd5 draws in all lines! A small sample: 6.Ke3 Kc6 7.b4 Kd5 8.Kd3 Kc6 9.Kc4 cxb4 10.cxb4 b5+ 11.axb5+ Kb6 12.Kd5 Kxb5 13.Ke5 f4! and Black draws as in Peters' subsequent (main line) analysis to 14...f4! (below).

6.Ke3 Kd5

Instead of my original intention of 6...f4+??, which was analyzed earlier.

7.Ke2 Ke4 8.b4 cxb4!

Worse is 8...Kd5 9.Kd3 f4 10.c4+! Kc6 (10...Kd6 11.b5 Ke5 12.Ke2 g4 13.Kd3 isn't any better) 11.b5+ Kd6 12.Ke4 Ke6 13.g3 (or the simple 13.Kf3) and black's defense breaks down. Analysis by Patrick Hummel.

9.cxb4 Kd4 10.a5 bxa5 11.bxa5 Kc5 12.Kd3

This was given as a White win by Mr. Hummel and John Watson, but Jack Peters points out that the position is a draw.

12...Kb5 13.Kd4 Kxa5 14.Ke5 f4!

This very important, but simple, move (found by Peters) was missed by a whole team of titled players. Black's King looks awfully far away, doesn't it?

15.Kf5 Kb6 16.Kxg5 Kc6 17.Kf6

A book draw follows 17.Kxf4 Kd7 18.Kf5 Ke7 since black's King gets to h8.

17...Kd7 18.Kg7 Ke7 19.Kxh7 Kf7 and now the point of 14...f4! is clear: White doesn't have a tempo move that will enable him to regain the Opposition. Thus, the game is drawn (20.Kh8 Kg6 21.Kg8! [21.h7?? Kf7, 0-1] 21...Kxh6 22.Kf7 Kg5 23.Ke6 Kg4 24.Ke5, =).

Remember, all this is merely meant to be a warning. The fact is, complex King and pawn endgames are a bit of a rarity and most masters (on up) love the idea of playing them. But they also know that such positions should be avoided if a safe, clear alternative is available.

The Pleasures of a Knight

I constantly hear players arguing over the relative values of Bishops and Knights. Which is really the stronger piece? The majority of voices point to the Bishop as the superior entity. The following quote from José Raúl Capablanca is particularly pointed: "The weaker the player, the more terrible the Knight is to him, but as a player increases in strength, the value of the Bishop becomes more evident to him and of course there is, or should be, a corresponding decrease in the value of the Knight as compared to the Bishop."

That's all well and good, but then how do we explain the following game?

Diagram 403

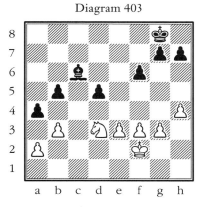

Capablanca - Reshevsky, Nottingham 1936

Black to move

Note the holes on b4, c5 and d4, plus the weak pawn on d5. If Black plays "normally" (...Kf7-e6) White will achieve a sweet "torture position": 1...Kf7 2.Nb4 axb3 3.axb3 Bb7 4.Ke2 Ke6 5.Kd3 Ke5 (5...Kd6 6.Kd4) 6.Nc2 with Nd4 and Kc3 to follow.

Due to this, Black tries to make use of his Bishop's long-range powers by creating an outside passed pawn on the kingside.

1...g5! 2.hxg5 fxg5 3.Nb4

Capablanca avoided 3.f4 gxf4 4.exf4 due to 4...d4! when Black would eventually lose his d-pawn, but his active Bishop will give him serious chances to save the game. The third World Champion was one of the greatest endgame players of all time and always avoided unclear situations in favor of "iron control."

3...axb3 4.axb3 Bb7

Black now hopes to play ...h5-h4 with an outside passed pawn.

5.g4

White prevents black's plan and now intends to swing his King over to d4 with total control. Refusing to die passively, Black realizes his only counterplay is based on an ...h5 advance. Thus ...Kh7-g6 and ...h5 will exchange pawns (always a good defensive idea in the endgame) and allow the King a measure of activity.

5...Kg7 6.Ke2 Kg6 7.Kd3 h5 8.gxh5+ Kxh5 9.Kd4 Kh4 10.Nxd5 Kg3

Diagram 404

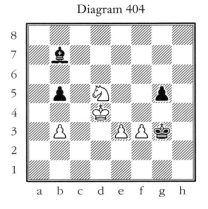

Black has lost a pawn but his active King and the limited remaining material gives him some practical chances to save himself. Nevertheless, White should win with best play.

11.f4 g4

Black loses after 11...Bxd5 12.Kxd5 g4 13.f5 Kh3 14.f6 g3 15.f7 g2 16.f8=Q g1=Q 17.Qh8+ Kg2 18.Qg8+.

12.f5 Bc8

Still twitching. Far worse is 12...Bc6 13.Nc7 (now black's Bishop can't stop white's f-pawn from promoting) 13...Kf2 14.f6 g3 15.f7 g2 16.f8=Q+ Bf3 17.Qg8 g1=Q 18.Qxg1+ Kxg1 19.e4 and it's all over.

13.Ke5 Bd7 14.e4

Now 14.Nc7 doesn't work: 14...Bxf5! 15.Kxf5 Kf3 16.Ne6 g3 17.Nf4 Kxe3, =.

However, it's not clear to me that 14.e4 is really necessary. More straightforward is 14.f6 Be8 15.Ke6 Kh4 (or 15...Kf3 16.Ke7 Bh5 17.Nf4 g3 18.Nxh5 g2

19.f7 g1=Q 20.f8=Q+ Kxe3 [20…Ke2 21.Nf4+ Kxe3 22.Ne6] 21.Qf5 with an easy win) 16.Ke7 Bh5 17.Nf4 g3 18.b4 Kg4 (18…Kg5 19.Nxh5 g2 20.Nf4 g1=Q 21.Nh3+) 19.Nxh5 g2 20.f7 g1=Q 21.Nf6+ Kh3 22.f8=Q Qxe3+ 23.Kd6 when 23…Qd4+ 24.Nd5 and 23…Qb6+ 24.Kd5 are both hopeless.

14…Be8

Diagram 405

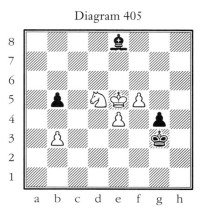

15.Kd4??

This blunder throws the win away. Bondarevsky showed that White could still claim victory by 15.f6! Kf3 16.Nf4 g3 17.Kf5 Bd7+ 18.Kg5 Be6 19.Nxe6! g2 20.f7 g1=Q+ 21.Kf6 and White wins. This theme of allowing Black to promote first comes up more than once.

15…Kf3 16.e5 g3 17.Ne3 Kf4?

Also losing is 17…Bd7 18.e6 Bc8 19.e7 Bd7 20.f6 Be8 21.Nf5—Alekhine.

However, Bondarevsky found a draw: 17…Bf7!! 18.e6 Bg8 19.e7 (or 19.b4 Kf4!) 19…Bf7 20.f6 Kf4! when White can't improve his position.

18.e6 g2 19.Nxg2+ Kxf5 20.Kd5 Kg4 21.Ne3+ Kf4 22.Kd4, 1-0 since Black has no defense against e7 followed by swinging the Knight to c7.

The "explanation" for Capablanca's obvious favoritism towards Bishops while he used his Knight to good effect against Reshevsky is simple: Bishops tend to be better in the majority of cases (i.e., open positions, passed pawn races where the Bishop's long-range abilities crush the slow Knight, etc.), but Knights have their own set of advantages:

➤ They can land on light and dark squares. This means that nothing is safe from them!

➤ Knights are more flexible than Bishops.

➤ Knights are often superior in closed positions.

▶ Knight-hops confuse amateurs and masters alike! After I managed to draw a pawn down endgame (multiple pawns and two Knights each) against the strong IM Georgi Orlov, he lamented, "Hop, hop, hop! The Knights are hopping all over the place! How could I possibly figure out what was going on?"

What this means is that the master has an open mind and understands that many positions are highly favorable for Knights. He might prefer the Bishop in a general sense, but won't hesitate to rush into a Knight vs. Bishop endgame if he feels the horse will reign supreme.

Our next example shows what happens when a "Bishop is better than a Knight" mentality becomes set in stone (or in this case, in metal).

Diagram 406

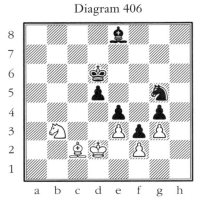

Mephisto Computer - Silman, Los Angeles 1989
Black to move

At the time, computers hadn't quite made their mark at the highest levels of tournament chess. This event was historic in that Mephisto did very well against several strong players and Deep Thought dragged down Bent Larsen and myself (Larsen didn't take the machine seriously, while I was "introduced" to the computer's incredible defensive skills in the final round—I outplayed it, achieved a position that would have given me excellent winning chances against any human, and then ran into a "non-human" defensive wall while in time pressure).

Though my loss to Deep Thought was traumatic (and costly!), I managed to uphold the integrity of the human race earlier in the same event against Mephisto. The game was a long, grueling affair that demanded accurate play and tremendous amounts of energy. I managed to win a pawn and began the long Cat and Mouse process of torturing the cursed bucket of bolts in the resulting endgame. In the diagrammed position, I played ...

1...Ba4

It was here that I discovered a glitch in the machine. Any experienced human would understand the tremendous flexibility of a Knight in such a position, but the machine was programmed to believe in the superiority of Bishops over Knights. Thus, it allowed me to take on b3 and enter a winning Knight vs. Bishop endgame.

2.Ke1?? Bxb3!

I wasn't going to let it change its mind!

3.Bxb3 Kc5 4.Ba4 Nf7

Diagram 407

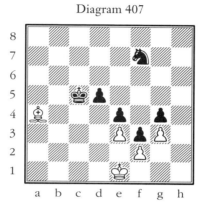

The only fly in the ointment is black's vulnerable pawn on g4. Thus, I swing my Knight to e5 where it defends g4, deprives the Bishop of the d7-square, and also threatens to decisively leap into d3 (targeting f2) or c4 (pressuring e3 and making a …d5-d4 push serious business) at the appropriate time.

5.Bb3 Ne5 6.Bc2 Nc4 7.Ba4 d4 8.Bc2 Kd5 9.Bb3 Kc5 10.Bc2 dxe3 11.fxe3 Nxe3 12.Bxe4 Kd4 13.Bg6 Nc4 14.Kf2 Nd2 15.Bf5 Ne4+

Diagram 408

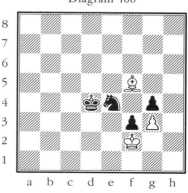

Nothing is safe from the mighty Knight! Now it chases white's King off of f2 and threatens the pawn on g3. As will be seen in the next note, it will also train its sights on f1, breaking any effort White makes to stop the f-pawn from turning into a Queen.

This highlights the Knight's main advantage over a Bishop: it can control any color and thus potentially place pressure on any square on the board.

16.Bxe4

A sad necessity, but 16.Kg1 Ke3 17.Bxg4 f2+ 18.Kg2 Nd2 promotes my remaining pawn.

16...Kxe4

The rest is basic King and pawn ending fare.

17.Kf1 Ke3 18.Ke1 f2+ 19.Kf1 Kd3 20.Kxf2 Kd2 20.Kf1 Ke3, 0-1.

The edge in flexibility that a Knight often has over a Bishop is graphically shown in our next game, played between two World Champions.

Diagram 409

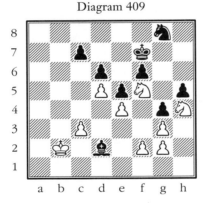

Smyslov - Euwe, Groningen 1946
White to move

Black is in serious trouble. The reasons for this:

➤ White's King is more active than black's.

➤ The white Knight will dominate black's Bishop.

➤ Black has potential pawn weaknesses on c7, f6, and h5 (that weakness will move to g4 if White plays f3 followed by fxg4). White will push his f-pawn to f3, so that will only leave g3 in need of defense. Simply put: Black has far more weak pawns than White does.

➤ In general two Knights don't work well together. However, in this case black's Knight is dominated and, if it moves, an exchange will take place that will leave

White with a crushing Knight versus a rather impotent Bishop.

▶ The c3-c4-c5 pawn lever allows White to break through on the queenside in many different variations.

▶ Correctly handling a Knight takes more skill than correctly handling a Bishop. As a result, lower rated players fear Knights—in a way, mastery of Knights is the test that separates the men from the boys.

1.Kc2 Be1

Smyslov analyzes 1...Bg5 (intending to transpose into a King and pawn endgame) and shows that it also loses: 2.Kb3 Bxh4 3.gxh4 Ne7 4.Nxe7 Kxe7 5.Kc4 f5 6.f3 f4 7.Kb5 Kd7 8.c4 Kd8 9.Kc6 Kc8 10.c5 dxc5 11.Kxc5 Kd7 12.Kc4 Ke7 13.Kb4 Kd6 14.Kb5 g3 15.Kb4 Ke7 (15...c6 16.dxc6 Kxc6 17.Kc4 Kd6 18.Kb5 wins) 16.Kc4 Kd6 17.Kb5 Kd7 18.Kc5 Kc8 19.d6, winning all of black's pawns.

Perhaps this is true, but John Watson feels that 5...f5 is a bad move since it later deprives the e5-pawn of some much-needed protection. Instead, he recommends 5...Kd7 6.Kb5 Ke7 7.Kc6 g3! 8.f3 (8.fxg3 f5!, =) 8...Kd8 9.c4 Kc8 10.c5 dxc5 11.Kxc5 Kd7. His logic is shown by the position that results from the following moves: 12.Kb5 Kd6 13.Kb4 c6 14.dxc6 Kxc6 15.Kc4 Kd6 16.Kb5 Kd7 17.Kc5 Kc7 18.Kd5 Kd7, =, since black's e5-pawn is solid thanks to black's f-pawn remaining on f6.

This fits nicely into the chapter, All King and Pawn Endgames Are Confusing. Whatever the truth might be, our focus here is on the upcoming Knight vs. Bishop battle, which shows the Knight running rings around its "faster" foe.

2.f3

White intends to play c4 and then march his King all the way to c6. Black would like to "greet" the white King by moving his own monarch to d7, but then Ng7+ followed by Nxh5 would follow. As a result, Black has no choice but to exchange a pair of Knights.

2...Ne7 3.Nxe7 Kxe7 4.fxg4 hxg4 5.Nf5+ Kf7 6.c4 Kg6 7.Kb3 Kg5

Black desperately seeks counterplay on the kingside. Trying to defend on the queenside by 7...Kf7 also falls on its face (see diagram 410 on the next page):

Diagram 410

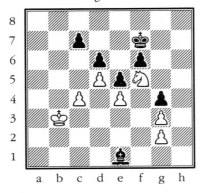

8.Ka4 Ke8 9.Kb5 Kd7 10.Nh6 Bxg3 11.Nxg4 Bh4 12.Nh6 Bg5 13.Nf5 Bd2 14.Ka6 Kc8 15.Ka7 Bf4 16.Ka8 Bd2 17.g4 Bf4 18.Ne7+ Kd7 19.Nc6 Kc8 20.Na7+ Kd7 21.Kb7 wins according to Smyslov. Let's verify this (note how the Knight dominated both the black King and black Bishop): 21...Be3 22.Nc6 Bc5 23.Nb8+ Kd8 24.Kc6 Bd4 25.Na6 Bb6 26.Nb8 and now:

➤ 26...Bd4 27.Nd7.

➤ 26...Be3 27.Nd7 Bg5 28.Nf8 and Ne6 will prove decisive.

➤ 26...Ke7 27.Nd7 Ba5 28.c5 Bb4 (28...dxc5 29.Nxc5 Bb6 30.Nb7 Kf7 31.d6) 29.Kxc7 dxc5 30.Nb8! Ba5+ 31.Kc6 c4 32.Kc5 c3 33.Nc6+ Kd7 34.Nxa5 c2 35.Nb3 and Black must resign. White's Knight gives the impression of being everywhere at once, while the Bishop seems ponderous and completely ineffective.

8.Ka4 Bxg3

The only chance, otherwise White just marches his King to c6 and feasts on black's queenside.

9.Nxg3 Kf4 10.Nh5+ Kxe4 11.Nxf6+ Kf5

Black doesn't do any better with 11...Kf4: 12.Kb5 e4 13.Nxe4 Kxe4 14.Kc6 g3 15.Kxc7 Ke3 16.Kxd6 Kf2 17.Ke5 Kxg2 18.d6 Kf3 19.d7 g2 20.d8=Q g1=Q 21.Qd3+ when White forces the trade of Queens (21...Kf2 22.Qd4+ or 21...Kg2 22.Qg6+), leaving himself with an extra baby Queen on c4.

After 11...Kf5 Black intends to push his e-pawn to the ends of the Earth. How can the Knight deal with this threat?

12.Ne8!

White's super-Knight goes in the opposite direction, seeking a quick lunch before dealing with the e-pawn.

12...e4 13.Nxc7 e3 14.Nb5 Kf4

He didn't like the look of 14...e2 15.Nd4+ followed by 16.Nxe2.

15.Nc3 Kg3 16.c5, 1-0. An impressive endgame that shows us just how light on its feet a Knight can be.

Our final example gives us more fancy hoof-work by a Knight.

Diagram 411

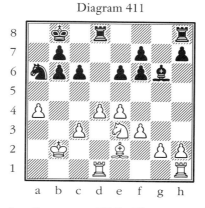

Bernstein - Suesman, U.S. Championship 1938
White to move

White's superior pawn structure and centralized pieces make an obvious impression. However, White has an idea here that allows him to add one more advantage to his quiver of plusses: he can create a crushing Knight vs. a poor Bishop scenario.

1.Bxa6! bxa6 2.a5!

The point. White clears away the one defender of the c5-square, which will turn into a wonderful home for white's Knight.

2...b5

This lets White rule the position with an iron grip thanks to the holes on b4 and c5 (lovely resting places for white's Knight and King). Like it or not, Black should have tried either 2...bxa5 or 2...Kb7.

3.Ng4!

By using tactics aimed at the pawns on f6, f7, and c6, White forces his Knight onto the dream c5-square.

3...f5 4.Ne5

Threatening a fork on c6.

3...Kc7 5.exf5 exf5

Ugly, but 5...Bxf5 6.Nxf7 was even worse.

6.Nd3 Kb7 7.Rhe1 Rhe8 8.Nc5+ Ka7

Diagram 412

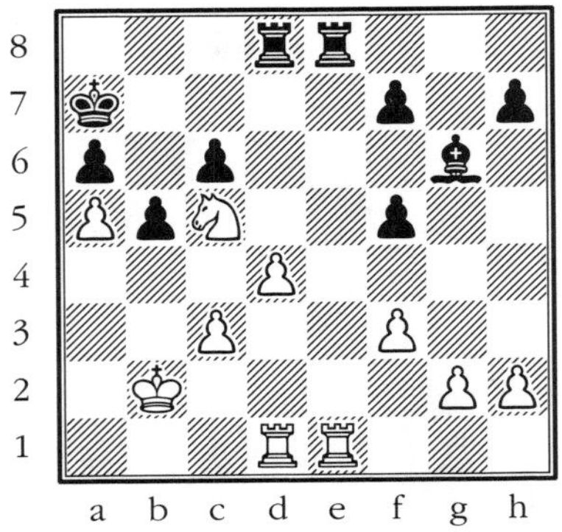

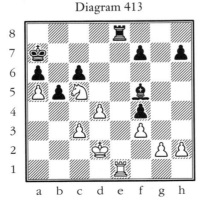

An experienced player will always head for a position like this. A Knight this good (along with black's passive King and the target on a6) will bring home the full point almost every time.

9.Kc2

The famous German player Fritz is gung ho for 9.Ka3 f4 10.Rxe8 Rxe8 11.d5 cxd5 12.Rxd5 Re2 13.Rd7+ Kb8 14.Nxa6+. However, I think Bernstein's choice is by far the more "human" move (Note that "human" doesn't necessarily mean "best." It's just a good, practical decision). The idea is simple: He intends to move his King to d2 and then swap off all the Rooks. The resulting minor piece endgame is winning for White, while if Black retains a Rook he will allow White to invade the 7th rank. What's particularly nice about this plan is that there is no risk involved—White doesn't want to allow Black any counterplay.

9...f4+ 10.Kd2 Bf5

The alternative, 10...b4, lets White decisively invade on the 7th rank: 11.cxb4 Rxd4+ 12.Kc3 Rxd1 13.Rxd1 Re3+ 14.Kc4 Re2 15.Rd7+ Ka8 16.Rc7 Rxg2 17.Rxc6 Rxh2 18.Rxa6+ Kb8 19.Rb6+ Ka8 20.b5 h5 21.Rd6 and it's all over.

11.Rxe8 Rxe8 12.Re1

Diagram 413

12...Rg8

Though 12...Rxe1 13.Kxe1 is indeed losing for Black, picking the right plan might be harder than one might suppose. In my view, White can make this easy on himself if he realizes that he's a King up—black's King is frozen to the defense of a6. Thus, all White has to do is find a way to penetrate into black's camp with his King: 13...h5 14.Kf2 h4 15.g3 fxg3+ 16.hxg3 hxg3+ (16...h3 17.g4 is easy) 17.Kxg3 Bc8 (Passive play offers no hope either: 17...Bg6 18.Kf4 Bb1 19.Ke5 Ba2 20.f4 Bc4 21.Kf6 Bd5 22.Ke7 f5 23.Kd6 Be4 24.Kc7 Bf3 25.Ne6 Bd5 26.Nd8 and it's time for Black to give up) 18.Kf4 Kb8 19.Ke5 Kc7 20.f4 f5 21.d5 cxd5 22.Kxd5 and Black is out of options.

13.Re7+ Ka8 14.Re2 Bc8

14...Ka7 15.Ke1 followed by Re7+ and Kf2 is a trivial win.

15.Nd3 Be6 16.Nxf4

This not only wins a pawn but it also defends g2. Now white's Rook is free to roam.

16...Bc4 17.Re7 Rd8 18.Nd3, 1-0.

The position after 18...Bxd3 19.Kxd3 c5 20.Rxf7 b4 21.Rc7 is completely lost.

The King is a Fighting Piece!

The King is an extremely strong piece, but many players lose sight of this fact due to the necessity for it to hide during the middlegame. Experienced tournament competitors, though, are well aware of the need to let their King flex its muscles once an endgame is reached. In fact, many games are saved or won when one side manages to activate their King, while the other King sits smugly at home doing nothing.

Though the "Use your King in an endgame!" concept is given regular lip service from class "D" on up, few realize just how important it is. Hopefully the examples that follow will boil your blood and make you want to reach for your King and kick it into dance mode.

Diagram 414

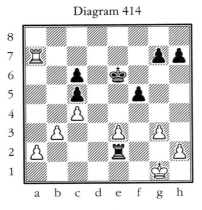

Lilienthal - Smyslov, Leningrad 1941

Black to move

The Bulgarian chess saying, "I make your pawns look like your grandmother's teeth," seems a good way to describe black's structure—his pawns are weak and many of them appear to be doomed.

Though things look bad for Black, he'll be able to save himself by following two classic endgame concepts:

▶ In the endgame, make your King a fighting piece!

▶ Keep your Rook active at all costs.

408

1...g5 2.Rxh7 Rxa2 3.Rh6+ Ke5 4.Rxc6

No better was 4.h4 g4 5.h5 (5.Rxc6 Ke4 6.Rxc5 f4!, =) 5...Ke4 6.Rf6 Rb2 (6...Ra1+, =) 7.h6 Rxb3 8.h7 Rb1+ 9.Kg2 Rb2+ with an instant draw since 10.Kf1 allows 10...Rh2.

4...Ke4!

Black's King, which is extremely active, has turned into a berserk fighting unit of death, while white's pathetic leader is trapped on the back rank, begging for its life.

5.Rxc5

White is three pawns up, but one King down.

5...f4!

Sacrificing another pawn to ensure the safe advance of the King.

6.exf4

6.Kf1 Ra1+ 7.Ke2 f3+ 8.Kf2 Ra2+ is another way to make a draw.

6...Kf3

Diagram 415

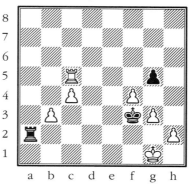

Now black's King is safe from checks while White is threatened by immediate mate.

7.h3

Suicide could still occur by 7.h4 Ra1+ 8.Kh2 Ra2+ 9.Kh3?? g4 mate.

7...Ra1+, ½-½.

Our next example shows Larry Christiansen enjoying superior King position, then sacrificing a pawn to make it even better!

Diagram 416

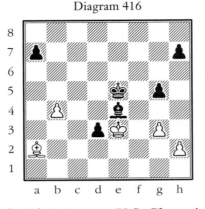

D Gurevich - Christiansen, U.S. Championship 2000

Black to move

Black's a pawn up and has the better King position, but his d3-pawn is vulnerable and there are no obvious breakthroughs happening any time soon. The way Black turns this into a forced win is very instructive.

1...Bd5! 2.Bb1

Trading would leave White with a losing Queen endgame after 2.Bxd5 Kxd5 3.Kxd3 g4 4.Kc3 h5 5.Kd3 a6 6.Kc3 Ke4 7.Kc4 Kf3 8.Kc5 Kg2 9.Kb6 Kxh2 10.Kxa6 h4 11.b5 hxg3 12.b6 g2 13.b7 g1=Q 14.b8=Q+ Kg2 15.Qa8+ Kf2 16.Qf8+ Ke2.

2...d2!

Black sacrifices his extra pawn to increase the domination of his King. This, in turn, will allow black's King to make contact with (and eventually win) the b-pawn.

3.Kxd2 Be4!

Ending the threat of 4.Bxh7 by offering up another King and pawn endgame.

4.Ba2

Now the exchange of Bishops is even worse for White than it was before: 4.Bxe4 Kxe4 5.Kc3 g4 6.Kc4 Kf3 7.Kb5 Kg2 8.Ka6 Kxh2 9.Kxa7 Kxg3 10.b5 Kf3 11.b6 g3 12.b7 g2 13.b8=Q g1=Q+ 14.Ka6 Qa1+ 15.Kb7 Qb2+ 16.Kc8 Qxb8+ 17.Kxb8 h5.

4...Kd4

Black's King is a dominating piece. Next on his agenda is:

➤ Place all his pawns on dark squares so they will be immune from the white Bishop's intentions.

➤ Force the b-pawn to advance to b5 so the c5-square will
become available to the black King. He will then surround and
win it by ...Kc5 mixed with the Bishop moving to the f1-a6
diagonal.

Diagram 417

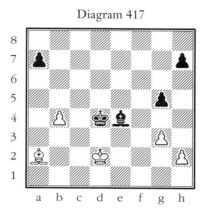

5.h4 h6 6.hxg5 hxg5 7.Be6 Bd5

Giving black's King access to the c4-square.

8.Bd7

As always, the trade of Bishops leads to a lost King and pawn endgame: 8.Bxd5
Kxd5 9.Kd3 g4 10.Ke3 Kc4 11.Kf4 Kxb4 12.Kxg4 a5.

8...Kc4 9.b5 Kd4 10.Ke2 Kc5 11.Ke3 Bc4 12.Ke4 Bxb5 13.Be6 a5

Black has won the b-pawn and should now win the game. However, care must
be shown: White would love to pick up the pawn on g5 and then sacrifice his
Bishop for black's remaining pawn.

14.Bb3 Kb4 15.Bd1 Ba4

Nothing wrong with this, though 15...Bc4 16.Ke3 Bb3 17.Bg4 Kc3 would
lead to white's quick resignation.

16.Bg4

Here Black suffered a meltdown: **16...Kc3 17.Ke5 Bb3** (17...Bc6 wins) **18.Bd7
g4** (18...Kb4 was a winner) **19.Kf4 Bd1 20.Be8 Kb4 21.Ke3 Ba4 22.Bh5 Bd7
23.Kd2 Kb3 24.Kc1 Ka2**, ½-½. Apparently he forgot that white's King could
scoot back to the queenside and take advantage of the fact that the a-pawn is a
"wrong colored rook-pawn" (If white's King can reach a1 he could make a draw
by sacrificing his Bishop for the g-pawn.).

Sadly, he had an immediate win after 16.Bg4 by 16...Bc2+ 17.Ke3 (17.Kd4 a4
18.Be6 a3 19.Ba2 Bb3 20.Bb1 Bg8 with ...Kb3 and ...Kb2 to follow) 17...Kc3
18.Bd7 a4 19.Bxa4 Bxa4 20.Ke4 g4 21.Kf4 Bd1 and White must resign.

Most young players today aren't familiar with Salo Flohr. That's a shame, since he was a powerful positional player and was also blessed with fantastic technique. In our next game, Flohr uses both his pieces (his King and Rook) to the maximum. His Rook seems to dance rings around its Black counterpart, while his King almost single-handedly rules the board.

Diagram 418

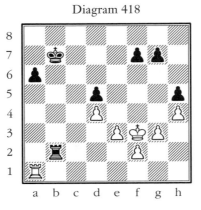

Flohr - Petrov, Semmering 1937

White to move

A glance might convince some players that Black is doing well; he has a Rook on the 7th rank and a passed a-pawn. However, Black is actually in serious trouble. How can this be? How can a white advantage be logically explained? The answer is simple: White's pawn structure is superior, and his King will prove to be far more active than black's (which is too far away from the kingside to defend its pawns there)!

1.Ra5!

A very nice Rook maneuver. The threat against d5 forces black's reply.

1...Rb5 2.Ra2!

Now black's Rook is denied the 7th rank and f2 is no longer under attack. This frees the white King for a triumphant march into black's kingside.

2...g6

It's possible to push the a-pawn, but after 2...a5 3.Kf4 Ka6 4.Ke5 Rb1 5.Kxd5 Kb5 6.Kd6, White wins: 6...a4 7.Ke7 Kb4 8.d5 Rd1 9.d6, etc.

3.Kf4 f6

Trying to prevent white's King from breaking through.

4.g4 hxg4

White wins material after 4...a5 5.gxh5 gxh5 6.Kf5.

5.Kxg4 Rb1

It seems that White threatened h4-h5, and this prevents it. However, what if Black ignores the "threat" and instead plays the logical 5...a5, simply shoving his passed pawn? It turns out that white's threat wasn't h4-h5 at all, but rather f4-f5! Thus, after 5...a5 6.f4! Black's busted: 6...Rb3 7.f5! gxf5+ 8.Kf4 and wins.

6.Ra5!

There's that wonderful Rook maneuver again!

6...Rb5 7.Ra1!

White's 1st rank is now more important than his 2nd rank. The way white's Rook zips to a5 then backtracks to whatever rank is crucial at that moment is nothing less than striking.

7...Rb2 8.Kf3

Threatening to win black's g-pawn by Rg1.

8...Rb6 9.Rg1 f5

Black has defended g6, but now the e5- and g5-squares have been opened up for white's King.

10.Kf4

Diagram 419

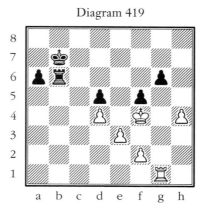

10...Re6 11.Rb1+ Ka7

Or 11...Rb6 12.Ra1 Rb2 13.f3 Rb3 14.Ra5! Rb5 15.Ra3 (Amazing! This same maneuver has been used to control the 2nd rank, then the 1st, and now the 3rd.) 15...Rb2 16.Ke5 Rh2 17.Kxd5 Rxh4 18.e4 fxe4 19.fxe4 and white's two connected passed pawns will win the day.

12.h5 Re4+ 13.Kg5 Rg4+

I think Black could have put up more resistance by 13...gxh5! 14.Kxf5 h4! with a rather odd position.

Diagram 420

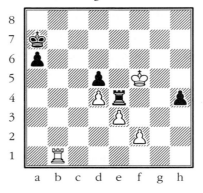

The variations concerning 15.Kg5 are extremely complex and outside the scope of this discussion. However, I suspect white's best chances can be found with 15.Kf6 when Black has:

- 15...h3 16.Rh1 Rh4 17.Ke6 Rh5 18.f4 Kb6 19.f5 Kc7 20.f6 Kd8 21.e4! dxe4 22.d5 and Black's dead, though I'll let you analyze a bit and convince yourself of that.

- 15...a5 16.Rb5 Ka6 (16...a4 17.Rb4!) 17.Rxd5 a4 18.Rc5 Kb6 19.Rc8 Kb5 20.Rb8+ Kc4 21.Ra8 Kb5 (21...Kb3 22.d5 wins for White) 22.Kf5 Re7 23.Rh8 Rf7+ (23...Kc4 24.Rxh4 a3 25.d5+ Kxd5 [25...Kb3 26.d6] 26.Rd4+ Kc6 27.Ra4 Rf7+ 28.Ke6 Rxf2 29.Rxa3 Kc7 30.Rd3 with a winning position—*Nalimov TableBase* claims mate in 38!) 24.Ke6 Rxf2 25.Rh5+! Kc4 26.Rxh4 a3 27.d5+ Kb3 28.d6 a2 29.d7 a1=Q (Worse is 29...Rf6+ 30.Kxf6 a1=Q+ 31.Rd4 Qa6+ 32.Ke7 Qb7 33.e4 when White wins: 33...Kc3 34.Rd5 or 33...Qc7 34.Rd6! Kc4 35.e5 [threatening Ke8] 35...Qb7 36.Ke6 and Black must resign) 30.d8=Q Qa6+ 31.Ke5 when White is clearly better.

Amazing stuff, and I barely scratched the surface. This should give you a real wake up call as to just how complicated endgames can be!

14.Kf6 gxh5 15.Kxf5

White's plan is clear: he wants to create two connected passed pawns in the center.

15...Rg2 16.Ke5 Rg5+

16...Rxf2 let's White achieve his goal after 17.Kxd5.

17.Ke6 h4 18.Rh1 Rh5 19.f4

Diagram 421

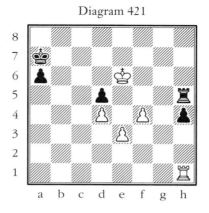

White didn't manage to get his two connected passed pawns, but it turns out that this single passer will do more than both of black's rook-pawn runners. Why is one pawn better than two? Because it's being escorted by white's King, while black's monarch is still on a queenside vacation.

19...Kb6

19...a5 20.f5 a4 21.f6 is easily winning for White.

20.f5 Kc7 21.f6 Kd8 22.Rf1! Rh6

22...Ke8 runs into 23.Rb1 Kd8 24.Rb8+ Kc7 25.f7.

23.Kf7!, 1-0. The threat is Kg7 followed by f6-f7 and f8=Q. A beautifully played endgame by the great Flohr.

I'm finishing this section with a famous King and pawn endgame by Rubinstein, who is widely thought to be one of the greatest endgame players of all time. The reason for its inclusion is obvious—one rarely gets to see such a dominating King!

Diagram 422

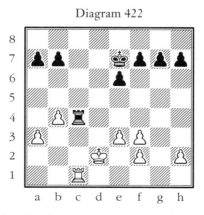

Cohn-Rubinstein, St. Petersburg 1909

Black to move

White has just played his Rook to c1, which is a horrible mistake since it allows Black to trade into a winning King and pawn endgame.

1...Rxc1 2.Kxc1

Why is this endgame winning for Black? Aside from his superior pawn structure, the answer is simple: *Black's King will dominate white's!* In general, you don't want to rush into a King and pawn endgame if your opponent's King can take up a far superior position than your own.

2...Kf6

Many players blindly rush their King to the center, which (I must admit) is usually the right thing to do. However, in this case black's superiority is on the kingside, so he makes a dash to that embattled area where it will target the pawns on h2, f2, and f3 for extinction.

3.Kd2 Kg5 4.Ke2

White's King tries to shore up his weaknesses on the kingside, but the vast superiority of the black monarch will eventually drag him down. However, trying to create a pawn race also ends in dismal failure: 4.Kd3 Kh4 5.Kd4 Kh3 6.Kc5 Kxh2 7.Kd6 Kg2 8.Kc7 h5 (Black can gain a tempo with 8...b5, but it's not really necessary: 9.Kc6 h5 10.Kxb5 h4 11.Ka6 h3 12.Kxa7 h2 13.b5 h1=Q 14.b6 Qa1 15.b7 Qxa3+ 16.Kb6 Kxf3 17.b8=Q Qb4+ 18.Kc7 Qxb8+ 19.Kxb8 Kxf2) 9.Kxb7 h4 10.Kxa7 h3 11.b5 h2 12.b6 h1=Q 13.b7 Qa1 14.b8=Q Qxa3+ 15.Kb7 Qb4+ 16.Kc7 Qxb8+ 17.Kxb8 Kxf3 and it's time for White to resign.

4...Kh4 5.Kf1 Kh3 6.Kg1

Diagram 423

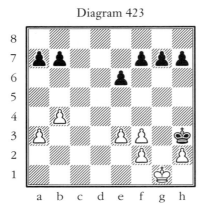

Just in time! However, the difference in King placement is glaringly apparent.

6...e5

A good move that stops the f3-pawn from safely moving to f4. Thus, the normally desirable 6...b5 (fixing white's queenside pawns and squirreling away a useful tempo move via ...a6) would be met by 7.f4.

7.Kh1

Other possibilities:

➤ 7.e4 (not very challenging) 7...g5 8.Kh1 h5 9.Kg1 h4 10.Kh1 g4 11.fxg4 Kxg4 12.Kg2 h3+ 13.Kg1 Kf3 and wins—analysis by Hans Kmoch.

➤ Speelman and Mestel say, "The best chance was 7.a4 b6 8.b5. Now the winning plan used in the game wouldn't work as Black doesn't have the tempo-gaining ...a6 in reserve (this is explained in the note to white's 12th move). However, he can still win by another method: 8...f5 9.Kh1 g5 10.Kg1 h5 11.Kh1 h4 12.Kg1 e4 13.fxe4 fxe4 14.Kh1 (14.f3 exf3 15.e4 g4 16.e5 g3) 14...Kg4 15.Kg2 h3+ 16.Kg1 Kf3 17.Kf1 g4 and wins."

7...b5

It's always useful to fix enemy pawns, especially if you are able to retain a tempo move like ...a6.

8.Kg1 f5 9.Kh1 g5 10.Kg1 h5 11.Kh1

White is completely helpless and must sit tight and hope Black can't find a way to break through.

11...g4

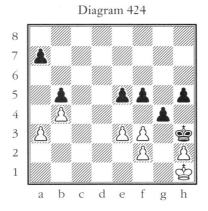

Diagram 424

The deathblow finally comes and, not surprisingly, there isn't a defense. Of course, 11...h4, as in the note with 7.a4, was also winning.

12.e4

This makes things easy. Far trickier is 12.fxg4 hxg4 13.Kg1 f4 14.exf4 exf4 15.Kh1

Diagram 425

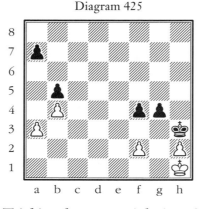

Trickier than one might imagine

Hans Kmoch wrote that 15...g3?? 16.fxg3 fxg3 17.hxg3 Kxg3 was winning, and a glance might make us agree with him since what can stop black's King from marching over to the queenside and eating white's remaining pawns? Speelman and Mestel, though, showed this to be an illusion. White draws: 18.Kg1 Kf3 19.Kf1 Ke3 20.Ke1 Kd3 21.Kd1 Kc3 22.a4! (The key defensive trick. Taking on a4 leaves Black with two rook-pawns. Of course, if we move things over one file [WH: K-e1, P-b3, c4; BL: K-d3, P-b7, c5], Black would win easily—Silman) 22...a6 23.axb5 axb5 24.Kc1 Kxb4 25.Kb2, =.

Once again, our friends Speelman and Mestel show us the correct way for Black to continue from diagram 425. 15...f3 16.Kg1 Kh4 and now:

➤ 17.Kh1 Kg5 18.h3 gxh3 19.Kh2 Kg4 20.Kg1 Kf4 21.Kh2 Ke4 22.Kxh3 (22.Kg3 h2) 22...Kd3 23.Kg4 Ke2 24.Kg3 and here we must return to Speelman and Mestel's comment in the analysis to 7.a4: "Now the winning plan used in the game wouldn't work as Black doesn't have the tempo-gaining ...a6 in reserve." This is the position they were referring to. After 24.Kg3 we have a Trebuchet, meaning that whoever has to move their King loses. Fortunately for Black, he has that all-important tempo move 24...a6 available, when White must resign.

➤ 17.Kf1 Kh5! (Very nice! Black wants his King on g5 after White plays Ke1. That way the flexible black Monarch retains the choice of going after h2 via ...Kh4, or penetrating in the center via ...Kf4—Silman) 18.Ke1 Kg5 19.Kf1 (Not what he wanted, but 19.Kd2 loses immediately to 19...Kh4 20.Ke3 Kh3 21.Kf4 Kxh2 22.Kxg4 Kg2—Silman) 19...Kf4 20.Ke1 Ke4 21.Kd2 Kd4 22.Kc2 Kc4 23.Kd2 Kb3 24.Ke3 Kxa3 25.Kf4

Kxb4 26.Kxg4 a5 and wins—analysis by Speelman and Mestel. I (Silman) should add that this is a nice illustration of the old "opposite corner rook-pawn rule" where whoever promotes first wins since he covers the queening square of the other pawn: 27.h4 a4 28.h5 a3 29.h6 a2 30.h7 a1=Q, etc.

12...fxe4 13.fxe4

No better is 13.fxg4 hxg4 14.Kg1 e3 15.fxe3 e4 16.Kh1 g3—analysis by Kmoch.

13...h4 14.Kg1 g3 15.hxg3 hxg3, 0-1. The finish could be: 16.f4 exf4 17.e5 g2 18.e6 Kg3 19.e7 f3 20.e8=Q f2 mate.

Queen and Pawn Endgames (Passed Pawns Rule!)

Passed pawns are important in all endgames, but they have the greatest impact in Queen endings. Why is this the case? Let's look at the following series of Kingless diagrams.

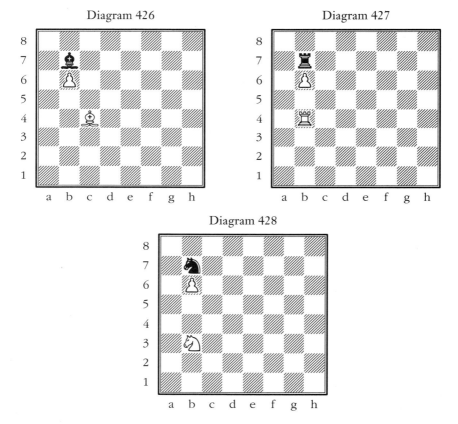

Diagram 426

Diagram 427

Diagram 428

In all these diagrams, we have a position where each side has the same piece (Knight vs. Knight, Bishop vs. Bishop, or Rook vs. Rook), White is a pawn up, and the defender's piece is blocking the enemy passed pawn. In each case, the blockade of the passed pawn can't be broken.

Let's compare the following Kingless diagram with the previous three:

Diagram 429

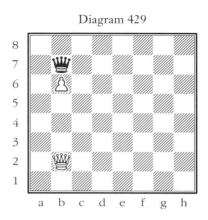

Here White can break black's blockade by Qb5/Qb4, Qc5, and Qc7.

This series of four diagrams has shown us that, in positions with Bishop vs. Bishop, Knight vs. Knight, or Rook vs. Rook, without Kings or other pieces or pawns helping, a firm blockade can't be broken. However, in a Queen ending, this defensive blockade can easily be torn down by the stronger side's Queen and pawn.

> **RULE**
>
> Passed pawns have the greatest impact in Queen endgames because a blockade of an advanced passer is very difficult, if not impossible, to maintain.

The following examples should "brutally" push this rule home.

Diagram 430

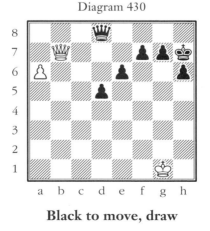

Black to move, draw

> **RULE**
>
> In a Queen endgame, a passed pawn's value is dependent on how advanced it is. When both sides have passed pawns, the player with the fastest passer (even if he's a pawn or two behind) often has a marked advantage.

Though Black is no less than four pawns ahead, white's single pawn on a6 is so powerful that Black is forced to scramble for the draw (1...Qg5+ forces perpetual check).

Understanding the rule connected to diagram 430 allows you to save positions that appear lost, simply because you'll know that it's not a material count that matters, but rather the creation and subsequent speed of a passed pawn.

Diagram 431

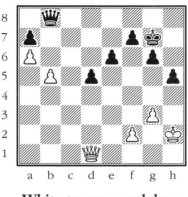

White to move and draw

White is two pawns down, apparently for nothing. All of black's pawns are safe, his King is secure, and white's queenside majority seems to be going nowhere fast. But, as has already been stated, material often takes a back seat to passed pawns in Queen endgames. Since white's only plus is his queenside majority, he *must* create a passed pawn in that sector, no matter what the price!

1.Qd4+ Kg8

White's task is even easier after 1...Kh7?? 2.Qf4! when it's not clear how Black can save the game: 2...Qb6 (2...Qxf4 3.gxf4 d4 4.Kg1 intending b6 is an easy win for White, while 2...Qe8 3.Qc7 is also grim for the second player.) 3.Qxf7+ Kh6 4.Qf8+ Kh7 (4...Kg5? 5.Qf4 mate) 5.Kg2 d4 6.Qf7+ Kh6 7.Qb7 Qc5 8.b6!, winning.

2.b6!

Diagram 432

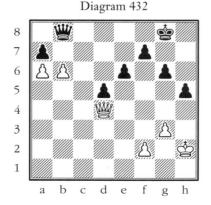

Sacrificing a pawn (which puts him three behind!) in order to create a far advanced passer. Also adequate is 2.Qc5 with the idea of Qc6-b7.

2...axb6 3.Qa4 Qa7

Avoiding the losing race that occurs after 3...d4? 4.a7 Qa8 5.Qa6 d3 6.Qxb6 Kh7 7.Qb8 Qf3 8.a8=Q Qxf2+ 9.Qg2, 1-0.

4.Qe8+ Kg7 5.Qc8

Suddenly it's clear that white's a6-pawn—soon to be unblocked by Qb7—is light years ahead of black's whole armada.

5...b5

Realizing that the tide has turned, Black bails out and plays for perpetual check.

6.Qb7

The most striking way to force the draw. Of course, 6.Kg2 is a bit less extreme: 6...Qd4 7.Qb7 Qe4+ 8.Kg1 h4 9.gxh4 Qg4+, =.

6...Qxf2+ 7.Kh1 Qxg3

Diagram 433

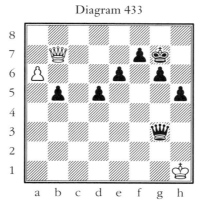

Six pawns to one, yet Black must play for the draw!

8.a7 Qe1+, ½-½.

Since blocking a far advanced passed pawn is often impossible in a Queen endgame, the defender often resorts to perpetual check as his main "survival mode" weapon. To combat this, there are two basic ways for the stronger side to avoid the perpetual and try for the full point.

➤ *Dual Purpose Queen*: The Queen escorts the pawn down the board and simultaneously covers the only road available to its King.

■—▶ ***Doubled Pawn Protective Cover***: The doubled pawns around the stronger side's King act as a wall, blocking any and all checks.

Let's look at each of these concepts in action.

Diagram 434

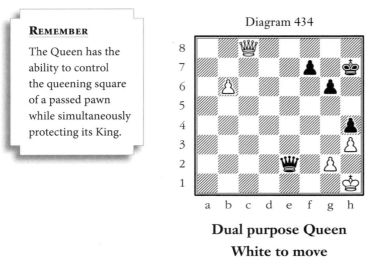

Dual purpose Queen
White to move

White's monster b-pawn will win the game unless Black can generate some counterplay against white's King. Black to move would allow 1...Qd1+ (1...Qe1+ 2.Kh2 Qg3+ 3.Kg1 Qe1+, etc. is an immediate draw) 2.Kh2 Qd6+ followed by 3...Qxb6. However, the whole "King safety" problem can be taken care of by one simple move.

1.Qc7!

White's Queen becomes master of the h2-b8 diagonal (which means that when white's King moves to h2 it will be immune from harm) while simultaneously forcing through the b-pawn by b7 and b8=Q (the fact that it attacks f7 also doesn't hurt!).

1...Qe1+ 2.Kh2 Qa5

The only chance.

3.Qxf7+ Kh8

Far easier for White is 3...Kh6 4.Qf4+ g5 (4...Kh7 5.b7) 5.Qd6+ with b7 to follow. By staying on the h2-b8 diagonal, White leaves Black no hope of saving the game.

4.Qe8+ Kh7 5.Qe7+

And not 5.b7?? Qc7+ followed by 6...Qxb7. On e7 the Queen covers the c7- and e5-squares, making it hard to check along the sensitive h2-b8 diagonal.

5...Kh6 6.Qxh4+

Though hardly necessary, why not pocket a free pawn and then return to the same position a little bit richer?

6...Kg7 7.Qe7+ Kh6 8.b7 Qa7 9.Qf8+ Kh7 10.b8=Q, 1-0. Note how the new Queen takes up the task of defending the diagonal.

Diagram 435

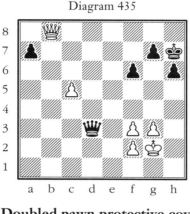

Doubled pawn protective cover
White to move

In this position white's doubled f-pawns form a perfect "anti-check seal" against the attentions of the black Queen. Note that if we took the doubled pawn on f3 and made it "healthy" by placing it on h2, Black would be able to annoy his opponent via checks on d5 and/or e4.

Since the King is safe, White can go about the business of promoting his pawn.

1.c6, 1-0. Black can't bother white's King or stop the c-pawn's decisive advance.

Let's see an illustration of these ideas at the highest level.

Diagram 436

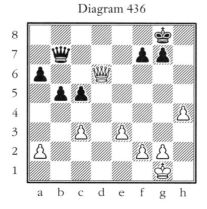

Rubinstein - Capablanca, St Petersburg 1914
Black to move

Black's a solid pawn down, his c-pawn is loose, and white's Queen is more actively placed than black's. One might think that a superb endgame player like Rubinstein will reel in the full point, but Capablanca is aware of the principles illustrated in this section and knows that he must use his queenside pawn majority to create a passed pawn or face certain defeat. If this calls for the sacrifice of another pawn or two, so be it!

1...b4!

Immediately striving to make a passed pawn.

2.c4!

This is white's best winning try. In the actual game White played 2.Qxc5 when, after 2...bxc3 3.Qxc3 Qb1+ 4.Kh2 Qxa2 (the powerful passed a-pawn will soon force White to take a draw by perpetual check) 5.Qc8+ Kh7 6.Qf5+ g6 7.Qf6 a5 8.g4 a4 9.h5 gxh5 10.Qf5+ Kg7 11.Qg5+ Kh7 12.Qxh5+ Kg7, the game was agreed drawn.

An instructive position arises that beautifully illustrates our "a passed pawn is more important than material" philosophy after 2.cxb4 Qxb4 3.Qxa6 c4 4.Qa8+ Kh7 5.Qe4+ Kg8 6.Qe8+ Kh7 7.Qxf7 c3.

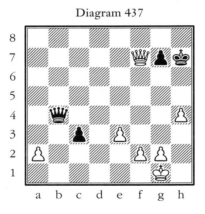

Diagram 437

Even though White is ahead by three big pawns, the c-pawn is too strong— White must take a perpetual check.

2...Qc8!

Simply bad are 2...a5?? 3.Qd8+ Kh7 4.Qxa5 and 2...b3?? 3.axb3 Qxb3 4.Qxa6.

Tempting but inaccurate is 2...Qe4? 3.Qxc5 Qb1+ 4.Kh2 Qxa2 5.Qxb4 Qxf2 6.Qe7! with a winning position.

This leaves us 2...Qa7 which, apparently, should (along with 2...Qc8) prove adequate: 3.g4 (3.Qd8+ Kh7 4.Qa5 Qe7 5.Qxa6 and now 5...Qxh4 6.Qb5 Qe7 is okay, but I prefer 5...Qe4, =. I'll let you figure out the variations here!)

3...a5 4.h5 a4 and, as always, the passed pawn will prove to be equivalent to a small nuke:

Diagram 438

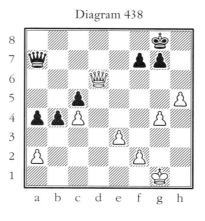

5.g5 b3 6.g6 Qa8 7.axb3 a3 8.Qd7?? (8.gxf7+ Kxf7 9.Qg6+ Kg8 10.h6 Qa7 11.h7+ Kh8 12.Qe8+ Kxh7 13.Qh5+ is a draw by perpetual check and would be the sane way to play for White) 8...a2 9.gxf7+ Kf8 and Black wins.

The idea behind 2...Qc8 is twofold: Black intends both 3...Qf5 with ...Qb1 and ...Qxa2 to follow, and also 3...a5 followed by 4...a4 when a passed pawn will soon be born.

3.Qb6

This freezes black's a-pawn and, apparently, ties black's Queen down to the defense of both a6 and c5.

3...Qf5!

Refusing to buy into the "defend your pawns passively" myth.

4.Qxa6 Kh7!

Diagram 439

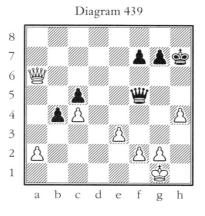

It's interesting how Black, now two pawns down, can play a quiet move like this and still assure himself of good chances. The idea behind 4...Kh7 is clear:

he wants to avoid an unpleasant back rank check after the Queen eventually penetrates to b1 or c2.

5.Qa7

As usual, allowing Black to create an advanced passed pawn is a bad idea: 5.Qb7 Qb1+ 6.Kh2 Qxa2 7.Qxf7 b3 8.Qh5+ Kg8 9.Qd5+ Kh7 10.Qxc5 b2 and White should bail out with perpetual check.

5...f6!

Another calm move, telling White that he has no good way to improve his position. Also possible was 5...Qe5!? with the usual idea of giving up lots of pawns to create an advanced passed b-pawn.

6.Qe7

Also fine for Black is 6.Qa4 Qb1+ 7.Kh2 Qb2 with annoying threats.

The most dangerous move is probably 6.e4 when 6...Qxe4?? 7.Qxc5 is winning for White. However, 6...Qe5! 7.Qf7 Qa1+ 8.Kh2 Qxa2 gives Black enough counterplay to draw.

6...Qb1+ 7.Kh2 Qxa2

Diagram 440

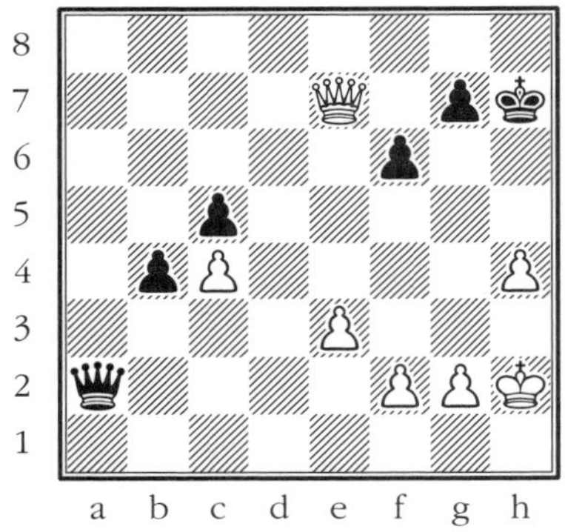

Another monster passed pawn

8.Qe4+ Kh8 9.Qe8+ Kh7 10.Qh5+ Kg8 11.Qxc5 b3 when, as we've seen time and again, the strength of the passed pawn, mixed with a Queen's ability to torment the enemy King, should allow Black an easy draw. (Some of the variations were culled from those by Paul Keres in the classic *The Art of the Middle Game*.)

Part Nine

Endgames for Pure Pleasure

Contents

While Parts One through Eight are part of a detailed study program, Part Nine (Endgames for Pure Pleasure) is something anyone of any rating can enjoy. Who doesn't find the sight of an entombed or dominated minor piece almost comic in nature? And who doesn't stare in wonder at startling tactical thrusts in any phase of the game?

My favorite "finding pleasure in the endgame" subject, though, surrounds the eternal "Who was the greatest of all time?" question. Here I picked five players whose endgame prowess is the stuff of legends. This allows us to analyze what part of the endgame each of the five excelled in, and see examples of endgame mastery at levels few will ever rival.

Have fun! I hope the earlier parts of this book, and this section in particular, allow you to see the endgame as I do: mysterious, of great practical importance, and most of all beautiful.

Entombed and Dominated Minor Pieces

One of my favorite patterns in chess is the domination or actual entombing of an enemy minor piece. While rendering a piece helpless can often result in an uninteresting (one-sided) beating (due to the fact that the side with the entombed piece is, for all intents and purposes, a piece down), at other times the paralysis of a piece creates a rather eye-pleasing effect.

In general, pawns are the prison bars that entangle Bishops, leaving the once mighty pieces trapped in a tiny cell. Knights, on the other hand, can easily become dominated (literally frozen) by Bishops. Of course, the noble steed isn't immune to the "pen-building" properties of the pawns and, like the Bishop, can easily find itself imprisoned in a cage.

First, let's enjoy a medley of basic entombments and dominations.

Diagram 441

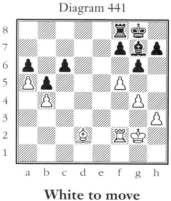

White to move

An experienced player wouldn't hesitate to play **1.f6 Bh8 2.g5**, entombing black's Bishop and leaving himself effectively a Bishop up in the resulting endgame. Black would be a pawn ahead, but his game is hopeless because the Bishop on h8 will never see the light of day.

431

Diagram 442

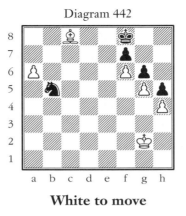

White to move

The position in diagram 442 is another no-brainer. White plays **1.Bd7** when **1...Na7** leaves the Knight trapped on a7 and the King trapped in its kingside tomb. White would then march his King to b6, pick off the Knight, and then promote his a-pawn.

Diagram 443

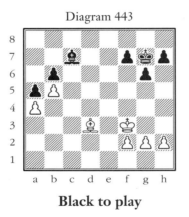

Black to play

The game is completely drawn—the presence of Bishops of opposite colors, and the fact that both side's queenside pawns can't be threatened by the enemy minor piece, doesn't leave either player with anything to hope for. However, miracles are occasionally known to occur in chess, and **1...Bxh2??** instantly changes that assessment! After **2.g3** the Bishop is trapped and lost by Kg2 and Kxh2.

The position in diagram 444 is clearly lost for White. Yes, the Bishop on c6 is a monster, and yes, Black has more space on the queenside and kingside. But the main reason that White is doomed is that the c3-Knight is going to be caged.

Diagram 444

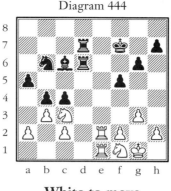

White to move

1.Nb1 (1.Na4 Nxa4 2.bxa4 Bxa4 is easy for Black) **1...c3!** leaves the b1-Knight entombed and "a piece down" in the upcoming endgame battle.

Now that we've gotten a taste for minor piece imprisonment, let's see how such things pan out in actual play.

Diagram 445

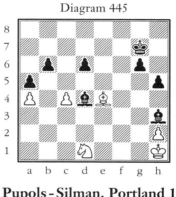

V Pupols - Silman, Portland 1985
White to move

This comic position is overkill, but it also makes an excellent illustration of a dominated Knight. Black has just played ...Bc5-d4, taking away all the Knight's squares and effectively freezing it in place. Of course, white's misery goes far beyond this one indignity—his King is trapped in a corner (that's two "caged" white pieces!), Black is two pawns up, and black's King is free to roam the board.

This is one of those occasions where resignation really is the best move, but White decided to linger in his death agony.

1.Bf3

Black threatened 1...Bg4 when 2.Bc2 allows 2...Bf3 mate.

1...Kf6

Why not let the King take part in the festivities?

3.Be2 Ke5 4.Bf3 h4 5.Be2 Kf4 6.Bd3 Bg4

Threatening both 6...Bxd1 and 6...Bf3 mate.

7.h3 Bxd1, 0-1.

Diagram 446

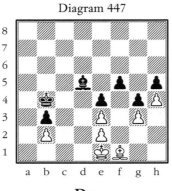

Eddy - Silman, Anchorage 1993
Black to move

This position looks like it should be a fairly simple win for Black since he's, in effect, a Bishop ahead. Due to this, black's only real question is whether or not he can penetrate into the queenside with his King after the exchange of Rooks. If he can (while also retaining a queenside pawn), it's game over. If he can't, it might be a draw. Here are three typical positions that Black will be sure to avoid.

Diagram 447

Draw

Diagram 448

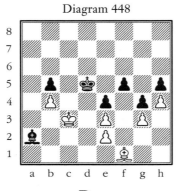

Draw

Diagram 449

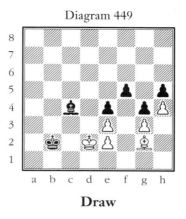

Draw

In the first two illustrative diagrams (447 and 448), black's King can't enter the white position and the game is drawn. In the third diagram (449), black's King has managed to penetrate but all the queenside pawns are gone. This too, is a draw.

With these failures in mind, black's play from our starting diagram (446) is easy to understand: he will exchange Rooks when his King can penetrate into the queenside, and he will be sure to retain a queenside pawn.

1...a5

This gains space and also shows that Black is in no hurry. White is completely helpless so Black should only begin the decisive phase (i.e., trading the Rooks) after he's optimized his King and pawns.

2.Ke1 Bb3 3.Kf2 Rc1 4.Bg2 g5 5.h3 g4 6.h4 b5 7.Bf1 Ke6?

Failing to embrace a true Cat and Mouse mentality. This well-intentioned but lazy (and hasty!) move allows White a bit of counterplay by Rd8. Though the position after 8.Rd8 would still be quite lost, why give the "helpless" opponent anything at all?

The older (more patient) Silman would have avoided any bother by 7...Rc8! (taking the d8-square away from white's Rook) 8.Bg2 (Ah, the sweet sight of the helpless opponent doing absolutely nothing!) 8...Ke6 9.Bf1 Rc2 10.Ke1 (10. Rd8 is now hopeless thanks to 10...Rxb2) 10...Rxd2 11.Kxd2 b4 when we end up back in our actual game.

By the way, Black passed on 7...Rc2?? due to 8.Rxc2 Bxc2 9.b4 axb4 10.axb4 Ke6 11.Ke1 Kd5 12.Kd2 when White achieves one of our drawing illustrative diagrams.

8.Bg2

White should have played the last gasp 8.Rd8 and hoped for the best.

8...Rc2!

Black can now exchange Rooks in optimal fashion.

9.Ke1

The other choices were no better:

➤   9.Rxc2 Bxc2 10.b4 axb4 11.axb4 Kd5 12.Ke1 Kc4 and black's
King picks up white's b-pawn.

➤   9.Rd8 Rxb2 10.Rh8 Bc4 11.Bf1 Ra2 12.Rxh5 Rxa3 and it's all over.

9...Rxd2 10.Kxd2 b4!

Diagram 450

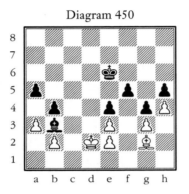

The Bishop on b3 and pawn on b4 form a wall against white's King. This allows
the black King to calmly march to a4 or c4 and enter the white position.

**11.axb4 axb4 12.Bh1 Kd5 13.Bg2 Kc4 14.Bf1 Ba4 15.Kc1 Kb3 16.Kb1
Bb5**

Forcing White to make a highly unpleasant decision: give up e2 or let black's
King into a2 or c2.

17.Kc1 Ka2 18.Kc2 Ba4+ 19.Kc1 Bd1!

Diagram 451

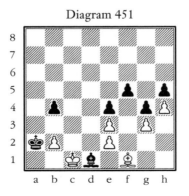

There were many ways to win, but this is the most fun. It graphically shows
just how bad the entombed Bishop really is.

20.Bg2

After 20.Kxd1 Kxb2, White would be powerless to stop the promotion of the b-pawn.

20...Bxe2 21.Kc2 Bd3+ 22.Kc1 b3 23.Bh1 Bf1, 0-1. White's poor Bishop was first entombed, and now dominated.

Diagram 452

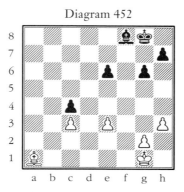

Kujovic - Stryjecki, World Youth Championship 1999
Black to move

One might think that things are not so bad for White since material is even and black's King is no better than white's. However, this evaluation drastically changes after black's first move.

1...Ba3!

Suddenly white's Bishop is stuck on the uninspiring a1-square! Though it seems that black's Bishop isn't doing much either, the fact is that it can leap into action on c1 or anywhere along the a3-f8 diagonal in a flash, while white's Bishop is a useless hunk of plastic/wood.

2.Kf2 Kf7 3.Kf3 e5 4.Ke4

Also losing was 4.e4 h5 5.g4 Kf6 and now:

➤ 6.h4 Ke6 (as soon as a white pawn moves to a dark square, the black King dashes over to the queenside) 7.g5 Kd6 8.Ke2 Kc5 9.Kd2 Kb5 10.Kc2 Ka4 11.Bb2 Bc5 when ...Bf2 followed by ...Bxh4 is completely decisive.

➤ 6.Kg3 Kg5 7.gxh5 (on 7.h4+ Black revels in the fact that a white pawn is on a dark square and rushes over to the queenside, as in our previous variation and as in our actual game continuation) 7...Kxh5 8.Kf3 Kh4 9.Kg2 g5 10.Kh2 g4 11.hxg4 Kxg4 12.Kg2 Kf4 13.Kf2 Kxe4, 0-1.

4...Ke6 5.g4 h5 6.gxh5 gxh5 7.h4

Placing a pawn on a dark square doesn't seem right, but 7.Kf3 Kf5 is just as hopeless: 8.e4+ (8.Ke2 e4 9.Kf2 Kg5 10.Kg3 Bc1 11.h4+ Kf5) 8...Kg5 9.Kg3 h4+ 10.Kf3 Bc1 when White is in zugzwang and must resign.

7...Bc1 8.Kf3 Kd5 9.e4+ Kc5 10.Ke2 Kb5, 0-1. White didn't need to experience the horror of 11 Kd1 Bf4 12.Bb2 Ka4 13.Kc2 Be3 (13...Bg3 is simpler, but further Bishop domination is hard to resist!) 14.Ba1 Ka3 15.Bb2+ Ka2 16.Bc1 Bxc1 17.Kxc1 Kb3 18.Kd2 Kb2 and enough is enough.

Diagram 453

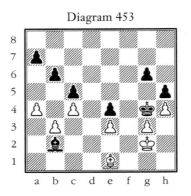

F Say-Peters, Los Angeles 1990
Black to move

It only took one move to make White lay down his arms.

1...Be5!

White resigned since his Bishop would end up in a comic situation after …

2.Bf2

There's no relief from 2.a5 bxa5, 2.b4 cxb4, or 2.Kf1 Kf3.

2...Bc3 3.Bg1 Be1 4.Bh2 a5, zugzwang.

Diagram 454

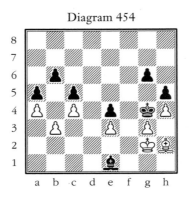

If you're Black you laugh, if you're White you cry. Of course, any move White plays leads to material loss. Thus, White resigned.

Tactics

Everyone loves the rush of a beautiful or surprising tactical shot. Many players think such things only reside in the realm of the opening and middlegame. However, it turns out that the endgame is rich in tactics, tricks, combinations, and the need for extremely deep calculation.

The forty examples below are grouped in order of difficulty. You can cover up the answers and try to solve them yourself, or you can just play them over and marvel at their beauty.

Simple Tactics

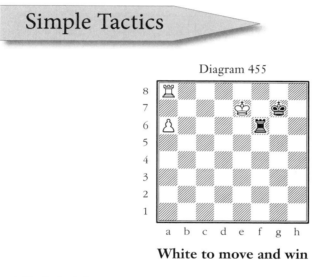

Diagram 455

White to move and win

1.Rg8+!, 1-0.

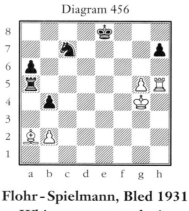

Diagram 456

Flohr – Spielmann, Bled 1931
White to move and win

1.g6!, 1-0. White makes a new Queen after 1...Rxh5 2.g7!

Diagram 457

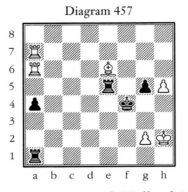

Donner - Spanjaard, Holland 1961

Black to move and win

1...Rh1+! 2.Kxh1 Kg3, 0-1. White's enormous army can't deal with the threat of 3...Re1 mate.

Diagram 458

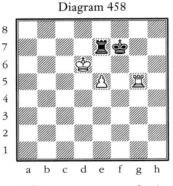

White to move and win

1.Rg7+, 1-0.

Diagram 459

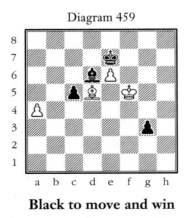

Black to move and win

1...c4!, 0-1. White's Bishop can't deal with both pawns (2.Bxc4 g2), and 2.Ke4 allows 2...g2.

Medium Tactics

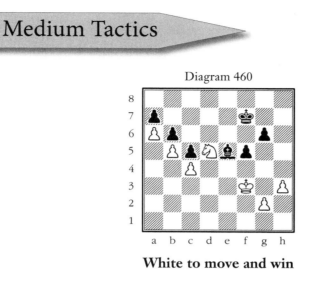

Diagram 460

White to move and win

1.Nxb6! Ke6 2.Na4 Bd6 3.b6 Bb8 4.b7 Kd7

Holding onto the c-pawn by 4…Kd6 allows white's King to invade the kingside by 5.Kf4 followed by 6.Kg5.

Of course, 4…Bd6 doesn't really guard c5 at all, as shown by 5.Nxc5+.

5.Nxc5+ Kc6 6.Na4

White's Knight and c-pawn stops the black King from attacking a6. Now all White has to do is break through on the kingside and it's game over.

6…Kd7

6…g5 7.g3 followed by 8.h4 gives White a passed h-pawn.

7.g4, 1-0.

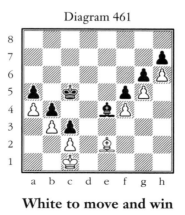

Diagram 461

White to move and win

Black's King is ready to march to e3 and begin feasting on white's kingside pawns. One might peg the second player as the likely winner, but a "small" tactical device has been overlooked that turns the game in white's favor.

1.Bh5!!

And not 1.Bc4?? Bd5.

1...Bd5

1...gxh5 2.g6 forces the creation of a new white Queen.

2.Bxg6! Bg8 3.Bxf5 Kd4 4.g6 hxg6 5.Bxg6, 1-0.

Diagram 462

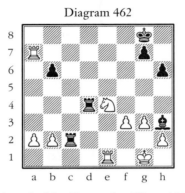

Averbakh - Ragozin, Kiev 1954

White to move and win

1.Nf6+!, 1-0. 2.Re8 mate follows.

Diagram 463

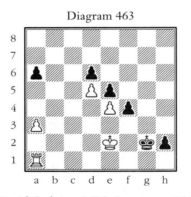

Duif Calvin - NN, Internet 2005

White to move and draw

1.Rh1! Kxh1

1...f3+ doesn't make any difference: 2.Ke3 (2.Ke1 amounts to the same thing)
2...Kxh1 (2...f2 3.Ke2!) 3.Kf2 a5 4.a4 stalemate.

2.Kf2 f3 3.Kf1 a5 4.a4 f2 5.Kxf2 stalemate.

Diagram 464

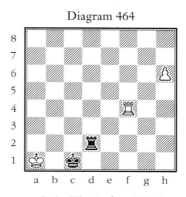

A.A. Troitsky, 1924

White to move and win

1.h7 Rh2

Or 1...Rd8 2.Rc4+ Kd2 3.Rd4+! Rxd4 4.h8=Q

2.Rf1+ Kd2 3.Rf2+! Rxf2 4.h8=Q with a theoretical win.

Hard Tactics

Diagram 465

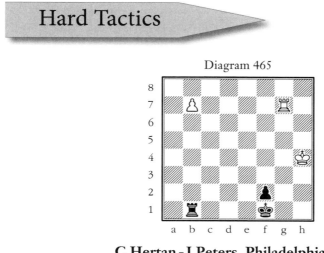

C Hertan - J Peters, Philadelphia 1979
Black to move and win

Black is aiming for a Queen vs. Rook endgame win, something that White must avoid by checking, threatening to win the f-pawn, and/or keeping black's King in front of his pawn.

1...Ke2 2.Re7+ Kf3 3.Rf7+ Kg2

Threatening 4...Rxb7!—white's moves are all forced.

4.Rg7+ Kh2! 5.Rf7 Rb4+

Black's plan is clear: he will combine threats of ...Rxb7 with pushing white's King backwards until ...Rxb7 pins the Rook to its King!

6.Kh5 Kg2 7.Rg7+ Kh3 8.Rf7 Rb5+ 9.Kh6 Kg3

Again threatening 10...Rxb7.

10.Kh7

Giving in to the inevitable. Black's concept would be strikingly fulfilled after 10.Rg7+ Kh4 11.Rf7 Rb6+ 12.Kh7 Rxb7.

10...Rxb7 11.Rxb7 f1=Q 12.Rg7+ Kh4 13.Kg8 Qf5 14.Rh7+ Kg5 15.Re7 Kh6 16.Rf7 Qc8+, 0-1. It's all over, since 17.Rf8 Qe6+ 18.Kh8 (18.Rf7 Kg6) 18...Qe5+ mates.

Diagram 466

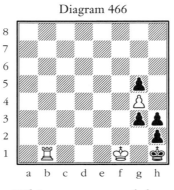

White to move and draw

1.Re1! (The only good move!) **1...g2+ 2.Kf2+ g1=Q+ 3.Kf3! Qxe1** stalemate.

Diagram 467

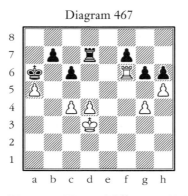

Karpov - Hort, Tilburg 1979

White to move and win

1.g5! hxg5 2.h6 Kxa5 3.h7 Rd8 4.Rxf7 b5 5.cxb5 Kxb5 (5...cxb5 6.Rg7 Rh8 7.d5) **6.Rb7+ Ka6 7.Rg7 Rh8 8.Ke4 Kb5 9.Kf3 Kc4 10.Rd7 Kd3 11.Kg4 Rxh7 12.Rxh7 Kxd4 13.Rd7+!**, 1-0.

Diagram 468

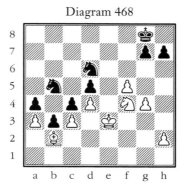

Euwe - Averbakh, Zurich 1953
Black to move and win

1...Nxa3! 2.Bxa3 Nb5 3.Bc1 Nxc3 4.Ne2 Nb1!, 0-1.

Diagram 469

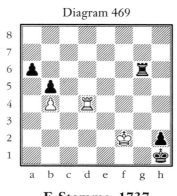

F. Stamma, 1737
White to move and win

1.Rd1+ Rg1 2.Rf1! Rxf1+ 3.Kxf1 a5 4.bxa5 b4 5.a6 b3 6.a7 b2 7.a8=B mate.

Diagram 470

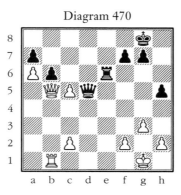

Smyslov - Guimard, Mar del Plata 1962
White to move and win

1.cxb6!! Re1+

This wins the white Queen.

2.Rxe1 Qxb5 3.bxa7

Unfortunately for Black, the passed a7-pawn will promote.

3...Qc6 4.Rb1 Kh7 5.Rb8, 1-0.

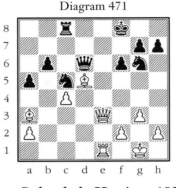

Diagram 471

Fine - Golombek, Hastings 1935/36

White to move and win

White has pressure against the black King, which means that he would normally try and retain the Queens so his attacking chances would be enhanced. However, in the present case White sees that transposition into an endgame leads to immediate material gains thanks to tactical considerations—namely the poor position of the black King and the pin along the a3-f8 diagonal.

1.Qe6! Qxe6

Of course, 1...Nxe6 2.Bxd6+ leaves White a piece up.

2.Rxe6 Rb8

2...Ne7 3.Rxb6 followed by Rb5 is decisive.

3.Rxb6!, 1-0 since 3...Rxb6 4.Bxc5+ wins a piece.

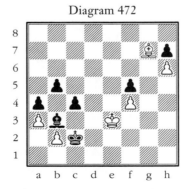

Diagram 472

Ljubojevic - Karpov, Milan 1975

Black to move and win

1...b4! 2.axb4

The actual game continuation was less interesting: 2.Kd4 c3 3.bxc3 bxa3 4.c4 a2 5.Kc5 Kb1 6.Kb4 a1=Q 7.Bxa1 Kxa1 8.c5 Kb2 9.c6 a3 10.c7 Be6 11.Kc5 a2 12.Kd6 Bc8, 0-1.

2...c3 3.bxc3

The win is also a sure thing after 3.Bxc3 a3, though Black does have to use a little care: 4.bxa3 Kxc3 5.Kf2 Kb2 6.Ke3 Ba4 7.Kd4 Kxa3 8.Ke5 Kxb4 9.Kxf5 Kc5 10.Ke6 Bb3+ 11.Ke7 Bc2 12.Ke6 Bd1! 13.f5 Bg4 14.Ke5 Kc6 15.Ke6 Bh3 16.Kf6 Kd6.

3...Bc4!

The nice point. By blocking the c-pawn, Black doesn't allow white's Bishop to cover a1.

4.b5 a3 5.b6 a2 6.b7 a1=Q 7.b8=Q

White has managed to make a Queen of his own, but now his King gets mated.

7...Qg1+ 8.Kf3 Bd5+ 9.Ke2 Qg2+ 10.Ke1 Qg3+ 11.Ke2 Bc4 mate.

Diagram 473

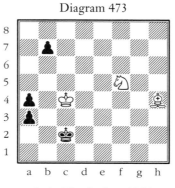

A.A. Troitsky, 1897
White to move and win

1.Nd4+ Kb1

White's minor pieces permanently stop black's pawns (meaning that they will eventually be captured) after 1...Kd2 2.Nb5 a2 3.Bf6 Kc1 4.Na3.

2.Nb5 a2 3.Na3+ Kb2 4.Bf6+ Kxa3 5.Ba1 b5+ 6.Kc3 b4+ 7.Kc4

The same mate occurs after 7.Kc2 b3+ 8.Kc3 b2 9.Bxb2.

7...b3 8.Kc3 b2 9.Bxb2 mate.

Diagram 474

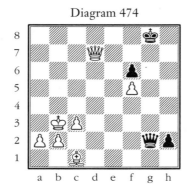

Simagin - Bronstein, Moscow 1947
White to move and win

Black is about to make a second Queen so one might think that giving perpetual check is a more or less forced. However, White has a lovely tactical trick that cements the victory.

1.Bg5!! h1=Q

A "show me" move. However, 1...fxg5 2.f6 is horrible, while 1...Qxg5 2.Qd8+ Kh7 3.Qc7+ followed by 4.Qxh2 leaves White with a winning material advantage.

2.Qe8+

2.Qe6+ mates one move faster, but who cares?

2...Kg7 3.Qg6+ Kf8 4.Qxf6+ Kg8 5.Qd8+ Kg7 6.Qe7+ Kg8 7.Qe8+, 1-0.
It's all over after 7...Kg7 (7...Kh7 8.Qg6+ Kh8 9.Bf6 mate) 8.f6+ Kh7 9.Qf7+ and 10.Qg7 mate.

Diagram 475

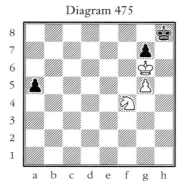

Vesely - Antos, Czechoslovakia 1968
White to move and win

It seems the Knight must run to the queenside and stop black's passed a-pawn. However, if he does that the resulting position on the kingside holds for Black.

Seeing that the basic Knight stop doesn't get the job done, White looks into mating patterns that often occur when a King is trapped in a corner. This allows him to find a very pretty win.

1.Kf7! a4

1...Kh7 2.g6+ Kh8 3.Kf8 followed by 4.Ne6, 5.Nd8, and 6.Nf7 mate.

2.Ng6+ Kh7 3.Ne5 a3 4.g6+ Kh6

4...Kh8 5.Kf8 with 6.Nf7 mate to follow.

5.Ng4+ Kg5 6.Ne3

Now the kingside situation is winning for White so he rushes to stop black's pawn.

6...a2 7.Nc2, 1-0. After 7...Kh6 8.Na1 the g-pawn is lost.

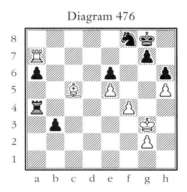

Diagram 476

Taimanov - Averbakh, Leningrad 1947

White to move. Is the obvious move good?

How would you assess this position and which move would you choose if you were White?

A glance might give the impression that Black's about to lose after …

1.Ra8?

But this turns out to be a mistake. Better was 1.Rb7 Ra5 2.Bxf8 Kxf8 3.Rxb3 Rb5 4.Rd3 Rb8 5.Rd6 Ra8 6.Rxe6 a5 7.Rd6 a4 8.Rd2 a3 9.Ra2 Ke7 10.Kf3 Ke6. Analysis by Averbakh, who feels this position is drawn due to the fact that white's Rook is passive and, after …Ra4, neither his pawns nor his King are going anywhere.

1...Rb4!!

This eye-opener completely turns the tables.

2.Rxf8+ Kh7

The threat of …b2 forces White to give up his Bishop.

3.Bd4 Rxd4 4.Rb8 Rd3+ 5.Kf2 a5 6.f5!

Getting some counterplay just in time. White would have lost quickly if he had allowed Black to advance his a-pawn to a4.

6...Rd5 7.fxe6 Rxe5 8.Rxb3 Rxe6 and Black, being a pawn up, had good winning chances (and indeed he won in the end after a long battle).

Diagram 477

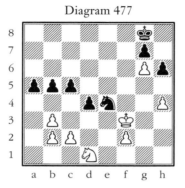

Bonner – Medina, Haifa 1976

Black to move and win

Here's a rather odd example of a Knight's "problem" in dealing with a passed rook-pawn.

1...Nc3!!

A lovely and very surprising move! White's Knight is trapped and thus he must capture on c3.

2.bxc3

2.Nxc3 dxc3 3.bxc3 a4 also allows the pawn to make a touchdown.

2...a4 3.cxd4 cxd4 4.c3 a3, 0-1.

Diagram 478

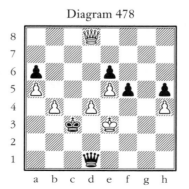

Topalov – Kasparov, Linares 1999

Black to play and win

1...Qg1+ 2.Ke2 Qg2+ 3.Ke3

3.Ke1 Kd3 mates.

3...f4+!!, 0-1. After 4.Kxf4 Kd3! 5.Qg5 (5.Qg8 Qxg8 lasts a few moves longer) 5...Qf2 is mate.

Diagram 479

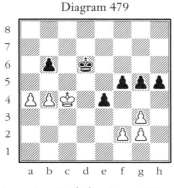

Weinstein - Rohde, Lone Pine 1977

Black to move and win

One might think that White must be better due to his outside passed pawn. Indeed, in the actual game White made use of this fact to create a classic Fox in the Chicken Coup situation: 1...h4?? 2.gxh4 gxh4 3.Kd4 Ke6 4.a5 bxa5 5.bxa5 Kd6 6.a6 Kc6 7.Ke5 Kb6 8.Kxf5 Kxa6 9.Kxe4, 1-0.

However, it turns out that Black could have won by force:

1...f4! 2.gxf4

No better are 2.Kd4 e3 3.fxe3 f3 4.gxf3 h4 and 2.a5 bxa5 3.bxa5 h4 4.Kd4 e3 5.fxe3 f3 6.gxf3 h3 7.a6 Kc7. In both cases black's h-pawn can't be stopped.

2...gxf4 3.Kd4 e3 4.fxe3 f3 5.gxf3 h4 and White must resign.

Diagram 480

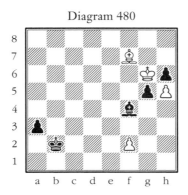

Hindle - Möhring, Tel Aviv 1964

Black to move and win

1...Be3!

The tempting 1...g4 2.Kf5 g3 3.fxg3 Bxg3 4.Kg4 Be1 5.Kh3 a2 6.Bxa2 Kxa2 is a draw since black's rook-pawn is of the wrong color.

2.Kxh6

Of course, 2.fxe3 g4 promotes a pawn.

2...g4+ 3.fxe3 g3 4.Kh7 g2 5.h6 g1=Q 6.Kh8 a2 7.Bxa2 Kxa2 8.h7 Qg6 9.e4 Qf7, 0-1.

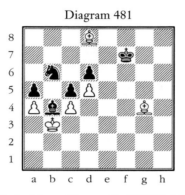

Diagram 481

Kobaidze - Cereteli, USSR 1969
Black to move and draw

1...Ke8!

Telling White that he doesn't need the Knight to draw!

2.Bxb6 Ke7, ½-½. Black just moves his Bishop back and forth along the e1-b4 diagonal and dares White to make some form of progress (which he obviously can't).

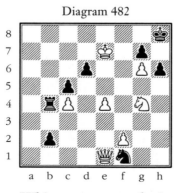

Diagram 482

White to move and win

1.Qxb4! cxb4 2.Nxh6!

2.Kf8 b1=Q 3.Nxh6 amounts to the same thing.

2...b1=Q

Black also gets mated after 2...gxh6 3.Kf7 h5 4.g7+ Kh7 5.g8=Q+ Kh6 6.Qg6 mate.

3.Kf8!

The threat of Nf7 mate forces Black to chop on h6.

3...gxh6 4.g7+ Kh7 5.g8=Q mate.

Diagram 483

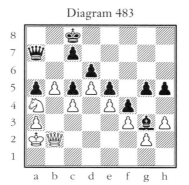

A Petrosian - Hazai, Schilde 1970

Black to move and Swindle

Black is lost due to the weakness of his a5-pawn. White intends Qd2 (hitting a5 and preventing a later ...Be1) followed by Kb3, Nc3, Ka4, and (if necessary) Na2-c1-b3. Realizing that there is no defense to this plan, Black tries to throw White off by ...

1...Qb6! 2.Nxb6+??

And White goes for the bait! Instead, he should have ignored the Greek gift and simply continued with the above plan.

2...cxb6

Threatening 3...h4.

3.h4 gxh4 4.Qd2

White probably felt he would now win by Qd1-h1-h3. However, he's in for a shock.

4...h3! 5.gxh3

Else ...h2 follows.

5...h4, ½-½.

Diagram 484

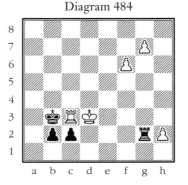

Teschner - Richter, Berlin 1951

Black to move and win

1...Ka4!

And not 1...Ka2?? 2.Rxc2 since 2...Rxc2 3.g8=Q is check, or 1...Kb4?? 2.f7 when the f-pawn queens with check.

2.g8=Q c1=N+!, 0-1. Note that 2...Rxg8?? 3.Kxc2 would have allowed White to draw. After 2...c1=N+ White gave up because 3.Rxc1 bxc1=N+! 4.Ke4 Rxg8 5.Kf5 Nd3 6.f7 Rf8 7.Kf6 Ne5 8.Kxe5 Rxf7 followed by ...Rh7 and taking the h-pawn leaves a simple King vs. Rook position.

Diagram 485

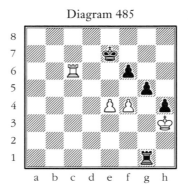

Silman - Yermolinsky, World Open 1991

White to move and draw

Yermolinsky was sure he was going to win at this point. He failed to see my next move, which sacrifices a second pawn in order to force a positional draw.

1.e5!

This prevents Black from getting two connected passed pawns.

1...Rg3+ 2.Kh2 fxe5

2...gxf4 3.Rxf6 (White also draws by 3.exf6+ Kf7 4.Rc4) 3...f3 4.Kh1! leaves Black unable to improve his position.

3.fxg5 Rxg5 4.Kh3 Rh5 5.Ra6 Rh8 6.Rb6 Kd7 7.Ra6

Diagram 486

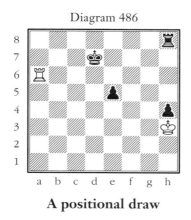

A positional draw

7...Rh5 8.Kg4 Rh8 9.Kh3 e4 10.Ra4 Re8 11.Kxh4 Kc6 12.Kg3 Kb5 13.Ra2 e3 14.Kf3 Kc4 15.Ke2, ½-½.

Very Hard Tactics

Diagram 487

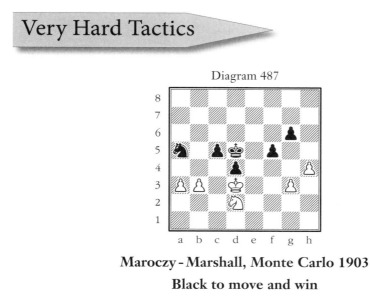

Maroczy - Marshall, Monte Carlo 1903

Black to move and win

Geza Maroczy was one of the finest endgame players of all time. However, the crazed tactician Marshall was also very strong in this final stage of the game. In the present example, we get a taste of Marshall's ability to calculate deeply and accurately.

1...Nxb3!!

A real surprise. Why? Isn't the ...c5-c4+ fork pretty obvious? Yes it is, but the resulting position leaves White with an outside passed pawn, which could easily turn the tide in white's favor.

2.Nxb3 c4+ 3.Kc2 cxb3+ 4.Kxb3

Has Marshall miscalculated and, in his search for beauty, forgotten that outside passed pawns usually rule the roost in King and pawn endgames?

4...Ke4! 5.Kc2

The straight race by 5.a4 doesn't get the job done since after 5...d3 6.a5 Ke3 7.a6 d2 Black will queen with check. Instead, Maroczy wisely blocks the d-pawn with his King before pushing the a-pawn.

5...Ke3

And not 5...d3+?? 6.Kd2 when White wins thanks to his outside passed pawn which will allow him to make use of the Fox in the Chicken Coup routine (i.e., while black's King is dealing with the a-pawn, white's King takes the d-pawn then rushes over to the unguarded kingside to eat everything in sight).

6.Kd1 Kf2 7.a4 Kxg3 8.a5 f4 9.a6

9.Ke2 f3+ 10.Kf1 d3 is no help to White.

9...f3 10.a7 f2 11.Ke2

11.a8=Q f1=Q+ 12.Kd2 Qg2+ 13.Qxg2+ Kxg2 leads to an easily winning King and pawn endgame since Black will win white's h-pawn and then get his King in front of his remaining pawn.

11...d3+

11...Kg2 wasn't possible due to 12.a8=Q with check!

12.Kd2

12.Ke3 f1=Q 13.a8=Q Qe2+ 14.Kd4 d2 is also hopeless. Also bad is 12.Kf1 d2.

12...f1=Q 13.a8=Q Qg2+ 14.Qxg2+ Kxg2 15.Kxd3 Kg3

For those that have studied the earlier lessons in this book, this King and pawn endgame should be kid stuff!

16.Ke3 Kxh4 17.Kf3 g5 18.Kg2 Kg4 19.Kh2 Kf3 20.Kh3 g4+ 21.Kh2 Kf2 22.Kh1 Kg3

Avoiding 22...g3?? stalemate!

23.Kg1 Kh3, 0-1 since 24.Kh1 g3 25.Kg1 g2 is game over.

Diagram 488

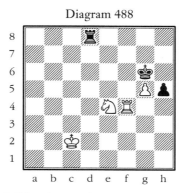

Ribli - Oszvath, Hungary 1971
Black to move and draw

White's a solid Knight ahead. However, Black is able to create a surprising positional draw. Two of his trumps are:

➤ White's King is cut off from the field of battle.

➤ White can't win if he loses his final pawn.

1...h4!

Giving up his pawn and leaving himself a piece and a pawn down!

2.Rxh4

White also fails to get anywhere with 2.Rf6+ Kh5 3.Rh6+ (3. g6 Rg8 wins the pawn) 3...Kg4 4.g6 Kf5 5.g7 Rg8 and the pawn can't be retained.

2...Kf5

Now black's idea is clear: White's King is still trapped away from the embattled area, the Knight can't move without losing the pawn, the pawn will be eaten if it dares to move, and the white Rook can't move without losing the Knight.

3.Kc3 Rd1 4.Kc4 Rd8 5.Kc5 Rd3 6.Kc6 Rd1

Black is happy to move his Rook back and forth along the d-file (making sure he avoids 6...Rd4?? 7.Ng3+) since White isn't able to improve the position of his pieces.

7.Kc7 Rd3 8.Rh1

White finally gives it a shot.
8...Re3!, ½-½. Seeing that Black avoided 8...Kxe4?? 9.Rg1 (getting the Rook behind his passed pawn) 9...Ra3 10.g6 Ra8 (10...Ra7+ 11.Kd6 Rg7 12.Ke6) 11.g7 Rg8 12.Kd6 Kf5 13.Ke7 and White wins, peace was agreed since 9.Rg1 Rxe4 10.g6 Re7+ 11.Kd8 Rg7 leaves nothing to play for.

Diagram 489

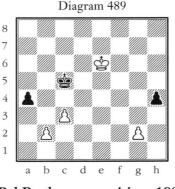

Pal Benko composition, 1988

White to move and draw

Black intends to gobble up white's b-pawn and make a new Queen. Since White can't prevent this, one might guess that Black will win. However, White can save the game by a very strange maneuver.

1.Kd7!

1.Kf5? Kc4 2.Kg4 Kb3 3.c4 Kxc4 4.Kxh4 Kb3 5.g4 Kxb2 6.g5 a3 7.g6 a2 8.g7 a1=Q 9.g8=Q Qh1+ 10.Kg5 Qg1+.

1...Kc4 2.Kc7 Kb3 3.Kb8 Kxb2 4.c4, ¹/₂-¹/₂. After both sides promote their pawns and Black chops with his Queen on g2, we get a TableBase draw.

Diagram 490

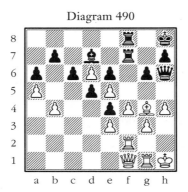

Rubinstein - Cohn, Carlsbad 1911

Black to play. Is 1...g5 a good idea?

Black's position is extremely uncomfortable (he has no space, his Bishop is absolutely horrible, and white's d6-pawn is a nightmare), but he thought he saw a way to end his troubles tactically.

1...g5? 2.fxg5 Rxf2 3.Qxf2 Qxh4+ 4.gxh4 Rxf2

Black must have entered this thinking "I've exchanged pieces and have a Rook on the 7th. My position has really improved!"

5.Rd1

This must have burst his bubble. It turns out that Kg1 is crushing since an exchange of Rooks leaves White with a winning Bishop endgame.

5...Kg7

5...Rb2 6.Rf1 allows White to decisively penetrate along the f-file: 6...Kg7 7.Rf6 Rxb4 8.Bxe6 Bxe6 9.Rxe6 and it's all over.

6.Kg1! Rf8 7.Rf1 Rxf1+ 8.Kxf1, 1-0. Black has no answer to white's plan of Kf1-e2-d2-c3-d4-c5-b6 when ...Bc8 is met by Kc7. Note that 8...Kf8 (trying to bring the King over the queenside, though this would lose even if he was able to achieve it) 9.Bh5! creates an impenetrable wall since 9...Be8 10.Bxe8 Kxe8 11.h5 forces the promotion of a pawn.

Diagram 491

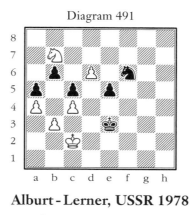

Alburt - Lerner, USSR 1978
White to move and win

At first glance one could easily think that Black is better. After all, his King is far more active than white's, and his passed e-pawn seems more dangerous than white's on d6 (which is firmly blocked by black's Knight). On top of all that, white's Knight seems out of play on b7. Yet, White can force a win by taking advantage of the black King's absence from the queenside.

1.Nxc5!!

I'm sure Mr. Lerner couldn't believe his eyes!

1...bxc5 2.b4 axb4

Other moves fare no better:

> 2...Nd7 3.bxa5 Kf2 4.a6 e4 5.a7 e3 6.a8=Q e2 7.Qe4 e1=Q 8.Qxe1+ Kxe1 9.a5 Nb8 10.Kc3! (Not falling for 10. a6 Nxa6 11.d7 Nb4+ 12.Kb3 Nc6 13.Ka4 Kd2 14.Kb5 Nd8 15.Kxc5 Kc3 when both 16.Kd5 Kb4 17.c5 Kb5 and 16.Kb5 Kd4 17.c5 Kd5 lead to draws) 10...Ke2 11.a6 Nxa6 12.d7, 1-0.

➤ 2...cxb4 3.c5 b3+ 4.Kxb3 Kd4 (4...Ne4 5.Kc4) 5.c6 Ne4 6.d7
Nc5+ 7.Kc2 Ne6 8.c7 wins.

**3.a5 e4 4.a6 Kf2 5.a7 e3 6.a8=Q e2 7.Qf8 e1=Q 8.Qxf6+ Kg3 9.Qg5+
Kh3 10.Qd2 Qa1**

White also prevails against 10...b3+ 11.Kc3 Qa1+ 12.Kxb3 Qb1+ 13.Ka4.

**11.d7 Qa4+ 12.Kb1 Qb3+ 13.Kc1 Qa3+ 14.Kd1 Qb3+ 15.Ke2 Kg4
16.Qd1!**

Not falling for 16.d8=Q?? Qf3+ 17.Ke1 Qh1+ 18.Kf2 Qh2+ 19.Ke3 Qf4+
20.Kd3 Qf5+ with a draw by perpetual check.

Though 16.Qd1 is completely decisive, I should add that Mr. Fritz preferred
16.Qd3 Qb2+ 17.Ke1 when 17...Qe5+ 18.Qe2+ and 17...Qc1+ 18.Qd1+ both
force immediate resignation.

16...Qxc4+ 17.Ke3+, 1-0.

Diagram 492

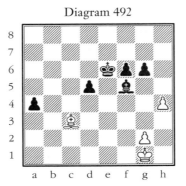

Topalov - Shirov, Linares 1998
Black to move and win

If white's King can get to e3, black's pawns will be firmly blocked and the
game will be drawn. Thus, Black must get his King to e4 before white's reaches
e3. There is only one way to do this:

1...Bh3!!

Absolutely brilliant! The generic 1...Be4 2.g3 Kf5 3.Kf2 only leads to a
draw.

2.gxh3

Since 2.Kf2 Kf5 3.Ke3 Bxg2 leaves Black three pawns up.

2...Kf5 3.Kf2 Ke4 4.Bxf6

White also loses after 4.Ke2 a3 5.Kd2 d4 6.Ba1 f5.

4...d4 5.Be7 Kd3! 6.Bc5 Kc4 7.Be7 Kb3, 0-1. The finish could easily have
been 8.Bc5 d3 9.Ke3 Kc2 10.Bb4 a3 when a pawn turns into a Queen.

Diagram 493

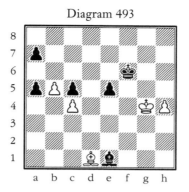

Shirov‑Andersson, Biel 1991

Black to move and win

1...Bxh4!! 2.Kxh4

Black also wins after 2.Bc2 Be1 3.Kf3 Kg5 4.Bd1 Bc3 5.Ba4 Kh4 6.Bd1 Kh3 7.Ba4 Bd4 8.Bc2 Kh2 9.Bd1 Kg1 etc.

2...Kf5 3.Kg3 Ke4 4.Kf2 Kd3 5.Ke1 Kxc4 6.Kd2 Kb4 7.Kc2 e4 8.Bg4 a4 9.Bf5 e3 10.Be6 c4, 0-1.

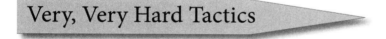

Very, Very Hard Tactics

Don't even think about solving these last two positions! Just play them over and enjoy their raw, lovely complexity.

Diagram 494

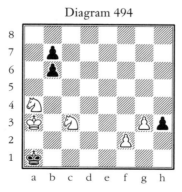

Pal Benko composition, Magyar Sakkelet 1972

White to move and win

Pal Benko's endgame compositions simply blow my mind. You can stare at them for months and never solve them. However, that doesn't matter! What *does* matter is simply looking at the amazing path to victory that Benko weaves and marveling at its sheer beauty.

1.Nb5!!

A real key move which fully deserves two exclamation marks. The Knight jump to b5 is counter-intuitive since it allows the black King to escape from the mating net and, in addition, it takes the Knight further from the threatening pawn, apparently allowing it to promote. Is this key move necessary? Wouldn't 1.Ne2 lead to a White win? No, 1.Ne2 fails to 1...h2 2.Nac3 b5 (the note after black's 1st move shows what happens if Black promotes to a Queen here) 3.Nd4 b4+! 4.Kxb4 Kb2 and Black escapes since his King is out of the trap.

1...Kb1

The best try. The tempting 1...h2 loses beautifully after 2.Nac3 h1=Q 3.Nd4 Qc1+ 4.Kb3 Qb2+ 5.Kc4 b5+ 6.Kd3 Qxf2 7.Nb3+ Kb2 8.Nd1+. It's now clear that the black Queen was led into a trap. Due to all the possible forks, she would have been lost whether she captured the f-pawn or not.

2.Nac3+ Kc2 3.Nd4+! Kd3!

The obvious 3...Kxc3 runs into 4.Ne2+! (A very important move! The obvious 4.Nf3? fails to 4...b5!, when Black can draw.) 4...Kc4 (4...Kd2 fails to 5.Ng1 h2 6.Nf3+, while 4...Kd3 5.Nf4+ is also easy for White.) 5.g4 h2 6.Ng3 Kc3 7.Ka4 Kc4 8.g5 b5+ 9.Ka5, and White wins since he will queen with check.

4.Nd1!!

This is the only way to win. White fails to achieve the victory after 4.f4 Kxc3 5.Ne2+ Kd3, and Black wins because White no longer can play Nf4+. If White had tried 4.f3 instead of 4.f4, then 4...Kxc3 5.Ne2+ Kd2 wins since 6.Ng1 h2 7.Nf3+ isn't possible. White can try 4.Nf3, but he still fails to win the game: 4...Kxc3 5.Ka4 Kc4 6.g4 b5+ 7.Ka5 b6+! 8.Ka6 b4 9.g5 Kd5 10.g6 Ke6 11.Ng5+ Kf6 12.Nxh3 b3 13.Nf4 b2 14.Nd5+ Kxg6 15.Nc3 Kf5, with a draw.

4...h2 5.f4 Kxd4

And not 5...h1=N 6.f5, winning for White.

6.Nf2 Kc3

6...Ke3 7.Ng4+ wins for White.

7.f5 b5 8.f6 b4+ 9.Ka2 Kc2 10.f7 b3+ 11.Ka3 b2 12.f8=Q b1=Q 13.Qf5+, 1-0.

Diagram 495

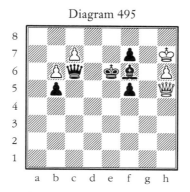

Pal Benko composition, Sakkelet 1987
White to move and win

White seems to be in trouble since he's a piece down. He faces mating threats and his passed pawns appear to be frozen in their tracks.

1.Qd1!

White threatens 2.Qd8! Bxd8 3.cxd8=N+!.

1...Qa8

If Black tries 1...Qe8!?, White must avoid 2.Qd8? since the position would be a draw after 2...Bxd8 3.c8=Q+ Kd5 4.b7 Qe7! 5.b8=Q (White gets nowhere with 5.Qxf5+ Kc6 6.b8=Q f6+.) 5...f6+ 6.Kg6 Qe8+. However, White still has a win by answering 1...Qe8 with 2.Qe2+ Be5 3.Qxe5+ Kxe5 4.b7 Qc6 5.c8=Q Qg6+ 6.Kh8 Qxh6+ 7.Kg8 Qg6+ 8.Kf8 Qh6+ 9.Ke8 Qh8+ 10.Kd7, and Black must resign.

2.Qd8!

2.Qb3+ Ke7 3.Qe3+ Kd6 4.Qd3+ isn't nearly as strong.

2...Bxd8 3.b7!

Diagram 496

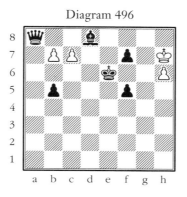

A remarkable situation: the two pawns beat the Queen and Bishop.

3...Qxb7 4.cxd8=N+ Ke7

The game comes down to a race between the passed pawns. Black's alternative is 4...Kd5 5.Nxb7 f4 6.Na5 Ke4 (Black also gets caught after 6...f3 7.Nb3 f2 8.Nd2 b4 9.Kg7 b3 10.h7 b2 11.h8=Q f1=Q 12.Qd8+ Kc6 13.Qc8+ Kd6 14.Qb8+ and 15.Nxf1) 7.Nb3 Ke3 8.Nd4! Kxd4 9.Kg8, and the h-pawn queens with check.

5.Nxb7 Kf8

Black tries to trap the white King and then push his own passed pawns.

6.Nc5 f4 7.Nd7+ Ke7 8.Kg7 f3 9.Nf6

Weak is 9.Nb6? due to 9...Ke6.

9...f2 10.Nd5+ Ke6 11.Ne3, 1-0.

The Five Greatest Endgame Players of All Time

What "something extra" did the players on this short list have that other all-time greats didn't? Every World Champion and true World Championship Candidate was a giant among grandmasters, and it must be stated that chess legends of this stature were magnificent at every stage of the game. But each player's style is unique, and each player tends to excel in one area more than others. For example, Alekhine, Tal, and Kasparov would head the list if we were searching for the greatest calculators and attackers. Petrosian and Karpov would be our choices if we were looking for sublime positional skills.

On this list, though, we are limiting ourselves to those few who reached the highest heights in technique and endgame mastery. Such talent in this area of chess isn't merely learned; it requires a "feel," an artistic touch that few ever achieve.

Putting together such a small list was anything but easy since a case can be made for the inclusion of several players. Who would have argued if I had placed Karpov here? And players like Alekhine, Botvinnik, Reshevsky, Petrosian, and Korchnoi also possess(ed) magnificent endgame skills. Ultimately, I decided to stick with the classical choices, Lasker, Rubinstein, and Capablanca, with the addition of Smyslov and Fischer.

Hopefully, this sampling will inspire chess fans to read more about chess history, and to study the games of all the players I've just mentioned—Kasparov's *My Great Predecessors* series is an excellent way to do this. Remember that chess is more than just a competitive game. Its history is rich in pain and triumph, and the writings and games of the great masters can both inspire the student to new heights, and leave one in awe at the depth of artistic beauty they've created.

Emanuel Lasker
(The 2nd World Champion)
The Art of Endgame Defense

Dr. Emanuel Lasker (1868-1941), the legendary German World Champion who held the title from 1894-1921, had a rather unusual style. His openings were poor, and his middlegame play, while powerful, didn't have the fluid feel of Rubinstein's. His strengths, though, combined to create a player that dwarfed the world's best during his prime years, and instilled fear into the hearts of his competitors long after he gave up the crown to Capablanca. These strengths were: An untiring fighting spirit, endless optimism, a magnificent tactical vision, unsurpassed defensive skills, and an almost flawless command of the endgame.

Our first example shows Lasker overwhelming Frank Marshall from a position that the American attacking genius probably expected to draw. Somehow, Lasker made it look easy.

Diagram 497

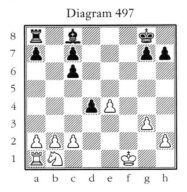

Marshall - Em. Lasker, New York 1907

Black to move

Capablanca said, "In this position it is black's move. To a beginner the position may look like a draw, but the advanced player will realize immediately that there are great possibilities for Black to win, not only because he has the initiative, but because of white's underdeveloped queenside and the fact that a Bishop in such a position is better than a Knight. It will take some time for White to bring his Rook and Knight into the fray, and black can utilize it to obtain an advantage. There are two courses open to him. The most evident, and the one that most players would take, is to advance the pawn to c5 and c4 immediately in conjunction with the Bishop check at a6 and any other move that might be necessary with the black Rook. The other, more subtle, course was taken by Black."

1...Rb8 2.b3 Rb5!

The Rook is very active on the 5th rank, and can torment white's pawns by moving to a5, c5, e5 or even h5.

3.c4

This makes sense because it avoids attacks against c2 and also closes down the a6-f1 diagonal (which black's Bishop might well have made use of). However, the resulting positions turn out to be remarkably difficult for White to deal with.

Defenses like 3.Nd2 Rc5 4.Nc4 Ba6 5.Ke2 Bxc4+ 6.bxc4 Rxc4 7.Kd3 Rc3+ 8.Kxd4 Rxc2, 3.Nd2 Rc5 4.c4 dxc3 e.p. 5.Nf3, and 3.Nd2 Rc5 4.Nf3 Rxc2 5.Nxd4 were all possible (and might well have been better than what was actually played), but they look risky and one can understand why Marshall avoided them.

3...Rh5 4.Kg1 c5 5.Nd2 Kf7

Diagram 498

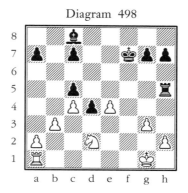

Black's plan is now clear: he wants to play ...Bg4 (dominating the Knight) and then bring his King up to e5. After that, ...d4-d3 followed by ...Kd4 is very strong.

6.Rf1+

A mistake that forces Black to continue with his plan. He should have tried for queenside counterplay with a3 followed by b4.

6...Ke7 7.a3 Rh6!

A fine move that renews the Rook's flexibility by leaving the 5th rank for the wide open 6th. Now ...Ra6 looms on the horizon.

8.h4

8.b4 fails to 8...Ra6 9.Rf3 Bg4 10.Rb3 Bd1 11.Rb1 Bc2 12.Rc1 d3.

8...Ra6

Probing at the weakness on a3. If he can get White to play a3-a4, then ideas of freeing himself with b3-b4 would be a thing of the past.

9.Ra1 Bg4 10.Kf2 Ke6

Diagram 499

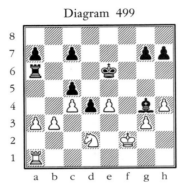

A nice picture: Black's King is better than white's, his Rook is far superior to the thing on a1, and the Bishop is dominating the Knight.

11.a4

11.Nf3 doesn't help: 11...Bxf3 12.Kxf3 Ke5 when the threat of ...Rf6+ gives Black a winning game.

11...Ke5 12.Kg2 Rf6

White is completely helpless.

13.Re1 d3 14.Rf1 Kd4

Black's plan is a major success. I'm sure Marshall was wondering how he had allowed such a horrible position to occur!

15.Rxf6 gxf6 16.Kf2 c6 17.a5 a6

The first zugzwang. Any pawn move hangs something, a Knight move gives up e4, and Ke1 allows the decisive ...Kc3 when White would be forced into heavy material losses.

18.Nf1 Kxe4 19.Ke1 Be2 20.Nd2+ Ke3 21.Nb1 f5

Taking his time and not allowing White any counterchances. White is helpless, so why not make everything perfect before beginning the final phase?

22.Nd2 h5

Another zugzwang. White must step back to b1.

23.Nb1 Kf3 24.Nc3 Kxg3 25.Na4 f4 26.Nxc5 f3 27.Ne4+ Kf4 28.Nd6

The last several moves were all forced. Now both 28...Ke3 and 28...Kg3 (threatening ...f2+) would be parried by 29.Nf5+.

28...c5!

One final zugzwang! 29.Kd2 f2 and 29.Kf2 d2 both lose immediately, while 29.Nb7 Ke3 leads to mate. That only leaves the suicidal advance of the b-pawn.

29.b4 cxb4 30.c5 b3 31.Nc4 Kg3 32.Ne3 b2, 0-1. This game was from a fifteen game match they played in New York. Though Marshall was considered to be one of the world's best players in 1907, Lasker mercilessly routed him 8 wins to none, with 7 draws.

Though he excelled in all kinds of endgames (as we've just seen!), his ability to save poor or even lost endgame positions has never been equaled through the span of chess history.

Diagram 500

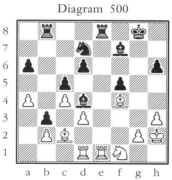

Em. Lasker - Dus Chotimirski, Moscow 1925
White to move

Lasker's position is completely lost! Let's see what Reuben Fine had to say: "White's light-squared Bishop is stalemated, his pawn structure hopelessly weak, his other pieces (with the exception of the dark-squared Bishop) have little or no freedom. In such positions, Lasker's conception of chess as a struggle has valuable practical applications: Lasker makes the win as difficult as possible for his opponent, and he seizes upon any slight chance which his opponent may regard as unimportant."

1.Rxe8+!

An important move that cuts down on black's options since now he must take back with his Bishop (1...Rxe8?? 2.Bxb3 is something White can only dream of!). The immediate 1.Bb1 would have allowed 1...Bh5! (1...Ne5 2.Ng3 gives

White undeserved play) 2.g4 fxg4 3.Rxe8+ Rxe8 4.Ng3 Bg6 5.hxg4 Nb6 6.a5 Na4 with a dead win.

1...Bxe8 2.Bb1 Ne5

The entombed Bishop on b1 makes it seem that the position should be won by itself. Thus, it's understandable that Black didn't want to let white's pieces make noise after 2...Bxb2 3.Ne3 Bg6 4.Bxd6 Re8 5.Nd5 (though 5...Bd4—centralizing and stopping any d3-d4 nonsense—leaves White in a bad way).

However, this hesitation to "wage war from a position of strength" ultimately comes back to haunt Black.

3.Ng3

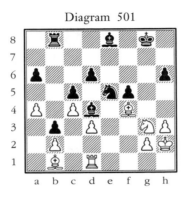

Diagram 501

3...Bg6?

Bogoljubov claimed a Black win after "3...Bd7 4.Rd2 Nf7 5.a5 Re8 6.Ne2 Bf6 with ...Bd8 and ...Bxa5 to follow". While this does favor Black (what doesn't?), White can answer 6...Bf6 with 7.d4 when his position is far better than it initially was.

Instead of all this delicacy on black's part, it was time for him to cash in with 3...Bxb2! when 4.Nxf5 Bxa4 leads to complicated play (just what Black was trying to avoid!), but both 5.Nxh6+ Kh8 (which is hopeless for White) and 5.Nxd6 Rf8 should ultimately allow Black to prevail.

Note how Dus Chotimirski became lazy due to his crushing position, while Lasker's play forced his opponent to either wake up and play well or lose much of his advantage.

4.Rd2 Rb4?!

He still could have retained an advantage with 4...Nf7, guarding d6 and h6, and also allowing the dark-squared Bishop to retreat if it's attacked by white's Knight.

5.Ne2 Rxa4?

Keeping the dark-squared Bishop by 5...Bf2 still gave Black some chances.

6.Nxd4 cxd4 7.c5!

Diagram 502

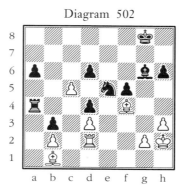

Suddenly White is getting real counterplay.

7...Ra1?

Like a wounded animal, I would guess that Black couldn't understand what was happening to him. After the move played, White actually emerges with the superior game. Instead of this meltdown, he could have tried 7...Bh5 (threatening ...Ra1 since White can't guard his Bishop with Rd1 anymore) 8.cxd6 Nd7, but 9.Rf2! intending 10.Rf1 seems fine.

Black's last chance to keep some pressure was 7...Be8! 8.cxd6 Nf7 9.Rd1 Bb5 (and not 9...Ra1? 10.Bc2!), keeping ...Ra1 in reserve.

8.cxd6 Nd7 9.Rd1

Threatening Bc2!

9...Bf7 10.Re1

Also possible was 10.Bxh6, but that lets Black gain a tempo for queenside counterplay by 10...a5 11.Re1 a4. One fun possibility is: 12.Bg5 a3 13.bxa3 Rxa3 (not 13...b2? 14.Bh4) 14.Re7 Nf8 15.Rb7 Ra1 16.Rb8 Be6 17.Bh6 Rxb1 18.Rxf8+ Kh7 19.Re8 b2 20.Rxe6 Rh1+ 21.Kxh1 b1=Q+ 22.Kh2 Qb3 23.Rf6 (or 23.d7 Qxe6 24.d8=Q Qe5+ with a draw by perpetual check) 23...Qxd3 24.d7 Qb5 24.d8=Q Qe5+ with a draw by perpetual check.

Lasker's choice forces Black to deal with some straightforward threats—not an easy thing for Dus Chotimirski to face since his confidence was likely smashed to jelly by this time. 10.Re1 is also safe since, in case of perfect Black play, White can always force a draw.

10...a5 11.Re7 Nc5??

Black cracks and manages to complete his nightmare by losing a position that was once won. He had to play 11...Nf8 when 12.Re1 Nd7 13.Re7 Nf8 would be drawn.

12.Be5! Ra4

12...Rxb1 13.Bxd4 Ne6 (13...Rc1 14.Bxc5 Rxc5 15.d7) 14.d7 Nd8 15.Re8+ also loses for Black.

13.Rc7 Ne6 14.d7 Rb4 15.Rc8+ Kh7 16.Rh8+ Kg6 17.Re8

Lasker's technique is brutal. He wants to get every last drop of juicy goodness from the position.

17...Rb6 18.Bf4!

Not settling for 18.Rxe6+ Rxe6 19.d8=Q Rxe5.

18...Nxf4 19.d8=Q Rc6 20.Re7, 1-0. Poor Dus Chotimirski must have been emotionally devastated after this loss.

Our final example sees our hero walking on the precipice of defeat. To save this game, he creates a problem-like draw over the board that had never been seen before.

Diagram 503

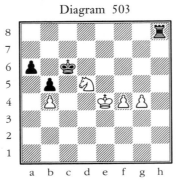

Emanuel Lasker - Edward Lasker, New York 1924
White to move

Visually White seems to be doing well—his two connected passed pawns seem very dangerous. The reality of the situation, though, is quite different. White's kingside pawns are far slower than one might suppose due to the Rook's defensive powers, while ...a6-a5 will create a passed pawn for Black, which the Knight will have serious trouble dealing with.

The immediate threat is 1...Re8+ 2.Kd4 Rd8, winning the pinned Knight. Thus, White moves it to safety.

1.Ne3 Re8+ 2.Kd4 Rd8+ 3.Ke4!?

This keeps the King close to his kingside pawns. However, the published analysis of 3.Kc3!? doesn't seem particularly compelling. Edward Lasker said he intended 3...a5 4.bxa5 Kc5 5.g5 b4+ 6.Kc2 b3+ 7.Kb2 Rd2+. This analysis contains a couple flaws. The first blip is, instead of 5.g5, 5.Nc2, when I don't see how Black can win. However, even after 5.g5 b4+ 6.Kc2 b3+, White should avoid the blunder 7.Kb2?? and instead give 7.Kc3 a try when, once again, I'm not sure Black can force a win.

In *My Great Predecessors, Part I*, Kasparov or Plisetsky simply say, "If 3.Kc3, then 3...Rd6! is unpleasant." The position after 4.g5 Kd7 5.f5 Ke8! (this King move avoids lots of unpleasant checks in many variations) is a very interesting one.

To say the position is "unpleasant" in diagram 504 is a bit funny, since the whole endgame is unpleasant for White, whether he plays 3.Ke4 or 3.Kc3. The real question is, can Black win by force after 3.Kc3? The idea of 3...Rd6 is clear: to allow White to advance his pawns so they become vulnerable to attacks by black's Rook and King (The King will swing over to the kingside via ...Kd7, ...Ke7, etc.).

To make matters worse, Knight moves will allow Black to target b4 by ...Rc6+ followed by ...Rc4. Naturally, 3...Rd6 also allows black's King to run to the kingside by stepping behind the Rook, thus keeping the d-file a no-fly zone for white's King.

Diagram 504

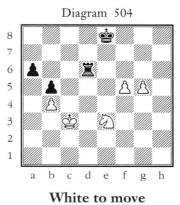

White to move

One illustration of the problems White faces is: 6.Ng4 (6.Kc2 Rd4 7.Kc3 Rf4 really *is* extremely unpleasant!) 6...Kf8 7.Ne3 Rd8 when White is in a mini-zugzwang since a Knight move allows ...Rc8+ followed by ...Rc4 while a King move lets the Rook into d4. Nevertheless, can even these facts guarantee victory? One important line: 8.Ng2 Rc8+ 9.Kd4! Rc4+ 10.Ke5 Rxb4 11.Nf4 and I don't believe Black can win.

Diagram 505

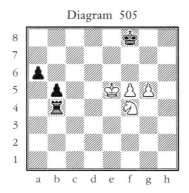

For example, 11...Rb1 12.Ne6+ Kg8 13.f6 Rg1 14.Kf5 b4 15.g6 Rf1+ 16.Ke5 b3 17.f7+ Rxf7 18.gxf7+ Kxf7 19.Ng5+ Ke7 20.Ne4 b2 21.Nd2 a5 22.Kd4 and White successfully stops the pawns.

I'll leave a truly in-depth analysis of the position after 3...Rd6 to someone more inclined to spending weeks fishing for its secrets. After all, this section of the book is titled Endgames for Pure Pleasure, and not The Pain of Drowning in Chess Variations.

3...a5

With white's King away from the queenside, the passed b-pawn that this move creates will cost White a high price to stop.

4.bxa5 b4 5.a6!

Diagram 506

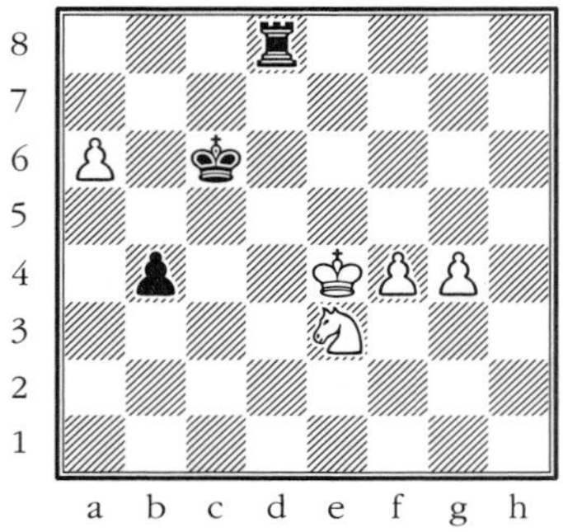

Forcing Black to deal with the a-pawn and thus gaining enough time to set up his upcoming defensive scheme. Alekhine correctly pointed out that 5.g5 b3 6.Nc4 Kc5 7.Nb2 Rd2 8.Nd3+ Kc4 9.Ne5+ Kc3 wins for Black.

5...Kc5!

5...b3 6.Nc4 Kb5 7.Nb2 Kxa6 8.Ke3 Kb5 9.g5 Kb4 10.g6 Kc3 11.Na4+ Kc2 12.f5 Re8+ 13.Kf3 Re5 (13...Rf8 14.g7 Rxf5+ 15.Kg4 Rf1 16.Kg5, =) 14.Kf4 Ra5 15.Nb2! Kxb2 16.g7 Ra4+ 17.Kg3 Ra8 18.f6 Kc3 19.f7 b2, =.

6.a7! b3!?

It's not clear if this allows a draw or not, so perhaps the Fritz suggestion of 6...Ra8!? (mentioned in *My Great Predecessors, Part I*) was the way to go. This whole endgame is so complicated that many of the positions have yet to be analyzed to definite conclusions.

7.Nd1 Ra8 8.g5 Rxa7 9.g6

Diagram 507

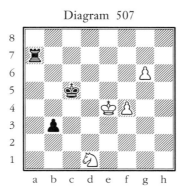

9...Rd7

My Great Predecessors, Part I once again bows to computer analysis, which suggests that 9...Kd6 wins. They mention 10.Kf5 Ke7 and show that things look grim for White. However, simply 10.Kd4! Rc7 11.g7! Rxg7 12.Kc4 sets up the same defensive formation that occurred in the actual game.

10.Nb2 Rd2 11.Kf3!

White is saved by his central King. Now 11...Rxb2?? loses to 12.g7.

11...Rd8 12.Ke4 Kd6 13.Kd4!

Rushing to the queenside so the King can deal with the black pawn, but sacrificing his own remaining pawns to do so.

13...Rc8 14.g7! Ke6 15.g8=Q+ Rxg8 16.Kc4 Rg3

Diagram 508

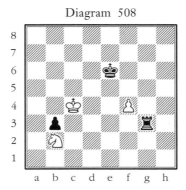

Black must hold onto his b-pawn since most Rook vs. Knight endgames (with no pawns) are easily drawn.

Edward Lasker (in his classic little book, *Chess for Fun and Chess for Blood*) wrote: "This is the move I had calculated would win my game after all. The other contestants also believed I had now a fairly easy win as White could not capture my pawn. I remember I left the room at this stage to stretch a little and was congratulated upon my victory by Bogoljuboff and others who were in the pressroom and told me the story of the game was ready to be released. However, when I returned to the table, a rude shock awaited me."

The only other move worth consideration is 16...Rb8. Shereshevsky (from his excellent book, *Endgame Strategy*) gave the following explanation as to why the game is drawn: "After 16...Rb8 Black again loses his pawn: 17.Kc3 Kf5 18.Nd3 Rb6. Now 19.Kb2 is bad due to 19...Ke4, but if White coolly waits with 19.Nb2 Kxf4 20.Na4 Rb8 21.Nb2 Black has no possibility of winning. As soon as the black King reaches e1 with the white King at c3 and Knight at b2, there immediately follows Na4 ...Kd1 Kb2, forcing the win of the pawn by Nc5."

17.Na4 Kf5 18.Kb4 Kxf4 19.Nb2!

Diagram 509

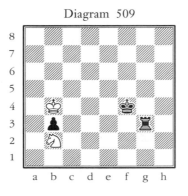

Edward Lasker: "I was certainly surprised when I saw this move. Examining the position carefully, I soon realized that I had no way of driving white's King away. And I could not cross the 6th rank without exposing the pawn to capture! The first thing I did was to rush back to the pressroom and tell the reporters that they should kill their story. I was afraid they might have already released it, for everyone had been telling them I had an easy win. Then I returned for another analysis of the position. If I could reach d2 with the King by playing him in back of my Rook, I could still win. And I made a last attempt."

19...Ke4 20.Na4 Kd4 21.Nb2 Rf3 22.Na4 Re3 23.Nb2 Ke4 24.Na4 Kf3 25.Ka3!

Edward Lasker: "This foils my plan. After ...Ke2 white would play Kb2 and I could never approach."

25...Ke4

25...Ke2 26.Kb2.

26.Kb4 Kd4 27.Nb2 Rh3 28.Na4 Kd3 29.Kxb3 Kd4+, ½-½. This game took over thirteen hours to complete!

Akiba Rubinstein

(Uncrowned King)
Master of Rook Endgames

The great Polish Grandmaster Akiba Rubinstein (1882-1961) is the only player on this list that wasn't a World Champion. Though one of the world's four or five strongest players from 1907 to 1922, his results from 1907 to 1911 demonstrated that he was second only to Lasker, and his total domination in 1912 (four 1st prizes in four powerful events) led some to believe (then and now) that he was Lasker's superior at that time. A match between the two was finally arranged for October 1914, but the advent of World War I prevented what would have been an amazing battle between two chess titans.

What made Rubinstein great was his tremendous opening preparation, balanced positional skills that allowed him to squeeze/attack/out-maneuver/push you off the board at will, and an unsurpassed mastery of Rook endgames. In particular, his credo of "Do not hurry!" served him very well in the endgame, as we'll soon see.

Our first example is against no less an opponent than Emanuel Lasker!

Diagram 510

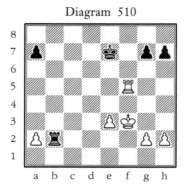

Rubinstein - Em. Lasker, St. Petersburg 1909
White to move

A pawn up, Rubinstein's first order of business is in tying his opponent down to the weakness on a7.

1.Ra5! Rb7 2.Ra6

A very important idea that the student can use in many Rook endgame situations. White's Rook hits a7, thus forcing black's Rook into a passive defensive role. The Rook on a6 also stops the enemy King from any active undertaking.

2...Kf8 3.e4 Rc7 4.h4 Kf7 5.g4

Having rendered his opponent helpless, White now makes use of his extra e-pawn and also begins to annex kingside space. Ultimately the advance of kingside pawns will, he hopes, create an entry square on g6 or f6 for white's King.

5...Kf8 6.Kf4 Ke7 7.h5 h6

Black weakens the g6-square. However, 7...Kf7 8.Kf5 Ke7 9.g5 Kf7 10.e5 Ke7 11.g6 h6 12.Re6+ is also winning for White, as analyzed by Lisitzin:

Diagram 511

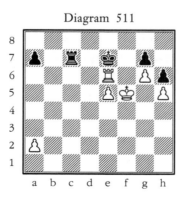

12...Kd7 13.Rf6!! Ke8 (13...gxf6 14.g7 Rc8 15.exf6 leaves Black unable to stop white's pawns) 14.Rf7 Rxf7+ 15.gxf7+ Kxf7 16.e6+! and wins since he will stalemate black's King,

force him to give up a pawn, which will then mate him: 16...
Ke7 17.Ke5 Ke8 18.Kd6 Kd8 19.e7+ Ke8 20.Ke6 a6 21.a3 a5
22.a4 g5 23.hxg6 e.p. h5 24.g7 h4 25.g8=Q mate.

➤ 12...Kf8 13.Rd6 Ke7 14.Ra6 Rb7 (14...Kd7 15.Rf6 wins as
above, or 14...Kf8 15.Ke6 Ke8 16.a4 planning a5, Rd6, a6,
etc.) 15.Rc6 Rd7 16.Rc8 followed by 17.Rg8, winning g7 and
the game.

8.Kf5 Kf7

Black can't let white's King into g6.

9.e5

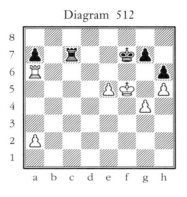

Diagram 512

Notice how the e-pawn protects the white King from checks along the 5th
rank.

9...Rb7 10.Rd6 Ke7 11.Ra6 Kf7 12.Rd6

Time pressure or Cat and Mouse? Cat and Mouse is the likely answer since
one doesn't get many chances to torture a completely helpless Lasker! In other
words, why hurry the execution when you can let your opponent suffer!

12...Kf8 13.Rc6 Kf7 14.a3, 1-0. At this point I enjoy saying to my students,
"And here, upon seeing this crushing move, Black resigned!" The look on
their uncomprehending faces is always priceless. But this move actually has an
important point! After 14...Kf8 (or 14...Re7 15.e6+ Kg8 16.Kg6 Re8 17.e7
followed by Rd6-d8 is easy) 15.Kg6 the annoying 15...Rb4 would be possible
if the a-pawn still stood on a2. However, with a3 in, Black can't avoid serious
material losses due to the threat of Rc8+.

Our next example of Rubinstein's Rook endgame mastery shows the great
Pole making use of his main Cat and Mouse credo: "Take your time" and "*No
counterplay allowed!*"

Diagram 513

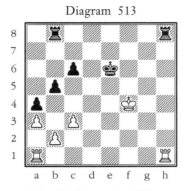

Levenfish - Rubinstein, Vienna 1912

Black to move

Black has excellent winning chances thanks to the road along the a2-g8 diagonal that will take black's King straight to the weak pawn on b2. By mixing an attack against b2 with threats against white's King, Black will be using the Principle of Two Weaknesses (b2-pawn and vulnerable King) in instructive fashion.

35...Kd5

Starting the journey to b3.

36.Rhd1+ Kc5!

One would have thought that Black would play the immediate 36...Kc4, when 37.Rd4+ Kb3 38.Rb4+ Kc2 39.Rg1 c5 40.Rg2+ Kb1 41.Re4 Rbf8+ 42.Ke3 (42. Kg3 Rhg8+ is also easy) 42...Rh3+ 43.Kd2 Kxb2 wins.

Far tougher is the very nice defense found by Mr. Fritz: 37.Rd2 Kb3 38.Rad1 Rbe8 39.Kg5! Ref8 40.Kg6! Rhg8+ 41.Kh7 Rg3 42.Rh1 Rfg8 43.Rhh2 when a Rook exchange (which would win for Black) isn't possible, white's King prevents Rook mates on h8, while enemy Rook checks on the rest of the h-file are stopped by the Rook on h2.

Diagram 514

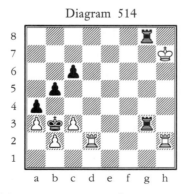

Fritz creates a tough nut to crack

Fortunately, Black can avoid this by answering 37.Rd2 with 37...Rhf8+! when White doesn't have the time to set up the Fritz defensive formation: 38.Kg5 Rf3 39.Kg6 (39.Re1 Rg8+ 40.Kh4 Kb3 41.Ree2 Rf1 wins immediately) 39...Rg8+ 40.Kh7 Rfg3 41.Rh1 R3g7+ 42.Kh6 Rg2 and wins.

Rubinstein made the decision to move his King to c5 instead of c4 because it's a much better practical decision. Here's why:

- He's in no hurry (don't forget Cat and Mouse!), he can play ...Kc4-b3 whenever he wishes to.

- Why leave c6 undefended in some lines when you can safely move to b3 on your own terms?

- Why add to the number of calculations you have to make by giving White a Rook check on d4? Note how Rubinstein refuses to give his opponent any counterplay at all!

- In some lines where black's Rook powers its way to the 7th rank, black's King will have the option of moving back to b6 or forward to c4. Thus, 36...Kc5 is more flexible than 36...Kc4.

37.Rd2 Rhf8+

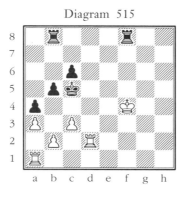

Diagram 515

38.Kg3

A zugzwang occurs after 38.Ke3 Rbe8+ 39.Kd3 Rd8+ 40.Kc2 Rxd2+ 41.Kxd2 Rf2+ 42.Kd3 (42.Kc1?? Rf1+ wins a Rook) 42...Rxb2 since any Rook move loses the a3-pawn to ...Ra2, while a King move allows ...Kc4.

Playing for our earlier Fritz defensive formation is a total flop: 38.Kg5 Rf3 39.Kg6 Rg8+ 40.Kh7 Rfg3 41.Rf1 (the same hopeless situation is reached after 41.Rad1 R3g7+! 42.Kh6 Rg2 43.Kh7 R8g3 when White is forced to swap Rooks) 41...R3g7+! 42.Kh6 Rg2 when the threat of ...Rh8 mate forces White to take on g2 and give Black the 7th rank.

38...Rb7!

Simply threatening mate in two!

39.Kh2

Both 39.Rg2 Rg7+ (which transposes into the actual game) and 39.Rd4 Rg7+ 40.Rg4 Rxg4+ 41.Kxg4 Rf2 42.Rb1 Kc4 are completely hopeless.

39...Rh7+ 40.Kg1 Rg7+ 41.Rg2 Rxg2+ 42.Kxg2 Rd8

Diagram 516

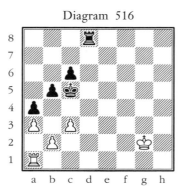

43.Kf3

The pawn endgame after 43.Rf1 Rd2+ 44.Rf2 Rxf2+ 45.Kxf2 Kc4 is resignable.

43...Rd2 44.Ra2

Why is White playing on? He would also suffer horribly after 44.Rb1 Kc4.

44...Rd1

There were other ways to win, but this is the most humiliating.

45.Ke2 Rh1 46.Kd3 Rg1

Keeping White in a box and forcing him to either move his King and allow black's King to c4, or give up a pawn by pushing the b- or c-pawn. The third and best option, resignation, seems to have been overlooked by White.

47.c4 Rg3+, 0-1. After 48.Kc2 Kxc4, ...Rg3-g2+ will nuke white's position once and for all.

Our final example of Rubinstein's endgame skills is against the great Alekhine. The classic battle that follows leaves one with a sense of awe at the Polish player's tremendous strength.

Diagram 517

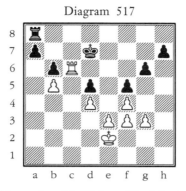

Rubinstein - Alekhine, Carlsbad 1911
Black to play

1...Re8?

The first thing that both sides have to do is determine if the pawn endgame after 1...Rc8 2.Rxc8 Kxc8 is viable for Black. The answer is no: 3.e4 h6 (3...fxe4 4.fxe4 dxe4 5.g4 Kd7 6.Ke3 Ke6 7.Kxe4 h5 8.gxh5 gxh5 9.Kf3 Kd5 10.f5 and white's passed pawns take care of themselves) 4.e5 g5 (4...Kd7 5.g4 Ke6 6.Kf2 Ke7 7.gxf5 gxf5 8.Kg3) 5.g4 (5.fxg5?? hxg5 gives Black a drawing fortress since white's King can never penetrate.) 5...fxg4 and now not 6.fxg4?? Kd7 7.f5 since, though it looks very impressive, white's King can't participate and thus the game's a draw.

Instead of the horrific 6.fxg4, White can force a win by 6.fxg5 hxg5 7.Kf2! (7.fxg4?? once again leaves white's King with no way to get in) 7...Kd7 8.Kg3 gxf3 9.Kxf3 Ke6 10.Kg4 and it's all over.

This means that Black is left with two other choices: passive defense (which is rarely a good idea when you're defending a Rook endgame) or the active counterplay supplied by 1...a5. Marin points out that this draws by force: 2.Rxb6 Kc7 (2...a4?? 3.Ra6 Rxa6 4.bxa6 Kc7 5.Kd3 wins) 3.Rc6+ Kb7 4.Kd2 a4 5.Kc2 Re8 6.Rc3 Kb6.

Having missed this opportunity, Alekhine faces endless pain as Akiba leaps into "torture mode."

2.Kd3

Why is White so much better here? There are several reasons:

- ▶ White's Rook is more active than black's.

- ▶ White's one queenside pawn holds back black's two.

- ▶ Black's King is busy stopping Rook penetrations on c8 and/or c7. Thus white's King is far more mobile.

- ▶ The g3-g4 move will create new weaknesses in black's camp.

▬▬▶ Black is passive and can't do anything but wait for White to improve his position—Rubinstein's fondest fantasy!

2...Re7 3.g4 Re6 4.Rc1

Apparently the exchange of Rooks is winning: 4.Rxe6 Kxe6 5.gxf5+

Diagram 518

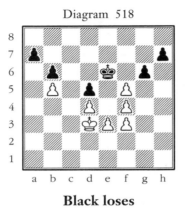

Black loses

5...gxf5 (No better is 5...Kxf5 6.Ke2 h6 7.Kf2 h5 8.Kg3 Kf6 9.e4 Ke6 10.Kh4 Kf6 11.exd5 Ke7 12.f5 gxf5 13.Kxh5 Kd6 14.Kg5 Kxd5 15.Kxf5 Kxd4 16.f4 Kc5 17.Ke6 Kxb5 18.f5 a5 19.f6 a4 20.f7 a3 21.f8=Q and wins. Analysis by Silman) 6.e4 Ke7 (6...fxe4+ 7.fxe4 dxe4+ 8.Kxe4 gives White a two passed pawns vs. one position) 7.e5 Ke6 8.Ke3 Kf7 9.Kf2 Kg7 10.Kg3 Kf7 11.Kh4 Kg6 12.e6 Kf6 13.Kh5 Kxe6 14.Kg5 h5 (14...Kf7 15.Kxf5 Kg7 16.Kg5 Kf7 17.Kh6 Kg8 18.f5 Kf8 19.Kxh7 Kf7 20.f6 Kxf6 21.Kg8 Kf5 22.Kf7 Kf4 23.Ke6) 15.Kxh5 Kd6 16.Kg5 a5 17.bxa6 e.p. Kc6 18.Kxf5, winning (analysis by Marin). This is proven by 18...b5 19.Ke6 b4 20.f5 b3 21.f6 b2 22.f7 b1=Q 23.f8=Q Qe1+ 24.Kf6 when the Queen endgame is hopeless for Black.

Why did Rubinstein avoid this? Quite simply, he knew that all King and pawn endgames are confusing (as explored in Part Eight). If that was the only way to win, he would have gone for it, but why take the chance that he was missing a defensive nuance in the King and pawn endgame when he could quietly dole out the slow, patient death that the Rook endgame offered.

4...Re7 5.Rh1 Ke6 6.Rc1 Kd7 7.Re1 Rf7 8.Ra1 Kd6 9.Rc1 Kd7 10.Rc6

Vintage Cat and Mouse! Rubinstein begins to wear down his opponent by, seemingly, doing nothing.

10...Rf8 11.Ke2

Finally he begins his true plan. His King heads for h4 where it hopes to penetrate into the enemy position, or force Black to create new weaknesses in his efforts to prevent it.

11...Rf7

The pawn endgame after 11...Rc8 is still lost: 12.Rxc8 Kxc8 13.gxf5! gxf5 14.e4 with play similar to that which occurs from diagram 518.

12.Kf2 Rf8 13.Kg3 Re8 14.Rc3 Re7 15.Kh4

Threatening Kg5

15...h6

Diagram 519

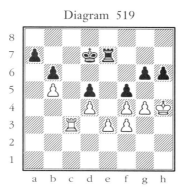

New weaknesses along the 6th rank

Black had to keep white's King out of g5, but now the 6th rank becomes seriously weakened. Thus, White brings his King back to guard e3 and then begins to "dance" between threats against g6, h6, and a7 with his Rook.

16.Kg3

Intending Kf2 (defending e3) followed by Rc6, immediately taking advantage of the new weaknesses on the 6th rank.

16...h5

Alekhine realizes (a bit too late!) that he must create some form of counterplay. Thus he avoided 16...Re8 17.Kf2 h5 18.Ra3 when the horribly passive 18...Ra8 would be forced.

17.Kh4

As always, Rubinstein makes a point of keeping his opponent's counterplay to a minimum. The immediate 17.gxh5 gxh5 18.Kh4 allows 18...Rg7 when White still wins, of course, but why give black's Rook free reign so quickly? Play might continue: 19.Kxh5 Rg3 20.Ra3 Rxf3 21.Rxa7+ Kd6 22.Rb7 Rxe3 23.Rxb6+ Kc7 24.Rc6+ Kd7 25.Kg5 Re4 (25...Rb3 26.Kxf5 Rxb5 27.Rc5 is easy for White) 26.Kxf5 Rxd4 27.Ke5 Re4+ (27...Rb4 loses quickly to 28.Rd6+ followed by 29.Rxd5) 28.Kxd5 Rxf4 29.Kc5 Rf1 30.Kb6 etc.

17...Rh7 18.Kg5 fxg4

This sets a cute trap, which Rubinstein avoids.

19.fxg4

Not falling for 19.Kxg6?? g3 20.Kxh7 and now the very tempting 20...h4?? only draws: 21.Ra3 h3 22.Rxa7+ Ke6 23.Rg7

Diagram 520

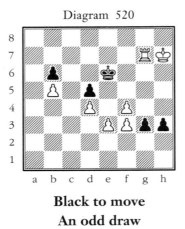

Black to move
An odd draw

23...h2 24.Rg6+ Kf7 (and not 24...Kf5?? 25.Kg7! h1=Q 26.Rf6 mate) 25.Rg7+ with a perpetual check.

Instead of 20...h4??, Black wins by 20...g2! 21.Rc1 h4 when 22.Ra1 no longer draws against best play:

Diagram 521

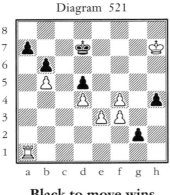

Black to move wins

➤ 22...h3?? 23.Rxa7+ lets White draw as he did against 20...h4.

➤ 22...Kc8?? allows a problem-like situation to occur: 23.f5 h3 24.f6 h2 25.f7 h1=Q+ 26.Kg7 we arrive at the insane position in diagram 522.

Diagram 522

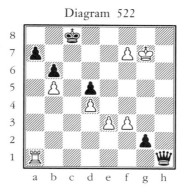

Black to move, only a draw

26...g1=Q+ (or 26...Qxa1 27.f8=Q+ with a draw by perpetual check) 27.Rxg1 Qxg1+ 28.Kf6 Qxe3 29.f8=Q+ Kd7, =.

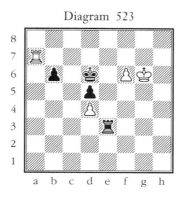

(from diagram 521) 22...Kd8! 23.f5 h3 24.f6 h2 25.f7 when 25...h1=Q+?? 26.Kg7 is a draw, but 25...Ke7! 26.Rxa7+ Kf8 wins on the spot.

Great stuff!

19...hxg4 20.Kxg4 Rh1 21.Kg5

Black's Rook has finally gotten out of its box, but white's powerful King and pressure against a7, d5, and g6 will prove decisive.

21...Rb1

White also wins after 21...Rg1+ 22.Kf6 Kd6 23.Rc6+ Kd7 24.Ke5.

22.Ra3 Rxb5 23.Rxa7+ Kd6 24.Kxg6 Rb3 25.f5 Rxe3 26.f6

Diagram 523

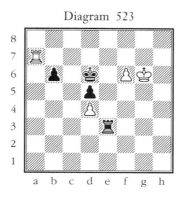

White's active King and far advanced f-pawn guarantee victory, though some subtle play is still required.

26...Rg3+ 27.Kh7 Rf3

Or 27...Rh3+ 28.Kg8 Rg3+ 29.Rg7.

28.f7 Rf4

Black's last stand. His idea is to check along the 4th rank until white's King blocks its own pawn on f8. Then he'll capture the d4-pawn, give up his Rook for white's remaining pawn, and draw by running his b- or d-pawn down the board as fast as he can.

29.Kg7 Rg4+ 30.Kf6!

Diagram 524

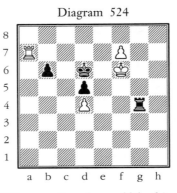

Brilliant refutation of black's plan

Very nice! White will thwart black's idea by chasing the enemy Rook off the 4th rank with his King, and only then allow himself to be herded to f8 since in that case the d4-pawn will no longer be under attack.

30...Rf4+ 31.Kg5! Rf1 32.Kg6!

Willingly heading for f8.

32...Rg1+

32...Rf4 fails to 33.Ra8.

33.Kf6 Rf1+ 34.Kg7 Rg1+ 35.Kf8 Rd1 36.Ke8 Re1+ 37.Kd8 Rf1 38.Rd7+ Kc6 39.Ke8

Flawless technique! Black's only hope is to swing his King to c4 and gobble the d-pawn. Rubinstein's maneuver has prevented this since 39...Kb5 would run into 40.Rxd5+.

39...Rf4 40.Re7 Kb5

Is Black going to get white's d-pawn after all?

41.Rc7!

No! As always, Rubinstein refuses to give his opponent the slightest hint of counterchances.

After 41.Rc7, Black resigned due to the following maneuver: 41...Re4+ 42.Kd7 Rf4 43.Ke7 Re4+ 44.Kf6 Rf4+ 45.Ke5 Rf1 46.Kxd5. A magnificent demonstration of endgame mastery!

José Raúl Capablanca
(The 3rd World Champion)
Crystal Clarity

José Raúl Capablanca (1888-1942) is considered by most to have been the greatest natural talent in the history of the game. He didn't put much time into opening study, and much preferred a night on the town to the tedious task of chess analysis. Nevertheless, when he sat down to play, everything just seemed to magically "click." His plans and moves were crystal clear, and no less a player than Alekhine said that he had never seen anyone else with such a "flabbergasting quickness of chess comprehension."

Looked upon as an unbeatable "chess machine," the legendary Cuban was most famous for his endgame skills. However, he didn't play to reach an endgame per se; instead, Capablanca tended to see the whole game as one living organism, with whatever set of advantages he obtained often flowing logically right into an endgame.

Diagram 525

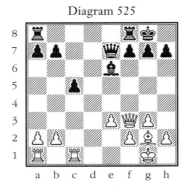

Marshall - Capablanca, New York 1909

Black to move

This middlegame position has one outstanding feature for Black: his queenside pawn majority.

1...Rab8 2.Qe4 Qc7 (Unpinning his Bishop and thus avoiding the threat of Bh3.) **3.Rc3 b5 4.a3 c4 5.Bf3** (Lasker said that black's advantage could be kept to a minimum by 5.Rd1 Rfd8 6.Rcc1.) **5...Rfd8 6.Rd1 Rxd1+ 7.Bxd1 Rd8 8.Bf3 g6 9.Qc6 Qe5 10.Qe4 Qxe4 11.Bxe4**

Diagram 526

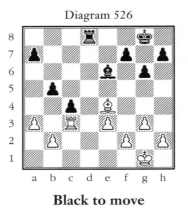

Black to move

Having zipped through eleven moves, we find that the basic nature of the position hasn't changed at all, *except* for the fact that we now have an endgame which is won for Black—black's middlegame play was completely devoted to achieving this kind of "queenside majority rules the world" position! Note that the pawns have become threatening, black's Bishop is perfectly placed to support them, and black's Rook dominates its counterpart since it owns the only open file.

11...Rd1+

"Very important. Black must stop the approach of the white King by means of Bc2 followed by Kf1, etc." Analysis by Capablanca.

12.Kg2 a5 13.Rc2 b4

Black's moves seem effortless, giving the impression that anyone can do it.

14.axb4 axb4 15.Bf3 Rb1

Diagram 527

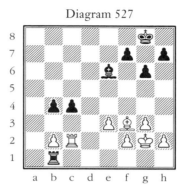

16.Be2

Kasparov points out that 16.Rd2 also failed: "16...Ra1! 17.Be2 Ra2 18.Kf1 c3 19.Rd8+ Kg7 20.bxc3 Ra1+ 21.Rd1 (21.Kg2 bxc3 22.Bd1 Ra2) 21...Rxd1+ 22.Bxd1 b3 23.Ke1 b2, winning." Of course, 24.Bc2 is met by 24...Ba2.

16...b3 17.Rd2

17.Rc3 Rxb2 18.Bxc4 Rc2!

17...Rc1 18.Bd1

18.Kf3 loses nicely: 18...Rc2 19.Rd4 c3 20.bxc3 b2 21.Rb4 Bd5+ 22.e4 Rxc3+ 23.Kf4 Bb3.

18...c3 19.bxc3 b2 20.Rxb2

Not a happy decision, but 20. Bc2 Rxc2 was even worse. The rest is a demonstration of Capablanca's usual brutal technique—once he had an opponent on a hook, few ever escaped.

20...Rxd1 21.Rc2 Bf5 22.Rb2 Rc1 23.Rb3 Be4+ 24.Kh3 Rc2 25.f4 h5 26.g4 hxg4+ 27.Kxg4 Rxh2 28.Rb4 f5+ 29.Kg3 Re2 30.Rc4 Rxe3+ 31.Kh4 Kg7 32.Rc7+ Kf6 33.Rd7 Bg2 34.Rd6+ Kg7, 0-1.

Diagram 528

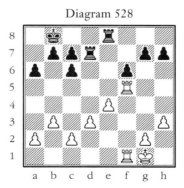

Capablanca - Janowski, New York 1913

White to move

This game shows that Capablanca had completely mastered the ideas of patience and avoidance of counterplay. White's three advantages: more active Rooks, space, and superior pawn structure. Apparently, this is all the Cuban genius needed to grind out a win.

1.g4

White's Rooks look impressive on the half open f-file, but they can't do damage if they can't penetrate into the hostile position. 1.g4 is the first step towards that penetration, since a well-timed g4-g5 will blast open the f-file.

1...b6

Intending to gain space via ...c6-c5.

2.b4!

Nowadays this is a well-known idea in such positions. White's one pawn freezes the a6- and c6-pawns and effectively kills black's whole queenside pawn mass! In other words, one pawn kills four!

2...Kb7 3.Kf2

If there's no threat, then Capablanca will happily improve the position of his King. White's philosophy is clear: don't rush, stop all queenside counterplay, centralize the King, and slowly but surely prepare to blast open the f-file by g4-g5.

3...b5

An ugly looking move that creates a serious threat: Black wants to play ...Kb6 followed by ...a6-a5, with counterplay on the a-file.

4.a4!

Refusing to give his opponent anything at all! Now 4...Kb6 walks head first into 5.a5+, while 4...bxa4 5.Ra1 followed by Rxa4 leaves black's queenside shattered.

4...Rd4 5.Rb1 Re5?!

This ultimately loses with hardly a whimper. Though 5...bxa4? 6.Ra5 Re5 7.Ke3 Rd6 8.Rxa4 is winning for White, Black could have made use of his final active chance and tried 5...a5!

Diagram 529

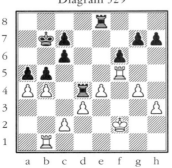

Best is then 6.axb5 Rxb4 and now 7.bxc6+ Kxc6 8.Ra1 a4 9.Ra5 Rb2 gives Black far more counterplay than he deserves. Thus, instead of 7.bxc6+, correct is 7.Rxb4! axb4 8.Rc5 Re6 9.Ke3 Kb6 10.Rxc6+ Rxc6 11.bxc6 Kxc6 12.Kd4! and the King and pawn endgame is very unpleasant for Black.

Diagram 530

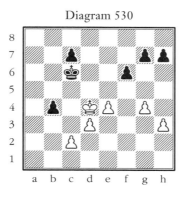

Here's a sample of what might occur: 12...Kb5 (12...Kd6? 13.Kc4 c5 14.Kb5 g6 15.Kb6 h6 16.Kb5 and Black will eventually run out of moves and be forced to pitch his c-pawn) 13.Kd5 c6+ 14.Kd6 c5 15.Kd5 Kb6 (15...g5? 16.Ke6 c4 17.dxc4+ Kxc4 18.Kxf6 Kc3 19.e5 Kxc2 20.e6 b3 21.e7 b2 22.e8=Q b1=Q 23.Qe4+, 1-0) 16.h4 h6 17.Ke6 Kb5 18.Kf7 c4 19.dxc4+ Kxc4 20.Kxg7 Kc3 21.Kxf6 Kxc2 22.e5 b3 23.e6 b2 24.e7 b1=Q 25.e8=Q with a winning Queen and pawn endgame.

6.Ke3

The King chases the Rook from its active position and White takes total control of the game.

6...Rd7 7.a5!

Diagram 531

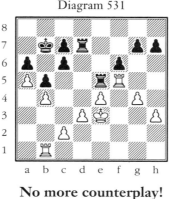

No more counterplay!

Ending black's dreams of queenside counterplay once and for all.

7...Re6

Equally depressing are 7...c5 8.bxc5 Kc6 9.d4 and 7...Rxf5 8.gxf5. For those that want a taste of the kind of slow torture that Black would be forced to endure after this latter try: 8...Re7 9.h4 Kc8 10.Rg1 Kd7 11.d4 Ke8 12.c3 Kf8 13.Kf4 Rd7 14.h5 Rd8 15.Ke3 (Also very strong is the obvious 15.e5 fxe5+ 16.dxe5 Rd2 17.h6!, but I find the alternative plan of pushing the c-pawn to be quite instructive) 15...Re8 16.Rc1 Ke7 17.c4 bxc4 (17...Kd6 18.cxb5 cxb5 19.d5 Ra8 20.Rc6+ is beyond awful) 18.Rxc4 Kd6 19.Rc2 Re7 20.Kf4.

8.Rbf1

With black's counterplay permanently suppressed, White goes right back to his plan of "conquest along the f-file."

8...Rde7 9.g5 fxg5 10.Rxg5 Rh6 11.Rg3

Threatening 12.d4 followed by 13.e5, so Black tries to stop this by bringing his Rook back to the e-file.

12...Rhe6 12.h4 g6

12...Rh6 13.Rg4 is certainly no improvement.

13.Rg5 h6 14.Rg4

A new weakness has been created on g6.

14...Rg7 15.d4 Kc8 16.Rf8+ Kb7

Also unattractive is 16...Kd7 17.Ra8.

17.e5 g5 18.Ke4 Ree7 19.hxg5 hxg5 20.Rf5

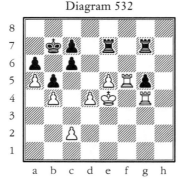

Diagram 532

Here's a quick checklist giving white's plusses:

▬▶ More active King!

▬▶ More active Rooks!

▬▶ Far superior pawn structure!

▬▶ About to win material!

Black could resign here with a clear conscience. The rest was kid-stuff for Capablanca.

20...Kc8 21.Rgxg5 Rh7 22.Rh5 Kd7 23.Rxh7 Rxh7 24.Rf8 Rh4+ 25.Kd3 Rh3+ 26.Kd2 c5

Desperation is all that's left to him. Another form would be 26...Ke6 27.Ra8 Kd5 28.Rxa6 Kxd4 29.Rxc6 Rh2+ 30.Kc1 Kxe5 31.Rxc7 and it's over.

27.bxc5 Ra3 28.d5, 1-0. As usual, Capablanca made this endgame appear remarkably easy.

Okay, so Capablanca was able to make "lower tier" grandmasters like Marshall and Janowski look bad. How did he do against a monster like Lasker? Well, let's take a look!

Capablanca had lost to Lasker in 1914 and, due to the war, they didn't play again until a match for Lasker's title was arranged in 1921. To be fair to Lasker, he was no longer in his prime, out of practice, and suffered horribly from Cuba's stifling heat (Capablanca, of course, was well accustomed to it). After fourteen games, the Cuban challenger was leading four wins to none (two were lost by very basic blunders) and Lasker, on his doctor's advice, resigned the match, thus making Capablanca the new World Champion.

Here was the situation (after the final game) in Lasker's own words: "Towards the end of the fourth hour, just before the time control, I was almost exhausted and with several obvious errors I ruined my entire strategic plan. I was looking at the board as through a mist, and my head ached suspiciously. This was a warning to me, and I heeded it."

Before you think that Capablanca was "given" the title by crushing a used up old man, consider this: three years later the best players on the planet competed in one of history's strongest events ever: New York 1924. Now fifty-five, the old lion shocked the world by winning the event with a mind-blowing score of 16-4, a point and a half ahead of the 2nd place finisher, Capablanca!

Diagram 533

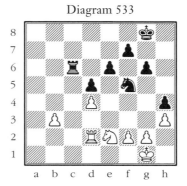

Em. Lasker - Capablanca, Havana 1921

Black to move

White's inferior pawn structure dooms him to eternal misery. Against a player of Capablanca's extraordinary endgame talents, the game can already be considered lost.

1...Rb6!

An accurate move that forces white's Rook into a clumsy position.

2.Rd3

Forced since both 2.Rb2 or 2.Nc1 lose a pawn to 2...Rb4.

2...Ra6!

Creating a new threat of 3...Ra1+ which would shut out the white King.

3.g4

Of course, White would like to try and hold this position intact without creating new weaknesses. However, this is simply asking too much from white's unhappy forces: 3.Rd1 Ra2 4.Kf1 Rb2 5.Nc1 Nd6 6.Re1 (6.Ke1 Ne4 7.f3 Nc3 8.Rd2 Rb1 9.Rc2 Nb5 is certainly no better) 6...Rd2 7.Ne2 Nb5, winning material.

Another line, pointed out by Kasparov, is 3.Nc3 Ra1+ 4.Kh2 Rc1 5.b4 Rc2 6.Kg1 Rb2 7.b5 Rb4.

3...hxg3 e.p. 4.fxg3

His life wouldn't have been any easier after 4.Nxg3 Ra1+ 5.Kh2 (Worse is 5.Kg2 Nh4+ 6.Kh2 Rb1) 5...Nd6 6.Kg2 Rb1 when white's pawn structure is even more fragmented than it was in the game.

4...Ra2 5.Nc3 Rc2!

Threatening 5...Nxd4.

6.Nd1 Ne7!

Heading for c6, where it eyes the d4-pawn and the b4-square.

7.Nc3

7.b4 loses the pawn to ...Rc1 followed by ...Rb1.

7...Rc1+ 8.Kf2 Nc6 9.Nd1

Diagram 534

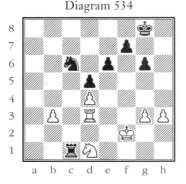

This sets a nice trap, but perhaps 9.Ne2!? would have put up more resistance.

9...Rb1!

Avoiding 9...Nb4? 10.Rd2 Rb1 11.Nb2 Rxb2? 12.Rxb2 Nd3+ 13.Ke2 Nxb2 14.Kd2! Kf8 15.Kc2 trapping the Knight, when a draw results after 15...Nc4 16.bxc4 dxc4 17.Kc3 Ke7 18.Kxc4.

10.Ke2?

White had to try 10.Ke1, though one would expect Capablanca to eventually win after 10...Na5 11.Kd2 Rxb3 12.Rxb3 Nxb3+.

10...Rxb3!

This is typical of Capablanca, who often made use of "petite combinations" like this one.

11.Ke3 Rb4!

Retaining the Rooks makes black's task much easier. Why? Because the "army of two" (eventually to be joined by their King and pawns) can work together to harass white's King and keep the various weak pawns under constant pressure.

12.Nc3 Ne7 13.Ne2 Nf5+ 14.Kf2 g5 15.g4 Nd6

White's position has worsened. Now the h-pawn is fixed and will be permanently vulnerable.

16.Ng1 Ne4+ 17.Kf1

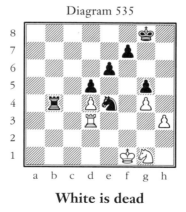

Diagram 535

White is dead

White can hold things together for a while, but once Black gets his King and pawns into the act white's resistance will crumble. However, note how Black handles the position: he suddenly goes into Cat and Mouse mode, torturing his opponent before finally lowering the axe.

17...Rb1+ 18.Kg2 Rb2+ 19.Kf1 Rf2+ 20.Ke1 Ra2 21.Kf1

21.Nf3 Nf2 picks up the pawn on h3.

21...Kg7 22.Re3 Kg6 23.Rd3 f6

Diagram 536

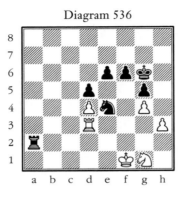

Finally getting on with it. Black will bring his King to d6 and then create a passed pawn by ...e5.

24.Re3 Kf7 25.Rd3 Ke7 26.Re3 Kd6 27.Rd3 Rf2+

A bit more Cat and Mouse! It seems that Capablanca is having so much fun watching his opponent suffer that he doesn't want the game to end.

28.Ke1 Rg2 29.Kf1 Ra2 30.Re3 e5 31.Rd3 exd4 32.Rxd4 Kc5 33.Rd1 d4 34.Rc1+ Kd5, 0-1. 35.Rd1 Ng3+ 36.Ke1 Rg2 37.Nf3 Re2 mate would have been a picturesque finish.

Comparing Capablanca and Lasker, an obvious question arises: "Who was the superior endgame player?" Let's allow Capablanca to share his opinion (given after a brilliant tournament victory in San Sebastian, 1911): "The endings were up to the highest standards, some players thinking that I played them better than Lasker himself, until then reputed to have no equal. I do not believe that I played them better, but just as well."

Vasily Smyslov
(The 7th World Champion)
Simplicity

Smyslov (1921-2010) was the second in a long line of Soviet grandmasters to win the highest title. His autobiography titled, *In Search of Harmony*, sums up his style and his chess philosophy. Crediting his father for the skills he eventually became known for, I find these words of Smyslov's to be extremely interesting: "He instilled in me a love for so-called 'simple' positions, with the participation of only a few pieces, I was able to gain a deep feeling for what each piece is capable of, to sense their peculiarities, their strength and impotence in various different situations on the board, the limits of their capabilities, what they 'like' and what they 'don't like' and how they behave. Such a 'mutual understanding' with the pieces enables a player to see that which often remains concealed to purely logical analysis. It is then that the innate ability of a player, which I call a sense of harmony, manifests itself."

With words like "simplicity" and "harmony" being tossed about, it's easy to imagine Smyslov as a dry player who craved boring positions. However, nothing can be farther from the truth. The 7th World Champion was an excellent opening theoretician in his prime, and many new, dynamic ideas and even whole systems bear his name today. A positional player, he possessed a deep chess intuition that allowed him to navigate complex looking situations with a minimum of calculation.

Though at home in both quiet and complicated middlegames, his main strength was the endgame, and he claimed that his talents in this phase directly contributed to his World Championship Match victory over Botvinnik in 1957.

Smyslov's ability to find simple, to-the-point solutions to complicated endgames is nicely demonstrated in our first example.

Diagram 537

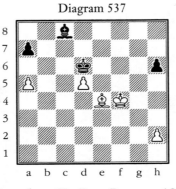

Smyslov - Xu Jun, Lucern 1985

White to move

White is a pawn up, but the d-pawn is firmly blocked (and in need of defense!) and his King is having trouble reaching the juicy pawn on h6. However, the 64-year-old endgame genius makes the process look easy.

Some key points:

➤ White doesn't want to allow black's King to move to e5.

➤ Black can't let white's King land on e5, since then the blockade against the d-pawn will be broken.

➤ Trading Bishops, even if it loses the d-pawn, usually leads to a winning pawn endgame since white's King is closer to the h-pawn than black's is to the a-pawn.

➤ To win, White must figure out a way to safely get his King to f5 where it will target h6 for assassination. This goal can only be achieved through the use of zugzwang.

1.Bf5!

Temporarily breaking black's hold on the f5-square and forcing the defender's Bishop to a less flexible diagonal.

1...Ba6

Forced. Two quick ways to lose would be:

➤ 1...Bb7?? 2.Be6 Bxd5 (else White plays Kf5) 3.Bxd5 Kxd5
4.Kf5 Kc5 5.Kg6 Kb5 6.Kxh6 Kxa5 7.Kg5 Kb4 8.h4 a5 9.h5
a4 10.h6 a3 11.h7 a2 12.h8=Q and we get a well-known
situation where the promotion of one rook-pawn prevents the
promotion of the other!

➤ 1...Bxf5?? 2.Kxf5 Kxd5 3.Kg6 Ke5 (going after white's a-pawn
puts Black even farther behind in the race than he was in the
previous variation) 4.Kxh6 Kf6 5.a6 Kf7 6.Kg5 Kg7 7.Kf5 and
White marches over to the queenside and captures the pawn
on a7.

2.Be6

Defending the d-pawn and threatening a decisive penetration by Kf5.

2...Bd3 3.Bf7

White needs to show some fancy footwork if he wants to break through to
h6. For example, the straightforward 3.Kg4 (threatening 4.Kh5) can be foiled
by 3...Bg6.

3...Ke7

Also possible is 3...Bc2 when 4.Kg4 (threatening 5.Kh5) 4...Ke7 (4...Bd1+
5.Kf5) 5.Be6! Bg6 (worse are 5...Kf6 6.Kh5 Kg7 7.d6 Bd1+ 8.Bg4, 1-0, and
5...Bd1+ 6.Kf5 Bc2+ 7.Ke5 when White has landed on the winning e5-square)
6.Bf5 Bf7 7.Be4 Kf6 (7...Kd6 8.Kf5 and White's successfully broken through)
8.Kf4 Bg8 9.d6! Be6 (9...Ke6 10.Bd5+!) 10.Bf3 Bd7 11.Bg4 has led to the successful breaking of the blockade against white's d-pawn.

Diagram 538

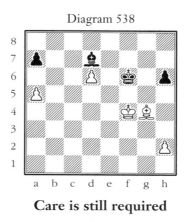

Care is still required

Incredibly, play is still somewhat complex, and surprising pitfalls exist: 11...Bb5
12.d7? (So natural and so wrong. I'm not sure White can win after this move)
12...Ke7 13.h4 Bc6 14.Ke5 Bb5 15.d8=Q+ Kxd8 16.Kf6 Be8 17.Kg7 h5 18.Bf5

Kc7 19.Bg6 Bc6 20.Bxh5 Kd6 21.Bg6 Bf3 22.a6 (22.h5 Bxh5 23.Bxh5 a6 wins the a5-pawn and forces a draw) 22...Kc6 23.h5 Bxh5 24.Bxh5 Kc7 25.Kf6 Kb8 26.Ke5 Kc7 27.Kd5 Kb8 and Black has miraculously created an unassailable fortress (see diagram 253 in Part Six)!

Diagram 539

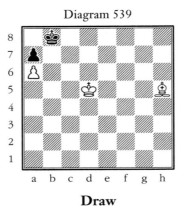

Draw

Fortunately for White, the win is fairly easy after the accurate 12.Ke4! (Targeting black's a-pawn for death. Note how the d6-pawn keeps black's King from coming to the defense of the queenside) 12...Bc6+ (12...Kf7 13.Ke5 when 14.Bh5+ will end things quickly) 13.Kd4 Bb7 14.Kc5 Kf7 (or 14...Be4 15.Bc8 when the a7-pawn will fall) 15.Bd7! Kf6 16.Kb5 Ke5 17.Bc6, 1-0.

4.Bh5 Kd6

4...Kf6 5.Bg4 Bc4 6.d6 takes us to the note to black's 3rd move.

5.Bf3

Diagram 540

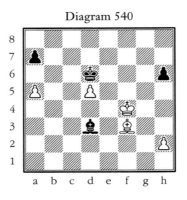

Believe it or not, the end is near! One might be justified in asking what White has achieved—isn't his Bishop on the same diagonal (h1-d5) that it started on? However, now black's Bishop has been herded to the b1-h7 diagonal, and a well timed Be4 will shatter that control and give white's King access to the coveted f5-square.

5...Bc2

Tucking the Bishop away on the kingside doesn't work either: 5...Bh7 6.Bg2! (Forcing black's Bishop off of h7. The immediate 6.Be4 Bg8 7.Kf5 fails to 7...Bh7+.) 6...Bg6 7.Be4 Bf7 8.Kf5 and White has achieved the desired position.

6.Be4 Bd1 7.Kf5

At last!

7...Be2 8.h4

It doesn't hurt to get this pawn a bit closer to its queening square (as long as it stays on a safe dark square!).

8...Bh5 9.Kf6 Be2 10.Bg2!

Very accurate. Now a later ...Ke5 won't attack the Bishop.

10...Bg4 11.Kg6 h5

Note that without 10.Bg2, Black could now play 11...Ke5, hitting the Bishop with tempo, before guarding his h-pawn.

12.Kf6!

Still denying black's King access to e5.

12...Be2 13.Be4 Bg4 14.Bh1 Be2 15.Kf5

White's King is heading back to f4 (all the while covering e5!) where it can support the Bishop's move to f3, winning the h5-pawn.

15...Bg4+ 16.Kf4 Be2 17.Bf3!, 1-0. The King and pawn endgame after 17...Bxf3 18.Kxf3 Kxd5 19.Kf4 Kc5 20.Kg5 Kb5 21.Kxh5 Kxa5 22.Kg5 leaves White way ahead in the race, while 17...Bb5 18.Kg5 Be8 19.Bxh5 is also game over.

An impressive display, no doubt, but let's amp up the voltage a bit and see how Smyslov completely outmaneuvers his opponent in our next position.

Diagram 541

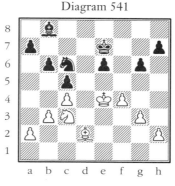

Smyslov - Golombek, London 1947

White to move

White is better due to his more active King and his superior pawn structure (two pawn islands to black's three). To increase his advantage, White must place his Knight on g4 and his Bishop on c3, dominating the enemy Knight. Any trade of white's Bishop for black's Knight will increase the first player's chances because the black Bishop has very little mobility while the white Knight can dance to almost any square on the board. Once White gets his Bishop to c3 and his Knight to g4, the threat of Nf6 will force black's h-pawn to move to h5. This, in turn, weakens the g-pawn. When this is done, White will train his sights on g6 and, if necessary, freeze it in its tracks by h3 followed by g4-g5.

1.Nd1!

Vacating the c3-square for the Bishop while intending to swing the Knight to f2-g4-f6.

1...Bd6

Black wasn't enticed by 1...e5 since, aside from the fact that the d5-square is seriously weakened and made accessible to the white King and white Knight via Ne3-d5, the creation of a kingside pawn majority would be much simpler to achieve after 2.f5.

2.Nf2 Nd8

White wasn't worried about 2...Nd4 since 3.Bc3 would force it into immediate retreat.

3.Bc3 Nf7 4.Ng4

Heading for f6 where it will attack h7. Keep in mind that any advance of black's h-pawn will seriously weaken the pawn on g6.

4...h5?!

There was no reason to push this pawn until it was actually attacked. Now white's advantage takes on very serious proportions.

5.Bf6+!

Diagram 542

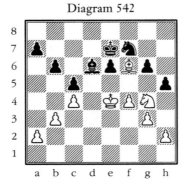

Smyslov plays very accurately. The Bishop's leap to f6 stops Black from trying any ...g6-g5 ideas.

5...Kd7 6.Nf2 Bc7

Too passive. He had to try 6...Be7 7.Bc3 g5 8.fxg5 Nxg5+, though White would retain a considerable advantage with 9.Kf4.

7.Nd3 Kc6 8.Ne1

Bad would be 8.Ne5+?? Bxe5 since it wouldn't be possible to attack g6 without the white Knight, while the black Knight would keep white's King out of e5 and g5.

With 8.Ne1 White intends to swing the Knight around to h4, where it will target g6 for destruction.

8...Nd6+ 9.Kd3

The bold 9.Ke5 would be answered by 9...Kd7 and not 9...Nxc4+?? 10.Kxe6 when the threat of Kf7 is decisive.

9...Nf5 10.Nf3 Kd7

Black decides against 10...b5 since 11.cxb5+ Kxb5 12.Ng5 would win material.

11.Ke4

Threatening 12.Ne5+ Bxe5 13.Kxe5 followed by a Bishop move and Kf6, when white's King penetrates into the enemy camp.

11...Nd6+ 12.Ke3

White's King is heading for f2 where it will defend g3. Then h2-h3 followed by g3-g4 will force the black Knight into a passive position.

12...Nf5+ 13.Kf2 Bd6 14.h3! Bc7 15.g4 hxg4 16.hxg4 Nh6 17.Kg3

Diagram 543

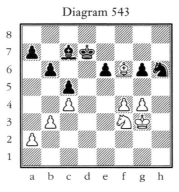

Hard to stand up to white's slow torture

17...Nf7

White wins easily after this final display of passivity. Black had to try 17...Ke8 when 18.Be5 Bd8 19.Bb8 a6 (19...Nf7!? might be stronger) 20.Ne5 g5 21.Nc6 Bf6 22.Be5 Bxe5 23.Nxe5 gxf4+ 24.Kxf4 leaves White with an outside passed pawn in the Knight endgame.

18.g5

The annoying and highly destructive threat of Nh4 is once again "on."

18...Bd8

Of course, 18...Nd6 is met by 19.Ne5+.

19.Kg4 Bxf6 20.gxf6 Kd6 21.Ne5!, 1-0. Black would have nothing left to play for after 21...Nd8 22.Kg5.

The following endgame was a key moment in Smyslov's match against Botvinnik for the World Championship, and demonstrates how deeply and flawlessly he could play these positions.

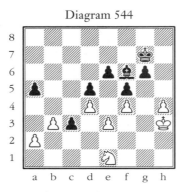

Diagram 544

Botvinnik - Smyslov, Moscow 1957

Black to move

1...Kh6

The game was adjourned at the diagrammed position and this was Smyslov's sealed move. Later, he had this to say: "The game was adjourned and the following morning Goldberg, Botvinnik's second, sent me an offer of a draw. The b3-pawn and the Knight at c2 create a defensive line which the black King is unable to cross. However, Black has a plan of penetrating with his King to the queenside, using zugzwang motifs, via the 1st rank. And so the game continued."

2.Nc2 Be7 3.Kg3?

Kasparov pointed out that White could have drawn by exchanging off black's a-pawn: 3.a3 Kh5 4.b4 axb4 (4...a4 fails since he won't have time to take the h-pawn after 5.b5) 5.axb4 Bxh4 6.b5 Bd8 7.Kg3 g5 8.fxg5 Kxg5 9.Kf3 Bb6

10.Ne1 (10.Nb4! also appears to draw) 10…Kf6 11.Ke2 f4 12.Kd3! fxe3 13.Nc2!
e5 14.Nxe3 Ke6 15.Nxd5! Kxd5 16.dxe5 Bd4 17.b6 and Black can't avoid the
draw since he loses his final pawn.

After the mistaken 3.Kg3, black's magnificently precise play eventually drags
his opponent down to defeat.

3…Kh5 4.Kf3 Kxh4 5.Ne1 g5 6.fxg5 Kxg5 7.Nc2 Bd6 8.Ne1

According to Smyslov, 8.a3 no longer works since "8…Kh4 9.b4 a4 10.b5 Bc7
11.Ne1 Kg5 12.Nc2 Ba5 13.Ne1 Bb6 14.Nc2 Kf6 and the pawns on the a-file
improve black's winning chances."

8…Kh4

Diagram 545

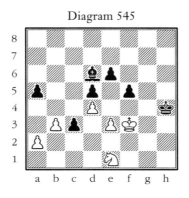

The beginning of a beautiful journey by the black King. The game R Schutt-J
Peters, Los Angeles 1989 (diagram 360) comes to mind.

9.Nc2 Kh3 10.Na1

As in our note to white's 8th move, 10.a3 Kh2 11.Kf2 Be7 12.b4 a4! is still
strong.

10…Kh2 11.Kf2 Bg3+

This forces white's King to give ground and allows black's King to move a file
closer to the white's e-pawn and ultimately to the queenside.

12.Kf3

The same thing results from 12.Kf1 Bh4 13.Ke2 Kg2.

12…Bh4 13.Nc2 Kg1 14.Ke2

14…Kf1 can't be allowed.

14…Kg2 15.Na1 Be7 16.Nc2 Kg3 17.Ne1 Bd8 18.Nc2 Bf6

Diagram 546

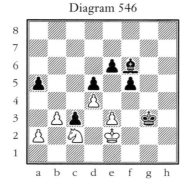

Our first zugzwang! White can't move his Knight due to the threat of ...f5-f4, and he doesn't want to play 19.Kd3 since that would allow ...Kf2.

19.a3

19.Kd3 Kf2 and now:

 20.a3 Be7 21.b4 a4! is a theme we've seen before.

20.Kxc3 Ke2 21.a3 e5 22.b4 exd4+ 23.exd4 Bd8 is completely overwhelming. Analysis by Fritz.

20.Na1 Ke1 21.Nc2+ Kd1 22.Na1 Be7 23.Nc2 Bd6 24.Na1 Kc1 25.Kxc3 Bb4+ 26.Kd3 Kb2 27.Nc2 Kxa2 wins. Analysis by Smyslov.

19...Be7 20.b4

Let's allow Smyslov to tell us what happens after the advance of the a-pawn: "20.a4 Bd6 21.Ne1 e5 22.dxe5 Bxe5 23.Kd3 (23.Nc2 d4! 24.exd4 Bd6 25.Ne3 f4 26.Nf5+ Kg4 27.Nxd6 f3+ and one of the pawns queens) 23...d4! 24.exd4 Bd6 25.Nc2 (25. Kxc3 Bb4+) 25...f4 26.Kxc3 f3 27.Ne3 f2 28.Kd3 Kf3 29.Nf1 Bf4! (A lovely example of a Bishop dominating a Knight!—Silman) 30.d5 Kg2 31.Ke2 Kg1 and Black wins."

20...a4 21.Ne1 Bg5 22.Nc2 Bf6

Diagram 547

A second zugzwang!

23.Kd3

Since any Knight move allowed 23...f4, white's only alternative was: "23.b5 Bd8 24.Ne1 Ba5 25.Nc2 Kg4 26.Ne1 Bc7 27.Nc2 (27.Nd3 c2 28.Kd2 Ba5+ 29.Kxc2 Kf3, or 27.Kd3 Bb6 28.Ke2 f4 29.exf4 Bxd4) 27...Bb6 28.Nb4 f4 29.exf4 Bxd4 30.Kd3 (30.Nd3 Kf5 31.Kf3 Bb6) 30...Bb6 31.Kxc3 Kxf4 32.Nc6 (32.Kd3 Ke5 33.Nc6+ Kd6) 32...Ke3 33.Kb4 d4 34.Ne5 d3 35.Kxa4 (35.Nc4+ Kd4) 35...d2 36.Nc4+ Ke2 37.Nxd2 Kxd2 38.Kb4 e5 39.a4 e4 40.a5 Bd8 41.b6 e3 and Black wins."—Smyslov.

23...Kf2 24.Na1 Bd8 25.Nc2 Bg5

A third zugzwang! Since 26.Na1 Bxe3 won't do, and since 26.Kxc3 Ke2 27.b5 Bd8 28.Kb4 Kd2 29.Na1 Kxe3 is resignable, that only leaves the advance of the b-pawn.

26.b5 Bd8 27.Nb4 Bb6 28.Nc2 Ba5

Diagram 548

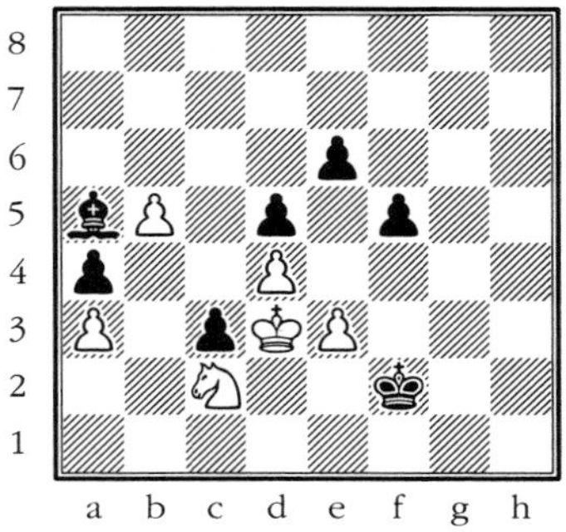

Our fourth and final zugzwang! Every legal move either hangs a pawn, or allows black's King to decisively step on e1.

29.Nb4 Ke1! and White resigned due to 30.Nc2+ (30. Kxc3 Ke2) 30...Kd1 31.Na1 Kc1 32.Nc2 Kb2.

Robert Fischer
(The 11th World Champion)
Master of Bishop Endings

Photo by Dr. Richard Cantwell.

The legendary American grandmaster (1943-2008) was an aggressive, "try to win at all costs" kind of player. Possessing opening preparation that was ahead of its time, the work ethic of an Alekhine, the technique of a Capablanca, and a will to win that terrified literally everyone he faced, Fischer bulldozed through the world's best players on his way to the highest title.

Though Fischer played ultra-sharp openings like the King's Indian and the Najdorf as Black, and 1.e4 as White, don't make the mistake of pegging him as an attacking player—his was a style based on iron logic and deep positional ideas, and he was always happy to leap into an endgame, secure in the knowledge that few could challenge him in this stage of the game.

Fischer's love of Bishops was well known, and his magnificent handling of them in the endgame has never been equaled. Our first example is an excellent illustration of Fischer's incredible chess education.

Diagram 549

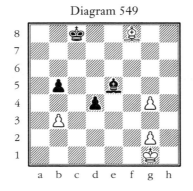

Taimanov-Fischer, Buenos Aires 1960
Black to move

Poor Taimanov suffered in several games due to Fischer's skill in Bishop endgames. His comments, from his excellent book *Taimanov's Selected Games*, give us a taste for what he went through in the game:

"I got into time trouble and before the control I missed a sure win. But in the adjourned position I still had winning chances—Fischer faced a difficult defense. My colleagues took bets: 'Bobby won't save the game, such accuracy is required!'

"And indeed, when after tactical complications the game went into an ending, where Bobby was a pawn down, one sensed that the correct decisions would not come easily to Fischer, and that he was balancing on the edge of the abyss. But then the critical, most important position was reached, and … Bobby suddenly began playing quickly and faultlessly, like an automaton—he rattled off more than a dozen difficult moves within a minute, and the draw became inevitable. Stunned by such a finale, I asked him: 'Bobby, how did you manage to find this saving path, and so quickly?' 'I didn't need to find anything,' said the contented Fischer with a smile, 'a few years ago your magazine *Shakhmaty v SSSR* published a detailed analysis of this ending by Averbakh, and I remembered all the variations perfectly well.'"

1...Bg3

The Bishop and d-pawn will form a block to the white King that will force White to part with a g-pawn in exchange for black's d-pawn. The resulting position, though seemingly dangerous for Black, is in fact a forced draw.

2.Kf1 d3 3.Bb4

3.g5 Kd7 4.g6 Ke6 5.g7 Kf7, =.

3...Kd7 4.Be1 Bf4

Threatening 5...d2, winning a piece.

5.Bc3 Bg3 6.g5 Ke6 7.g6 Ke7

7...Bh4?? fails to 8.Be5! Be7 9.Kf2 Bg5 10.g3 Bh6 11.Bf4 Bg7 12.Ke3 Kf5 13.Kxd3 Kxg6 14.g4 and wins.

8.Be1

Having sidetracked black's King, it's time to free his own monarch from its cage.

8...Bf4 9.Bh4+ Kf8 10.g3

10.Bf6? Bg3, =.

10...Bd6 11.Kf2 Bc5+ 12.Kf3 Kg7 13.Bg5 Kxg6 14.Bf4

A very interesting try (discovered by IM Jack Peters) is 14.Be3!? Bb4 15.g4 Kf6 16.Bf4. However, Black holds: 16...Ke6! (White wins after 16...Kg6?? 17.Ke3 d2 18.Ke2) 17.Ke3 d2 18.Ke2 d1=Q+ 19.Kxd1 Kd5 20.Bg5 Ke5 21.Kc2 Ke4 22.Bf6 Ba5 23.Be7 Ke5 24.Kd3 Bb6 25.Bg5 Bc5 26.Kd2 Ke4 27.Bf6 Bf8 28.g5 Kf5 29.Kd3 (29.Kc3 Bc5, =) 29...Bc5 30.Kc3 Bf8 31.Kd4 Bb4 32.Kd5 Bd2 33.Kc5 b4 34.Kc4 Kg6 35.Be7 Kf5 36.Bd8 Bc3 37.Bf6 Bd2 38.Be7 Ke6, =.

14...Kh5 15.Ke4 Kg4 16.Kxd3 Kf3

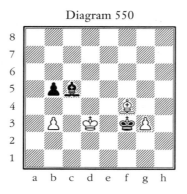

Diagram 550

Knowledge never hurts!

Fischer no doubt was playing fairly rapidly at this point, well aware that the unavoidable exchange of the g-pawn for his b-pawn would lead to a position that he was well acquainted with.

17.Bc7 Bf2 18.Bd6 Be1

A little dance ensues. White takes his time (a bit of Cat and Mouse) before finally winning black's b-pawn in exchange for his g-pawn.

19.Kd4 Kg4 20.Kc5 b4 21.Kb5 Kf5 22.Kc4 Ke6 23.Bc7 Kf5

He doesn't want to allow the pawn to advance to g4.

24.Kd3 Kg4 25.Bd6 Bc3 26.Kc4 Be1 27.Bxb4 Bxg3

Fischer takes no more than sixty seconds for the rest of the game!

28.Bc3 Bd6 29.Kd5 Be7 30.Bd4

Threatening Bc5 followed by b4-b5.

30...Bb4

Forcing white's King to give ground if the pawn is to safely advance.

31.Kc4 Ba5 32.Bc3 Bd8 33.b4

It turns out that (from diagram 551) if Fischer had played 33...Kf5 (instead of his hyper-accurate 33...Kf4), a position from the game Capablanca-Janowski, New York 1916 would have been reached after 34.Kd5. Amazingly, Janowski resigned! At that time, analysts erroneously justified Janowski's decision by presenting the following line: 33...Kf5 34.Kd5 Bb6 (It turns out that 34...Kf4! would still have drawn) 35.Bd4 Bc7 36.b5 Bd8 37.Kc6 Ke6 38.Bb6 Bg5 39.Bc7 Be3 40.Bd6 Bf2 41.Bc5 Bg3 42.b6 Bf4 43.b7 Bg3 44.Bb6 Bb8 45.Bc7 Ba7 46.Kb5 Kd7 47.Ka6 and White wins.

Diagram 551

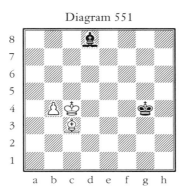

33...Kf4!

It was only years after the aforementioned Capablanca game that Fischer's defensive scheme (bringing the King over the top of the pawn instead of in front of it) was discovered.

34.b5 Ke4 35.Bd4 Bc7

White's King will again have to give ground in an effort to advance his pawn to b6.

36.Kc5 Kd3 37.Kc6 Kc4!

The point of black's play. The pawn isn't going anywhere.

38.Bb6 Bg3 39.Ba7 Bc7!, ½-½.

Our next example is a complicated ending (once again Fischer possesses his favorite Bishop!) where Fischer mixes mathematical precision and fine art, creating one of the greatest endgame performances of all time.

Diagram 552

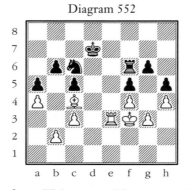

Fischer - Taimanov, Vancouver 1972

White to move

White's advantage is clear: the Bishop is far more active than the Knight, white's Rook is more active than its counterpart, black's King has no way into the enemy position while white's has a path down the f1-a6 diagonal, and black's kingside pawns are all on light-squares, meaning they will be permanently vulnerable to attack by the Bishop.

1.Bb5 Rd6

Black is hoping to trade Rooks and then swing his Knight to d6 where it will create a complete blockade by depriving white's King of access to the c4-square. White doesn't mind the swap of Rooks, but he'll only allow this to happen once he prevents the Knight maneuver to d6.

2.Ke2!

It's important that white's King can recapture on d3 after a Rook exchange on d3. For example, 2.Rd3?? Rxd3+ 3.Bxd3 Nd8! when Black forms an unbreakable blockade after 4.Bc4 Ke7 5.Bd5 Kd6 6.Bg8 Ke7 7.Ke3 Nb7 8.Kd3 Nd6 (note that 9.b4 Kf6 10.bxa5 bxa5 still leaves White with no way to enter).

2...Kd8

After 2...Rf6 there follows 3.Kd3 Rd6+ 4.Kc4 Rd2 5.Rd3+ Rxd3 6.Kxd3 Kd6 7.Bxc6 Kxc6 8.Kc4 Kc7 9.Kd5 Kd7 10.c4 when Black must allow White to clean out his pawns on one side of the board (10...Kc7 11.Ke6 or 10...Ke7 11.Kc6).

3.Rd3 Kc7 4.Rxd6 Kxd6 5.Kd3

White now threatens to trade Bishop for Knight and get a winning King and pawn endgame.

5...Ne7

5...Kc7 6.Bxc6 Kxc6 7.Kc4 Kc7 8.Kb5 was given by Marin: 8...Kb7 9.c4 Kc7 10.Ka6 Kc6 11.Ka7 Kc7 12.b3 Kc6 13.Kb8. Very nice, but far simpler is 8.Kd5 Kd7 9.c4 when we have the note to black's 2nd move—Black will lose all his pawns on one side of the board.

6.Be8

Starting a magnificent sequence where the Bishop ties the Knight down to the defense of its pawns while simultaneously forcing black's King back so that its own monarch can advance.

6...Kd5 7.Bf7+

Kicking the King back so white's can claim c4.

7...Kd6 8.Kc4 Kc6 9.Be8+

Again pushing black's King backwards so that white's can move up to b5. The fact that the Bishop is dominating the enemy King and Knight at the same time is remarkable.

9...Kb7 10.Kb5 Nc8 11.Bc6!+

This bully of a Bishop once again forces the black King's hand—he must give up control over either a6 or c6. It's also important to point out that Fischer could have ruined his masterpiece by 11.Bxg6?? Nd6 mate. This kind of helpmate in an endgame has become known in some American circles as a "Nigel Short."

11...Kc7 12.Bd5

Threatening Ka6

12...Ne7

Black also loses after 12...Nd6+ 13.Ka6 and now:

➤ 13...Ne4 14.Bf7 Nxg3 15.Bxg6 Kc6 16.Be8+ Kc7 17.Kb5 Ne2 18.Bxh5 Nxf4 19.Bf7! dominates black's Knight. He can resign after both 19...Nd3 20.Bg6 or 19...Kd6 20.Kxb6.

➤ 13...c4 14.Bg8 Kc6 15.Bh7 Ne4 16.Bxg6 Nxg3 17.Be8+ Kc5 18.Bf7 Ne2 19.Bxh5 Nxf4 20.Bd1!—Kasparov. It might seem clear to Mr. Kasparov, but let's check out a few more moves: 20...Nd5 21.h5 Nf6 22.h6 f4 23.Bf3 Nh7 24.Be4 Ng5 25.h7 Nf7 26.Bg6 Nh8 27.Bh5 and the pesky Bishop continues to dominate black's pieces.

Diagram 553

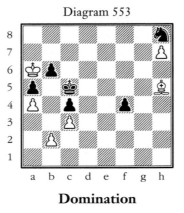

Domination

The game might finish: 27...Kc6 28.Bf3+ Kc5 29.Kb7 Ng6 30.Bh5 (There are other ways to win, but I love this theme!) 30...Nh8 31.Kc7 b5 32.axb5 Kxb5 33.Kd6 Ka4 34.Bd1+ Kb5 35.Ke7, 1-0.

13.Bf7 Kb7

Black seems to have managed to keep white's King off of a6, but now the Bishop regroups and manages to create a lovely zugzwang.

14.Bb3 Ka7 15.Bd1 Kb7

Forced. A Knight move allows the decisive Kc6.

16.Bf3+ Kc7

16...Ka7 17.c4! powers the white King into black's camp: 17...Ng8 18.Kc6 Nf6 19.Kd6 Ne4+ 20.Ke5 Nxg3 21.Kf6, winning.

17.Ka6

Diagram 554

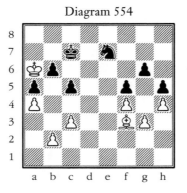

Success! Next up, bringing the Bishop back to f7 or e8 so it can continue to bind the Knight.

17...Nc8 18.Bd5 Ne7 19.Bc4!

This allows the Bishop to go to f7 with gain of tempo.

19...Nc6

19...Kc6 20.Bb5+ Kc7 21.Be8 will lead to the same position as the game.

20.Bf7 Ne7 21.Be8

Diagram 555

Zugzwang

This might well be the greatest Bishop of all time. Having completely outma-
neuvered the whole black army, it now creates a winning zugzwang!

21...Kd8

Black has no other move.

22.Bxg6!

The heroic piece now sacrifices itself in service to its King.

22...Nxg6 23.Kxb6 Kd7 24.Kxc5

White gets two protected passed pawns on the queenside vs. a rather clumsy
Knight. Two things can happen: one of the queenside pawns will promote, or
the pawns will be stopped but white's King will infiltrate the kingside and clean
out those pawns as well!

24...Ne7 25.b4 axb4 26.cxb4 Nc8

Trying to hold off the pawns by 26...Kc7 also fails: 27.b5 Kb7 28.a5 Nc8
(28...Ng8 29.Kd5 Nf6+ 30.Ke6 Ne4 31.Kxf5 Nxg3+ 32.Kg6) 29.Kd5 Na7
30.Ke6 Nxb5 31.Kxf5 Nd4+ 32.Kg6 Ne2 33.f5 Nxg3 34.f6, 1-0.

27.a5 Nd6 28.b5 Ne4+ 29.Kb6 Kc8 30.Kc6 Kb8 31.b6, 1-0. One possible
finish could be: 31...Nxg3 32.a6 Ne4 33.a7+ Ka8 34.b7+ Kxa7 35.Kc7 and the
pawn queens with check. This perfect performance put Fischer up 4-0 in their
match, which he ultimately won by the unheard of score of 6-0!

Just in case you think that Fischer was a one minor piece kind of guy, let's see
how he handles a Knight.

Diagram 556

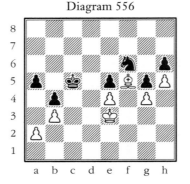

Damjanovic - Fischer, Buenos Aires 1970
Black to move

Here we have a classic case of a flexible Knight vs. a "ghost" Bishop (i.e., a Bishop that can move all over the board without ever being able to make contact with an enemy piece or pawn). It might appear that Black has no way to penetrate into white's camp, but the truth of the matter is that White is dead lost.

1...Kb5

Preparing to advance the a5-pawn.

2.Kd3 a4 3.bxa4+

It turns out that 3.Ke3 a3 is extremely strong since it fixes the a2-pawn, which suddenly becomes a serious target: 4.Kd3 Kc5 5.Ke3 Ne8 6.Kd3 Nd6 (threatening ...Nb5-c3 winning the a2-pawn) 7.Bd7

Diagram 557

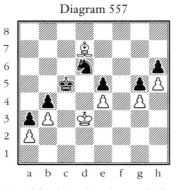

Has black's plan been foiled?

7...Nc4! 8.Be8 (Accepting the inevitable, since 8.bxc4 b3 forces the creation of a new Queen.) 8...Nb2+ and it's all over since 9.Kc2 let's the black King in by 9...Kd4, while 9.Ke3 Nd1+ followed by ...Nc3 picks up the a2-pawn.

3...Kxa4

Fischer has calculated the rest out to white's resignation.

4.Kc4 Ka3 5.Kc5 Kxa2 6.Kxb4 Kb2 7.Kc5 Kc3 8.Kd6 Kd4 9.Ke6 Nxe4 10.Kf7

Of course, 10.Bxe4 Kxe4 11.Kf6 Kf4 12.Kg6 e4 doesn't give White any chance at all in the race.

10...Nf2 11.Kg6 e4 12.Kxh6

The alternative was 12.Bxe4 Kxe4 13.Kxh6 Kf4 14.Kg7 Nxg4 15.Kg6 and now black's clearest (and most fun!) way of winning is 15...Nh6!

Diagram 558

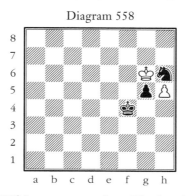

White to move, but Black wins

16.Kxh6 g4 17.Kg7 g3 18.h6 g2 19.h7 g1=Q+ 20.Kf7 Qa7+ 21.Kg8 (21.Kg6 Qd4 followed by ...Qh8) 21...Kg5 22.h8=Q Kg6 and White gets mated in a few moves. You'll be familiar with this entertaining "let him Queen then mate him" endgame if you studied Part Six.

12...e3 13.Kg7 e2 14.h6 e1=Q 15.h7 Qe7+ 16.Kg8 Ne4!, 0-1. A good time to give up since 17.h8=Q+ falls on its face due to 17...Nf6+, winning white's Queen. That only leaves 17.Bxe4 Kxe4 18.h8=Q Qe8+ 19.Kg7 Qxh8+ 20.Kxh8 Kf4 when black's g-pawn will soon promote.

We've seen Fischer's skill with Bishops. We've seen that he could wield a mean Knight. And we've seen his enormous endgame knowledge. Let's finish our study of Fischer by taking a look at how he fares in an ultra-intense position when the pressure of a World Championship is hanging over his head.

Diagram 559

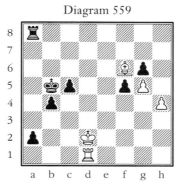

Spassky - Fischer, World Championship, Reykjavik 1972

White to move

A very complicated position: White has a Bishop for three strong queenside pawns. This is obvious. What make things difficult to figure out are the following questions:

➤ With white's Rook (which eyes a1), King and Bishop all defending the queenside, just how threatening are black's queenside passers?

➤ How big a part will black's fourth passed pawn on f5 play?

➤ White has the option of pushing his h-pawn and creating a passed pawn of his own.

An interesting aside is that chess engines like Fritz and Deep Junior give Black an overwhelming advantage here (the poor things don't realize that the position is balanced, a draw being the proper outcome). That should give the reader a glimpse into just how hard it was to play this endgame correctly.

1.h5!

An excellent move. White understands that passive defense won't save the game, so he sacrifices a pawn (giving Black an unprecedented fifth passed pawn in the process!) in order to create his own passed g-pawn.

1...c4

Creating the threat of ...c3+ (blocking the Bishop's control of the a1-h8 diagonal) followed by ...a1=Q. Black sees that he can capture white's pawn next move, since neither 2.h6 nor 2.hxg6 is playable (as shown in the note to white's second move).

2.Ra1

Forced. The two moves that White would prefer to play both lose:

2.h6 c3+ 3.Kd3 a1=Q 4.Rxa1 Rxa1 5.h7 Rd1+ 6.Kc2 Rh1 7.h8=Q Rxh8 8.Bxh8 Kc4 when the three passed pawns easily beat white's Bishop. Analysis by Gligoric.

2.hxg6 c3+ 3.Bxc3 Rd8+ is game over since 4.Kc2 Rxd1 5.Kxd1 (5.g7 Rc1+! 6.Kxc1 bxc3 7.g8=Q a1=Q+ forces mate, while 5.Bb2 a1=Q 6.Bxa1 Rxa1 7.g7 Ra8 is also 0-1) 5...bxc3 forces white's immediate resignation.

2...gxh5 3.g6 h4! 4.g7!

An old analysis by Purdy gave 4.Bxh4 b3 5.Kc3 Rg8 as winning. However, instead of 5.Kc3??, 5.Bf6! is a hard nut to crack: 5...Rd8+ 6.Kc3 Rd3+ 7.Kb2 Rg3 8.g7.

Kasparov's answer to 4.Bxh4 is superior to Purdy's: 4.Bxh4 Rg8 5.Rxa2 Rxg6 6.Ra8 c3+ 7.Ke2 Rg2+ 8.Kd3 Rd2+ 9.Ke3 Rd6! "One of the Black pawns would have inevitably queened."

4...h3 5.Be7 Rg8

The following Botvinnik quote is quite interesting: "Fischer finds a paradoxical solution: he stalemates his own Rook, but blocks white's passed pawn and ties his Bishop to it. Now five passed pawns are fighting against the white Rook. Nothing similar had previously occurred in chess. Spassky was astounded and he lost. Soon Smyslov found a draw for White, but would he have found it at the board, sitting opposite Fischer?"

6.Bf8!

This move, which entombs black's Rook, is white's only good reply. Two losing possibilities:

➤ 6.Rxa2?? Rxg7 is completely hopeless for White.

➤ 6.Bf6 h2 7.Kc2 Re8! 8.Rh1 Re2+ 9.Kd1 Rg2 10.Rxh2 Rg1+ 11.Kc2 c3 and Black wins. Analysis by Kasparov.

6...h2

A better try than 6...c3+ 7.Kd3 h2 8.Rf1 f4 9.Rd1 f3 10.Kd4 f2 (Three passed pawns are poised to promote on their 7th rank, but the Rook stops them all in their tracks.—Silman) 11.Kd3 Kc6 12.Kc2 a1=Q (Else the black King won't be able to penetrate to the kingside.—Silman) 13.Rxa1 Kd5 14.Kd3 c2 15.Kxc2 Ke4 16.Rf1! Kf3 17.Bc5 with a draw. Analysis by Soltis.

7.Kc2 Kc6

So far we've heard from Kasparov, Botvinnik, Gligoric, Purdy, and Soltis. We might as well let Smyslov toss his voice into the mix too: "An exceptionally original position: Black's Rook is shut out of the game, but the five(!) passed pawns guarantee him at least equal chances."

8.Rd1!

A key defensive idea. The Rook stops the black King from marching over to the kingside.

8...b3+ 9.Kc3

Diagram 560

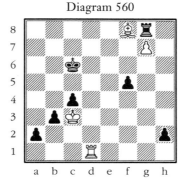

Fully adequate, but simpler was 9.Kb2! f4 (9...h1=Q 10.Rxh1 Kd5 11.Rd1+ Ke4 12.Rc1 Kd3 13.Rd1+ and Rc1, =) 10.Rd6+ Kc7 11.Rd1! f3 12.Kc3 f2 13.Kb2 with a draw. Analysis by Gligoric.

9...h1=Q!

Sacrificing this pawn is the only way to pull white's Rook off the d-file and let black's King make a last desperate dash to the kingside, where it will try to help the f-pawn promote.

Less critical is 9...f4 10.Rd6+ Kc7 11.Rd1 f3 12.Kb2, =. Analysis by Purdy.

10.Rxh1 Kd5 11.Kb2

White is still keeping the draw in sight. Another way to split the point is 11.Rd1+ Ke4 12.Re1+ Kf3 13.Kb2! f4 14.Rc1! Ke2 15.Rxc4 f3 16.Rc1 f2 17.Kxb3 f1=Q 18.Rxf1 Kxf1 19.Kxa2, =. Analysis by Kasparov.

11...f4 12.Rd1+ Ke4 13.Rc1 Kd3 14.Rd1+??

Spassky finally cracks from the pressure of the game and the occasion. A draw could have been assured by 14.Rc3+ Kd4 (14...Ke2 15.Rxc4 f3 16.Rc1, =) 15.Rf3 c3+ 16.Ka1 c2 17.Rxf4+ Kc3 18.Rf3+ Kd2 19.Ba3! Analysis by Gligoric. Timman takes it a bit further: 19...Rxg7 20.Rxb3 Rc7 21.Bb2, =, Timman, and not 21.Kxa2?? Ra7! when Black wins.

As was so common with Fischer's endgames, one mistake (even a very small one) was all it took to turn what seemed like a defensible position into a complete wreck.

14...Ke2! 15.Rc1 f3

White finds himself a tempo down in the important drawing lines (shown best in the note to white's 11th move) where he takes on c4, brings his Rook back to c1, takes on b3 with his King, and then gives up his Rook for black's f-pawn. Now 16.Rxc4 f2 17.Rc1 f1=Q 18.Rxf1 Kxf1 doesn't give White time to chop off the b3-pawn.

16.Bc5 Rxg7

Kasparov points out that "Now and on the next move the crude ...f3-f2 also won, but Fischer has his own way to the goal."

17.Rxc4

Diagram 561

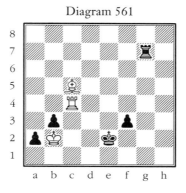

17...Rd7 18.Re4+

White would also have to resign quickly after 18.Rc1 Rd1.

18...Kf1 19.Bd4 f2, 0-1. The end would have been: 20.Rf4 Rxd4 21.Rxd4 Ke2 22.Re4+ Kf3 23.Re8 f1=Q 24.Rf8+ Ke2 25.Rxf1 Kxf1 26.Ka1 Ke2 27.Kb2 Kd3 28.Ka1 Kd2 29.Kb2 a1=Q+ 30.Kxa1 Kc3 31.Kb1 b2 32.Ka2 Kc2. A magnificent struggle!

Beyond Master
(Recommended Endgame Books)

Once you achieve a 2200 + rating and have mastered all the material in this book, simple experience and analysis of grandmaster games will painlessly improve your understanding of this final phase of the game. However, if you've become addicted to endgame study and wish to continue your "technical" education, the following books should prove both useful and enjoyable.

Reference

Fundamental Chess Endings by Karsten Müller and Frank Lamprecht. London: Gambit Publications, LTD, 2001.

This encyclopedic tome is the best reference book ever written on the endgame, and will promise you some guidance no matter what kind of endgame situation you're looking for. Perfect for those that want a book that shows every possible kind of endgame, but don't expect heavy explanation or soul.

Dvoretsky's Endgame Manual by Mark Dvoretsky. Milford, CT: Russell Enterprises, Inc., 2003.

Okay, this isn't anything like *Fundamental Chess Endings*, which is a true reference work. Dvoretsky's wonderful book covers an enormous amount of material though, and everything is explained and nicely presented. Many won't like me listing this as "reference." But, in my view, its size and complexity earn it a spot in this category. This isn't a book I would read from beginning to end. Instead, I would turn to a particular section whenever that subject interested me.

Rook Endgames

Practical Rook Endings by Victor Korchnoi. Zürich: Edition Olms, 1999.

Though not as practical as *Survival Guide to Rook Endings*, Korchnoi's book is wonderfully complex and informative.

The Survival Guide to Rook Endings by John Emms. London: Everyman Publishers, 1999.

An excellent exploration of all kinds of Rook endgames. In-depth and practical.

Learn from the Best

Capablanca's Best Chess Endings: 60 Complete Games by Irving Chernev. New York: Dover, 1982.

The title speaks for itself. You can't go wrong by immersing yourself in the technical know-how of the Cuban legend. The notes, of course, are not computer checked. This means that quite a few errors are present, that allows you to challenge everything Chernev says and see who's right.

Vasily Smyslov: Endgame Virtuoso by Vasily Smyslov. London: Cadogan Books, 1997.

Lots of Smyslov endgames with notes by the legend himself. How can you go wrong?

General Endgame Reads

Botvinnik On The Endgame by Mikhail Botvinnik. Translated by Jim Marfia. Coraopolis, PA: Chess Enterprises, 1985.

A small (80 pages) and out of print book that is an easy, relaxing, and instructive read.

Chess Endgame Lessons by Pal Benko. 1990.

A compilation of Benko's endgame columns that first appeared in *Chess Life* magazine, this self-published monster is filled with so much fascinating and extremely instructive material that one could lose oneself in it for months and months. Since it's almost impossible to find, making the effort to compile these lessons from old issues of *Chess Life* would be time well spent. If I were allowed just one endgame book on a desert island, this would be it, hands down!

Endgame Secrets: How to Plan in the Endgame in Chess by Christopher Lutz. London: B.T. Batsford, LTD., 1999.

This is a serious endgame workbook. Be ready to put in some blood, sweat, and tears, and your efforts will pay dividends.

Technique for the Tournament Player by Mark Dvoretsky and Artur Yusupov. London: B.T. Batsford, LTD., 1995.

A top-notch book on technique, it takes the reader though many different subjects, such as: How to Study the Endgame, Exploiting an Advantage, and Techniques of Grandmaster Play, to name just a few.

Bibliography

Bán, Jenö, *The Tactics of End-Games*. Translated b Jenö Bochkor. Mineola, NY: Dover, 1997.

Benko, Pal, and Jeremy Silman, *Pal Benko: My Life, Games, and Compositions*. With an opening survey by John Watson. Los Angeles: Siles Press, 2003.

Chernev, Irving, *Capablanca's Best Chess Endings: 60 Complete Games*. New York: Dover, 1982.

ChessBase. *DVD-Endgame Turbo 2, Nalimov Tablebases*. Hamburg: ChessBase GmbH.

ChessBase. *MegaBase 2005*. Hamburg: ChessBase GmbH.

Chess Informant. 91 vols. Beograd, Yugoslavia: Chess Informant, 1966-2004.

Classification of Chess Endings: The Best Endings of Capablanca and Fischer. Beograd, Yugoslavia: Chess Informant, 1978.

Dvoretsky, Mark, *Dvoretsky's Endgame Manual*. Milford, CT: Russell Enterprises, Inc. 2003.

Emms, John, *Starting Out: Minor Piece Endgames*. London: Gloucester Publishers (Everyman Chess), 2004.

Emms, John, *The Survival Guide to Rook Endings*. London: Everyman Chess 1999.

Fine, Reuben, revised by Pal Benko, *Basic Chess Endings*. New York: Random House, 2003.

Flear, Glenn, *Starting Out: Pawn Endgames*. London: Gloucester Publishers (Everyman Chess), 2004.

Griffiths, P.C., *The Endings in Modern Theory and Practice*. New York: Charles Scribner's Sons, 1976.

Kasparov, Garry, *Garry Kasparov On My Great Predecessors*.With the participation of Dmitry Plisetsky. 4 vols. Gloucester Publishers (Everyman Chess), 2003-2004.

Lissowski, Tomasz, and Adrian Mikhalchishin, *Najdorf: Life and Games*. With game commentaries by Miguel Najdorf. Translated by John Sugden. London: B.T. Batsford Ltd., 2005.

Marin, Mihail, *Learn From the Legends: Chess Champions at Their Best*. Gothenburg, Sweden: Quality Chess, 2004.

Müller, Karsten, and Frank Lamprecht, *Fundamental Chess Endings*. London: Gambit Publications, LTD, 2001.

Nunn, John, *Tactical Chess Endings*. London: George Allen & Unwin, 1981.

Reinfeld, Fred, *Practical End-game Play*. Philadelphia: David McKay Company, 1940.

Shereshevsky, M.I., *Endgame Strategy*. Translated by K.P. Neat. Oxford: Pergamon Press, 1985.

Silman, Jeremy, *Essential Chess Endings Explained Move by Move*. Dallas: Chess Digest, Inc., 1988.

Silman, Jeremy, *How to Reassess Your Chess: The Complete Chess Mastery Course, 3rd Ed*. Los Angeles: Siles Press, 1993.

Silman, Jeremy, *The Reassess Your Chess Workbook: How to Master Chess Imbalances*. Los Angeles: Siles Press, 2001.

Smyslov, Vasily, *Vasily Smyslov: Endgame Virtuoso*. Translated by Ken Neat. London: Cadogan Books, 1997.

Taimanov, Mark, *Taimanov's Selected Games*. Translated by Ken Neat. London: Cadogan Books, 1995.

Ward, Chris, *Starting Out: Rook Endgames*. London: Gloucester Publishers (Everyman Chess), 2004.

Index of Names